MANAGING NETWORKS IN TRANSITION ECONOMIES

INTERNATIONAL BUSINESS AND MANAGEMENT SERIES

Series Editor: **Pervez N. Ghauri**

Published

GHAURI & OXELHEIM
European Union and the Race for Foreign Direct Investment in Europe

HYDER & ABRAHA
Strategic Alliances in Eastern and Central Europe

CONTRACTOR AND LORANGE
Alliances and Co-operative Strategies

GEMÜNDEN, RITTER & WALTER
Relationships and Networks in International Markets

GHAURI & USUNIER
International Business Negotiations

HAVILA, FORSGREN & HÅKANSSON
Critical perspectives on Internationalisation

MOROSINI
Managing Cultural Differences

NAUDE & TURNBULL
Network Dynamics in International Marketing

BUCKLEY & GHAURI
The Global Challenge for Multinational Enterprises

HÅKANSSON AND JOHANSON
Business Network Learning

LI
Managing International Business Ventures in China

Forthcoming titles

YANG
Intellectual Property and Doing Business in China

HENNART & THOMAS
Global Competitive Strategies

Other titles of interest

FATEMI
International Trade in the 21st Century

DUNNING
Globalization, Trade and Foreign Direct Investment

MONCARZ
International Trade and the New Economic Order

KREININ
Contemporary Issues in Commercial Policy

Related journals sample copies available on request

European Management Journal
International Business Review
International Journal of Research in Marketing
Long Range Planning
Scandinavian Journal of Management

MANAGING NETWORKS IN TRANSITION ECONOMIES

BY

MARTIN JOHANSON

Uppsala University & Mid Sweden University, Sweden

2004

ELSEVIER

Amsterdam – Boston – Heidelberg – London – New York – Oxford
Paris – San Diego – San Francisco – Singapore – Sydney – Tokyo

ELSEVIER B.V.	ELSEVIER Inc.	**ELSEVIER Ltd**	ELSEVIER Ltd
Sara Burgerhartstraat 25	525 B Street, Suite 1900	**The Boulevard, Langford**	84 Theobalds Road
P.O. Box 211	San Diego	**Lane, Kidlington**	London
1000 AE Amsterdam	CA 92101-4495	**Oxford OX5 1GB**	WC1X 8RR
The Netherlands	USA	**UK**	UK

First edition 2004

Library of Congress Cataloging in Publication Data
A catalog record is available from the Library of Congress.

British Library Cataloguing in Publication Data
A catalogue record is available from the British Library.

ISBN: 0-08-044461-X

⊗ The paper used in this publication meets the requirements of ANSI/NISO Z39.48-1992 (Permanence of Paper). Printed in The Netherlands.

Working together to grow
libraries in developing countries

www.elsevier.com | www.bookaid.org | www.sabre.org

ELSEVIER   BOOK AID
             International   Sabre Foundation

Contents

Introduction

The present study examines the transition from a planned economy to a market economy in Russia. In light of the fact that one of the main problems perceived by Russian firms during the transition is the management of their relations with the contexts, mainly customers and suppliers, a network approach is used as the theoretical framework. A case study of Tipografiya, the largest printing house in Novgorod, covers the period from 1986 to 1998 and addresses change and stability in Tipografiya's network.

Chapter 1

Transition Economies and Networks

> The real voyage of discovery consists not in seeking new landscapes, but in having new eyes.
>
> Marcel Proust

Background

From the moment in 1985 when Mikhail Gorbachev was appointed General Secretary of the Communist Party of the Soviet Union, much attention has been paid to the economic situation in that country. A few years later, on 31 December 1991, the Soviet Union ceased to exist and was replaced by 15 independent states. One of these was Russia. During the last 10 years Russian society has been subjected to a furious rate of change. From being a planned economy, the plan and the plan's authorities were abolished, prices liberalised, and Russia has moved towards a general definition of a market economy. It has been a painful and complicated process with extensive economic, political, and social tensions. Waves of hopes, expectations, and optimism have been mixed with threats and horror scenarios. In this unstable environment, industry has tried to survive and develop. This picture is the frame and the point of departure for this study.

This study is about stability and change during the transition from a planned to a market economy. Although a vast number of researchers during the Soviet period studied whether an economy could be planned, surprisingly few have empirically studied what happens when the economy is not planned any longer. From that, it follows that the problem of this study has its roots in the change in how the economy is governed. The transition from a planned economy to a market economy is defined as containing several institutional changes (for reviews see Eliasson 1998; Fischer & Gelb 1991; Peng & Heath 1996), all of them affecting exchanges between firms. These changes re-allocated the means in order to attain the new "re-considered" and "re-defined" ends in the economy and thereby affected the firms and the contexts in which they operated.

Transition is defined in this study as going from one economic system to another. In Russia, it means leaving a system where the exchanges between firms are planned by one set of authorities and the prices are fixed by another set, for a market economy. The transition can either be viewed as two states, where one type of governance of the economy is replaced with another type of governance, that is, when the transition is assumed to have reached an end when specific conditions, defined in advance, have been achieved. This perspective implies that the transition from a planned economy to a market economy can be planned. However, leaving the planned governance of an economy and moving to a market economy requires that several steps be taken and I will therefore view the transition as various change processes. In the light of Peng & Heath's (1996: 493) statements that "It seems that more research should be directed toward the firm in planned economies in transition [...] At this stage, perhaps empirical efforts should be focused on qualitative field studies in these countries," the aim of this study is to highlight the effect of the transition on something already existing and to focus on the behaviour of firms in the marketplace during the transition.

> The overall purpose of this study is to investigate the change processes of a firm and its context, in the light of the change of governance of the Russian economy, from a planned to a market economy.

The Firm and the Context in Transition

One of the reasons for the transition from a planned to a market economy was the relative failure in planning the exchange between the firms in the economy. Therefore, it is not surprising that the transition is perceived by management as mainly a market problem, that is, as the firms and the managers having problems in handling their relations with the surrounding environment. Markets in transition economies are often characterised by:

- Differences between old and new relations and networks.
- Importance of personal relations.
- Changes in relations and networks.
- Difficulties in managing relations and networks.

The Differences Between Old and New Relations and Networks

As a result of the extensive institutional changes the Russian economy underwent, some researchers discuss and compare the old relations and networks, which were established already during the planned economy, with those relations and networks that have emerged during the transition to a market economy (Huber & Wörgötter 1998; Salmi 1996; Sedaitis 1997). According to Huber & Wörgötter (1998) and Sedaitis (1997), the old relations and networks are different from the current ones, and Huber and Wörgötter, moreover, observe that they are separate entities. Salmi (1996), on the other hand, says that the new networks in industrial markets originated from the old networks and that the new evolving relations in the transition largely build on the old ones. This was the case even for small firms, which were often spin-offs from big firms, and the management would tend to utilise the relations from their old workplaces.

However, there are diverging views about what happens with the existing relations and networks during the transition. Huber & Wörgötter (1998) argue that two types of networks evolve: survival and entrepreneurial networks. The survival network consists of former state-owned firms, which strive for power and control in order to "obtain rent," whereas the actors from the entrepreneurial networks are either individuals from the former state-owned firms or new entrants. Sedaitis (1997) observes additional differences, noting that spin-off firms from former state-owned firms have higher network density than new private start-up firms, and it follows that their strengths are their skills to build institutions and to use relations to former colleagues. The networks of spin-off firms are inversely related to the volume of market sales but are positively related to compliance with the internal rules of the exchange. Start-up firms are more honed to pursuit of opportunities and excel as revenue generators. They are more dynamic, flexible, and able to respond quickly to shifts in market conditions. There seemed to be differences between relations established in the planned economy and those established after 1992 as the old networks tend to be more embedded in a complex set of personal relations, which are used to maintain power and dominance in the network, while the networks of newly established firms are more dynamic.

The Importance of Personal Relations

The importance of personal relations in the Russian economy was first observed by Berliner (1952); several researchers have since studied the role personal relations play in both legal and illegal business activities. Thus, it seems that the reason for the importance of personal relations can at least partly be viewed as a legacy of the planned economy, especially the shortages of goods, which were so significant and widespread. This means, for instance, that firms tend to rely more on personal relations than on the legal system to solve disputes and conflicts (Hendley 1997). However, in one of the few empirical studies,

Hendley *et al.* (1997) draw an opposite picture, in which professional, ethnic, family, social, and political relations had little importance, at least for former state-owned firms. The only factors that had any bearing were a common educational background or the result of the old official relations. Ledeneva (1998) argues that although the first wave of businessmen originated in personal relations, reforms tend to undermine the importance of personal relations, while they still seem to be important in contacts with tax authorities, customs, banks and district administrations.

But, the importance of personal relations can also be a result of the reforms; that is, due to the uncertainty and volatility in the Russian economy, firms tend to do business with those with whom they already have strong personal relations. In an environment characterised by high transaction costs due to opportunism, lack of a property-rights-based legal framework, lack of a stable political structure, and firms, which lack knowledge on how to buy and sell in a market, networks of personal relations are instrumental (Peng & Heath 1996). The best way to realise agreements and contracts is to do business with those whom one trusts. Consequently, the importance of personal relations is both a legacy of the planned economy and a result of the uncertainty and volatility caused by the reforms.

Difficulties in Managing Relations and Networks

In the light of the firms' lack of experience in managing relations with suppliers and customers and the deep production decline in Russia after the reforms were initiated, it is not surprising the firms have difficulties in managing relations. It seems, however, that despite the dismantling of the plan and the liberalisation of prices, insufficient supplies remain a big problem for Russian firms (Shama 1992). Relations to the suppliers changed character; in many cases they became bad or very bad (Filatotchev *et al.* 1996), and they made up the most serious problem in 1992 and remained so in 1995 (McCarthy & Puffer 1995). According to Gurkov (1996), this is in part because of a lack of means with which to purchase raw materials and semi-finished goods, and high debts to suppliers. The insufficient supplies meant that shortages remained high from 1991 to 1995 (Blanchard & Kremer 1997).

Russian firms do not only experience difficulties in managing relations to suppliers; relations with the customers have became worsened as well (Filatotchev *et al.* 1996) and are often perceived as a major constraint on firms, probably due to a sharp decrease in demand (Buck *et al.* 1998; Golden *et al.* 1995; McCarthy & Puffer 1995). At the same time, the firms perceive a higher level of competition (Golden *et al.* 1995; Shama 1992). Another serious problem linked to relations to suppliers and customers was that the firms experienced a financial recession, which forced many of them to begin to barter (Aukutsionek 1998; Commander *et al*. 2002; Gurkov 1996; Poser 1998).

Changes in Relations and Networks

The change of governance of the economy aims to cause change on the micro-level. Gurkov (1996) observes that Russians strove to change their products in order to satisfy customers, and the changes within their distribution channels confirm this observation; moreover, these changes towards an increased market orientation have led to better performance. Also, in this case the increased uncertainty is the triggering factor as it causes the firms to focus more extensively on the buyer, beginning to develop new products, conducting market research, and trying to satisfy customers (Golden *et al*. 1995).

Obviously, some researchers have advanced the idea that existing relations are maintained but transformed during the transition process. Salmi & Mattsson (1998) argue that the social network based on personal relationships and the network of production relations undergo an overlapping process, while Huber & Wörgötter (1998) observe that these two networks tend to exist in parallel rather than overlapping with each other, which means that the former state-owned firms will continue to do business with each other while the small newly founded firms will develop new networks.

Davis *et al*. (1996) observe an almost total collapse of networks between firms in different former Soviet republics after 1992. Moreover, they also found that firms' success is related to their ability to establish and maintain domestic and republic-specific networks. Gurkov (1996) confirms the collapse of former production relations, and counterparts that let the firms down were viewed as being the main reason for the failure of many firms. Blanchard & Kremer (1997) even argue that the lack of trust and reputation combined with weak contract enforcement, short-term horizons and opportunistic behaviour in the networks are reasons for the production decline in Russia at the beginning of the 1990s. Another explanation may be that the position of the customer in economic systems characterised by monopoly and shortages, such as in the planned economies, was weak. In such situations the exit option is inaccessible and the voice option is meaningless or counterproductive. According to Gurdon & Savitt (2000), the first option used by customers in the previously planned economies, when they got access to alternatives, tended to be to exit the relationship. Thus, exiting is a natural behaviour when barriers are removed and alternatives appear. In consumer markets this was found to be a quick process, but it is slower in industrial markets (Gurdon *et al*. 1999).

Theoretical Point of Departure

Independently of which of these perspectives is applied, it is obvious that the transformation of the Russian firms and market takes time and that a "continuous process of incremental change is now inevitable" (Filatotchev *et al.* 1996: 101). Moreover, most managers find that managing relations with customers and suppliers is probably the most serious problem and a major constraint on the firm's development during the transition process. A perspective is needed that grasps the fact that transition is a market process, which Snehota (1993: 17) viewed in the following way: "market process is the process of networking, that is, establishing, strengthening, weakening and dissolution of exchange relationships between market participants." Our knowledge about these processes in Russia is limited.

In the selection of an appropriate theory, two considerations were taken into account. The first was to find a theory that dealt with relationships and networks, and second, that this theory should incorporate both change and stability. In Western research on industrial marketing management, the term "networks" has its own distinct meaning. The basic premise for the concept of networks used here is derived from the findings of the Industrial Marketing and Purchasing Group (e.g. Ford 1990; Håkansson 1982; Håkansson & Snehota 1995; Turnbull & Valla 1986). It is not the first time a network approach has been used in studies of the transition economies in Eastern Europe and the former Soviet Union, but usually the focus has been on foreign firms entering the markets (Bridgewater 1999; Salmi 2000; Törnroos & Nieminen 1999) and the data have been gathered mainly at the Western firms. The existence of business networks within this tradition is based on the notion of combining heterogeneous resources in order to interlink activities and actors (Håkansson & Snehota 1995). In a wider context, business relationships are connected to each other through their interdependence and together constitute a structure, the business network, which is defined as a set of two or more connected business relationships (Anderson *et al.* 1994).

It is not coincidence that the Austrian school has been the second source of inspiration. It has a long and rich tradition when it comes to discussing and criticising both the attempts to plan the economy in the Soviet Union (Caldwell 1997) and the attempts to reform the planning system during the perestroika era (Boettke 1993). Moreover, its strong emphasis on dynamics and change suits this study's approach.

During the transition the main problem the firms perceived was in managing their relations with the contexts, mainly customers and suppliers. Moreover, theories are needed that can provide models necessary for understanding these processes. This is the reason that the network perspective is applied in this study. One of the characteristics of the network perspective is that it deals with stability, change, and the interplay between them. It seems logical to study the Russian market and Russian firms by applying the network perspective, for five reasons.

(1) The transition is largely a market problem, as institutional changes such as price liberalisation and dismantling of the plan and the plan authorities affect the firm's operations in the context, although to varying degrees.
(2) Several studies have found theoretical arguments for the use of a network perspective.
(3) A number of empirical studies have observed that Russian managers perceive relations with other firms as the main constraint and problem.
(4) The changes take place over time and are both intra-organisational and inter-organisational phenomena.
(5) There is a tension between the legacy of the planned economy and the beliefs and dreams about the future.

Key Assumption-Resource Heterogeneity

The European network perspective, which had its roots back in the 1960s (Johanson 1966), corresponded with my requirements. At the beginning of the 1980s, two key concepts, relationship and network (Hägg & Johanson 1982; Håkansson 1982), were launched. Hägg & Johanson (1982) defined the heterogeneity of resources as the theoretical point of departure. Initially, it was said that there are three sources for heterogeneity of resources. The first is the intangibility dimension, which refers to the heterogeneity being found in human beings and the fact that knowledge about the utilisation of resources is imperfectly distributed among the actors (Penrose 1959; Snehota 1990). Experience, human capital, personality, knowledge, and so on, are not only imperfectly spread among the individuals, but also different from case to case. To put it briefly, people are different and that is an important aspect of heterogeneity. The second source is the heterogeneity that can be found in nature (Hägg & Johanson 1982). For instance, the same raw material varies: pine from one region is often of a different quality from pine from the neighbouring region. Moreover, raw material has different physical locations. Third, over time new heterogeneity develops. Thus, the value is never definite in time and space (Håkansson & Johanson 1992). When individual A does something with material B there is an outcome which differs from when individual C does something with the same material.

Actually, it is the bounded knowledge about the use of resources, which is imperfectly spread among the individuals (Hayek 1945; Snehota 1990), that makes the resources heterogeneous, and could therefore be viewed as the key assumption in the network perspective. Thus, a resource is the combination of knowledge and an intangible or tangible element (Håkansson & Snehota 1995). Resources are characterised by scarcity, and their value varies depending on with whom and with which resources they are combined. The supply and scarcity of the resources are both an opportunity and an obstacle for the firm. A resource is something that has a value for someone. This means that one has to make a sacrifice to own, control, or at least have access to it.

The Firm and the Business Relationship

Two definitions of the firm follow from the discussion around the notion of heterogeneous resources. The first is Penrose's (1959: 33) classic approach to the firm. She said that the firm could be viewed as a "psychological predisposition on the part of individuals to take a chance in the hope of gain, and in particular, to commit effort and resources to speculative activity." Snehota's definition (1990: 42) is close. He described the firm as "a pattern of activities that link together a set of actors and resources with the purpose of exploiting exchange in a market." Two elements of the definitions are worth emphasising. First, both definitions contain a component describing the firm as a durable collection of heterogeneous resources. Second, they both claim that these resources must be at work (that is an activity must be performed). The third component of the definitions refers to the goal or objective of the firm. In Penrose's version, it is the hope of gain and for Snehota it is to exploit exchange in a market. Obviously, firms are constituted by a collection of resources, which are controlled and activated by the firm in order to do business.

There are two profound dimensions that distinguish a business relationship from other transactions: *long-term orientation* and *importance*. The first and most obvious is that the business relationship has an explicit time dimension. A relationship is durable and the firms buy and sell recurrently from specific counterparts (Hallén 1986). The next characteristic concerns the importance of the business with the counterparts. Keeping these two dimensions in mind, it still seems worthwhile to remind the reader that none of three governance modes — market, firm, and relationship — exists in its pure form (Bradach & Eccles 1989; Håkansson & Johanson 1993; Powell 1990). For instance, price is not unimportant in the relationship. Commitment and trust, generally viewed as driving mechanisms in the relationships, can prevail within a hierarchy. Power, rules, and norms, finally, are seldom absent in the market transaction. It is rather a question of degree and character.

Exchange and Use of Resources

Over the years, several attempts have been made to describe and explain the network's stable structure. One of the traditions advances the idea that there are two levels in the network (see Figure 1). These are "the network of exchange relationships between industrial actors and the production system where the resources are employed and developed in production" (Johanson & Mattsson 1992: 205). I call the two levels in the network the exchange level and the use level. This idea is based on the assumption that few resources actually are exchanged, but are used in combinations and almost all of them are used in order to execute the exchange. This division of the network can also be observed

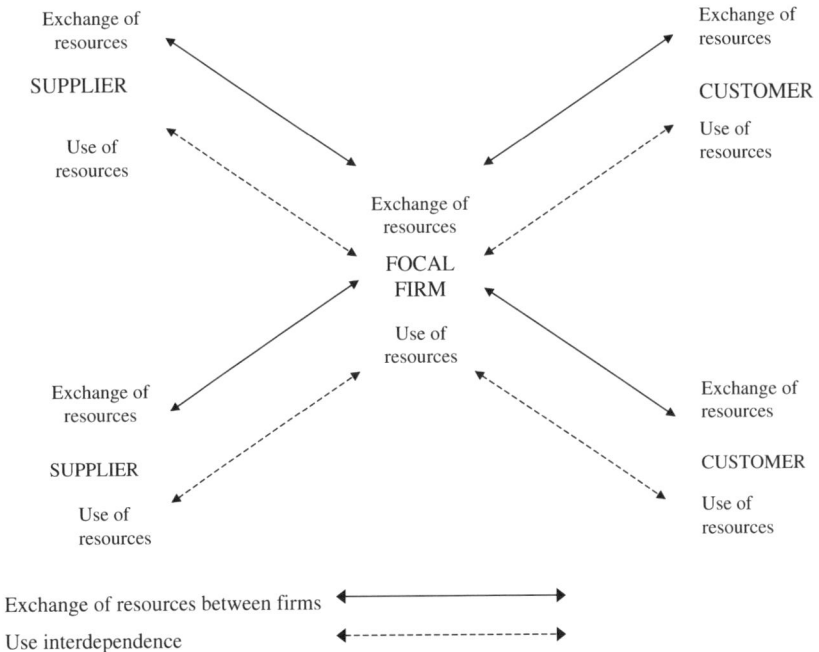

Exchange of resources

SUPPLIER

Use of resources

Exchange of resources

SUPPLIER

Use of resources

Exchange of resources

FOCAL FIRM

Use of resources

Exchange of resources

CUSTOMER

Use of resources

Exchange of resources

CUSTOMER

Use of resources

Exchange of resources between firms

Use interdependence

Figure 1: Relations between the actors and the use of resources (adapted from Johanson & Mattsson 1992).

in Lundgren's study of technological change (1991). The network level is a structure of actors that exchange resources, whereas the technological system is a cluster of interdependent technologies that are structured to whole systems, where various technologies are dependent on each other and interact with each other in different ways.

A firm cannot exist in a vacuum (Håkansson & Snehota 1989) — firms are always dependent on other firms' resources. It is understood that no firm can survive by exclusively combining its internal resources, but is always dependent on other firms' provision of resources, which causes a situation where the firm is exchanging resources with other firms (e.g. Cook & Emerson 1978). Therefore, as described by Emerson (1981), each actor or firm has both possessions and behavioural capabilities, and needs related to realisation of them. Firms will act so that needs are satisfied. The possessions and behavioural capabilities are resources if other specific firms value them. The firm approaches other firms in order to obtain the resources needed. In accordance with Alchian & Allen (1964), the economic exchange is seen as a reciprocal transfer of resources. Economic exchange implies a change of control of the resources involved. Thus, according to Snehota (1990: 58), "Values involved in exchange regard benefits from the rights to use the entities exchanged as resources for whatever specific purpose pursued by the parties [. . .] An economic exchange is essentially a barter, a mutual transfer of rights to benefit from the possession of a resource from one owner to another."

From these writings, an exchange situation can be understood to mean that the parties both give and receive value and that the focus is not on possession, but on the use of the transferred resources. The user defines the value of the resource (Snehota 1990). Both the exchange and transfer of resources between the actors is crucial for the firm. Barter trade is the best example of exchange of resources between two parties. Trade requires direct control, for instance ownership, which, in turn, requires that the resources traded are sufficiently tangible. The value of the resources in the exchange is determined by the relationship between the provider and user of the resources (Håkansson & Snehota 1995). Firms, through their relationships with other firms, are parts of networks where resources are exchanged between the actors.

Owing to the bounded knowledge, the market, which the firm approaches, is perceived to be characterised by uncertainty and complexity, which, in turn, make that market unpredictable. The uncertainty refers to the estimation and expectation of the present market, but also how the market will develop in a longer perspective. One way to cope with the complexity and uncertainty is to simplify extensively, which is to delimit the number of alternatives, exchange partners, and choose to repeat actions that were previously rewarded. In this case, it means continued exchange with those firms with which the focal firm already has experience. Even though the focus is on the interaction and the development of relationships between the actors, it starts from somewhere. The exchange might be viewed both as the start of the relationship and as a main dimension of the relationship.

In a critical note on the planning problem, Hayek argued (1945) that the use of resources is the economic problem that society has to face. Moran & Ghoshal (1999: 392) stretched the argument that resource use is the most important issue for the single firm and claimed further that "the creation of economic value, be it individuals or organisations, is a process that involves the use of resources." Control of resources in time and space is an important dimension, because control gives the firm the right to use the resource, but control also gives the firm the right to benefit from this use. Finally, these two interact so that the firm develops knowledge about how to use the resources more beneficially. The control of the resources gives the firm the opportunity to use them.

The less available a resource the more crucial is the degree of control (Håkansson & Johanson 1992). An actor can directly control resources, for instance by ownership, but resources can also be indirectly controlled, either by exchange or by sharing, through joint development with other actors. There are two ways to control resources. Firstly, there are resources that are owned (Håkansson & Johanson 1993a; Mahoney & Pandian 1992). They are mainly tangible, but there are exceptions, for instance, patents, brands, goodwill, quotas, licenses, and so on are intangible. With ownership, it follows that they are tradable, even though trade of course often means a change in value. Secondly, there are resources that are shared between various firms since they are developed in the interaction between the firms. Through the interaction knowledge and capabilities evolve that are context specific. The crucial component in these resources is intangible and embedded in the firms and thus not transferable to other contexts.

Håkansson (1992) listed six types of resources that the firm strives to control. The first type is raw and supplemental material. The second concerns technology, that is, knowledge and equipment necessary to utilise the knowledge. Third, is the control of supply of a specific strategic product. Fourth, is the control of financial means. The fifth is control over human resources, which may have a specific ability or be located in a strategic geographic area. The resources mentioned up to this point are usually controlled by ownership or long-term contract, but the sixth type differs from the first five, because it can be viewed as both a way to control resources or as a resource in itself. Access to specific relationships is a crucial way to control resources, as it covers not only internal resources but also the resources in the surrounding context. The first question one has to ask oneself is who is doing what. In a relationship, the division of activities between the firms is an indicator of how the relationship is structured, which turns it, at least partly, into a pattern of use of resources. Within this pattern, one use is followed by another. This means there is an interface between uses, which has to be understood.

Relationships are characterised by interdependence (Blankenburg-Holm *et al.* 1999; Kumar *et al.* 1995). Through performance of activities resources, which are controlled by firms in the relationships, are put in use. On each exchange episode in the relationship the firm's resources are mobilised vis-à-vis another firm's resources and they are brought together in an interface by various activities (Richardson 1972; 1995). Over time, "Two companies direct and orient some of their resources toward each other [. . .] A relationship between two companies can tie together more or less slightly some of their resources in a specific way" (Håkansson & Snehota 1995: 136). From a financial point of view, this can be defined as investment of resources towards specific counterparts. Over time, in a dynamic and interactive process the two firms' resources achieve complementarity, which improves efficiency and profitability. In parallel, it diminishes potential exchange opportunities, and consequently the transferability and substitutability in the relationship increases and so does the interdependence. Low substitutability and transferability means that the resources are not versatile, which means that resources combined, used, and exchanged in a relationship have less meaning in contexts other than the relationship (Håkansson & Johanson 1992). The relationship gives value to the two firms' resource collections, not only to the resource explicitly exchanged, but also to the resources deployed in the relationship.

Changes in the Network

Changes of Exchange and Use of Resources

Håkansson & Snehota (1995) claim that the main purpose of the firm is the creation and development of new resources. Development of new resources takes place over time and the history thus plays an important role in understanding change in networks. Consequently, path dependence is typical for the network. Lundgren (1991) assumes that technology could only be understood by understanding the past. Change and technological development must be studied in space and time, that is, both the structure and the dynamics must be taken into consideration. Moreover, he also sees two levels in industrial systems and like Johanson & Mattsson (1992) he suggests a circular relation between the exchange level and the use level. Every change is embedded in a specific context. The combined efforts of the different actors are a condition for technological development, which is an interactive and cumulative process between firms, where those involved learn by relating old experience to new impressions. Especially important are the small changes, often characterised by adaptation to the context, as the core of technological change.

Use of resources not only means efficiency, standardisation, and economisation, what March (1991) calls exploitation, it also involves exploration and innovation. For instance, use of resources (von Hippel 1988) can be a source for exploring new solutions to problems that occurred when using the resources. On the use level, firms search for and discover new, or until then unknown, ways to combine previously known resources. Firms also find resources, which until then had been unknown, and combine them with the resources already used and exchanged. Innovation and technological development are closely related to use of resources and from those it follows that the knowledge, which is a product of the change in use of resources, is costly to transfer. Consequently, it is a strength to solve one's own problems, but the combination of problem and solution when using resources makes this knowledge "sticky" (von Hippel 1998). On the use level, it means that activities such as transportation, distribution, production, communication, storage, payment, and resources such as equipment, organisation, expertise, patents, goodwill, brands, and people are combined in new ways.

Knowledge and Change

Building on Johanson & Mattsson (1985) and Johanson & Vahlne (1990), the crucial knowledge acquisition does not take place in the interaction between the firm and an anonymous market, but in the *relationship between firms, where resources are exchanged and used.* Thus, experience-based knowledge could be given a deeper and richer meaning if it is studied within the frame of a specific relationship. A firm's experience is directly related to its relationships with other firms. It reflects the firm's knowledge about relationships that are directly and indirectly related to it, and thus, is the platform for the firm's capabilities to use and exchange resources in the network. Experience is situation specific and a result of action in the past (Johanson & Vahlne 1990; Penrose 1959). Consequently it is difficult and costly to generalise and transfer to other contexts. It can only be acquired through concrete activities and it is not accessible for those who follow the network from outside.

Resource heterogeneity implies that, in principle, there is an endless number of possible resource combinations, and that there is always space for new combinations. In accordance with Penrose (1959), firms are driven by a desire to search and find more knowledge about the resources they have at their disposal in order to develop new combinations. The knowledge is not only generated within the firm, but is also an effect of individuals' increased experience and knowledge of the external world. Knowledge of markets and technology being developed by other firms of particular interest (Penrose 1959), because additional knowledge is assumed to improve efficiency and profitability, the unknown and unused are of crucial importance.

In a similar way, Håkansson (1993: 213) argues, "By knowing more about how the product can be combined with other products, and/or functions within the production process and/or functions when used by their customers, the user can increase the value of it [i.e. the product]. In order for the user to learn more about this they have to utilise the producer and his knowledge. But that is not enough. The possibilities of developing the interface between the actual product and other resources are certainly, if the product is not seen as given, but as a variable which can be changed." Through interaction, the firms become specialists in finding new resource combinations to use and exchange. This is both a conscious and unconscious learning process, where the boundaries of the firm's knowledge change. It goes on constantly.

There is no perfect market for experience — it is embedded in the relationship. Neither can it be fully controlled by the firm, since it cannot be owned. When a firm is interacting with a specific counterpart, it acquires experiences that give new meanings to old knowledge and provide new ways of using and exchanging resources. It is in line with Penrose's (1959) ideas that the intangible experience is obtained through interaction between individuals adding new value to earlier experiences. The procurement of knowledge often requires the establishment of long-term relationships (von Hippel 1988). The relevant environment of the relationship, where other actors are exposed, would be the set of opportunities perceived by the two parties. This is because use and exchange in one relationship often require adaptations in other connected relationships (Anderson *et al.* 1994).

Håkansson (1993) identified three types of learning in a network context. The firm learns by experimenting, by using other firms' knowledge, and finally, several actors can be involved in the process that is labelled joint learning. Joint learning is an interaction process, where two firms develop the skills and experience needed to utilise each other's resources. Joint learning implies mutual adaptations. The firms become specialists in producing joint values. Thus the team-effect, which is the result of human co-operation and the reason why firms exist (Alchian & Demsetz 1972), also occurs in business relationships, since they provide both stability and variety, which are crucial for learning (Håkansson 1993). Stability provides the time and opportunity for repetition, which is needed, as learning is a complex and multidimensional process. Stability is needed partly because the knowledge about how to use a resource is tacit (i.e. it is costly to transfer and difficult to understand for outsiders), and partly, because the parties jointly develop new knowledge (Håkansson & Snehota 1995). Variety, on the other hand, exists when actors have the possibility of relating their own resources and knowledge to that of others. New aspects of life, sometimes never known beforehand, are discovered and combined with existing experience.

Change Processes

Kirzner (1992) argues that change embraces both *search* and *discovery*, which are related to the knowledge gained during the process, and which, in turn, can be of three types. The first one is what the firm knows. This knowledge can be both experiential and tacit, and objective and explicit in nature. The second is the knowledge of which the firm is aware, but which it does not possess itself. Thus, the firm knows that it does not know. In this case, the knowledge could also be experiential and tacit, objective and explicit in character. Such knowledge is usually costly to find and/or to produce — the higher the degree of experience and tacitness the more costly to reproduce it. The difference between the first type and the second type of knowledge is that the firm possesses the first, while the second is not possessed by the firm and consequently has to be found. Recognising this type of knowledge implies searching for something, which the firm is able to define.

Finally, there is a third type of knowledge, which is unknowable for the firm. The firm does not know that it does not know. It can be defined as "sheer ignorance" (Kirzner 1997) until the moment the firm realises that it has discovered something previously unknowable. According to Kirzner (1997: 72), "what has occurred is that one has discovered one's previous (utterly unknown) ignorance. What distinguishes discovery [. . .] from successful search [. . .] is that the former (unlike the latter) involves that surprise accompanies the realization that one had overlooked something in fact readily available." The dictionary describes discovery as someone finding out something they did not know about before or being the first to discover a place, a substance, or fact that no one knew before (Collins Cobuild 1987).

Kirzner (1992) argued that discovery is a consequence of the firm's alertness, that is, firms may be more or less able to make discoveries. Barney (1986), on the other hand, claimed that discoveries could only be described as luck, whereas Hayek (1936) saw the discovery as a consequence of accidents. Simply put, discoveries are impossible to completely avoid. By combining these five

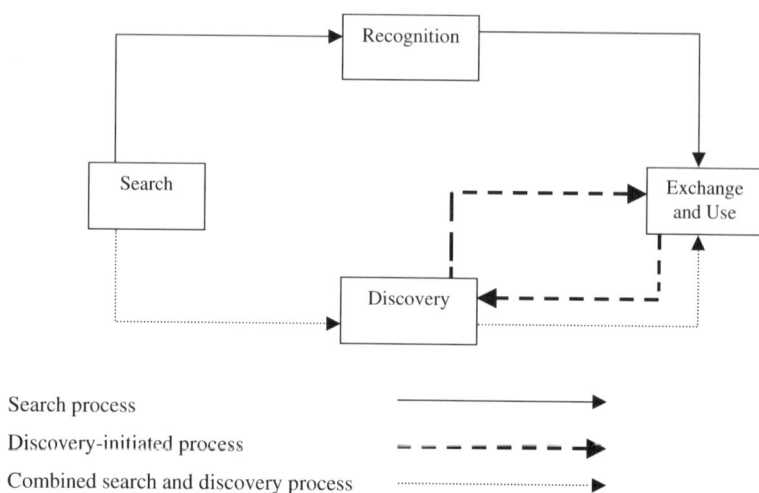

Figure 2: Components in the change processes.

components — search, recognition, discovery, exchange and use — I distinguish three change processes.

The first type could be called the search process and in this case, the change process is a linear route process (the continuous line search-recognition-exchange and use in Figure 2), which starts from search. Search is when the actor, either the authority or the firm, knows what both the ends and the means are, but does not simultaneously have control over both and so has to search for one or the other. Once the ends and the means are identified, the actor knows what he is searching for. Search means that the firm, based on its knowledge, has identified the ends or the means. However, it has still not been able to combine them, that is, it has to search for one of them in order to find them and to combine them and to exchange or use the resources. Thereby, search is the activity that ties what we know with what we believe that we will find. Recognition is the intended result of search. In this case, change is a conscious and planned process. For example, the firm may know the product but has not found the buyer or it may know the customer and the product but has to find the right way to produce the product. Thus, a precondition for search is that the actor knows either the ends or the means. The search process can only take place within the frames of the searching actor's knowledge.

But changes are often not planned. They sometimes happen by accident or are a coincidence. For example, when either the ends or the means (but not both) are not known and identified, or when neither are known, they may be unintentionally or unconsciously be combined. Sometimes (or rather usually) things take place that are largely outside the control of the firm. The firm discovers what was previously unknown or unknowable. Discovery is not completely random. Also, in this case experience and expectation make up the frame for what the firm actually can discover. One difference between search and recognition, on the one hand, and discovery, on the other hand, is that the latter is not intentionally planned. Discovery is the key concept in the remaining two processes.

The second change process appears from exchange and use in the relationships and is a kind of discovery. It follows the loop exchange and use-discovery-exchange and use (the thick dotted line in Figure 2). During either an occasional or repetitive exchange or in the use of an existing combination of resources, the firm discovers that a change is needed and/or might be beneficial for it. The discovery-initiated process begins in the prevailing structure of exchange and use of resources in the network and suddenly, the firms discovers something previously unknown, which changes either the exchange or the use or both. This is an unintentional change process. The firms are not looking for a change, but have to change due to the discovery, and since exchange or use is a precondition for this type of change, only the firm has the possibility of making this discovery.

Finally, there is a third change process, which can be called a combined process. This type of change (search-discovery-exchange and use) is reflected as the thin dotted line in Figure 2. It starts from search, but while searching, the firm discovers something else, which until then could have been unknowable. The discovery results in a new way of using and exchanging resources, even though they were expecting to find something different.

In the network, learning is a continuous process where firms acquire mutual knowledge about how to use and exchange resources. Adaptations and correction of negative discoveries are possible because of this mutuality. In this process of learning, search and discovery are instrumental for changes. Kirzner's (1992) focus is on the exchange level and how an alert firm is able to link two other firms, which do not know about the profitability in doing business with each other. By linking a buyer and a seller, the firm fills a structural hole in the network (Burt 1992). Exchanging resources or doing business (i.e. buying and selling) is the main activity on the exchange level and thereby finding and exploiting exchange opportunities is important for how the relationship changes on the exchange level. When the firm has control over either the ends or the means, but not both, this can be defined as exchange opportunity. This implies that the firm has identified either the customer or the supplier but has not yet been able to identify how to pay or which product to buy or sell or vice versa. Only if the ends and the means are found and combined in space and time does the exchange begin. Nevertheless, search and discovery exist and drive changes on both the use and exchange level.

To sum up, the network process is based on the joint experience the firms in the network acquire through interaction with each other. During this process, they mutually find ways of using and exchanging resources. Finding is sometimes an intended result where the firms search for already existing knowledge, but very often, this process contains discoveries.

Chapter 2

Method Section

The Unit of Analysis in Change

The problems in getting access to Russian firms are probably the main reason why so few empirical studies concerning firms' behaviour in the market have been conducted. In the light of that and the limited knowledge of what is actually happening in the Russian market it seems reasonable to concentrate on a single case study (Yin 1989). A case study, according to Yin (1989), is an appropriate strategy when it covers a unique or significant subject, which has been sparsely studied, but is of such importance that it deserves to be studied. Moreover, Yin mentions the revelatory case study, which is when the researcher has an opportunity to observe and understand a previously inaccessible subject. In the light of the small number of empirical studies conducted so far and the limited knowledge of what is actually happening in the Russian market it seems reasonable to concentrate on a single case study. This part of the study has a lot in common with pilot studies, where the researcher is forced to refine the methods for data collection and to develop the theoretical assumptions (Yin 1989).

The case selected for this study should meet the criteria of being a formerly state-owned firm still maintaining at least one important relation from the planned economy. Its relationships include both such that are kept since the planned economy era and new ones established during the transition to market economy governance. The unit of analysis in this study is the network of a firm called Tipografiya, which could be defined as the object and the context of the study.

In several articles, Pettigrew (1987, 1990, 1992, 1997) devoted time to processual analysis, where time and history are in focus. In accordance with Pettigrew (1997), the ambition was not to produce a case history but a case study. The latter reaches beyond the border of the case history in three aspects: (1) The researcher seeks pattern in the process and does at least try to compare case A with case B; (2) the researcher tries to find the underlying mechanisms, which create the patterns in the process; and finally (3) the main factor that turns a case history into a case study is that the exploratory inductive search after patterns goes hand-in-hand with a more deductive verification. Inspired by Van de Ven (1992), Pettigrew (1997) defined process as a sequence of individual and collective events, actions, and activities, which develop over time in a context. The processes take place in a context in which they are embedded. One process can be linear, directional, cumulative, and irreversible, while another is non-linear, radical, and transformational.

For the processual researcher both the result of the process and the process in itself are of interest. This approach suits the purpose of this study well, as the transition to a market economy was defined as a process and not as two positions, where a planned economy was replaced by a market economy. The aim was to explain what the links were between context and results in this process and how and why they developed. A processual analysis is needed if one has the ambition to understand the process, that is, not only what takes place over a specific period, but the dynamic that exists in the tension between past, present, and future. A processual analysis that follows the object forward in time is stronger than a processual analysis that is retrospective in character. Retrospective studies entail a bigger risk for ex-post rationalisation, simplifications, and linear reasoning.

In accordance with Eisenhardt (1989) and Yin's (1989) description, case studies combine different sources of data and methods of data collection, which leads to strong synergies. These include archives, interviews, questionnaires, and observations and the evidence gathered can be both qualitative and quantitative. Wider and richer material gives the researcher the possibility of studying more than one topic but above all, the observations are more reliable if several sources give the same evidence. Three methods were used: interviews, direct observations and documentation.

Qualitative Research Interviews

In this section, the focus is on the interview, which was the most important method for this study. As described by Kvale (1997), the questions had not only a descriptive form but also aimed at drawing out the informants' spontaneous stories. During the period from September 1996 to June 2000, I completed 35 interviews with people who, at that time, were employed at Tipografiya. One of the informants, the chief accountant Ludmila Khokholova, left the firm during the period of data collection. At the time, all those who were interviewed had a position as some kind of manager, with two exceptions, the interviews with Galina Belova and Svetlana Klimenko in September 1996. Galina Belova's title was dispatcher. In September 1996 Khokholova was on vacation and not available and Svetlana Klimenko was the deputy chief accountant. However, at the time of the second interview with

Klimenko she had already replaced Khokhololova as chief accountant. Although the respondents were on a low managerial level, the picture they drew in the case study is very much a managers' view of reality. Interviews with the employees at Tipografiya were mainly conducted in their workroom at the printing house in Novgorod. We were alone in the room and the interviews took from 30 to 70 minutes. In addition, three interviews with Nikolay Yevlapmiyev and one with Irina Kondratyeva were carried out in Sweden. All the interviews were conducted in Russian without an interpreter. Interviews, other than those in Sweden and the first one with Sergei Brutman, were tape-recorded and later transcribed into Russian.

Despite the well-defined purpose of each step of the interview, their character was similar to what Kvale (1997) calls qualitative conversation interviews. The qualitative research interview is half-structured, which means that it is neither an open conversation nor that it strictly follows a structured questionnaire (Kvale 1997). But, this does *not* mean that the qualitative interview misses focus and subject. The qualitative interview results preferably in words and not in figures. Its focus is in this case the firm's relationships with its customers and suppliers. The present study has exploratory aims and was open to unexpected answers and explanations. Almost all the interviews were tape-recorded and thereafter mainly typewritten, but a handful were also written down by hand.

The Set-Up of the Data Collection

Step 1 — The Quantitative Mapping of the Focal Firm's Network Structure

The purpose of the first interviews at the majority of the firms interviewed was to map the network structure within which the firm had operated during recent years. The structure was quantitatively mapped using a structured question guide (see Appendix B), which in the spring of 1996 was translated from English to Russian. The guide was used to get answers to the following questions: Which are the firm's most important customers and suppliers? What does the firm buy from its suppliers and sell to its customers? What types of investment has the firm made in its relations with customers and suppliers? What technology, in terms of machines, equipment, and expertise, exists and by whom is it used? Step 1 meant that Tipografiya's most important relationships were quantitatively mapped and identified. From the time of the first visit in September 1996 to the next, in January 1997, Tipografiya managed to find and supply the quantitative data for the period 1993–1995. These data were then updated and completed. A sub-purpose of this step was to study Tipografiya's organisation, its formal structure, ownership, financial status, number of employees and their tasks and authority and to find key-persons.

Step 2 — The Qualitative Mapping of the Focal Firm's Network Structure

During the first visit, I had already begun to deal with questions that were part of Step 2. Besides the relationships, which in September and November 1996 had only been partly identified and quantified, I also interested myself in the resources used in the relationships. Tipografiya's relationships with its customers and suppliers were the objects and I was looking for data concerning different types of activities and resources, such as manufacturing, storing, investments, payment, communication, and transportation and was interested in how they were working at that time. The aim was to draw a picture of how Tipografiya operated and related to its customers and suppliers. Open-ended questions were varied with more concrete and specific questions.

Step 3 — Investigation of Dynamics and Change in the Focal Firms' Network

If Steps 1 and 2 meant that Tipografiya's network structure was quantitatively and qualitatively mapped and described, the aim of Step 3 was to grasp the dynamics and the changes in the same network. In this step, I tried to identify both change and stability in Tipografiya's network, and the main purpose was to find the driving forces in these processes. A sub-purpose was to go back to the period before the quantitative data (that is before 1993), in order to find the stability and change in the planned economy. Step 3 constituted the biggest part of the data collection.

Processing of Data from the Interviews

The transcriptions are both de-contextualised and de-temporalised conversations (Kvale 1997), which, in this case, later were placed in a new context beginning with coding a large amount of data. The coding process may be characterised as a condensation and categorisation of a large volume of written text (Coffey & Atkinson 1996). During the processing of the data, fragments were brought together and thereby categories created, which had some common property or element. Coding and retrieving are activities usually connected with coding as an analytical strategy; an analysis that in this case emanated from a specific theory and a specific unit of analysis. I followed Seidel and Kelle's recommendations (1995) and began by: (1) noticing relevant phenomena, which was later followed by; (2) collecting examples of those phenomena; and completed by (3) analysing those phenomena in order to find commonalities, differences, patterns, and structures. Cutting and slicing up the data set, coding is more than just putting data into various categories. Instead, it is about identifying concepts, questioning data and categories, testing provisional relations among and within the data, and searching for antecedents and outcomes. The purpose of the study was to extend and enrich an already existing theory, but at the same time, I was open to new discoveries and was looking for similarities and dissimilarities, patterns and contrasts, and regularities and irregularities among and in the categories.

Direct Observations and Documentary Sources

In reality, the direct observations never constituted a conscious method for data collection. However, during the time at Tipografiya I had complete freedom to walk around, to study the building and the equipment, and to have short conversations with the employees and there is no doubt that the direct observations influenced the data collection. It was, however, something that emerged gradually, rather than a conscious choice of method. The excursions mainly took place on two occasions, in September 1996 and August 1999. I did not take notes or keep records during my walk around the firm, but the observations were filed as memories and impressions. Although they are not explicitly reported here, they were significant, as they strengthened observations and conclusions from the interviews.

Although analysis of documentary sources was not a predominant method, some documents were important for the work. As opposed to direct observation, using documentary sources was a conscious strategy. Two types of documents were used. The first type, different kinds of statistics, was used most extensively. They were mainly intended for internal use at Tipografiya. I was sometimes given photocopies of the originals and sometimes given the statistics in a typewritten form. The second type consisted of Tipografiya's annual reports, which were only used as background material.

Presentation and Analysis of the Case Study

The point of departure for the presentation of the study is the coding and this meant a structure consisting of two periods. The first period covered 1985–1991 and the second period 1992–1998. Within these two periods, two main blocks could be identified: one that focuses on the firm, its organisation and technology, and one that is devoted to the surrounding network. The part covering the period 1985–1991, gives a *structural* picture of Tipografiya's network. It is followed by an analysis. The major part of the case study is the second half, which in contrast to the first has a more dynamic character. It is a *processual narrative*, although it follows the same structure as Chapter 3. After the analysis of the second period, both periods are brought together in a more extensive analysis of the case study. The case is presented as a story. Quotations from the interviews are important for reliability and understanding and this is why the case contains so many quotations. With Tipografiya's approval, I chose to use the informants' real name or some other type of identifying information, thus making the case more interesting and its observations more evident (Pettigrew 1997).

The Case — Tipografiya and its Surroundings

Oblispolkom (the District Administration) in the Novgorod district, Tipografiya's owner, had a committee for printing matters, the *Komitet po Pechati i Informatsii* (KPI). The only role Oblispolkom played, as owner, was when it allocated resources for some investment. There were no annual board meetings and the top-management at Tipografiya seldom met representatives from Oblispolkom. Contact took place when Tipografiya gave KPI information about its plan fulfilment. Before mass privatisation started in Russia in 1992, legislation already permitted firms to be transformed into so-called leasing companies with preference of acquisition by the employees. The management at Tipografiya decided to start the privatisation process as a leasing company. Tipografiya's organisational structure around 1990 is depicted in Figure 3. In 1985, the director Oleg Porfiridov managed Tipografiya but at the beginning of 1989 he was replaced by Nikolay Yevlampiyev. Besides having the overall responsibility for operations, they also largely managed production. At the beginning of the 1990s, Yevlampiyev became more and more engaged in the purchasing of paper. He spent most of his time at the firm and strove to have some control over all types of activities. Tipografiya's organisational structure is to be found in Figure 3.

In 1991 a new chief engineer, Valery Polyanskiy, arrived. He inherited the task of the former chief engineer and became partly responsible for production as well as answering for the equipment and the renewal of the machine park. At that time, Nikolay Yevlampiyev felt that Tipografiya was lagging behind and needed to renew its technology. Besides that, Valery Polyanskiy started to manage the purchasing of ink, zinc, plates, and other consumables when Tipografiya was given the right to purchase freely the types of products mentioned above. Eight employees at the mechanical (engineering) workshop were placed under him. According to the

```
                    ┌──────────────────┐
                    │ Managing director│
                    │     Nikolay      │
                    │   Yevlampiyev    │
                    └──────────────────┘
```

┌─────────────────────┐   ┌─────────────────────┐   ┌─────────────────────┐
│   Chief-Economist   │   │   Chief-Engineer   │   │   Head of plan and │
│ Ludmila Khokhololova│   │ Valery Polyanskiy │   │ production department│
│   │   │   │   │   Irina Kondratyeva │
└─────────────────────┘   └─────────────────────┘   └─────────────────────┘

┌─────────────────────┐ ┌──────────────────┐ ┌──────────────────┐ ┌─────────────────────┐
│Accounting department│ │Valentina Andreyeva│ │Valentina Guseva │ │ Plan and production │
│   │ │   │ │   │ │   department   │
│   │ │ ┌──────────────┐ │ │ ┌──────────────┐ │ │   │
│   │ │ │Relief printing│ │ │ │ Bookbindery │ │ │   │
│   │ │ └──────────────┘ │ │ └──────────────┘ │ │   │
│   │ │ ┌──────────────┐ │ │ ┌──────────────┐ │ │   │
│   │ │ │Offset printing│ │ │ │ Pre-press   │ │ │   │
│   │ │ └──────────────┘ │ │ └──────────────┘ │ │   │
└─────────────────────┘ └──────────────────┘ └──────────────────┘ └─────────────────────┘

┌──────────────────┐   ┌──────────────────┐   ┌──────────────────┐
│   Mechanical   │   │ Stock room for │   │ Stock for finished│
│   workshop   │   │   paper   │   │   products   │
└──────────────────┘   └──────────────────┘   └──────────────────┘

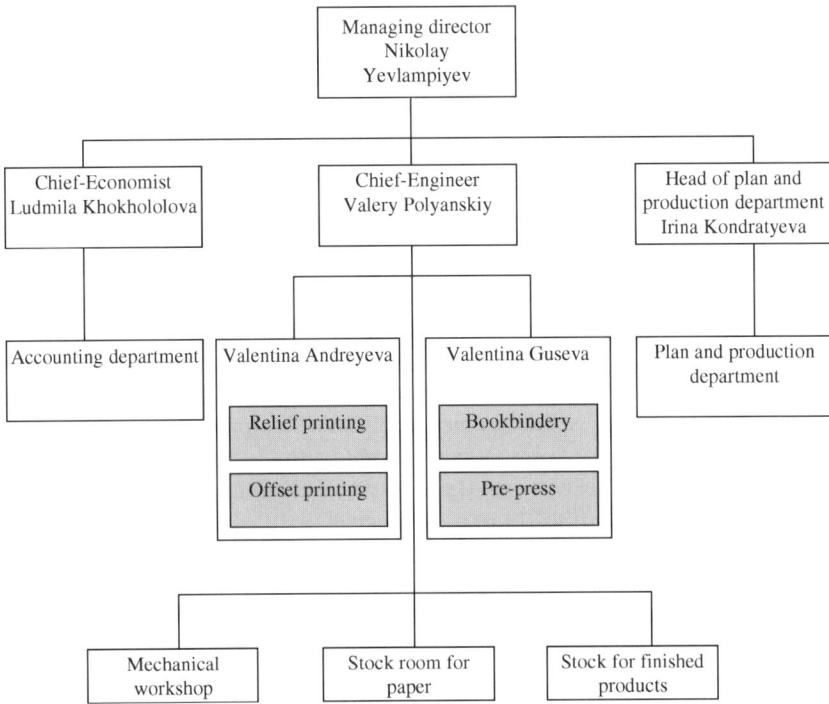

Figure 3: Tipografiya's organisation. *Source*: The organisational chart is my interpretation of Tipografiya's organisational structure around 1990. It is based on an interview with Irina Kondratyeva in September 1996.

chief engineer, the mechanical (engineering) workshop maintained and repaired Tipografiya's equipment, since it was so old. Valentina Andreyeva managed the relief printing and the offset printing shop while Valentina Guseva managed the composition room and the bookbindery. They were subordinate to the managing director, but in questions regarding technology and equipment, to the chief engineer. On the same formal level was the accounting department. The head of the department, Ludmila Khokhololova, had three bookkeepers to help her. Tipografiya had no traditional marketing or sales department; instead, the plan and production department was responsible for all contacts with the plan authorities and customers. The plan and production department was managed by Ludmila Yakovleva and was responsible for reception of plan orders, invoicing, calculations of prices, control and follow-up of production, and transportation arrangements.

Five people were working there in the middle of the 1980s: one engineer, who calculated among other things the price, two order receivers, one administrator, and the head of the department, Ludmila Yakovleva. At the end of the 1980s and beginning of the 1990s, when Ludmila Yakovleva was away on maternity leave, her deputy Irina Kondratyeva replaced her.

At the beginning of June 1997 Tipografiya celebrated its 220th anniversary. The firm had for a long time been located in the central area of the city of Novgorod, some two hundred meters from the railway station. The Novgorod district (*oblast*) is 55,300 square kilometers, larger than for instance, Denmark or the Netherlands, and has around 750,000 inhabitants, of whom one third, 250,000, live in the city of Novgorod. Around 50,000 live in Borovichi and Staraya Russa respectively.

The wood industry and the electronics industry have dominated the economy in the region. The latter suffered heavily from the economic crisis, which was a direct result of the package of economic reforms in 1992. Among other things, they meant a dramatic decrease in orders from the Ministry of Defence. Novgorod has a university, formed in 1993 when the University of Technology and the Pedagogical Institute merged. The city of Novgorod is situated about 200 kilometres from St. Petersburg and 500 kilometres from Moscow — generally, considered an advantageous position. Both the motorway and the railway between Moscow and St. Petersburg go through the city. The river Volkhov flows through the central parts of Novgorod and connects the city with the biggest lake in Europe, Ladoga, as well as the big lake Onega. The entire Russian river system can thus be used for transportation as the Volga can be reached from the Ladoga by a system of canals.

Over the last 10 years, the Novgorod district has experienced relatively positive economic development compared with almost the whole of the rest of Russia. In 1992 the region had a low ranking in terms of investment potential, 63rd out of 89, but in 1997 it had moved up to position six. Novgorod has been successful in attracting foreign capital. In 1997, the Novgorod region had attracted 2.5% of Russia's total foreign capital investment, but since it has only 0.5% of the total population it was second in terms of per capita investment. The region has also encouraged small business development and tried to attract domestic capital, but without the same striking results. Nevertheless, during the 1990s the Novogorod district experienced positive economic development compared with other parts of Russia (Ruble & Popson 1998).

Chapter 3

The Legacy — Networks in the Planned Economy

Products and Production

During the planned economy, Tipografiya produced two main products: forms and newspapers. The forms accounted for around 60% of the whole production and were mainly for the Soviet Post Office Administration, but Tipografiya also produced other types of forms for various firms and governmental organisations. A handful of local and regional newspapers constituted approximately 25% of the production. Seals and stamps, four-colour products, such as books, shared the remaining 15%. However, traditionally, Tipografiya specialised in production of different types of forms, including, to some extent, forms used on the local newspapers. The specialisation in forms was a decision made by politicians and civil servants, not by Tipografiya. Besides the newspapers and the forms, the production of books and labels produced considerable additional income. Tipografiya also printed writings pads and sold miscellaneous papers to a limited extent.

Tipografiya bought mainly eight products, of which six were different types of paper. Other than paper, the most important products were ink and matrices. In general, writing papers were used for forms, label papers for production of labels, and board for packaging of the local industry's production of TV-sets and furniture. Newsprint was used for printing the local newspapers, whereas offset paper and printing paper both had a wider field of application. A big stock of paper was viewed as a strength; it was an asset and a comfort if times were tough. The cost of paper was approximately 75% of current assets and the paper determined the quality of the end product. This meant that both price and quality of the paper were extremely important for Tipografiya.

Production was divided into two departments: The first consisted of two printing shops, one for offset printing and one for relief printing. The second production department was bookbindery and pre-press, the composition room. There was a stockroom where the paper was stored. It was managed by an employee who reported to the accounting department. Tipografiya also had an artist who was also the art director. Altogether there were approximately 100 blue-collar workers and 15 white-collar workers. During the last 10 years of the planned economy, the number of employees was stable. In 1992, 121 individuals were employed. Both production departments were located in one building in the central part of the city of Novgorod. The building had three floors. Composition and repro preceded the printing and was done by production of printing blocks in lead and by developing films. Tipografiya also produced stereotypes. Development of both films and production of plates was done manually. Photo equipment was produced in the Ukraine. The composition room was a large and demanding part of Tipografiya. Up to the beginning of the 1990s, composition was only done by hand. The composition room was the most intensive and lively department. Wages for printers were low and given the fact that it was not unusual for Tipografiya to have a shortage of staff, the company often had difficulties in producing on time. In the past, before the current management, it had happened that Tipografiya invited typesetters from other printing houses to help out.

At the end of the planned economy the first computers appeared. Tipografiya bought three computers in 1991. First, Valentina Guseva went to a computer exhibition in Moscow together with two employees, and then two of the composers were trained in Moscow. Only after that did Tipografiya buy the computers. Thereafter representatives from the computer supplier trained the composers at Tipografiya. The composition room worked in two shifts. While the composition was done the stock room on the ground floor prepared the paper needed for the specific order and took it to one of the printing shops. A special employee, who was responsible for the stock of paper, made the calculation and had control of the paper. She was subordinate partly to the plan and production department and partly to the accounting department, where she reported about consumables. This was the way it had been for a long time. It was perceived as important that the responsibility of the supervisors of the productions department should not be related to the paper. Furthermore, there was one person who managed the stock of finished products.

At the start of the study period in 1986, Tipografiya utilised two technologies for printing. The traditional relief printing shop accounted for the main part of the production during the 1980s and the beginning of the 1990s. The relief printing shop was situated partly on the first floor, but there was also a room with a few printing presses on the ground floor. Altogether, Tipografiya had eight relief printing presses, which had been supplied before 1986. Tipografiya printed the forms and newspapers in the relief printing shop as they were usually standardised and did not require any adaptations. The second technology used was offset, which first appeared at the end of the 1970s. The first offset printing press, Romajor 313, had been supplied in 1977 and in 1986 Tipografiya had a total of seven offset printing presses. Between 1986 and 1991, Tipografiya was supplied with two additional offset printing presses; in 1986, a Dominant 745 P and in 1991 one more Dominant 745. The last relief printing press had been supplied in 1984. As mentioned, Oblispolkom was the formal owner of Tipografiya. At that time, the aim was to modernise the equipment and the offset equipment was delivered by KPI. This was a governmental organisation, which undertook centralised purchasing for the graphics industry.

> We made an inquiry to them [Oblispolkom] and since it concerned a printing house, which was the biggest and most important in the district, they provided us offset machines (Valery Polyanskiy).
>
> Oblispolkom had an ambition to modernise the equipment. Everything was still centralised. For instance, KPI managed to come across some funding and equipment for the printing house. The main task of Oblispolkom's printing houses was to print the newspapers. All the revenues went direct to the district administration, which then distributed the money back to us, depending on our capability and power in relation to them (Nikolay Yevlampiyev).

They were the only authorities that could allocate resources for investments. Consequently, Tipografiya seldom made any of its own big investments in machines or equipment, and when it did happen, the decisions were always made by Oblispolkom and financed by KPI. Moreover, Tipografiya had no possibility of saving any money for investments in the future, since all profit was transferred to the government as taxes. At that time, offset technology was a revolution for the employees. They had no knowledge of handling both negatives and positives. When the offset equipment was installed, Tipografiya was still owned by Oblispolkom. But, since the printing house still belonged to the district administration and not the Communist Party's district department it was worse equipped than printing houses in the neighbouring district, Tver or Vologda, which belonged formally to the Communist Party. The party's priority was the development of its own printing houses. On the other hand, Tipografiya was better off than the small printing houses in the Novgorod district, which were municipally owned.

The printing shop for newspapers was located in a wing of the same building but a little aside. The offset technology was mainly used for smaller-volume orders. It was cheaper and the quality was better. The after-treatment consisted of paper cutters without computer programming and equipment for bookbindery. The equipment in the bookbindery was exclusively from a producer in the Ukraine. A minor part of Tipografiya's production was stamps and seals, which were of a low quality. When the products were printed, they were taken to a stock room for finished products on the ground floor. Common to all the equipment was the difficulty, and later, at the end of the period, the expense involved in purchasing spare parts, which forced Tipografiya to run a mechanical workshop. The mechanical shop was perceived as fulfilling an important function.

> They are busy all the time. It can be difficult to find spare parts and consequently we are forced to manufacture them. Furthermore, the spare parts are expensive. Earlier, we had to turn to KPI and they made a centralised inquiry and we waited and waited, while we were asking ourselves: Do we ever get the material or not? This was despite the fact that we had transferred money to them (Valery Polyanskiy).

Other Printing Houses

In the Novgorod district, there were two other firms offering more or less the same services and products as Tipografiya. They were both considerably smaller than Tipografiya and situated in Borovichi and Staraya Russa. During the perestroika the printing shop in Staraya Russa was allocated fairly modern equipment, a four-colour printing press Tsirkon-60, one Dominant colour printing press, and some offset equipment, by the plan authorities. The printing house in Borovichi had no modern equipment and had to rely solely on an old relief printing press. None of them was able to print Tipografiya's most important products — newspapers and forms — since only Tipografiya had the equipment and the knowledge needed for this type of printing.

Potential suppliers to the newspapers could be found in cities like St. Petersburg and Tver, all of them situated more than 200 kilometres from Novgorod. Tipografiya's knowledge about the two main competitors in the district was good, considerably better than their knowledge about the customers and the suppliers. The reason was that a number of people from Tipografiya had visited them and representatives from the two printing houses had been to Tipografiya. Furthermore, there was a printing house in the neighbouring district of Pskov, some 150 kilometres from Novgorod. This printing house had more or less the same equipment and technology as Tipografiya.

> We did not consider them our competitors. We called them colleagues. We knew them better than we knew our suppliers. But, after all, we had some knowledge about customers (Irina Kondratyeva).

Customers

Around 90% of Tipografiya's total sales went to three groups of firms. These three groups corresponded to the types of product Tipografiya printed. The first group was the local newspapers. The second group was the Soviet Post Office Administration's regional branches, which bought forms almost solely. Both these groups were relatively homogenous.

> The newspapers and the Post Office Administration were special customers. They were plan orders. We could never refuse to print the newspapers because we were printing forms, and we never did refuse. Above all, we tried never to refuse anyone, because we were the only printing house. But the production time could be three months, or even half a year (Irina Kondratyeva).

Besides the Post Office Administration, Tipografiya mainly operated locally within an area of 200 kilometres from the city of Novgorod. So, various local firms made up the third group of customers. If one excludes the Post Office Administration, approximately 90% of the turnover originated from local firms. The remainder came from customers either not located in the district or relationships not controlled by the plan authorities. The last type was more or less negligible until the end of the 1980s.

The plan and production department managed the customers but their contacts with them were limited. No one from the plan and production department ever paid the customers a visit, nor did they try to find new customers. The individuals at the plan and production department spent almost all the time at the firm. Consequently, the lack of knowledge both about existing and potential customers was obvious and activities to increase the knowledge were absent. All documentation was done by hand. The invoices were written by hand, since there was no computer in the department. After a plan order was received, a note of production was prepared and taken to the head of the paper store who prepared the paper needed and thereafter brought it to the composition room.

The order receiver gave the production specification to the printing shops and was responsible for the execution of the orders and monitoring that the production took place according to timetable. The accounting department received the money, controlled the payments, and wrote a pass that was given to the store for finished products, from where it was picked up by the customers. Tipografiya did not provide any transportation. Many of the customers picked up their products themselves without Tipografiya's involvement. Tipografiya did not have details of how this was done, if they utilised their own means of transport or turned to other firms. It goes without saying that the customers themselves carried out this activity and that Tipografiya was not involved in the physical distribution nor did the employees really care about it either. However, there was one exception, the Post Office Administration, but more about that later.

The Novgorodskaya Pravda

Since Tipografiya was Oblispolkom's printing house, its main task was to print the local newspapers. Tipografiya printed the Novgorodskaya Pravda, during the Soviet regime the most influential and biggest newspaper in terms of circulation in the Novgorod district. It was the official organ of *Obkom* (the Communist Party's regional committee) and was published six days per week and had a circulation of 75,000. It was cheap and was distributed mainly to its subscribers.

> The newspapers were always on the first place, maybe because of political apprehension. The newspapers, the order for the Post Office Administration, and the colour production were important — everything was printed on different printing presses and therefore they did not disturb each other. And moreover, we were practically never in a hurry, because we were the only one (Irina Kondratyeva).

The management of the Novgorodskaya Pravda purchased the paper and supplied it to Tipografiya. Tipografiya had no option concerning the choice of suppliers, nor did it have any relations with the purchasing of paper. The newspapers rented a stock room at Tipografiya where they stored the paper. The Novgorodskaya Pravda paid Tipografiya once a month, but not for the newsprint. At the end of the month Tipografiya sent an invoice to the editorial offices according to the agreement.

The planned edition varied according to the number of subscribers. Subscriptions and distribution of the newspaper were done through *Soyuzpechat*, which was a governmental organisation and from Soyuzpechat the plan order was passed to the Novgorodskaya Pravda and Tipografiya. Tipografiya delivered the newspapers to a small room, which was rented by *Gazetno-Zhurnalnaya Ekspeditsiya* from Tipografiya. Gazetno-Zhurnalnaya Ekspeditsiya was a department at the Post and distributed all papers to the subscribers. When Gazetno-Zhurnalnaya Ekspeditsiya picked up the newspapers, it meant the end of Tipografiya's responsibility. The physical transportation of the newspapers to Sojuspechat's newsstands was also done by Gazetno-Zhurnalnaya Ekspeditsiya. At the beginning of the 1990s,

Sojuspechat changed its name to *Rospechat*, but the Gazetno-Zhurnalnaya Ekspeditsiya continued to transport and deliver the newspapers to the subscribers and also to the retailer Rospechat.

This was the way it had been for a long time, but at the beginning of the 1990s a change began, when a new newspaper, the *Novgorodskiye Vedomosti*, was launched. The Novgorodskaya Pravda used to come out every day and in the beginning, the Novgorodskiye Vedomosti came out only once per week. Tipografiya printed the Novgorodskiye Vedomosti from the very beginning but continued to print the Novgorodskaya Pravda. In 1990, a third newspaper, the *Novgorod*, was founded on the base of the Novgorodskaya Pravda. From the very beginning, Tipografiya printed the Novgorod and also had direct contact with the paper's management.

The Novgorodskiye Vedomosti

The Novgorodskaya Pravda was closed by the authorities in 1991 when, in contrast to the Novgorodskiye Vedomosti and the Novgorod, it actively supported the coup d'état in August of that year, by publishing the statements of the perpetrators of the putsch. The Novgorodskiye Vedomosti and the Novgorod, on the other hand, took sides against these statements. The attempt failed and as a result, all newspapers that supported the coup were closed, among them the Novgorodskaya Pravda.

> In connection with the coup of 19 August 1991, the Novgorod-skaya Pravda supported the perpetrators, while the Novgorodskiye Vedomosti began to be published every day in the form of "war declarations". The Novgorodskiye Vedomosti described in a chronicle everything that happened. Yes, it was interesting to read the chronicle. The Novgorod published information that was not even broadcast on TV (Irina Kondratyeva).

Until then, the Novgorodskaya Pravda had been the biggest paper in the region, but the liquidation meant that all subscriptions were transferred to the Novgorodskiye Vedomosti, which suddenly became the main newspaper. It was controlled, owned, and financed by Oblispolkom. The papers were printed on the rotary and the sheet fed presses, of which three were old cylinder presses with manual feeding. Four of the production personnel worked with the newspapers, two on the first shift and two on the second. One did the composition and one the make up.

Tipografiya printed the Novgorodskiye Vedomosti four times every week all the year round, but other than that, had few contacts with the editorial staff. Among the managers, Ludmila Yakovleva, who was the head of the plan and production department, and Valentina Guseva, the supervisor for the composition room, sometimes met the representatives from the Novgorodskiye Vedomosti, although that did not happen often. The relief printing shop, which Valentina Andreyeva managed, had some contacts with the Novgorodskiye Vedomosti. The Novgorodskiye Vedomosti had a constant presence at Tipografiya. A supervisor was working at Tipografiya and he controlled every issue of the newspaper and had the final responsibility for each publication. Furthermore, four proofreaders from the Novgorodskiye Vedomosti worked at Tipografiya, although not at the same time. From the beginning, the Novgorodskiye Vedomosti was considered Tipografiya's most important customer. The Novgorodskiye Vedomosti was the biggest consumer of paper and represented the biggest income, although it was not the most profitable.

Tipografiya's advantage vis-à-vis the Novgorodskiye Vedomosti was that there was no alternative supplier. The daily circulation of the Novgorodskiye Vedomosti was approximately 50,000–60,000 in 1991. During the period of the planned economy there was a well-defined and stable price list, which fixed the prices between Tipografiya and the Novgorodskiye Vedomosti, but when inflation started in the final years of the planned economy, Tipografiya's suppliers began to increase the prices. The price list was abolished, since it meant operating at a loss. Tipografiya then began working based on cost price plus a small profit margin. This took place in 1991 and 1992 and Irina Kondratyeva was in charge of the pricing. The written contract that regulated the relationship between the Novgorodskiye Vedomosti and Tipografiya dated back to the Soviet economy. One common factor for all the newspapers was that they were themselves buying the paper. The cost of the paper never appeared in Tipografiya's bookkeeping or annual report. The only cost Tipografiya had for this was the stock room for paper and the employee who was working there.

> The paper does not go through our bookkeeping. It is a cost, but you do not find it in our annual report. More or less all the newspapers buy their own paper (Svetlana Klimenko).

The Novgorod

The Novgorod was also quite a young newspaper, founded in 1990, and it quickly came to an agreement with the *Gorispolkom* (City Administration — in other words, not the owner of the Novgorodskiye Vedomosti) that it should finance a daily circulation of 87,000. This volume was distributed free to all households in Novgorod. The paper published the television programmes daily, which was the main reason people read it. The Novgorod was printed in the relief printing department. The main product of course, was the paper, but forms and various leaflets were also produced. The paper used an 8-16-column format.

The editorial office was situated just a few buildings from Tipografiya, in the central part of Novgorod. Despite this geographical closeness, contact between the firms was not extensive and the one who had most contacts with the Novgorod was Valentina Andreyeva, the supervisor at the relief printing shop. The plan and production department had contacts with the Novgorod when a change of circulation and volumes was in the pipeline. That department was also in charge of all financial issues, such as invoicing and re-negotiation of the annual agreement. In this case, the contacts were always with the deputy editor-in-chief.

The Novgorod also purchased the paper and kept it in stock in Tipografiya's facilities: a practice followed from the beginning. Tipografiya did not interfere with the Novgorod as long as the quality of the paper was acceptable, and it did happen on occasion that it was not. As in the case with the Novgorodskiye Vedomosti, the Novgorod had its own supervisor working every day at Tipografiya checking the quality of each issue, and two proofreaders. The same distribution company, Gazetno-Zhurnalnaya Ekspeditsiya, picked up the newspapers at Tipografiya and delivered them to Soyuzpechat, which took care of the retail trade. At the end of the month Tipografiya sent an invoice to the newspaper's editorial offices according to the agreement. There were never any delays with the payment.

Tipografiya printed two other regional newspapers — the *Shimskiye Vesty* and the *Zvezda* — and had two more papers, the *Chto? Gde? Kogda?* and the *Novgorodskiy Universitet* as customers. Their circulations were much smaller and they had no staff based at Tipografiya, but otherwise the composition, purchasing of paper, production, and transportation were organised in the same way as the large papers throughout the whole period.

The Soviet Post Office Administration

Besides the local newspapers, the *Soviet Post Office Administration* and its regional branches over the country were the biggest and most stable customers. Tipografiya printed various types of forms for the Soviet Post Administration over the whole period. The forms were standardised in terms of quality of the paper, size, and layout and did not change over the years. The forms, which were used in the post offices, differed in that they were printed on different types of paper. *Lensvyazsnabkomplektatsiya* (LSSK) was the main organisation for all the regional branches of the Post Office Administration in the Soviet Union. The distribution of the forms was governed by LSSK. Approximately 60 different types of forms existed for the Post Offices. Tipografiya used to print ten types of forms, while other printing houses printed the remainder. Tipografiya was not permitted to print these other forms. At Tipografiya these products had always been regarded as the most profitable. The forms were annually depicted in the Ministry of Transport and Communication's catalogue. Neither Tipografiya nor the regional branches had any possibility of influencing the design of the forms.

> We did not participate in the planning. We absolutely could not choose what to do. For instance, now we produce 80 types of forms. Then we produced 10, but when we wanted to produce 11, I had to go to Petersburg and plead for a long time. We could not influence the quality or the volumes (Irina Kondratyeva).

All the regional branches sent their orders, where they specified the volumes of each type of form for the coming year, to LSSK in Leningrad. At the end of the year, LSSK distributed a list with over 100 cities all over the Soviet Union. The most important of these were the Leningrad district, the Sverdlovsk district, the Komi republic, the Arkhangelsk district, the Lipetsk district, Vladivostok in the Primorskiy Kray, and the Kemorovo district. Nikolay Yevlampiyev and Ludmila Yakovleva gave the following picture of the relationships with regional branches of the Post Office Administration:

> At that time, we worked with LSSK in St. Petersburg. It was planned and the plan was sent to us every year. We printed forms for the post offices, but also various parcels. We sent away 20 railway wagons monthly to different regions: Sakhalin, Pskov, Yekaterinburg etc. I can give you the following example: We sent a container to Sakhalin. A girl with whom I used to study at the institute managed a printing house at Sakhalin. I asked her: "Is it really true that you cannot print these forms?" The value of the forms was just one third of the cost of transportation. Her answer: "But, we are a planned economy, you have to supply. We do not have the right to print these forms in Sakhalin. You deliver and if it is not enough, then you have to print more of them." Or another example: I went to my parents in Astrakhan, a southern region, and there I found the forms that we printed, but they were printed in Saratov,

while we were printing for Saratov. In other words, there was no competition, absolutely no competition (Ludmila Yakovleva).

Tipografiya was annually, at the beginning of every year, allocated detailed production plans by LSSK, which specified products and quantities that were planned to be produced and thereafter delivered to customers.

> It was specified to whom, what, how much, and which design and we sent it away. After that, we were obliged to produce what was required spread quarterly over the year. They knew that when a new year began we would send forms; we had to do that. There were no changes (Ludmila Yakovleva).

The plan also included prices and salaries, which did not change over the years.

> There was no inflation, no increases of prices. Maybe, the prices increased a little bit over five years, due to the paper, but it was negligible. In general, the prices were stable. The quality of the forms and the technology was worse, since we printed on the relief printing presses. We printed constantly on the relief printing presses (Ludmila Yakovleva).

When Tipografiya had received the production plan, it had to produce the decided quantity when it was convenient, but by the quarter allocated over the year. The forms were printed almost exclusively on the relief printing presses, but sometimes, on the offset machines. Sometimes, there were deviations from the plan. For instance, sometimes Tipografiya produced too many of some type of form and in that case, could offer the surplus to one of the regional branches. In such a case, the regional branch and Tipografiya would set up the agreement without interference from LSSK.

> Occasionally, it happened that the machine did not work. I then called, for instance, Voronezh, and told them that we had, for instance, form number 58 for small retail shops in the countryside, which they use when they give the bank their money. We had many such forms and I offered to send them the forms. They agreed so we sent more than was in the plan and they paid. There were big deviations from the plan, but it was after concrete organisations had made an agreement (Ludmila Yakovleva).

It also happened that Tipografiya ran out of paper and had to make up the deficit on its own. The lack of financial resources made it difficult to do illegal business in the black market. The authorities did not require efficiency from Tipografiya, but, on the other hand, due to lack of financial resources Tipografiya had limited resources to buy on the black market. Almost all the revenues went directly to Oblispolkom, which then distributed the money back to Tipografiya, depending on Tipografiya's capability and power. This did not mean that Tipografiya did not try to push, charm, convince, or threaten the plan authorities in order to solve some problems where they were dependent on the authorities. Tipografiya never went to the branches, nor did they come to Tipografiya. Some communication existed but it was only on the telephone and mainly concerned transport, delivery times, and some logistics. The relation to LSSK was a little different. LSSK was the plan authority, which regulated the relations between Tipografiya and the regional branches. The employees called LSSK "Mailbox 760" and sometimes some of their representatives came to Tipografiya, but it was either for control or when problems had occurred. It also happened that the managing director went to Leningrad. No one else from Tipografiya ever went there.

> It was called Mailbox 760. Our management, the managing director went there. We did not have any problems with or questions for them. I never went there but we communicated by phone. They sometimes came to us, when there were some mistakes in our bookkeeping or other problems, trips for acquaintances (Ludmila Yakovleva).

Over the years, few changes took place. The same contact pattern held, which meant that all contacts were made by telephone and at each branch there was a special contact person with whom Tipografiya communicated. Deliveries were made in trains and containers in the same way. Tipografiya concluded agreements with the railway.

> We concluded agreements with the railway and if we did not manage to dispatch the containers, penalties threatened us. We gave the railway information about which forms, how much and where we should deliver at the beginning of every month. The railway required a strict fulfilment of the timetable, that is 20 containers should be dispatched. We dispatched the containers and depending on what we loaded, we wrote the invoice and sent it to them by mail. When they received the invoice they paid, that is we

sent off the invoice after we had dispatched the load. As a rule, the money arrived for us (Ludmila Yakovleva).

At the beginning of each month, Tipografiya gave the railway information about volumes and destinations and the railway required Tipografiya to fulfil the timetable. After that, the containers were sent away and the plan and production department wrote the invoice and sent it by mail. The regional branches paid immediately when they received the invoice and they were almost never late with the payment. If Tipografiya was late with the deliveries, penalties threatened.

> I do not remember any situation with penalties. The punishments were of a moral nature, not financial. When we did not fulfil the plan Obkom called the director and organised some slight. He usually took me: he thought I was the guilty one. It was not pleasant. Furthermore, there were internal plans for the composition room, the printing departments, and the book bindery. I made up these plans. In cases of plan fulfilment, they got a good bonus. A department that did not manage to fulfil the plan got a smaller bonus or none at all. In reality, it meant that one department had better orderliness and the other departments worse (Irina Kondratyeva).

Transportation was the same to all the regional branches, with one exception, the Leningrad district, where a van picked up the forms when the order was produced. It transported the forms to Leningrad where they were first kept in stock by the Leningrad district and then distributed to their offices. No one knew to whom the van belonged and no one really cared. Furthermore, no one knew or was interested in what happened to the forms when they arrived at the customers.

> We did not know who ordered from the Post Office Administration. During the centralised system one did not need that kind of information (Irina Kondratyeva).

LSSK provided paper to Tipografiya, but Tipografiya did not have any freedom to choose quality, quantity, transportation, or supplier. This was done by LSSK. Tipografiya tried to keep a large stock of paper in order to have some freedom and not be so dependent on the suppliers, but the plan and production department had to make reports about the paper. Tipografiya paid LSSK and not the supplier for the paper immediately the paper had been delivered. The calculators also fixed the prices based on the type of paper and the official price list. In spite of the fact that the paper was always delivered directly from the producer, Tipografiya's contacts with them were limited. In general, it made no difference from whom the paper was delivered, and according to Nikolay Yevlampiyev the reason was the following:

> We did not care from where or which type of paper was supplied to us: Partly, because it was a constant deficit, we were happy if we got the paper at all and partly, because we, of course, knew that we could not influence the choice of paper or supplier. Moreover, we never paid for the paper (Nikolay Yevlampiyev).

Tipografiya had neither responsibility for nor influence on the quality of the paper used in its relations with the Post Office Administration, and the Post Office Administration did not have any complaints about Tipografiya. However, Tipografiya always knew which firm was the supplier. The suppliers took care of the physical transportation, usually by train, and Tipografiya received the paper a couple of days after notice of delivery. In the price for the forms, only expenses in terms of physical work carried out by Tipografiya were included; thus expenses for raw material, for instance inks and paper, bought by Tipografiya, were not included. The customers probably paid LSSK for them. Tipografiya was paid when the products were produced not when they were delivered, and no credit was given.

Almost all information that was exchanged between Tipografiya and the regional branches was channelled through LSSK. The volume and the quality of the information were low and the information seldom flew directly between Tipografiya and the regional branches. It happened just a few times per year and in these cases, exclusively by phone. However, Tipografiya had contacts with some specific individuals at each regional branch. Although their relationship had a long history, representatives from the two firms had never met, which was typical for all the branches of the Post Office Administration. Tipografiya's knowledge about them was poor and no one really tried to learn more about them.

> We knew the firms in Novgorod better. We could not avoid them, even if we wished (Nikolay Yevlampiyev).

During these years, the system of payment between the two firms changed. In 1991, Tipografiya successively started to require prepayment from all customers. It happened when the whole Russian economy ended up in deep financial crisis.

Another influential factor was the late payment of invoices on a number of occasions by the Leningrad district.

Other Customers

Tipografiya was already the dominating printing house in the Novgorod district during the planned economy. There were different opinions at Tipografiya about which firm was the biggest and most important customer, but the biggest customers were by tradition the four local electronic industries *Kvant, Elkon, Start,* and *Transvit,* the manufacturer of furniture, *Novgorodmebel, and Akron,* which produced fertilisers. A number of the local industrial firms belonged to the defence industrial complex and consequently their biggest customer was the Ministry of Defence. All these remaining customers made up somewhere between 7 and 10% of Tipografiya's production. Kvant produced television sets and each television set required documentation, a guarantee certificate, instructions, and schemes. Tipografiya printed all kinds of documentation for them. Elkon produced kinescopes for television sets and Tipografiya printed forms for them. Tipografiya used to print instruction and labels for Start, but not packages. Start produced radio electronic equipment. Two other traditional customers for Tipografiya were Transvit and Novgorodmebel. Tipografiya used to print forms for them, as well as an internal newspaper, which came out once every half year, for Transvit. In Novgorodmebel's case, Tipografiya printed their labels and instructions for assembly of the furniture.

Other firms besides these ten customers bought constantly and quite extensively from Tipografiya before 1992. *Akron,* which was a big chemical firm, producing mainly fertilisers, bought big volumes of forms. The liqueur and vodka plant, *Alkon,* which was situated in the same block as Tipografiya, bought labels for their vodka bottles. Alkon was the only customer that actually bought labels from Tipografiya during the planned economy. They accounted for 1–2% of the total sales. For the *Rybokombinat* (Fish kombinat), Tipografiya printed long labels. There was no offset technology in the district besides Tipografiya's offset presses. Only Tipografiya was able to print in four-colour. For some customers with their printing presses in-house Tipografiya printed four-colour products and for others, without printing facilities, Tipografiya printed other products as well. There was a distribution (*Snabzheniye*) department at each company. As a regular representative from that department came to Tipografiya and placed the order, Tipografiya knew that person well. They came to Tipografiya's plan and production department.

> The same person came from the factories all the time, so we knew them very well. They came to our order department. The printing house did not work out the price list. The calculation for the products was distributed in a centralised way. The prices were centralised but the orders were decentralised, except for the Post Office Administration. The wages were clearly defined. The paper belonged to the customer. We did not buy paper at all (Nikolay Yevlampiyev).

It was not part of a planned distribution system, but nor was it based on formal agreements and contracts. A representative from the firm came to Tipografiya with a binder with samples and gave it to the plan and production department, where the staff planned when it would be possible to print.

> It was not planned orders. They came to us with binders with samples. We planned when we could print, this week or next week. We had so many orders that we had a queue. We had reception when we received orders only two days per week. There were no physical queues in the corridors. The firms came with their binders and we put them in a pile in our offices and executed them in queue order (Ludmila Yakovleva).

Tipografiya received customers only two days per week and it actually had a constant queue of orders. There were no physical queues in the corridor but customers usually had to wait a long time for their product. Some of the customers even brought the paper themselves. Tipografiya actually made an agreement with the biggest customer, Kvant, every year, which was continued the following year. It was a general agreement and did not contain any specific details. Corrections from the general agreement were made with each specific order. Up to the beginning of the 1990s, there was an established price list, from which no one could deviate. The printing houses did not work out the price list. The calculation of the wages and of the prices for the products was distributed in a centralised way.

> We were working according to the governmental price list — there were specific small books, printed by the government, but according to the party's committee in the city. We had a price list for the all the products. We did not know or even care of they counted. I do not know how the ministry fixed the prices. The committee distributed the corresponding instructions and from

there everything came to the printing houses. It was the Ministry for the Printing Industry; I remember exactly what it was called. I do not know if we had any relations with *Goskomtsen* [the State Committee on Prices in the Soviet Union]. Maybe Goskomtsen was connected to KPI, but all the decisions came to Tipografiya from KPI. Everything followed the price list. Once we had to count over the prices for seals and stamps again. I do not remember according to which principle, but it was terribly difficult to reach an agreement (Irina Kondratyeva).

The prices were centralised but the orders were decentralised. From 1991, when the economic reforms were introduced and inflation appeared, Tipografiya began to calculate prices based on a prime cost principle.

Suppliers

Tipografiya had a stable supplier structure; however, this did not mean that they had close relationships with the suppliers. When Tipografiya needed paper or consumables, it had to turn to KPI, which made centralised inquiries. Thereafter Tipografiya had to wait, very often for a long time, even though they had already sent the money.

When the paper was finished, we turned to KPI. The prices on the paper were absolutely centrally fixed, that is, they were the same at all kombinats. It was plan orders (Irina Kondratyeva).

KPI was completely responsible for the supply of consumables such as inks, offset plates, and stereotypes, and partly responsible for paper, but the goods were delivered direct from the producers.

For both the forms and the newspapers, the customers supplied us with paper. When we printed forms for Vladivostok the Mailbox in St. Petersburg supplied us with paper. It was planned that we should have a big stock of paper, which was delivered by train. We reported. We had an enormous net of reports concerning the paper. It was the task of our department. The accountant calculated. Different types of paper were supplied: board and newsprint. The accountant calculated the value of each sheet and we fixed the price for each form (Ludmila Yakovleva).

When Tipografiya was transformed into a leasing company in 1991, it also gained some freedom and responsibility to take care of the purchasing of paper itself, and in 1992 Tipografiya finally began to purchase paper without plan orders. The only exception was the Post Office Administration, where LSSK still provided paper. This also meant that Tipografiya had to be more active. The reason for that was greater freedom to purchase outside the plan and the fact that the firm had to take full financial responsibility for the purchasing operations. As paper, without comparison, represents the greatest cost, the chief engineer, Nikolay Yevlampiyev, decided to take control of it. He was responsible for purchasing other consumable material but also for investment and maintenance of machines and equipment. The managing director estimated that the purchasing activities took approximately 10% of both his and the chief engineer's time. According to the managing director, no criterion other than price was used in the choice of the supplier. Tipografiya preferred to buy large quantities and to keep them in stock for long periods.

There was a large number of paper and pulp producers in northwestern Russia. However, Tipografiya traditionally bought only from five or six of them. Consequently there was a large supply of paper in the region. In general, there were five big traditional suppliers to Tipografiya. *DAO Bumaga Arkhangelsk* produced writing paper for forms and writing pads. *Syktyvkarskiy TBK* made newsprint, offset paper, printing paper, and writing paper. As for the newspapers, they bought the paper themselves. *Okulovskiy TsBK* produced wrapping paper and *Solikomskiy TsBK* newsprint, but the last time Tipografiya bought from them was in 1993. *AO Kondopoga* produced newsprint, which Tipografiya bought directly from them. All the suppliers had to produce according to the governmental standard called gosstandarty, and the authorities regulated the prices. In spite of the fact that the paper was always delivered directly from the producer, Tipografiya's contacts with them were extremely limited. Nikolay Yevlampiyev had been to the biggest supplier DAO Bumaga only once, and that was before he began to work at Tipografiya.

> I was there a long time ago, before I began to work at Tipografiya.
> I was then a representative for the mass media department of the
> District Committee of the Communist Party. I have never been to
> Syktyvkar (Nikolay Yevlampiyev).

He had never been to the second most important supplier, Syktyvkarskiy TsBK. The suppliers of paper, altogether six or seven huge paper and pulp kombinats, all specialised in some types of paper. Although Tipografiya always knew which firm was the supplier Tipografiya did not care from where or which type of paper was supplied. Partly because there was a constant shortage of paper, all printing houses had to be satisfied if they had a sufficient quantity of paper, and partly, because Tipografiya knew that they could not influence the choice of paper or supplier, especially as Tipografiya only paid for the paper sometimes.

> If there was a deficit of paper or inks, and it happened, it was insignificant. There were no serious stops of production. We had good stocks. For instance, we still had enough offset plates, which we bought in 1991, two years after the price collapse. Inks were sometimes even destroyed. It is true; it seldom happened that there were interruptions because of the paper (Irina Kondratyeva).

Still, it did sometimes happen that Tipografiya ran out of material and that the official plan system could not provide sufficient material. In these cases, according to Irina Kondratyeva, Tipografiya had to go outside the official distribution system and use personal contacts:

> We had a *snabzhenets* (provider of goods), Yelizaveta Georgiyevna, I do not remember her family name, an old woman, but very persistent. She worked here for more than 70 years. She could secure needed material. Also the director called someone, made up agreements. Later, when Yevlampiyev came, Polyanskiy began to do this. And when it comes to *blat*,[1] it has always been there. Someone came with an urgent order. He was sent to Polyanskiy and he found out what we could get in exchange. There were gifts: sweets and champagne. But, at least, I have never got big gifts (Irina Kondratyeva).

The suppliers took care of the physical transportation, usually by train, and Tipografiya received the paper a couple of days after notice of delivery. Contacts with the paper suppliers were limited. Nevertheless, the employees usually knew from where the paper had been supplied. Over time they had learned to identify the differences in quality between the paper from the various suppliers, and how to use them in production.

---

[1] Blat is discussed under the heading The unofficial economy in Chapter 4.

> We knew, for instance, the paper came from Kondopoga in Karelia, but there were no relationships with the suppliers (Valentina Guseva).

In general, the character of the relations was the same with all the paper suppliers; no one from Tipografiya had ever been to them. The relations were faceless and the main issues discussed concerned logistics. Tipografiya bought wagons of paper and it fell on the supplier to secure the transport of the paper, which was done by train. The expenses for transport were included in the price. As mentioned previously, from 1991 Tipografiya had the freedom to buy paper themselves, which they started to do, but with one exception. LSSK still provided paper for the forms, but Tipografiya paid for the paper. However, after a while Tipografiya decided to buy paper for the forms as well. Earlier all paper and pulp kombinats produced paper in accordance with federal standards set by Gosstandart.[2]

When it came to the supply of products other than paper, KPI usually allocated the consumable to Tipografiya. The usual way was that Tipografiya made inquiries through KPI. Their inquiries were sent to Moscow, turned into production orders, and distributed to the producers of the consumables. At the same time, KPI also had a small stock of various consumables, for instance, it received inks and Tipografiya collected ink from this stock. The biggest suppliers besides the suppliers of paper were *Poligrafresursy* and *Torzhorskiy Zavod Krasok*. The most traditional supplier of inks was Torzhorskiy Zavod Krasok, located in the neighbouring district of Kalinin (which in the 1990s changed its name back to Tver). Film was bought mainly from *Tasmy* in Kazan. Poligrafresursy had supplied matrices over a long period. Zinc was bought from *Moskovskiy Zavod Offsetnykh Materialov* and Poligrafresursy.

> We used zinc for the printing blocks and for the composition lead — a harmful production. They delivered stereotypes from Leningradskiy Shriftoliteyny Zavod. Its contents were lead, tin, and antimony. Metals for the linotype machines were bought. We composed the newspapers and then the metal melted and we used it once more. I never went to the supplier of stereotypes (Valentina Guseva).

---

[2] Gosstandart was the State Committee on Standards.

Chapter 4

Analysis of the Network in the Planned Economy

Hierarchy

Throughout the whole period from 1986 to 1991, Tipografiya had a limited number of customers and suppliers with which it frequently exchanged important products. From that it follows that it is meaningful to analyse the case in order to identify the logic in this network and the consequences of the network. A well-defined hierarchy was the main foundation for the whole Soviet Union. This was also the case in the Soviet network. Collins Cobuild (1987: 684) defines hierarchy as "a system or organization in which people or things have different ranks or positions depending on how important they are." Consequently, in a hierarchy each specific firm has its position, which is determined by someone else, which, in turn, has the authority and power to do that. It is important to underline that I am not viewing hierarchy as the same as the firm, which is what Williamson (e.g. 1975, 1985) did. Instead, I see hierarchy as a driving force in the Soviet network, which is closer to the ideas put forward by Cook & Emerson (1978) and Cook *et al.* (1983). In the case study, three dimensions are observed which had an impact on and fortified the hierarchy: the plan, the planning process, and the relationships between the plan authorities and the firms.

The Plan

I start with the best-known dimension of the planned economy, namely the plan (see Figure 4). The most fundamental feature in the Soviet economy, along with the fact that the whole industry was state-owned, was the idea of replacing the market with an administrative and central planning and control system. The firms regularly received quantitative plans specifying products, transportation, customers, suppliers and so on. In general, the plan was assumed to fulfil the same function as

```
                    COMMUNIST PARTY

                          |

                  POLITICAL INTENTIONS

                          ↓

                    PLAN AUTHORITY

                      /        \

            PLAN                    PLAN
          COMMANDS                COMMANDS

              ↙                        ↘

   SELLER  ←————————  EXCHANGE  ————————→   BUYER
```

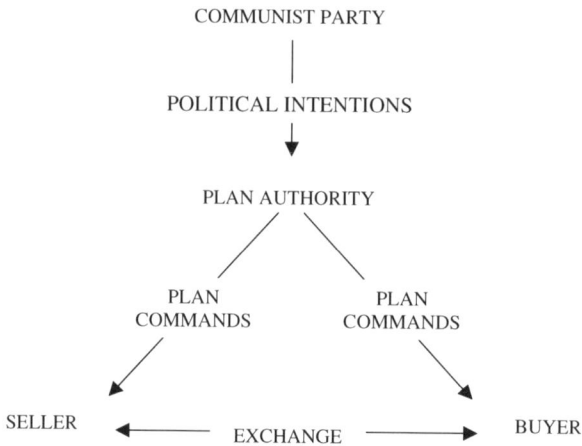

Figure 4: Plan governance of a production relation.

the market in market economies, that is to allocate resources in the economy, but the plan also functioned as to a tool for how and where to achieve progress. The authorities could allocate large amounts of resources to various industries, regions, or firms in order to achieve growth. Some of examples of these priorities were specific industries, such as the space industry and the defence industry, or specific projects, such as the Baykal-Amursky Magistral (BAM railway), but Soviet history is full of similar cases. However, if profit and business were the mechanism in the market economy, political intentions and priorities were the foundations for the plan.

The plan was a codified rule that required three conditions to be able to function. The *first aspect*, which was also the point of departure and the reason that a plan was assumed to function in reality, was that someone somewhere had perfect knowledge about all dimensions, both structural and temporal, in the economy. This was necessary so that the correct decisions, according to the political intentions, could be made. This was not enough however. The perfect knowledge and the political intention should either be united in one body or have an extremely strong link between them. Furthermore, having perfect knowledge was not sufficient, authority and power to realise these correct decisions were needed, as it was not those who had the political intentions and those who worked out the plans who should actually realise the contents of the plan.

The *second* aspect concerned the information encoded in the plan. The plan should contain all information necessary for the supplier and the customer and furthermore it was crucial that this information could only be interpreted in one way by the firms. Of course misunderstanding had severe consequences, which meant that the commands of the plan authorities had to be correctly communicated to the firms. Otherwise the plan could not be realised, and furthermore, it would destroy the possibility of other firms realising their plans.

The *third* aspect concerned the fact that some kind of incentive had to be tied to the plan, that is, if the firm did not obey or understand the plan, which meant that it did not fulfil it, the firm had to be punished or miss a potential reward.

In the case studied, there were four types of co-ordination of the network relations (see Table 1) and plan governance in various degrees. The table shows four dimensions of the relationship: counterpart, quality of the products, quantity produced and supplied, and the price of the products. The first group concerns

Table 1: Summary of the hierarchy in Tipografiya's network 1986–1991.

Counterparts	Quality, Quantity, Price
Tipografiya: The Post Office Administration	Based on an annual plan. Customers specified. Regulated prices set up by the authorities. Products were standardised.
Tipografiya: The newspapers	Annual agreement but regulated prices. No plan. Customers specified. The local and district administrations, for instance, Oblispolkom, influenced the relationships, but did not govern them by plan.
Tipografiya: Other customers	Spontaneous deals, which had a lower priority than the newspapers and the Post Office Administration. Customers not specified. Customers were geographically close to Tipografiya. Regulated prices.
The paper suppliers: Tipografiya	Despite paper being the most important product bought, the supply was mainly managed by other organisations. Suppliers specified. The newspapers bought the paper themselves, while LSSK provided the paper for production to the Post Office Administration.

the production of forms where the plan governed the relationships between Tipografiya and the regional branches of the Post Office Administration. LSSK completely defined which or how much of each product should be produced and exchanged between Tipografiya and the Post Office Administration. Furthermore, the price, the design, quality, and choice of paper to be used were determined by the authorities. The second type was the relationships to the newspapers, where there was no plan, and where the authorities played only an indirect and minor role. In this case too, the prices were centrally fixed. The third type referred to the relationships between the remaining customers and Tipografiya, where the only dimension beyond the control of Tipografiya and the customers was the price. The fourth type concerned the supply of paper, where LSSK completely determined prices, quantities, qualities, payment, and so forth when it came to paper used for production of forms. All Tipografiya had to do was answer the telephone when someone from the paper suppliers called and said that the paper was on its way and ensure that there was enough space in the stock room. Paper used in the production of other products were centrally ordered through KPI, but supplied from the producers according to the official price list.

In Tipografiya's relationships with its customers, the quality of the products supplied was determined in different ways. In its relationships with the newspapers and with the remaining customers, the quality of the products was determined by Tipografiya and the customers, whereas in the relationships with the regional branches of the Post Office Administration almost everything that concerned the products was decided by the Ministry for Communication. Neither Tipografiya nor the users could influence the quality. A third case was the paper supplied by various paper and pulp kombinats. Obviously, the paper standards were determined according to the general literature of the Soviet economy (Nove 1984).

The quality of the products was regulated through the application of the federal standard set by Gosstandart, which was a governmental standard. Even though the products were regulated, the firm had to make regular samples of the deliveries, and consignments were sometimes rejected for being of insufficient quality. There were no incentives to produce products of a higher quality level than stated in the federal standards, because the price was regulated and an increase in quality would just induce higher costs. Furthermore, if the firm manufactured products of higher quality, this would not affect the bonuses or the well-being of the firm. On the other hand, the buyer could reject products not meeting the standards set by Gosstandart. Rejections were deducted from the firm's production and could lead to the buyer's failure to fulfil its plan. Despite the federal standards, the firms often had to give priority to the production of quantity at the expense of quality.

Another dimension in the case that corresponds with the general view of the planned economy was the role of price in the economy. Ericson (1991: 19) claimed that the Soviet economy was characterised by an "exhaustive price control, yielding multiple and contradictory systems of centrally fixed, inflexible prices." Those prices that did exist were mainly used as control mechanisms. They were stable and fixed by Goskomtsen; the firms could not affect the price level. Prices only played a passive role in the economy and existed mainly for accounting, control, and measurement purposes. There was no possibility of the firms involved in any of the relationships being able to fix the prices, albeit, none of the informants mentioned Goskomtsen. It is striking that all prices were centrally fixed and out of reach for Tipografiya and therefore not something that could be used in the relationships with the customers. Prices on products were set on a cost-plus basis and included profits, turnover taxes, and handling charges. They were aimed to cover average costs in each branch of the economy. The intention was that each firm should be self-financed (Ericson 1991).

The Planning Process

The plan was a precondition for the hierarchy, but the plan was also a result of a process, the planning process, which was a set of activities that verified and strengthened the hierarchy. It is for that reason that I discuss the planning process separately from the discussion about the plan as a mode of governance. The plan was the result of the planning process and as such, it was definite. It placed an order, rightly or wrongly, which the receiver had to fulfil. The planning process, on the other hand, was a process over time where various actors played different roles. During the process the actors' knowledge and the information they had at their disposal was a point of departure for how the ends were specified and the means that were identified and allocated in order to realise those ends.

A number of governmental organisations existed in parallel to the firms. Their task was to regulate and co-ordinate the activities in the economy. According to Ericson (1991), over 20 state committees and other agencies with ministerial status answered for some specific aspect of the economy. The best-known authority was *Gosplan*, which had the task of developing a general plan and the methods and means to implement it. Gosplan did the planning all the way down to the production level, but the ministries had the actual executive power and made the plans for each firm concrete. *Gossnab* was responsible for the physical distribution of products to the industry. Gossnab controlled the fulfilment of the plan. The ministries had extensive power regarding the distribution of resources and the possibility of any firm exerting any individual influence over this was limited.

It speaks for itself that co-ordinating a whole economy by establishing various plans and commands was an overwhelming task. The planning was an iterative bargaining and negotiation process in which central agencies, branch ministries, and firms participated. However, at least in the case of Tipografiya, the firm did not take part in the planning process and none of the informants touched upon this issue, which means that Tipografiya's experience and knowledge were never utilised in the planning. The plan authorities were always assumed to have knowledge superior to Tipografiya's.

The process began with political decisions on the highest level of the Communist Party, the Politburo. Gosplan then analysed, interpreted, and compared such decisions with old information. In parallel, a year in advance, firms made estimates of their future needs and sent them to the plan authorities. The first round of the planning process resulted in a set of "control figures." They were communicated down the hierarchy of the economy and on the way, became more and more concrete until they were transformed into explicit plan commands. Organisations that were more operational, mainly producing firms, usually reacted to the commands by requiring more resources and thereby, according to Ericson (1991), revealed a lot about their own capacity. This information was utilised by the plan authorities when the firms' answer to the commands was sent back up in the hierarchy again. The results of the bargaining process were a set of commands to all branch ministries. Gosplan and Gossnab strained to produce at least rough tolerable demand and supply balances for all products and resources. These were, in turn, put together into a draft and sent to the political authorities for approval. The approved plan was returned to the administrative hierarchy where it was broken down into resource allocation, goals, instructions, and so on. In general, most of these commands were quantitative.

Relationships Between the Authorities and the Firms

Besides the plan and the planning process, the hierarchy was especially reflected in the relationships between the authorities and the firms. In the case study, I identified the fact that the authorities had two functions, which were related to the hierarchical dimensions of the network. The first function has already been discussed in part, that is, how the authorities, using their inherent power, codified rules and punishments that governed the relationships between the firms. One can even say that the firms were actually viewed as production functions, which were calculated by the plan authorities and aimed to meet quantitative production goals (Salmi 1996).

The second function, also evident in the case study, is the authority of an owner. Let me first deepen the analysis of an authority, LSSK, as a governor of relations and then return to Oblispolkom as an owner. As already discussed, the planned economy was characterised by order and commands given by the plan authorities. Their orders established all new relationships and terminated existing ones, which meant a mutual lack of possibility for the firms to choose customers and suppliers, thereby excluding almost all kinds of entrepreneurial activities. Finding exchange partners and linking firms were exclusive rights for the plan authorities. This is especially evident in the relationships between Tipografiya and the regional branches of the Post Office Administration, where the firms were one-sidedly dependent on the plan authority, LSSK. It also meant that Tipografiya's most extensive contacts were with LSSK and not with organisations that were defined as the customers and the users of the forms, namely the Post Office Administration's regional branches.

During the perestroika, which coincided more or less with the period covered in the case study, firms were gradually given the possibility of establishing contacts with customers and suppliers independently of the ministries. At this point, it was essential to have relationships with other firms that worked well. But, Tipografiya did not use this relative freedom, for instance, in relation to the paper suppliers or the local industrial customers, to establish new relationships or to try to change the products, transportation, production, storage, and so on in the existing relationships. It relied on old habit and preserved the network almost intact.

Both Tipografiya's and the Post Office Administration's resource dependence was managed by central control and monitoring. Consequently, the firms were not independent organisations, but operated more as production units (Salmi 1996). Their performance was measured in terms of the physical quantities produced (Dubini 1990), where, at least, Tipografiya was punished if it did not meet the plan goals. The interesting fact in this respect is that Tipografiya was not punished by the counterpart, but by the plan authority. This made the dependence one-sided and asymmetrical, even though the firms had a little room to manoeuvre; for example, they could negotiate with the authorities to reduce plan goals and have more resources allocated to them. The dependence on the plan authorities also concerned the extent to which and how the firms were rewarded. Ericson (1991: 19) said that the relationships were characterised by "incentives that are geared to meeting the plans and desires of evaluating superiors, and not to the economic consequences of decisions taken at levels below the very top." However, despite some possibilities, there is no doubt that the firms were completely dependent on the authorities and not the other way around.

Oblispolkom was the formal owner of Tipografiya. The case study describes three aspects where Oblispolkom had extensive influence over Tipografiya. First, Tipografiya's specialisation in forms and newspapers could be traced back to a time when no one from the present staff was working at the firm. For instance,

Nikolay Yevlampiyev estimated that Tipografiya had begun to print forms for the Post Office Administration some 40 years previously. The perception of Tipografiya's management was that Oblispolkom stood behind that decision.

Second, during the final years of the Soviet period an investment in two offset printing presses was made, which was not only made possible by Oblispolkom, but it was the driving force. Although Tipografiya was more passive, Oblispolkom identified the need and secured the funding.

Third, Oblispolkom was a passive rather than an active owner. The contacts between Tipografiya and Oblispolkom were limited. No board meetings took place; in fact, Tipografiya did not even have a board, and it was seldom that anyone from Tipografiya met any representative from Oblispolkom. Obviously, Oblispolkom participated neither in the daily running of Tipografiya nor in the long-term strategy discussion. It is not obvious in the case study which authority made the decision to close the Novgorodskaya Pravda, but it was a political decision, and it influenced Tipografiya, and illustrates how Oblispolkom used its hierarchical position towards the Novgorodskaya Pravda and thereby also towards Tipografiya.

To sum up the first observation; in the Soviet networks, hierarchy was a key word for two reasons. First, the mechanism for determining the position for each firm in the Soviet economy was the use of authority and rules, and breaking the rules was usually connected with penalties and punishment. Thus, each Soviet firm had well-defined positions in relation to other actors, both authorities and other firms. Second, most choices were made and all conflicts resolved at a superior level for the firms. Thus, the plan authorities had absolute and arbitrary control of norms, indices, and parameters of plan assignments, performance evaluations, and rewards and made all decisions for the firms. The firms had limited possibilities for influencing these decisions (Ericson 1991).

Static Network

If a strict hierarchical structure was the foundation for the whole of Soviet society, static networks became a natural consequence. Something is static when it "does not change or develop at all" and it "stays in the same position and does not move at all" (Collins Cobuild 1987: 1425). In line with this definition, a static network prevails when resources exchanged on the exchange level and the combinations of resources used on the use level remain the same for a long time. A static network means also that activities such as payment, transportation, production, storing, distribution, and so forth are performed in the same way by the same actors and towards the same counterparts over time. Furthermore, machines, equipment, premises, products, and other types of resources utilised by the actors to perform specific activities will not change in a static network. This means that in a static network both the structure as such, that is, the set of relationships, and the exchange and use of resources within these relationships remain the same and do not change.

In the case study, a few changes could be observed, but it was also evident that they were changes that had been ordered, as Tipografiya had little room to manoeuvre when it came to changing products, customers, suppliers, investment, technology, and so forth. Oblispolkom, LSSK, and KPI were responsible for the majority of the changes but they seldom met representatives from Tipografiya and in the light of that, one can ask oneself what they knew about Tipografiya's capabilities and needs. Furthermore, if one assumes that after all, they did have knowledge about Tipografiya, one wonders what they knew about Tipografiya's customers and suppliers and their operations. In Table 2, I summarise six dimensions of Tipografiya's static network. Thus, although the period from 1986 to 1991 has sometimes been described as a rather turbulent one, it is evident that for Tipografiya its network was static. Actually, the only aspect that disturbed the static nature of the network was that Tipografiya began to set by computer, which had consequences for their whole production process. Besides that, Tipografiya's network was static, which is also the second observation.

One important aspect that Ericson (1991) raised is that while the administrative superstructure was subject to rather frequent "reforms," the production structure and the interaction between firms changed very slowly. Firms were almost never shut down, relationships with customers and suppliers in the state sector very rarely changed, and capital stock and capacity were only abandoned due to breakdown and never for economic reasons (Ericson 1991). Furthermore, the authorities remained the same. The technology used was the same for a long period and competition was absent. Nor did laws and regulations change. The network in the planned economy was stable and predictable from both a temporal and structural view, which corresponds with the more general picture of the Soviet economy as even stagnation.

The main cause for the Soviet networks' remaining static over time was the hierarchy. According to Ericson (1991), the plan and the planning process concerned around 24 million products. This volume of process and information would have been manageable if the plan authorities had what was assumed, namely complete knowledge in space and time. However, if one believes that no one has complete knowledge (Hayek 1945) the planning process becomes rather tricky. Co-ordinating the whole economy by establishing various plans required an enormous amount of information. Ericson (1991) noted that that above all, in order to be able to manage all needed information during the planning process, simplifications were necessary. However, simplifying was not enough. Other measures had to be taken in order to be able to manage the information. The

Table 2: Summary of Tipografiya's static network 1986–1991.

Dimensions	Comments
Bought and sold products	The products bought, paper and ink, were the same, and of the same quality over the whole period. The only change was in the films needed for the computer setting. Otherwise there was no change. None of the three big products sold, the newspapers, the forms, or the products for the local industry, changed in terms of quality or quantity between 1986 and 1991.
Technology and production	During the period, two offset printing presses were bought and consequently the pre-press and Tipografiya's composition room began to be set by computer. Production was stable and the only change was that sometimes Tipografiya began to print small volumes on the offset machines instead of the relief printing presses.
Institutions	Prices, authorities and legislation, and regulations were stable over the years. The legislation in itself promoted and strengthened the stability.
Supplier relationships	The suppliers in Tipografiya's network were the same in 1986 as in 1991; none appeared and none disappeared.
Customer relationships	The customers in Tipografiya's network were the same in 1986 as in 1991; none appeared and none disappeared. Activities such as payment, transportation, storage, and communication were the same over the whole period without any changes.

planning process was easier to perform if the networks were stable and did not undergo changes. It speaks for itself that it was both easier to collect, interpret, and compare the information and also to assess and control the results of the plan if the networks were hierarchical and stable.

Ericson (1991) claims that one shortcoming was that all commands were built on the same information, which to some extent was outdated and obsolete. It seems reasonable, but static and hierarchical networks increased the chances that the information was valid, which in turn increased the probability that the contents in the plan corresponded to the political intentions. However, ensuring that the information was valid was not the only problem faced by the plan authorities. They also had to achieve consistency among all the detailed plans on all levels and between all organisations. In 1936 Hayek (1936: 38) had already noted that "it is essential for the compatibility of the different plans that the plans of the one contain exactly those actions which form the data for the plans of the other." This implies that the plan authorities had to have information and insight concerning all possible consequences of a change, which made the planning process even more difficult.

Thus, the static Soviet networks prevailed due to a paradox. Most changes in the economy were commanded and planned from above, based on the argument that the authorities had superior knowledge, but since they did not have what they claimed, namely perfect knowledge, the static network made the planning process easier and the plan more valid. In the light of this, it seems that the hierarchy in the Soviet network tended to have a positive effect on the static nature of the same network. This statement can also been seen in Hayek's comment (1945: 524–525): "The economic problems arise always and only in a consequence of change [. . .] the economic problem of society is mainly one of rapid adaptation to changes in the particular circumstances of time and place, it would seem to follow that the ultimate decisions must be left to the people who are familiar with these circumstances, who know directly of the relevant changes and of the resources immediately available to meet them." This means that by not changing the authorities did not have to face and manage the economic problem to the extent they would have in the opposite situation.

Obviously, changes in the Soviet network were neither appreciated nor encouraged by the authorities. From a network perspective, change can be said to have occurred when actors find and discover new ways of exchanging and using resources in relationships with other actors. Both finding and discovering, on the one hand, and using and exchanging, on the other hand, imply that change is a process containing several phases. In line with the previous discussion, the actors in the Soviet network were either the authorities or the firms. Consequently, theoretically, it is the authorities and/or the firms that find, use, and exchange the new resource combinations. The aim is to try to show why finding, exchanging, and using resources in new combinations in the Soviet network tended to be rare. A constraint in the Soviet network was that the hierarchy established what to find whereas exchange (partly) and use (completely) were tasks that the firms had to perform.

Change is, according to Kirzner (1992), a result of two types of activities: *search* and *discovery*. Change is sometimes a result of a plan, which seems to fit into the Soviet context. The authorities, in the spirit of their political intentions, established the ends and identified the means, which were communicated to the firms, which had the task of using the means according to the political intentions. Changes were initiated and controlled by the levels superior to the firms. Although theoretically search and discovery can be carried out both by the firm and the authority, exchange and use were always the task of the firms. It was not the role of the authorities to find ways to exchange and use resources.

Defining what to the search for was the task of the authorities, while exchange and use were the task of the firms. By this definition, one cannot search for the unknown. This is in line with Nove's observations (1984) on development of new technology. He found that research was usually isolated from practice. Formal research and development were performed by the Academy of Science, the ministries, or state committees and were remote from life, the problems the firms experienced and, most importantly, from the economic consequences of the new technology. According to Nove (1984: 167), new technology was based on the conviction that "central planners know what needs to be done." To that, one would like to add that they also strongly knew *how* to do it.

Berliner (1976) argues that the primary innovation function of the firm was to implement the innovations commanded from the authorities. Moreover, he means that the both potential users and the suppliers were resistant to new product and production technologies and there were several reasons for that. The user requirements were not incorporated into design decision and the user often found that new products did not fit his needs. Maintenance and support service were seldom provided by the supplier, meaning that the user have to deal with the problems that might occur. Berliner (1976: 218) claims that the innovation process built on the idea that perfect knowledge existed. However, the potential user could be expected to know the technical qualities of the new products and production technologies and the consequences if he implemented it; neither the innovator — the supplier — nor the potential user — the customer — had complete knowledge about the consequences of using the innovation, which means that both the supplier and the customer encountered a resistance to do business with the new product. This process was also rare in the Soviet networks. Both the firm and the authorities could of course, initiate the search, but changes had to be planned and the firms were not allowed to discover, find, and exchange or use resources in ways that were in conflict with the plans and the authorities' intentions.

The fact that change as a consequence of discovery was rare meant that the networks had no relationships where the activities were dissimilar and closely complementary (Richardson 1972), as these require close interaction. This in turn is a precondition for adaptation and increased co-ordination of the activities. This did not exclude the fact that individuals at Tipografiya learned more when they used the resources they controlled, but it does show that this knowledge was mostly related to their own organisation. Human interaction took place between people within Tipografiya. However, since change increases the uncertainty and the risk perceived, and since risk-taking was not rewarded in the planned economy, change was not in the interest of either the authorities or the firms. Change was not connected to any incentives for the firm. Actually, the only change that was welcomed by the firm was a change that made plan fulfilment easier to achieve. This change could take place within the firm or in the relationship, but under one condition: that the amount of resources allocated was the same. Usually, change meant tougher plan goals and/or fewer resources, which meant no improvement for the firm, unless the change was illegal (i.e. without the authorities having any knowledge about it). Change forced the firm to adapt to new conditions and to learn, which increased the uncertainty and the possibility of failure. Therefore, the firm tried to avoid changes.

The second type of change that was welcomed had its home in the illegal economy. This is a further indication of the static Soviet networks. There was limited space for change as a result of what Kirzner (1992) calls discovery. Change was mostly an intentional process, which was limited by the politicians and the knowledge and expectations of the authorities, and by the firms' room to manoeuvre when they came to realise that discoveries on the use level were limited and on the exchange level almost non-existent. Thus, discovery and change of exchange and use had to be within the frames of the authorities' intentions, and were, consequently, rare. Furthermore, the Soviet network also made the search activities difficult and hazardous, as search and finding were separated from use. In the end, it meant that it was easier to plan more or less the same thing that had been done previously, which conserved the static nature of the network.

There are, thus, three possible ways of achieving change. In western market economies these are performed mainly by the firms, but in the Soviet planned economy there was almost only one way and that way had to be initiated by the authorities. The firms' task was to absorb and put the change into use, which decreased the probability of change occurring. The firms learned and the networks changed on command. It follows from that that the firms' relationships were stable. Monitoring and control, the main mechanism in the hierarchy, thus facilitated the static network.

Anonymity

The hierarchy and the static network meant anonymity between the firms in the Soviet network. Anonymity is defined as "the state of not having your name or identity known, especially when you have done a particular thing" (Collins Cobuild 1987: 51). Obviously, someone's anonymity is a consequence of another not knowing. This section focuses first on the relationships between the plan authorities and the firms, and second, on the relationships between the firms. Ignorance of something is defined as a "lack of knowledge about it" (Collins Cobuild 1987: 720). In the context of the case study, ignorance means that the firms lack knowledge about other actors (both other firms and the plan authorities), their needs, and capabilities. Anonymity in the network also exists when an actor is ignorant of its counterparts' customers and suppliers, that is, the relationships connected with the actor's relationships.

Four types of actors are active in the case study: colleagues (i.e. other printing houses), customers, suppliers, and the authorities (see Table 3). The striking anonymity of the regional branches of the Post Office Administration has two

Table 3: Summary of the anonymity in Tipografiya's network 1986–1991.

Counterparts	Comments on Knowledge
Tipografiya: The Post Office Administration	Tipografiya standardised forms to over 100 regional branches and the knowledge about them was poor. The plan authority, LSSK, was better known and some interaction took place.
Tipografiya: The newspapers	Tipografiya had relatively few, but important, newspapers as customers. They were geographically closely located to Tipografiya and some of them had a constant presence there. Still, they were anonymous for Tipografiya who did not have much knowledge about them.
Tipografiya: The remaining customers	The remaining customers were a group of heterogeneous firms in Novgorod. The interaction was more extensive than in relation to the other customers and at least on a personal level, they knew each other well.
The paper suppliers: Tipografiya	The major part of the paper used in production by Tipografiya was not bought by them but by LSSK or the newspapers. Since Tipografiya had to use the paper, they knew very well the differences between the suppliers when it came to type of paper and quality of paper, but besides that, the paper suppliers were anonymous.

causes. The first was the high degree of plan-governance. LSSK governed the relationships with the branches of the Post Office Administration through the annual plan. Ericson (1991: 22) described the situation in terms of "the lack of legal alternatives to assigned economic relationships and the inability of any subordinates to alter any of these relationships legally." In the plan-governed Soviet economy, the firms were not allowed to establish or terminate production relationships. Once these were established, as in the case with the Post Office Administration's branches, the firms had minor possibilities for developing the relationships, but not on the exchange or the use levels. The firms' experience from the relationships was not used in the planning process and had no impact on the development. This caused ignorance about the counterparts, which over time resulted in anonymity. The main issue, which Tipografiya had to manage vis-à-vis the regional branches, was logistics. The firms were isolated from each other and did not perform any real exchange. Consequently, the environment was faceless and its actors anonymous. The second cause is rather obvious, namely the geographic distance. There are branches of the Post Office Administration in 119 cities spread all over the Soviet Union. Big geographic distance is an obstacle for interaction and development of identity, as even though together they comprised the biggest customer each one of them separately was less important.

Importance in terms of volumes or even quality of the products exchanged seems to affect the identity less positively than a close geographic distance and a low degree of plan-governance. The evidence for that statement lies in Tipografiya's relationships with the paper suppliers. Tipografiya's knowledge about the paper suppliers, although extremely important both from financial and quality points of view, was poor. No one from Tipografiya had ever been to any of the paper suppliers and no one expressed a real interest in learning more about them, although I believe that there is a natural difference between a firms' knowledge about its customers and suppliers, which the case verifies. A firm usually has a richer knowledge about its suppliers than about its customers and the reason is that the firm always has to manage a result of the supplier's capabilities, namely the product supplied. The firm has to handle the product supplied, and use it, which results in experience of at least one aspect of the supplier, that is, the product it produces and supplies. In the case, a number of employees at Tipografiya had to handle the paper daily, be aware of its quality, and manage it in various combinations with printing machines, ink, and so forth. In other words, several people had to learn about the suppliers through using the product they supplied to Tipografiya.

Rather surprisingly, the other printing houses and the local industrial firms had the weakest anonymity among these actors. Why was that so? The geographic distance from the local industry and the other printing houses was small, which had a negative effect on the development of anonymity. Nikolay Yevlampiyev's reaction was typical, when he said that they knew firms in Novgorod better, as the representatives from Tipografiya could not avoid them. The conclusions that could be drawn thus far are that the greater the geographic distance and the more plan-governance the less contacts and communication between the exchange partners and the more ignorance about the exchange partners' capabilities and needs, that is, the stronger the anonymity. Thus, when the firm's communication with other firms in the economy is weak, its social contacts delimited, its counterparts' capabilities and needs perceived as unimportant because the relationships are developed by mechanisms other than business, anonymity will appear and prevail among the firms, which is the third observation.

The firms' knowledge about other actors was deemed unnecessary in the Soviet network. The economy provided no incentives for firms willing to interact more closely with their counterparts (Mattsson 1993). The lack of incentives combined with a constant demand surplus meant that several activities like quality control, transportation, service, production of spare parts, training, and so on, were performed by the buyer or not at all. Or as Ericson (1991: 22) puts it: "Incentives oriented only toward implementing commands and directives and subject to apparently arbitrary control by superiors lead agents to avoid any change or risks, to shun innovation, to ignore information important to others, and to work to rules regardless of the impact on others. The logic of the system requires that initiative be punished ('initsiativa nakazuema'), making any attempt to change both personally risky and likely to fail." So, the conclusion is that the firms' resource dependence was handled through control and monitoring, made possible by an institutional framework the main tool of which was punishment, which, in turn, gave a low level of co-operation in most relationships.

From that follows that the hierarchy in the Soviet network positively affected the anonymity in the same network. But the anonymity was also a result of the static network, because when new technology appears and disappears, new firms are founded, laws and regulations are changed, uncertainty grows and it becomes more difficult and risky for the firms. In an unstable network, the main means of handling the growing uncertainty is to learn more about other individuals, firms, and authorities, which was not the case in the Soviet network. To sum up, a more hierarchical and static network offers less room for interaction and learning about other firms and over time the evolved mutual ignorance leading to that anonymity became embedded in the whole network.

The Unofficial Economy

I have so far discussed the existing and official relationships. Berliner (1957), Grossman (1977) and Ledeneva (1998) discussed the unofficial and illegal activities in the Soviet economy from different perspectives. There were numerous reasons why a parallel, sometimes overlapping, unofficial, and partly illegal, distribution system emerged. Ericson (1991) claims that a commitment to maximal resource utilisation, implying tautness and pressure in planning, and the lack of any liquidity or flexible response capability in the system were typical for the Soviet network. This meant that any kind of disturbance had severe consequences for the whole network, which very often resulted in situations where some firms had a surplus, while others had a deficiency of products. Regardless of this, business and trade between firms was strictly forbidden. If it occurred, the firms involved risked heavy penalties and in most cases, they did not have the financial means to pay extensive fines.

An important dimension of the unofficial distribution system was the purely personal influence on different exchange situations. In Russian this is called *blat*. The aim is to obtain some kind of favour, very often illegally, but not necessarily so (Ledeneva 1998). Blat existed in all kinds of activities in the firm, but mainly in areas related to exchange with other firms, especially those concerning the procurement of goods. Blat can be described as an illegal and informal exchange of resources where, at least, one of the counterparts does not own the resource it provides the exchange. Moreover, very often because of blat the resources are used in a context other than the one for which they were aimed. In addition, there was usually a time lag between the giving and getting of resources, which was possible because blat was often interwoven in a set of social relationships.

Closely related to the concept of blat was the function *tolkach*, which means pusher, and referred to a person sent out to push for the firm's interest, especially concerning supply, resource allocation, and production goals. The targets of this pusher were other firms, plan authorities, ministries, and even the Communist party. Berliner (1952) notices that if a large number of people engaged in blat, they must have expected others to be prepared to do the same or at least to accept that others did it. The stakes were high and thus, these situations were characterised by mutuality and trust.

Grossman (1977: 31) argued that breaking laws and regulations and bribing were commonplace for more or less the whole Soviet population. "The plethora of administrative superiors, controllers, inspectors, auditors, law enforcers, party authorities, expediters and just plain snoopers that beset every economic activity, legal or illegal, in the Soviet Union, anything done out of line requires the buying off of some and often very many people." Everything from small and unpretentious gifts to substantial bribes were commonplace in the contacts between representatives of firms and various authorities, which meant over time, a strong connection between the political-administrative authority, on the one hand, and a highly developed world of illegal economic activity, on the other, was developed.

The business climate has traditionally been characterised by the individuals' lack of freedom, instead relying more on control and authority. Since Russia never had the business legislation or ownership concept found in western societies, Russian business people have not had any rules to follow; instead the rules and laws have had a tendency to be contradictory and senseless. This was especially so during the communist regime. Nepotism, gifts, bribes, and price fixing were accepted in the unofficial economy and in traditional Russian business behaviour. Nor was the non-adherence to senseless laws and regulations considered unethical (Puffer & McCarthy 1995).

There is some evidence of blat, tolkach, bribes, gifts, and so forth in the case study. A woman called Yelizaveta Georgiyevna worked at Tipografiya and her tasks seemed close to the activities of a tolkach. The chief engineer Polyanskiy later replaced her. Both were involved in something that could be defined as blat. Thus these dimensions were definitely present; however, my impression is that they did not dominate the firm's operations, and were in fact, a small part of the total operations.

The Firm in the Soviet Network

By using observations from the case and support from the literature, I have so far argued that the Soviet network was characterised by anonymity. Plan-governance, large geographic distance, and to some extent importance and volume of the products seemed to encourage the development of anonymity. What did the actors know about other actors and what reason was there for them really to decrease the anonymity in the network? The answer is the reverse: they were concerned with business profit, value, growth, new markets, product development, and so forth. But these are not evident, neither the theory nor the case gives evidence for that, because the planning eliminated the competition (Hayek 1945), and also excluded co-operation. In a wider context there was indeed a dimension of competition, but the negotiations took place between the firms and the authorities and not between the firms themselves. The firms competed for the economy's resources and to be allocated as moderate plan goals as possible. Furthermore, the issue was not one of price and quality, but of plan goals and the resources allocated in relation to the plan (Dubini 1990), which is one of the reasons that the plan authorities had a stronger identity than most firms.

I have already thoroughly discussed the relations between the authorities and Tipografiya and argued and showed that in the relationship with the Post Office Administration the most extensive contacts were with neither the customers nor the suppliers, but with the plan authority. However, this did not mean that any need to know more about LSSK existed. No one except the managing director had ever been to LSSK. On a few occasions, a representative from LSSK came to Tipografiya, either for control purposes or to become acquainted. One can, of course, argue that over time, the firms and the plan authorities did not develop an anonymity vis-à-vis each other. But it is important to stress that this knowledge could never be strong because there were few rewards, such as business profit, value, growth, new markets, product development and so forth, that were tied to the process. The relationships between the firms and the plan authorities were characterised by one-sided power arbitrariness, a condition that was constant and predictable.

It has been argued that there were two reasons for the firms to learn more about the plan authorities. First, if the firm received insufficient materials (which was very often the case, as the physical resources were poorly distributed leading to constant lacks), it had the option of contacting the ministry and negotiating for additional resources. It was vital to have a close relationship with individuals at the ministry. A dispute could lead to the impossibility of receiving the required goods. Having good contacts made it possible, for example, to request faster deliveries. Second, if the firm did not fulfil the plan it was penalised. Furthermore, to be able to fulfil the plan, it was vital that the firm had the appropriate supply of products. Obviously, in both these cases there is some kind of deviation from the plan through negotiating and bargaining with the authority. In the case study, the managing director Yevlampiyev said that although Tipografiya did not have the financial resources to do business in the black market the firm had tried to influence the plan authorities. From that follows that the authorities' anonymity in general was weaker than the firms.

Thus far, I conclude that the anonymity of the firms was stronger than that of the authorities, although they also had quite a weak identity. In the light of that statement, the following question is reasonable: What did the actors actually know then? So far, one gets the impression that the only knowledge the firms had beyond the official plans concerned how to influence the authorities and how to deal in the black market. An answer to that question may start from the observation that firms were not allowed to establish or terminate relationships with other firms, because this meant that the managers attached more importance to the matters that they could influence and that had an impact on the firm's success. Product development, transportation, payment routines, and marketing activities were issues of subordinate interest for the firm. Instead, the managers' main task was to obtain and preserve power and control within the organisation (Holt *et al.* 1994; Vlachoutsicos & Lawrence 1990a, b) and their focus was on production, control, and monitoring the employees and stock of material: three aspects, which were crucial for the fulfilment of plan goals.

The Soviet firms had a highly hierarchical and functional structure and each department was part of a bigger department. Furthermore, the firm was characterised by the fact that the departments on the same level had limited communication. Communication in such firms was vertical, which resulted in a high degree of centralisation, which hampered the delegation of responsibility in the organisation (Vlachoutsicos & Lawrence 1990a, b). The organisation of the Soviet firm was authoritarian, that is, it lacked vertical reciprocity and interdependence, but it did not prevent the Soviet firms from functioning as open organisations. All the employees had direct access to the managers, and the top management spent a lot of time at the firm. Few employees had contacts outside the firm and it was the top management that had nearly all the external contacts, but as said before they were few. For instance, Luthans *et al.* (1993) showed that U.S. managers devoted twice as much time to external networking activities as Russian managers did. Managers rarely developed personal relationships outside their assigned domain, apart from engaging in activities relating to planning in conjunction with higher authorities. Obviously, the system encouraged the managers to engage in enhancing productivity within their units, while all matters regarding the relationship between departments were to be decided by a higher ranking manager.

The Legacy

The Soviet economy was structured like a network, but the firms bought and sold from each other over a long period for other reasons than in western market economies. It was not business or technological development that were the driving forces in the Soviet networks. Instead, these networks were anonymous, hierarchical, and static structures (Figure 5). However, the network was in different degrees hierarchicial, static, and anonymous. To sum up, there were five concerns in the development of an identity.

The *first* concern was the knowledge problem. By assuming that someone somewhere has, if not perfect, at least superior knowledge, one neglects the whole knowledge problem. In the Soviet network, it was assumed that it was possible for those with superior knowledge, those at the top of the hierarchy, to command new knowledge. Having superior knowledge implies that new knowledge is not needed and appreciated and if needed it should be commanded by those who are at the top. Developing new knowledge was consequently not viewed as a complex and complicated process, whereas in the western network perspective dispersed or bounded knowledge is a key assumption, which makes learning into a multidimensional and tricky process, and a reason for relationships above all

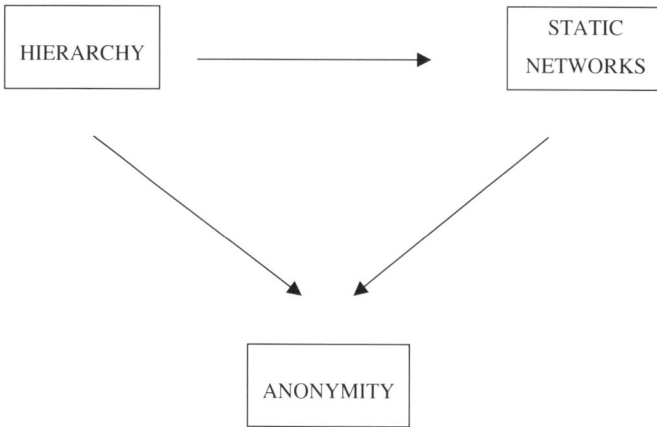

Figure 5: The logic of the Soviet network.

evolving (Snehota 1990). The *second* concern regards freedom to learn and to utilise the knowledge, which is related to Kirzner's discussion (1992) on search and discovery. It is obvious that in the planned economy a level superior to the firms commanded almost all types of changes, which excluded discoveries, in terms of, for instance, new products, other customers and suppliers, new ways of transportation, payments, and so on, in the economy.

The *third* concern is the incentive to learn. Interacting and learning more about others implies an incentive — either a reward tempts the firm or a punishment threatens. The planned economy only offered firms potential punishment, while business, growth, technological development, and so on, are incentives for firms in western networks. The risk of being punished and seldom rewarded, which was typical in the Soviet network, does not encourage experimentation and creativity, which, on the other hand, are essential ingredients in the traditional network perspective. Firms do not develop relationships for altruistic reasons, but for profit (Snehota 1990).

The *fourth* concern is interaction. One of the first main observations in the network tradition was the notion of interaction (Håkansson 1982). Relationships can facilitate room and time for interaction between several individuals and firms almost simultaneously. But when there are no rewards or freedom to interact firms will tend to do other things instead, in the Soviet case, concentrating on internal matters, which decrease the possibilities of learning more about and with the market. However, there is also a learning process, where the interaction takes place between the individual and an artefact. Repetitive use of, for instance, a physical resource supplied by a paper and pulp kombinat to Tipografiya forced, at least a few people to use this resource. Furthermore, they had to use it in a meaningful way. In the case, Tipografiya's employees knew from where the paper was supplied but never interacted with anyone from the supplier.

The *fifth* concern is variety and heterogeneity. To be able to learn one has to face other things, new things. Reflecting and comparing differences, the new and the old, is an important ingredient in the development of an identity. If these activities of reflecting and comparing are only performed within the boundaries of the firm, both incentives and the possibilities for development of anonymity in the network increase.

Chapter 5

Tipografiya's Network in Transition Economy

Organisation and Production Technology

Ownership and Management

In 1991, Tipografiya had already transformed into a so-called leasing company, with the final privatisation taking place in 1993 when Tipografiya first became a joint stock company and the employees acquired all the assets from the state. The assets were then depreciated to 78% of their previous value. A few years later, in 1996, the managing director, Nikolay Yevlampiyev, had the biggest block of shares (12%), while the other members of the management, the chief accountant, the chief engineer, and the head of the production and finance department, each had 3% respectively. Each of the remaining managers and supervisors owned a percentage of the shares, and the production personnel also had small stock holdings. There were also a few external shareholders, altogether owning 7%. They were mainly former employees who had retired since the privatisation started.

The former owner of Tipografiya, Komitet po Pechati i Informatsii, continued to exist, and was still attached to the District administration, but in 1997 had only one employee. After the privatisation, there were few contacts between the Komitet po Pechati i Informatsii and Tipografiya. Throughout the period from 1992 to 1998, Tipografiya owned the building and the land, as well as a building site in the central part of Novgorod. At the end of 1995, buildings constituted 55% and equipment 34.5% of the firm's assets in the balance sheet. The firm did not have any long-term loans, but current liabilities constituted 22% of the liabilities and equity. Of these 85% were accounts payable to customers. This was because Tipografiya had usually required prepayment from their customers. The accounts payable to suppliers were small, 0.7%. In comparison with the majority of the industry in the Novgorod district, Tipografiya had been in a rather advantageous financial situation since 1992. The period from 1992 to 1998 was characterised by financial recession, periods of hyperinflation, and a significant decrease in production. Still, Tipografiya had a relatively good level of liquidity and there were no delays in payment of salaries. The suppliers were usually paid in advance. Tipografiya did not have any debts and on the whole, was living on its own earned money and only needed to borrow money when it bought paper. In those circumstances, it could take out three-month short-term loans with a high annual interest rate.

Despite the decreased total production, the number of employees was generally stable over the whole period, although there was a slight decrease in numbers. In 1996, that number was 111 compared with 121 in 1992. The stability was a consequence of the policy not to reduce the employee complement. However, there were some small variations. The number of employees varied due to changes in tax legislation; in some years it was more beneficial to have more than 120 employees whereas in other years it was more beneficial to have less than that number. Tipografiya tried to adapt to these changes in the legislation, but still, in general, the number of employees was rather stable. Another reason for the stability was that smaller production volumes still required the same manpower.

The First and Second Re-Organisation

During the spring and summer of 1997, when Tipografiya celebrated its 100th anniversary, the company undertook its *first re-organisation*, which was completed in July 1997. The production and finance department was divided into three departments, called the *finance department*, the *marketing and advertising department*, and the *business centre*. The finance department became responsible for the relationships with the newspapers and also had the task of actively finding new customers. The marketing and advertising department was to take care of the more complicated products, preferably four-colour products, and the customers, who needed more attention and competence. The business centre had to manage the relationships with all the regional branches of the Post Office Administration, but also to execute small and urgent orders. In 1998, a second re-organisation was completed. In this second re-organisation the two production departments merged, and the name of the marketing and advertising department changed to the editorial and publishing department.

Production Process

Two developments, which started in the 1980s, were strengthened after 1992. Firstly, with composition the use of computers instead of setting by hand became more common, and secondly, offset technology became more important than relief technology. They completely changed work organisation and significantly increased the quality of the products. As noted in the previous section Tipografiya began to use computers for composing in 1991. Between 1995 and 1996, Tipografiya bought seven additional computers, but in 1996 the main part of the composition was still done without computers. Instead, the composition room produced its stereotypes, which meant that during the first years of the period composition was mainly done by hand.

Step by step, Tipografiya bought computers and by 1998, the company had 10 computers for composition and the bulk of the work was composed on computers. This development also meant that the first computers were replaced with more modern ones. The composition room had a Page Maker 4/86, a laser printer, a horizontal repro camera, and a drum scanner with low resolution. There were vacuum frames for both film and plates and development of films and plates was done manually. All the photographic equipment was produced in the Ukraine. Printing plates were used for the offset jobs. The plates were made out of metal on which a picture, an illustration, was applied. They were then taken to repro. Thereafter, the plates were slipped onto a cylinder. In 1997, Tipografiya bought colour separation equipment from Agfa. Until then this service had been bought from various firms in St. Petersburg. The colour separation equipment significantly changed the composition process and the organisation of the work. Moreover, the quality of the four-colour products improved.

In 1992, relief printing and offset printing technology were used. During the period Tipografiya bought two printing presses. In 1994 Tipografiya acquired a rotary press for production of the newspapers, and a year later it bought a Tsirkon 66. Both of these were offset machines. After 1995, the management tried to renew the equipment and several investments were made between 1994 and 1998. Above all computers, office machines, and equipment for colour separation were bought. The printing presses were used for different purposes. The four offset machines were used for black or two-colour production. Valentina Guseva considered them to be "old," and as some sections were not working they had to be used in two runs. The most recently bought Dominant 745 R was used for printing of labels and three-colour production. Presses of the brand Romajor were mainly used for four-colour production, but as they were designed for one-colour production, the paper had to be run four times. These machines were bought before 1992. The newspapers and forms were printed on the old relief printing presses. Tipografiya did not have the financial resources to renew the technology. Valery Polyanskiy confirmed this stagnation and the reason that this was still the case:

> I began to work at Tipografiya in 1991 and more or less all the production equipment is still here. The equipment was already old then. The only big acquisition that we have made is the

four-colour printing press. The reason is that it is too expensive (Valery Polyanskiy).

In 1998, Tipografiya re-organised its production. Valentina Guseva, who until then had been foreman of the composition room and the bookbindery, was appointed production manager, while Valentina Andreyeva, who had managed the relief printing shop and offset printing shop and who had been directly subordinate to Nikolay Yevlampiyev was now instead subordinate to Valentina Guseva. The mechanical shop still existed and was under the chief engineer Polyanskiy, who was busy with technology and equipment. According to Irina Kondratyeva the reason for this second re-organisation was the problem in keeping the production time. Delays were common and the managing director hoped to solve this problem through the re-organisation. The aim was not to make the operations more efficient. The boundaries between the departments were still abstract and vague and it was difficult to determine each department's efficiency.

Sales and Marketing Activities

Sold Products

Overall the production decreased significantly in terms of produced volumes from 1992 to 1998. Among the main products, only the production of newspapers increased and that was thanks to the Vechevoy Tsentr. The products sold by Tipografiya only changed little between 1991 and 1998. According to Table 4, one year after the beginning of the transition the forms made up 63.5% of the total sales. Half of those were forms for the Post Office Administration. The big decrease in the forms' share of the total turnover, from 63% in 1993 to 31% in 1998, was a result of Tipografiya losing these customers and an extensive decrease in small orders. At the beginning of the transition economy the forms were mainly printed in the relief printing shop but as the orders decreased, both in volume and numbers, it became more beneficial to print them on the offset presses. In parallel, Tipografiya developed four-colour printing (booklets and labels in table). The sales of newspapers were stable from 1993 to 1998 (see Table 4), which meant that their sales constituted a little less than 25% of the total sales, owing to the decrease in total sales in 1998 compared with 1993. The specialisation in forms and newspapers had a long history. Furthermore, none of the current members of the management worked at Tipografiya at the time those decisions were made.

While the sales of books, usually printed on the relief printing presses, were stable during the period from 1993 to 1998, the sales of labels decreased from

Table 4: Products sold 1993–1998.[a]

Products	1993	1994	1995	1996	1997	1998
Forms	63.5	45.4	37.6	35.7	36.1	31.4
Newspapers	12.6	22.2	22.4	22.4	23.5	27.3
Writing pads	–	0.4	4.3	9.5	7.7	3.2
Books	8.4	13.9	11.4	7.7	8.6	3.2
Labels	8.1	6.2	5.1	2.0	2.5	3.7
Booklets	0.8	2.4	4.4	5.8	4.2	13.7
Stamps and seals		4.0	3.3	4.1	6.9	6.8
Miscellaneous papers	6.6	–	8.8	10.3	7.9	7.9
Plates		0.8	0.8	1.1	6.7	0.4
Folders and certificates		4.7	1.9	1.4	1.9	3.0

Source: Author's own calculations based upon internal data from Tipografiya.

Note: Miscellaneous paper stands for strips for cash registers, papers for printers, and writing papers etc. In 1993 Tipografiya did not differentiate between stamps and seals, plates, folders and certificates. Miscellaneous papers were not sold.

[a] Share of total sales (%).

8.1 to 3.7%. The reason for this decrease was the fact that the local industry had not been satisfied with the quality of Tipografiya's production. Tipografiya did not produce writings pads and miscellaneous papers to any greater extent during the planned economy, but it opened a retail shop, Delovoy Mir, for stationery in 1994 (more about that later), and one of the aims was to sell these products there. After the retail shop was opened the sales of these two products accounted for something between 10 and 15% of the total sales throughout the period. Two other products produced by Tipografiya were also sold in the shop, namely stamps and seals and folders and certificates. Miscellaneous papers and stamps and seals had one thing in common: the firm's printing equipment was not utilised. Since 1996 stamps and seals had been produced on a laser graver. The paper was partly resold and cut, however, nothing was printed on the paper.

In the planned economy, Tipografiya's customer structure consisted of three groups of firms. This structure remained the same for the period from 1992 to 1998. The first group was the local newspapers. The second was the Russian Post Office Administration's regional branches. Both these groups were relatively homogeneous. They each accounted for approximately 25% of the sales. The third group was more heterogeneous and accounted for around 50% of the total sales. Of the total sales in 1995, 20% originated from other parts of Russia than the city and district of Novgorod. During the first quarter of 1995, 74.5% of the orders came from the city of Novgorod, 11.7% from the district of Novgorod, 10.4% from the St. Petersburg and Leningrad districts and 3.4% from other regions of Russia.

The structure concerning the big customers changed significantly during the 1992–1998 period. Tipografiya lost some of its more traditional customers and some of them were not supposed to come back, above all the defence industrial firms, but Tipografiya hoped that others, for instance the food industries would return if Tipografiya could improve the quality of the printing. Leaving the big customers, another development was the increase in the number of customers buying from Tipografiya and the increase of smaller orders. In 1995 there were more than 1000 customers, which was a big difference compared with the beginning of the 1990s, when Tipografiya had many fewer customers. Furthermore, a lot of orders were small, just 500–1000 units. In 1995, Tipografiya received 5,000 orders and the absolute majority of these bought only once from Tipografiya. So, since 1990, the number of orders and the number of customers grew, but sales and production decreased.

Organisation of Marketing Activities

In 1996 the sales and purchasing tasks were still carried out in the same way as they had been during the planned economy. The production and finance department was in charge of five main tasks: reception of orders, preparation of price lists, control of production times, invoicing, and follow-up of price calculation. Three people were working in the department: Irina Kondratyeva, Ludmila Yakovleva, and Galina Belova. Besides the Post Office Administration, the majority of the customers approached Tipografiya by themselves. The company did no outreach work and did not try to find new customers.

> Those who are coming are coming. I know those customers who are coming to us all the time. Since we are not receiving orders by phone we have to meet them. We have had a fax machine for a few years, but it is seldom used for this purpose (Galina Belova).

On the whole, at the beginning of the period, the lack of knowledge both about existing and potential customers was obvious and activities to increase it were limited. The individuals at the production and finance department spent almost all the time at the firm. The head of the department, Irina Kondratyeva, estimated that she spent 95% of her time at the firm. The remaining 5% consisted of contacts with the management of the newspapers, the district administration, and various federal organisations, for instance, the regional anti-monopoly committee. She was in charge of all the big customers and all invoices. The department wrote out invoices and sent them to the customers, who paid Tipografiya's accounting department. The other two individuals spent all their time at Tipografiya. Galina Belova, whose position was that of dispatcher, had never been to a customer, but she usually took care of all the customers who came to Tipografiya. She received the orders and prepared the necessary documentation, which in 1997 was still done by hand, as the production and finance department had no computer. On average, the dispatcher wrote 20 invoices per day. Galina Belova took the note to the head of the paper store, who prepared the paper needed and thereafter brought it to one of the two production departments. Galina Belova gave the production specification to the printing shops and she was responsible for the execution of the orders and ensuring that the production took place according to timetable.

> The customer comes with the order and we make out an invoice. Usually we wait while they are paying and then we promptly give the order to the head of the paper store. It happens that the customer calls us and asks how it is going and in these cases I try to find out and return to him with a correct answer (Galina Belova).

Production time was a sensitive question that was solved in the negotiation between the customer and Galina Belova. Some of the products, like business cards and greetings cards, could be printed the same day. Forms could usually be ready within three days. After that, Tipografiya waited until the accounting department had received and checked the payments. After production, the accounting department wrote a pass and gave it to the store for finished products, where the customer then picked it up. Tipografiya was not involved in the physical distribution and it goes without saying that almost all customers picked up their products themselves. Tipografiya did not know if they utilised their own means of transport or turned to other firms.

> This question has never been of any interest to me (Irina Kondratyeva).

Ludmila Yakovleva was Irina Kondratyeva's deputy and replaced her when she was absent. She wrote the invoices and made the necessary calculations, other than for big editions and four-colour production. Irina Kondratyeva was in charge of the latter. The managing director also had some contact with customer representatives. He usually met them at Tipografiya, but he seldom met their managing directors. The same was true for the chief engineer and the composition room supervisor.

> I meet customers only in exceptional cases, if it has to do with technological issues. I meet with representatives from the Post Office Administration and the newspapers only if they have complaints concerning quality (Valery Polyanskiy).
>
> We seldom have contacts with the customers. We meet only representatives from the newspapers and when we are printing books. Then we have direct contacts with the authors. In all other cases, the business center has the contacts with the customers. The composition room are only executors (Valentina Guseva).

Irina Kondratyeva was also deeply involved in the financial issues, which were not directly the task of the accounting department. Furthermore, she was in charge of the pricing. During the period, approximately 10% of the total turnover was in barter trade. The management decided at the beginning of the 1990s that Tipografiya should not do any barter trade, which at that time was common in Russia, despite the possibility that it might mean increased sales. Several customers' debts to Tipografiya grew extensively in the middle of the period and some of them paid with convertibles on some occasions.

> Our main task is to be sure that sales correspond with production for that reason we print only on order. Rybokombinat paid us with convertibles. Myasokombinat often wants to pay with sausages, but we do not want to do that. I remember when the regional branch of the Post Office Administration in Kazan wanted to pay us with film from Tasmy, which also is situated in Kazan. This was the only case when we did barter trade (Irina Kondratyeva).

The financial crisis, which was one of the reasons that barter trade became common in Russia, also meant that a lot of customers could not pay and therefore, around 1993 Tipografiya began to require prepayment. This requirement grew and in 1996 almost all customers had to prepay before Tipografiya would start production.

> We require 100% prepayment. We sometimes make exceptions for continuously returning customers (Ludmila Yakovleva).

The first and second re-organisation meant that all the contacts with the customers changed. After the summer of 1997 around 15 employees were active in relations with customers. For instance, Ludmila Yakovleva described the tasks of the marketing and advertising department in the following way:

> When we started in 1997 I went around among firms and told them that we are not a printing house for forms; we do colour printing. We organise excursions for school children and participate in exhibitions. We do market research and investigate which segment is coming to us, and who does not want to pay for advertising. We studied our market, systematically, administering questionnaires and analysing. We did research in 1997 or 1998, which showed that in the town we are perceived as a producer of forms. The conclusion was that we had to print in four-colour and [focus on] advertisements. The customers buying forms became fewer and we had to compensate with the production of advertising material. The forms are cheap and a customer buying products in four-colours compensates for an enormous number of forms. That was the way the need to open our department matured (Ludmila Yakovleva).

Newspapers

During the period, Tipografiya printed more than a handful of newspapers, of which two, the *Novgorodskiye Vedomosti* and the *Novgorod*, were predominant. The volumes were, with some small exceptions, stable, but the contacts with these two newspapers, especially the Novgorodskiye Vedomosti, were complicated over the whole period. The newspapers were printed on the rotary press, which was purchased in 1994, and on the sheet-fed presses, of which three were old cylinder presses with manual feeding. Four members of the production personnel worked with the newspapers, two on the first shift and two on the second. One person worked on the composition and one on the make-up.

Tipografiya also printed a third newspaper called the *Vechevoy Tsentr*. It was owned by Tipografiya and was founded in 1996. The Vechevoy Tsentr was completely financed by advertisements, became a big success, and was very profitable, although less profitable than the retail shop, Delovoy Mir, which was founded at almost the same time as the Vechevoy Tsentr. In 1997 and 1998, the Vechevoy Tsentr's share of the total turnover was 6.8 and 11.5% respectively, while the retail shop's share was 19.4 and 21.2%. Other newspapers printed by

Table 5: Tipografiya's sales to the local newspapers 1993–1998.[a]

Newspapers	1993	1994	1995	1996	1997	1998
Novgorodskiye Vedomosti	25,000	25,000	25,000	30,000	25,000	23,000
Novgorod	86,000	88,000	88,000	88,000	88,000	88,000
Zvezda	4,600	1,900	2,900	2,400	2,800	2,300
Shimskiye Vesti	2,000	1,100	3,500	1,200	–	–

Source: Author's own calculations based upon internal data from Tipografiya.
[a] Average circulation of each issue.

Tipografiya were the *Shimskiye Vesti,* the *Zvezda,* the *Chto? Gde? Kogda?* and the *Novgorodskiy Universitet.* Since the reforms started in 1992 the circulation of all the newspapers was relatively stable (Table 5). Changes concerned what had happened within the relationships with these customers.

The Novgorodskiye Vedomosti

At the end of the period of the planned economy the Novgorodskiye Vedomosti was already considered to be Tipografiya's most important customer. Irina Kondratyeva was the one at Tipografiya who had the most extensive contacts with the editorial office of the Novgorodskiye Vedomosti.

> In terms of money, at least concerning income but not profitability, the Novgorodskiye Vedomosti is our biggest customer. I cannot give you any more details about this customer, we only invoice them, and they do not pay regularly. As for the rest, we do not have any relations with them. For me there is no reason to try to improve the contacts (Irina Kondratyeva).

The Novgorodskiye Vedomosti was the biggest consumer of paper and stood for the biggest incomes, but not the biggest profit. From the time it was launched, the District Administration owned, controlled, and financed its operations. Tipografiya printed the Novgorodskiye Vedomosti four times every week all year round. As far as the Novgorodskiye Vedomosti was concerned, Tipografiya's advantage was that there were no alternative printing shops in the Novgorod district that had the printing press needed to print the newspaper. Instead, potential suppliers to the Novgorodskiye Vedomosti could only be found in cities such as Pskov, St. Petersburg, and Tver, all situated more than 200 kilometres from

Novgorod. Printing the Novgorodskiye Vedomosti in the neighbouring districts would cause difficulties and would be costly. A second alternative was for the Novgorodskiye Vedomosti to buy its own printing press. Tipografiya perceived this as less realistic because it was currently experiencing severe financial problems. The same was the case for the District Administration, although in the long run this was a scenario that could not be excluded. On the other hand, the Novgorodskiye Vedomosti was a large and important customer for Tipografiya, one that would be extremely difficult to replace if it disappeared. This kind of monopoly situation meant that the regional anti-monopoly committee defined Tipografiya as having a monopoly, which meant that this committee monitored Tipografiya and was prepared to intervene Tipografiya's relationships with all the newspapers.

Pricing and Calculation

Before the beginning of the transition there was a well-defined official price list. This determined the prices in the transactions between Tipografiya and the Novgorodskiye Vedomosti. When the prices were liberalised in 1992, hyperinflation started. Tipografiya's suppliers began to increase the prices and the price list was abolished, as it meant a loss for Tipografiya, which instead began using the cost price plus a small profit margin.

The circulation of the Novgorodskiye Vedomosti decreased from around 50,000–60,000 per issue in 1991 to around 23,000 per issue in 1998. There were two causes for that. Firstly, the consumers' financial position was much worse in 1998 than in 1991 and they could not afford to subscribe to the newspaper to the same extent as they had before 1992. Secondly, a competing paper, the Novgorod, had been launched in 1990. The decrease of subscribers resulted in the Novgorodskiye Vedomosti being short of available funds and piling up big debts to Tipografiya over the years. In parallel to the price list there was a written contract that regulated the relationship between Novgorodskiye Vedomosti and Tipografiya. This contract dated back to the planned economy, but during the transition strong disagreements appeared. Such disagreements usually concerned financial issues, as the Novgorodskiye Vedomosti was generally late with its payment, often six to seven months late. This situation, in turn, meant that the District Administration and the regional branch of the federal antimonopoly committee had to intervene and solve the conflicts that arose.

> The editor-in-chief is a difficult person. He constantly sues us and trails me around to different courts, since he has the opinion that

our prices are far too high. When he sues us, we meet frequently. He writes complaining letters to the district administration and they ask us to meet in order to solve the problems with the prices. The district administration commissions the antimonopoly committee to solve the problem. In 70% of the cases, they accept our version. That is the reason I meet him (Irina Kondratyeva).

After these conflicts in the beginning of the 1990s, the parties came to an agreement that the price should be fixed in an annual contract, which even regulated Tipografiya's profit margin. The head of the production and finance department, together with the Novgorodskiye Vedomosti's editor-in-chief or his deputy, annually renegotiated this contract. The contract stipulated that the profit margin could not exceed 25%. The profit was based on prime cost, that is, production cost, depreciation of equipment, direct salaries, energy cost, spare parts, consumables, and ink. A sum of 25% was then added to the total.

It is our smallest profit margin. Other customers give us 40%–50%. Emergency orders have the highest profit margins (Irina Kondratyeva).

In 1995, Tipografiya sold newspapers for 790 million roubles, out of which the Novgorodskiye Vedomosti accounted for made 260 millions (30%). The profit made from this relationship was estimated at 50–55 million roubles in 1995 by the head of the production and finance department:

and a lot of nervous breakdowns for our director and me (Irina Kondratyeva).

The Novgorodskiye Vedomosti continued to be late with its payment during the whole period from 1993 to 1998, but it continued to order from Tipografiya. During 1998, Tipografiya began to get paid by the Novgorodskiye Vedomosti by not paying its taxes. Since the newspaper was owned and financed by the District Administration it was possible to solve these financial issues via the taxes. The taxes that the Novgorodskiye Vedomosti should have paid to the district budget were given as a loan. The Novgorodskiye Vedomosti obtained a loan from the District Administration corresponding to the taxes Tipografiya should pay, which was later transferred to a joint account. In that way the debt to Tipografiya and the taxes Tipografiya should pay were settled per contra. The fact that the Novgorodskiye Vedomosti was owned and controlled by the District Administration meant that Tipografiya had to trust the newspaper.

They behave as though we are dependent on them. We are forced to trust them. The District Administration publishes the paper, so even when it does not pay us we have to behave carefully. Despite the enormous delays with the payments, our Managing Director has never had opportunity to declare that if they do not pay we will from tomorrow not print this paper. It has been the case with other newspapers, but it is not worthwhile to end up in a deep conflict with the District Administration. According to the agreements they have to pay us directly. Sometimes the delays are three–four months (Irina Kondratyeva).

Purchasing of Newsprint

One thing in common for all the newspapers was that they continued to purchase newsprint themselves and the only costs in which Tipografiya was involved was for the employee responsible for the stock room for paper. The editorial office searched for and acquired paper from different suppliers itself. However, in April 1998 the Committee for prices at the District Administration (the owner of the Novgorodskiye Vedomosti) announced a tender in order to find a paper supplier that could offer the best conditions to the Novgorodskiye Vedomosti. A big trading company, *Adept-Les-Holding*, won the tender and after that supplied Tipografiya with paper. Adept-Les appeared in the market at the beginning of the transition economy and was a spin-off from the *Oblastpotrebsoyuz* (Regional Consumer Association). Adept-Les was doing business in various fields, for instance, it traded with food and was running a travel agency. Adept-Les had also supplied paper to the Novgorod since 1998. Usually, Adept-Les acquired the newsprint by barter from the kombinat in Kondopoga.

> Adept-Les delivers timber, which is cut in Novgorod, to Kondopoga, and buys newsprint for the timber. It is convenient for the administration, since if you do not pay today, they will find paper anyhow. For us it was indifferent from where Adept-Les was buying the paper, as long as it was of satisfactory quality (Nikolay Yevlampiyev).

Communication

The Novgorodskiye Vedomosti continued to have constant presence at Tipografiya. A supervisor was working at Tipografiya and he checked every issue of the newspaper and had the final responsibility for each issue. Furthermore, four proofreaders from the Novgorodskiye Vedomosti were working in Tipografiya's premises, although not at the same time. The newspaper informed Tipografiya about all changes concerning circulation, volumes, and publishing days. The invoices were sent to the newspaper's office by a courier. Irina Kondratyeva's most extensive contacts were with the chief accountant at the Novgorodskiye Vedomosti, which was particularly the case when Tipografiya changed prices. Irina Kondratyeva calculated the prices and discussed them with the chief accountant. Besides Irina Kondratyeva, the relief printing shop had some contacts with the Novgorodskiye Vedomosti. Valentina Guseva met the paper's representatives from the editorial office, although it did not happen as often as in the planned economy.

Production Technology

In May 1997, Tipografiya began to print the other big newspaper, the Novgorod, with a new technology. Instead of using zinc for production of plates, Tipografiya began to use photo polymer. The background was that it became impossible to buy zinc in Russia and Tipografiya's stock was finished. Photo polymer gave a higher quality of photograph, but it was also more expensive than zinc. The change also meant that the newspaper had to be composed on computer and printed on the offset machines and not on the relief presses. But the Novgorodskiye Vedomosti refused to use the new technology, mainly for financial reasons.

> We do not print the Novgorodskiye Vedomosti on photo polymer plates, since it is more expensive. The Novgorodskiye Vedomosti does not want to pay for this, although it gives better quality. The Novgorodskiye Vedomosti does not pay any money. The other newspapers pay. Since the Novgorodskiye Vedomosti belongs to the District Administration, we get an exemption from taxes corresponding to its debts to us. Irrespective of this, its debts to us grow. We have not made a legal matter of this in order not to destroy the relation to the authorities. But it purchases zinc. It was our condition (Irina Kondratyeva).

The solution was that the Novgorodskiye Vedomosti decided to continue to use zinc, but that it, and not Tipografiya, would purchase the zinc. It also meant that Tipografiya would continue to print the Novgorodskiye Vedomosti on the relief printing presses. The Novgorodskiye Vedomosti intended to do the composing by itself and to deliver already prepared blocks to Tipografiya.

Since it has big debts to us, we told them that we would not buy zinc for it. We gave it some addresses in Moscow where it could buy zinc. We do not need zinc anymore (Nikolay Yevlampiyev).

Distribution

During the whole period the same organisations, Gazetno-Zhurnalnaya Ekspeditsiya and Rospechat, were responsible for the distribution of the Novgorodskiye Vedomosti and no changes took place in the distribution. Gazetno-Zhurnalnaya Ekspeditsiya was a subsection of the Post Office Administration and took care of the subscriptions to newspapers, including the Novgorodskiye Vedomosti. Rospechat was an organisation, which was in retail trade and a customer of Gazetno-Zhurnalnaya Ekspeditsiya. The Post Office Administration collected information about the demand for the newspapers, including among other thing subscriptions, single copies, and the editorial office's needs. Thereafter, the Post Office Administration gave Gazetno-Zhurnalnaya Ekspeditsiya instructions about where and how many newspapers should be distributed. Gazetno-Zhurnalnaya Ekspeditsiya rented premises at Tipografiya and was directly involved with the printed newspapers. It packed and distributed them according to the Post Office Administration's instructions. The newspapers were not stored at Tipografiya or at Gazetno-Zhurnalnaya Ekspeditsiya, but were sent away by Gazetno-Zhurnalnaya Ekspeditsiya immediately after printing.

It has always been that way, until 1992 and thereafter, and no changes are expected in the immediate future. Between 1995 and 1998 there were no significant changes in the distribution of the newspapers. In 1998 the Novgorodskiye Vedomosti began to publish a newspaper of twice the size, 16A3, on Fridays, instead of the previous 4A2. It hardly affected the circulation at all (Irina Kondratyeva).

The two re-organisations did not change the responsibility for the newspapers. Irina Kondratyeva, who during the period was the head of three departments at different times — the production and finance department, the finance department, and the PR and advertising department — continued to have responsibility for the newspapers from 1992 to 1998. In 1998, it still meant price negotiations and establishment of contracts with the Novgorodskiye Vedomosti, but also with the Novgorod, and the Zvezda.

The Novgorod

At the end of the planned economy, the Novgorod had already come to an agreement with the City Administration (not to be confused with the District Administration, i.e. the owner of the Novgorodskiye Vedomosti), saying that it would finance a daily circulation of 87,000 copies. The circulation remained stable throughout the whole period. Each issue was distributed free to all households in Novgorod. The newspaper published the television programmes daily, which according to Tipografiya was the main reason that people read the paper.

Communication

The Novgorod's editorial office was situated very close to Tipografiya, but despite the geographical closeness, the contacts between the firms were not very extensive. Valentina Guseva and Irina Kondratyeva were the ones with most contact with the Novgorod. The main topic discussed was usually the quality of the printing. Very often, the editor-in-chief claimed that the quality of the photographs was not satisfactory and Tipografiya shared his opinion. However, in order to solve this problem the production had to be moved from the old relief printing machines to the offset machines. This would, in turn, require offset machines capable of handling larger size of paper, which Tipografiya did not have.

Irina Kondratyeva had contact with the Novgorod whenever changes of circulation and volumes were imminent. Furthermore, her department was in charge of all financial issues, such as invoicing and re-negotiation of the annual agreement. In this case the contacts were always taken with the deputy editor-in-chief. In contrast to the Novgorodskiye Vedomosti and the other small newspapers in the region, the Novgorod paid the invoices according to the agreement and thus did not have to make prepayments. The agreement regulating the relationship between the Novgorod and Tipografiya was protected against inflation, which meant that Irina Kondratyeva attentively followed the general price development and revised the prices monthly in relation to Tipografiya's expenses for production of the newspaper. In the Novgorod's case, the price was calculated at prime cost with a mark-up of 33%. The same calculation was used in their dealings with all newspapers except with the Novgorodskiye Vedomosti, where the mark-up was 25%.

Purchasing of Newsprint

The purchasing of newsprint was the same as in the relationship with the Novgorodskiye Vedomosti. The Novgorod purchased the paper and kept it in stock in Tipografiya's facilities and Tipografiya did not interfere as long as the quality of the paper was sufficient. However, at times this was not the case. For instance, once in 1997 the Novgorod bought a wagon of newsprint from Kamskiy TsBK, but the paper did not fit as it was of a different smoothness than the one Tipografiya usually used. The Novgorod was forced to take back the paper and until the spring of 1998 it bought all newsprint from Kondopoga instead. After that Adept-Les began to purchase the newsprint, but it did not mean a change of producer, as Kondopoga was the most common supplier.

Production Technology

Until 1997 the Novgorod was mainly printed on the relief printing presses. The Novgorod's main product printed by Tipografiya was, of course, the paper, but forms and various leaflets were also produced. The newspaper was in an 8-16 column-format. During the spring of 1997, Tipografiya began to apply a new technology to the production of newspapers. The main change was in the use of plates of photo polymer rather than plates made of zinc, mainly because it had become impossible to find zinc in Russia.

> Probably, we will print all the newspapers on polymer. We must stop using lead and zinc. We still have some zinc in stock but it will be empty in one or two weeks. There is no zinc in the country. Life has forced us to begin to use polymer (Valentina Andreyeva).

Many printing houses had at that time already begun to use the new technology, and instead of printing the Novgorod on the relief printing presses, Tipografiya began to compose on computer and print them on the offset presses. This happened in May 1997. The assessment of Tipografiya's management was that the photo polymer plates produced a higher quality and greater possibilities, and moreover, that they were advantageous economically.

> The main reason is that there is no deficit on photo polymer plates. They are a little bit more expensive than zinc, but since they can be used much longer, they are stronger. For instance, one plate can be used for 300,000 issues; in the end they are not more expensive than the old technology (Nikolay Yevlampiyev).

However, the production personnel did not like the change. They were used to managing the old technology and wanted to continue with it. From the very beginning the newspaper was positive about the new technology. Valery Polyanskiy met with the Novgorod's management in the beginning when there were complaints but in June 1998 both Zinaida Prokofyeva and Valery Polyanskiy said that up to that time the Novgorod was pleased with the change.

Distribution

The Novgorod had its own distribution service, that is, its own delivery staff, which meant that the distribution differed a little from that of the Novgorodskiye Vedomosti. The paper was put in each mailbox in Novgorod, and the Novgorod's editorial office therefore did not need the services of the Post Office Administration. The Novgorod just made an agreement with the Post Office Administration about the services of Gazetno-Zhurnalnaya Ekspeditsiya. It packed the newspapers next to the printing machines and gave them to the Novgorod's editorial office. Thus, other than the photo polymer, there were no changes in the way of producing and distributing the Novgorod during the period. Irina Kondratyeva elaborates on this:

> Nothing has changed concerning the newspapers. The number of subscribers determines the circulation. The editorial office turns to Tipografiya and shows how many copies they need (Irina Kondratyeva).

The Vechevoy Tsentr

The first issue of Tipografiya's newspaper, Vechevoy Tsentr, appeared on 13th September 1995. The background was the big increases in energy costs for Tipografiya, which was a consequence of the liberalisation of prices in 1992. The increased energy costs forced Tipografiya to increase the prices for printing newspapers.

> The local newspapers screamed a lot and claimed that we were "rent seeking." The newspapers' leaders criticised me and we felt that we were defenceless. We can use Vechevoy Tsentr as our defence. Through Vechevoy Tsentr our voice can always be heard (Nikolay Yevlampiyev).

At that time, Tipografiya's management was giving a great deal of thought to how it should react to the situation. Several plans and ideas existed simultaneously.

During a business trip to Sweden, the managing director Nikolay Yevlampiyev went to a printing house with which he was acquainted and saw, for the first time, that they were printing a newspaper financed by advertising. It was decided that Tipografiya should launch a similar newspaper. However, Tipografiya did not have the staff (for instance, journalists) that were needed. After some time, a former editor of the Novgorod, Sergei Brutman, was employed and he was commissioned to launch the newspaper. Two other people joined him and they formed three private firms, which signed an agreement of co-operation with Tipografiya. They all had a background in the Novgorod. The Novgorod was also a free newspaper and from the beginning was already perceived as the only competitor to the Vechevoy Tsentr. This took place in 1995 and the editorial office began its work with just a typewriter. And so the first issue of the first newspaper in the district to be financed by advertisements appeared.

Foundation of Trading Company

Tipografiya also founded a trading company, where the founders were not responsible for each other's obligations; each one of the three founders was responsible only for himself and reported the result to the tax authorities at the end of the year. Each had his own assets, but they could also acquire assets together. In case of conflict, the assets and their value were portioned out. The assets could be sold and the income distributed among the founders. This trading company had an agreement with Tipografiya, in which it was said that the trading company should concentrate on publishing the Vechevoy Tsentr. Formally, the Vechevoy Tsentr was founded by and belonged to Tipografiya. The agreement also stated that the partner, Tipografiya, was entitled to financial control over the trading company's incomes and expenses. The trading company should report the results every third month to Tipografiya, which then approved and signed them. The agreement with Tipografiya meant that the profit was divided so that the three individuals shared 65%, while 35% went to Tipografiya. The editorial office was on the first floor close to the main entrance and Tipografiya's office section. From the beginning Sergei Brutman as manager made all the strategic decisions and Tipografiya seldom interfered in the development of Vechevoy Tsentr. A decision was made that the Vechevoy Tsentr should orient its operations towards and find its advertisers among small business enterprises, because they were less connected to the political and administrative power circles.

> We understand that they have no purchasing power. There is a moment when the prices for advertisements begin to destroy them (Sergei Brutman).

The Vechevoy Tsentr quickly became a great success and the initial aim to make their own voice heard, quickly became unimportant. Instead the newspaper generated large revenues and a good profit. The Vechevoy Tsentr became very important for Tipografiya.

> We always pay Tipografiya in cash. The majority of the advertisers paid in cash and did not transfer the money to our bank account. We daily handed a large amount of cash to the accounting department. Furthermore, we always pay the invoices the founder gives us. We often make prepayments (Sergei Brutman).

This meant that Tipografiya almost always had liquid funds, which could be used for payment of wages to their employees.

> We do not pay for the graphic products cash anymore, but through the bank, in order to save 5%. But, we give it in cash. I think it is favourable. The other newspapers pay badly and irregularly. It is difficult to stop the production of the newspapers. It is a stable order (Sergei Brutman).

From the beginning the Vechevoy Tsentr was produced by three people, of whom two were journalists. All kinds of work needed to be done in the editorial office; such as technical work, proofreading advertisements, composing texts and doing tests. It was not possible in such a small editorial office to split up the work into different areas of specialisation. The Novgorod was viewed as Vechevoy Tsentr's only competitor. They had more or less the same circulation and the same method of distribution. In the beginning the Vechevoy Tsentr's prices were 25% lower than the Novgorod's, but the difference then decreased and in 1998 the Vechevoy Tsentr's prices were around 20% lower than the Novgorod's. Coca-Cola in St. Petersburg was the Vechevoy Tsentr's biggest buyer of advertisements between 1995 and 1998. Wednesday was the most popular day for the purchasers of advertisements and the Wednesday edition contained only advertisements and no journalistic texts. The Vechevoy Tsentr's focus was on news from Novgorod. It gave priority to material about consumer protection, that is, the quality of products, services, and retail trade. A second focus was on peoples' opinion about various issues in Russian society. Tipografiya undertook regular telephone polls and published the results.

Circulation

The customers were those who advertised in the Vechevoy Tsentr, and Nikolay Yevlampiyev claimed that the quality was high and that a number of studies had shown that the results of advertising in Novgorod were best in the Vechevoy Tsentr. In 1995, the Vechevoy Tsentr's circulation was 60,000, which increased to 80,000, and in 1998 to 85,000, which was the biggest circulation during the period. When the financial crisis hit Russia in August 1998 the price of paper increased considerably and circulation was decreased to 80,000. The decrease affected some of the suburbs, which were excluded from the distribution list.

In 1995, the Vechevoy Tsentr appeared once a week, but in 1996, demand increased and it was issued twice a week, on Wednesdays and Fridays. The circulation grew to up to four times a week, which was appreciated by the customers, who were mainly private individuals. In August 1998, Tipografiya was forced to decrease the circulation and during the autumn of 1998 the Vechevoy Tsentr was printed just two or three times a week. At the beginning of 1998, the Vechevoy Tsentr began to use a free schedule, that is, each week three issues came out, but twice a month a fourth issue would be published.

> It was before the crisis. We stopped this practise after the crisis, since we had problems with the advertisers; the market for advertisements diminished. Then the market levelled out. Before that we did not need so many advertisements to cover the costs then, due to the increased prices for paper and printing material, the costs for each issue increased. We even had problems purchasing paper during the most tense period, when business was really bad. The paper producers were sitting on their paper and did not sell at all. It was during that period, in the winter, when the paper came out just twice a week (Sergei Brutman).

However, the Vechevoy Tsentr could, since the newspaper was distributed free, always vary the number of issues. Moreover, it did not have to grant credits because it had no subscribers. It was not so dependent on the demand in the market. The crisis in August 1998 made it more difficult for Vechevoy Tsentr to cover the expenses and because of that the advertisements took up more space in the newspaper compared to the period from 1995 to 1997.

Production Technology

From the beginning the Vechevoy Tsentr was printed on relief printing presses but in 1995–1996 the production was moved to the offset machines. The Vechevoy Tsentr was of a higher quality than the Novgorod, as between 1995 and 1998 the latter was printed on the relief printing presses, using zinc plates. The Vechevoy Tsentr had two networks: one local and internal for the editorial office and one connected to Tipografiya. The editorial office was connected to Tipografiya's composition room.

> First, at the time, when the composition room made the setting and the clean proof of the newspaper, we printed our material on paper and took it to the composition room. After that, we began to compose the texts ourselves on diskette. From that moment we began to send the files, which were ready, via the net and they developed the films with the help of the equipment and realised them at the montage (Sergei Brutman).

Purchasing of Newsprint

The newsprint was originally mainly produced by Kondopoga and was sometimes bought by Tipografiya and sometimes by the editorial office, depending on the circumstances. Each time the editorial office made an agreement with Tipografiya about who should purchase the paper the next time. Tipografiya and the Vechevoy Tsentr purchased paper together, since they purchased wagons of paper, which made bigger volumes cheaper, but exclusively from the intermediaries operating in the market around 1995–1996. The volume of the purchased paper depended on the partners' liquidity. In Russia the conditions were so uncertain that the producers of paper were sometimes reluctant to sell the paper immediately. Furthermore, Tipografiya and the Vechevoy Tsentr were stuck with agreements with various intermediaries.

> It is more beneficial, both for us and for Tipografiya, if we purchase the paper. When Tipografiya purchases the paper, they really sell it to us. Tipografiya cannot sell for a lower price than prime cost and there has to be an additional charge on the prime cost, which means higher prime costs for the issue. The higher the prime costs the lower the income at the end of the period when the books are closed. Tipografiya purchases all the other material. It sends us an invoice, the same as it does to all its customers (Sergei Brutman).

Distribution

The Vechevoy Tsentr was printed between 4 and 10 p.m. and distributed during the evening and night so that it could be in all the letterboxes by 8 a.m. in the following morning. This was better than the Novgorod where it was written that the newspapers should be in the letterboxes every Thursday, but the households only got them at around 5 p.m. on Friday. The Vechevoy Tsentr was assessed by the management at Tipografiya to be of the highest quality of all newspapers in the district.

By Russian standards, the circulation of the Vechevoy Tsentr was stable, but the fluctuations that took place were partly due to the extension of the distribution to small towns and villages or because the circulation had been decreased. For instance, the editorial office made attempts to distribute the Vechevoy Tsentr in, for instance, Borovichi and Khvoiny, located rather far from Novgorod. Although there were people from there who were working in Novgorod, it was not a success. Partly because small business was locally oriented (i.e. the firms from Novgorod did not see any value in advertising in other towns), and partly because of problems with the distribution, it was difficult for the Vechevoy Tsentr to control the work of the distributors. This meant that these towns were taken off the distribution list. So, in 1998 the Vechevoy Tsentr was distributed only in the city of Novgorod. The distributors were students, retirees, or the unemployed and each of them was responsible for one of the total of 30 districts. The newspapers were transported from the printing house to the districts in a van which originally belonged to the Association of Handicapped and which could be used free of charge by the editorial office's staff, since all of them happened to be registered as physically disabled. Later, the editorial office bought the van. The fact that the three people in the editorial office were registered as disabled also implied certain tax benefits.

Four Small Newspapers

Tipografiya also printed two other regional newspapers: the *Shimskiye Vesti* and the *Zvezda*. They had in common that they did not have to make prepayment for a long period of time, which resulted in the growth of their debts to Tipografiya. The Shimskiye Vesti was distributed in the town of Shimsk. It came out three times per week with a circulation of 3,000. In 1996, the relationship with the Shimskiye Vesti changed dramatically. The Shimskiye Vesti had piled up huge debts to Tipografiya, and Tipografiya threatened the Shimskiye Vesti to discontinue printing if it did not pay Tipografiya. The Shimskiye Vesti's management then approached a printing house in Staraya Russa, and Tipografiya sued the Shimskiye Vesti. The court obliged the Shimskiye Vesti to settle its debts, which it did. In December 1996, Tipografiya printed an edition of the Shimskiye Vesti for the last time. Tipografiya printed the Zvezda throughout the whole period. It was distributed in Novgorod but mostly on the outskirts and in surrounding villages around Novgorod. It was issued once a week and the circulation was around 3,500.

In addition, Tipografiya previously had two more newspapers as customers, the *Chto? Gde? Kogda?* and the *Novgorodskiy Universitet*, which also enjoyed the advantage of not having to make prepayments. The Chto? Gde? Kogda? was a weekly newspaper published by the local TV and Radio Company and its main content was the television and radio programmes. The Chto? Gde? Kogda? also had big debts to Tipografiya which it did not pay for a very long time. At this time Tipografiya made a decision that either everyone should pay or that they had to find another supplier. Tipografiya sued the Chto? Gde? Kogda? and in the end it paid its debts. Tipografiya printed the Chto? Gde? Kogda? for the last time in February 1996 and then the local TV and Radio Company founded its own printing shop and started to print the Chto? Gde? Kogda? itself. The Novgorodskiy Universitet turned to another printing house, but in 1998 it still had big debts to Tipografiya.

The Retail Shop — Delovoy Mir

An innovation during the period was the retail shop, which was internally called the sales department and externally called Delovoy Mir. It was first managed by Zinaida Prokofyeva. When she became head of the business center in 1997, Valentina Chugrinova replaced her. Initially, Zinaida Prokofyeva, together with two salesmen, worked in the shop. It was founded in 1994, when Tipografiya came to the conclusion that many customers did not want to have to wait long for their order and that a faster service should be offered to existing customers. This was also a time when the economy was in deep crisis and Tipografiya had to look for new ways of doing business in order to survive.

> Then he went to someone else. We founded the shop in order to satisfy the customers' wishes: forms and other consumer goods, immediately. The retail shop offers the product to the same customers as the printing house (Nikolay Yevlampiyev).

Firms and organisations were the absolute majority of the customers in the retail shop. There was also a growing group of private entrepreneurs, but their share of the sales was quite small. The retail shop sold forms and strips for cash registers, which Tipografiya produced, and various types of paper. The firm also produced writing pads, booklets, and folders of waste from their remaining production. In the beginning, 80% of the shop's turnover came from products produced by

Tipografiya, which was one of the aims at that time. The aim was to find if not a new market at least a new channel to the market for the existing products. After a while, Tipografiya began to buy stationery and sell it in the shop. The shares of products that were bought and those they produced themselves varied over the period. Usually 60% of the sales were from products they produced, and 40% came from products that Tipografiya bought and then resold in its shop. The share of products from in-house production was never smaller than 50%. The retail shop became an almost instantaneous big success and emerged, together with the Vechevoy Tsentr, as the main source of income. In the beginning the shop had 12 square metres at its disposal, but in 1998 the management decided to increase the shop area to 25 square metres.

> It is a very good and profitable business. We have also opened a newspaper stall in the city administration's building, where the tax inspection is. We will sell our products there; there are a lot of potential customers running around there (Nikolay Yevlampiyev).

The retail shop was also selling to shops in the neighbouring towns, for instance, in Borovichi, Kholmy, and Staraya Russa. The retail shop came to agreements with these shops and this business was also very profitable.

The Post Office Administration

Over the period from 1992 to 1998, the relationships with the regional branches of the Post Office Administration changed both in terms of volumes sold and the character of the relationships. Sales to the Leningrad district, which had always been one of Tipografiya's most important customers, underwent rather large quantitative fluctuations between 1993 and 1998. But the Leningrad district remained one of Tipografiya's biggest customers. During the planned economy the Yekaterinburg district was almost as big a customer as the Leningrad district, but it gradually decreased its purchased volumes during the period from 1992 to 1998. The Kemorovo district and the Lipetsk district represented an opposite development. They, together, with the Leningrad district, first increased their volumes over the previous five years, but in 1998 the Kemorovo district chose not to buy from Tipografiya.

During 1997 and 1998, Tipografiya began to observe a change in the relationships with some of the Post Office Administration's regional branches. Both the volume and the number of orders decreased (see Table 6). The Yekaterinburg district and Penza district decreased their orders in 1997, while

Table 6: Tipografiya's biggest customers within the Post Office Administration.[a]

Customers	1993	1994	1995	1996	1997	1998
KMTO UPS Leningrad district	3,100 (2.6)	1,300 (1.2)	7,300 (2.5)	11,800 (3.9)	5,900 (2.4)	4,509 (1.9)
OAO Upravleniye Promyshlennoy Komplektatsii Yekaterinburg	2,200 (2.4)	1,100 (1.2)	6,100 (1.6)	2,400 (0.9)	1,200 (0.5)	2,754 (1.0)
UFPS Komi Republic	1,900 (1.3)	1,100 (0.7)	3,500 (1.5)	1,200 (0.5)	–	–
UPFS Arkhangelsk district	200 (0.3)	3,100 (1.8)	2,400 (1.2)	1,100 (0.4)	–	2,335 (1.9)
Kts UPFS Lipetsk district	1,100 (0.7)	700 (1.0)	1,300 (0.8)	4,000 (2.1)	5,000 (2.9)	4,075 (2.1)
AO Elektrosvyaz Primorskiy Krai Vladivostok	6,500 (3.0)	1,000 (0.7)	2,700 (0.7)	2,600 (1.1)	900 (0.4)	–
TsMTO UFPS Kemorovo district	800 (0.6)	1,800 (0.6)	1,100 (0.4)	2,500 (1.6)	2,400 (0.1)	–

Source: Author's own calculations based upon internal data from Tipografiya.
[a] Thousand of units (share of the total sales in %).

the one in Vladivostok (Elektrosvyaz Primorskiy Krayi) stopped buying from Tipografiya entirely in 1998. This had already happened with UPFS in the Arkhangelsk district and UFPS in the Komi Republic in 1997. The reason for this development was obvious for Tipografiya:

> It is easy to explain and it is a development regulated by law. In the Soviet Union it was done through centralised plans. Many regional branches continue to buy from us by habit, despite big cost increases for transportation by railway. They are gradually realising that they can buy these forms in their own hometowns (Zinaida Prokofyeva).

The Leningrad District

The Leningrad district had always been considered to be the most important of the regional branches, but for a long time, the only direct contact Tipografiya had with the Leningrad district was the driver who regularly picked up the forms. After 1992, the deliveries began to take place once a month. Nobody at Tipografiya had any knowledge about from where the driver and the van came or to whom they belonged.

> Every month it sends a big van to us in order to pick up the forms. If they change the order they inform us beforehand (Irina Kondratyeva).

During 1996 a gradual change of transportation took place. On some occasions, Tipografiya sent its newly bought van and at other times the van from St. Petersburg came. In 1998, Tipografiya solely began to take care of the transportation. During the first months of 1997 the parties came to an agreement that henceforth Tipografiya should be in charge of the transportation and for that service it would add 1% to the price to cover the expenses. Irina Kondratyeva was in charge of the contacts with the Leningrad district and during 1993 she began to have more regular contact with the Leningrad district. The volume and quality of the information exchanged between the Leningrad district and Tipografiya also increased over the period. Between 1992 and 1996 the firms had contacts one–two times a month and the flow was direct and exclusively by phone. For a long time Tipografiya had the opinion that there was no need to communicate more closely with the Leningrad district.

> I did not need any information from Leningrad, since we are talking about standardised forms. There was no reason to go there.

> In general, the only information I needed was samples. And I
> even remember a case when we did not have any contacts with the
> regional branches; I asked Leningrad to send me samples, but they
> did not do that (Irina Kondratyeva).

When the two firms began to have direct contact, the main information that was transferred was the annual agreement. Tipografiya never needed any confidential information from the Leningrad district. The information exchanged was mainly concerned with which type of forms to produce. Irina Kondratyeva went to the Leningrad district for the first time at the end of December 1996. The visit surprised the district. She was the first representative from Tipografiya who had ever been to the Leningrad district.

> I brought champagne and caviar in order to celebrate New Year's
> eve with them. Their reaction was that, probably, I had some other
> reason to be in St. Petersburg, so they were very happy and flattered
> when they learned that I had come exclusively to meet them. They
> said that it would be much easier to talk on the phone and read my
> faxes now that we have met (Irina Kondratyeva).

After that, the system of payment between the two firms changed. During 1991–1993, Tipografiya successively started to require prepayment from all customers. In this period the whole Russian economy ended up in deep financial crisis. Also the Leningrad district had also on several occasions paid the invoices too late. First, Tipografiya required 50% prepayment, but in 1993 the firm decided to start production only if the customer made 100% prepayment. In 1996, Tipografiya gave up the requirement on prepayment from the Leningrad district, which was unusual in Russia at that time. For a long time, the Leningrad district was the only customer that was given that advantage. After Tipografiya had tried to do business with the Leningrad district without requiring prepayment, and this change had worked out fine, the top management decided to try to do the same with another old customer, namely the Yaroslavl district. It began on a partial basis, but when no problems occurred, Tipografiya increased the size of the credit to the Yaroslavl district. Yaroslavl was also a traditional customer; however, nobody from Tipografiya had ever been to that district or met any representatives from there. In 1996, Tipografiya gave very few customers credit. Besides the Leningrad district and the Yaroslavl district, credit was only extended to the City Administration in Novgorod. Tipografiya has since 1993 made a number of small investments, but none of these has been dedicated to the relationship with the Leningrad district. Instead, they concerned customers and products not related to the Russian Post Office Administration and its regional branches.

At Tipografiya, the production of forms was regarded as simple from a technical point of view, even though the forms were their most profitable products. The head of the production and finance department had the impression that Tipografiya still was the main supplier of forms to the Leningrad district, but she had no knowledge about which other firms supplied the district with forms. Moreover, Tipografiya had no knowledge about how the Leningrad district stored and distributed forms in St. Petersburg and the Leningrad district. Tipografiya knew very well that a large number of printing houses existed there able to print the forms, particularly as the forms were standardised. Nevertheless, Tipografiya believed that the Leningrad district would not turn to alternative suppliers, but continue to buy the bulk of the forms from Tipografiya.

> The only reason the Leningrad district is still buying from us is the credit line we give it. Any printing house would gladly take the offer since at around four tonnes per month it is rather a large quantity, even for a big printing house. I do not think that they buy only from us. If at the beginning of the year we offer a special range of forms, they return a signed agreement with the quantity required. Obviously, they do buy from other suppliers as well. If I offer them something new in the middle of the year, they always answer that they already have it in stock. Finally, at the beginning of the next year when I offer a wider line of forms, they are very keen to buy from us. But I think they are buying more than 50% from us (Irina Kondratyeva).

Tipografiya printed more forms for the Leningrad district in 1998 than in 1993 but its importance in terms of sales volume decreased slightly. Still, Tipografiya expected the relationship to live on. An expression of that was the fact that the two firms had already at the beginning of the autumn of 1996 come to an agreement on deliveries during 1997.

Other Regional Branches of the Post Office Administration

Besides the Leningrad district, Tipografiya annually concluded an agreement with approximately 30 regional branches to which the forms were transported by train. For instance, in 1995 Tipografiya concluded agreements with exactly 30 out of 75 regional branches. Throughout the period the forms were still depicted and standardised annually in the Ministry of Transport and Communication's catalogue and neither Tipografiya nor the regional branches had any possibility of influencing their design. Tipografiya's marketing activities were limited to advertising in the Russian Post Office Administration's journal.

The layout of the forms had not changed since 1992. The Russian Ministry for Transportation and Communication decided on all the minor changes that were made. During 1997–1998 there were some small changes in the design of the forms: the logotype and the organisation name were replaced. Writing paper quality was still used. Earlier the quality of the paper had been standardised, but in the middle of the period the printing shops and the Post Administration's offices were given the freedom themselves to decide the quality. Tipografiya then began to print the forms on a cheaper, lower quality type of writing paper. This measure was aimed at lowering the price, which was welcomed by the customers. When volumes decreased, Tipografiya moved the production from the relief printing shop to the offset equipment, although small orders were sometimes relief printed.

In 1992, LSSK, which until then governed all the relationships with the regional branches, began to play a new role in the relationship between Tipografiya and the regional branches of the Post Office Administration. Initially serving as an intermediary, Tipografiya then had to pay LSSK for its services. However, in 1994, Tipografiya perceived that LSSK's importance for the relationship was negligible and it took the step of terminating the contacts with LSSK and instead starting to do business directly with the regional branches of the Post Office Administration.

> We realised that we would lose this customer if we did not do anything. We had to change our relationship to the Post Office Administration (Nikolay Yevlampiyev).

The relationship with LSSK was rather easy to terminate and a few years later LSSK changed its profile and name and no longer dealt with printing. Tipografiya had no knowledge of or contacts with it whatsoever. After Tipografiya had terminated the relationship with LSSK, it negotiated an agreement with each regional branch once a year. The process began with Tipografiya distributing a standardised contract, where the price was stipulated, to all potential customers among the regional branches. If they intended using Tipografiya as a supplier for the following year, they specified, signed, and returned the contract.

> I have the addresses of all the regional branches, and once a year I send them a contract. But I do not go there (Irina Kondratyeva).

During the period Tipografiya was hit by the customers' complaints regarding quality. At Tipografiya, they believed that quality was not perceived as an important aspect of the product. Instead, the head of the production and finance department claimed that the only way to compete was to offer as low a price as possible. Several of the regional branches became interesting customers for other printing houses, which were viewed as competitors, although they were located in other regions in Russia. For instance, *Polex* from Nizhny Novgorod was a trading company, which had no production facilities of its own. Polex appeared in the market in the middle of the 1990s and attracted a number of Tipografiya's old customers among the regional branches. Tipografiya had not the slightest idea about where Polex printed the forms, but it was obvious that Polex was offering a much lower price than Tipografiya and that Polex took care of the transport of the forms. By tradition Tipografiya did not want to deal with that service. However, the success of Polex meant that Tipografiya started to think about whether it should also offer transportation, at least to the branches in the surrounding districts. Otherwise, the printing house in Kostroma was the most traditional competitor. It had more or less the same equipment, knowledge, and technology and the quality of the end products was approximately the same. The management at Tipografiya had the opinion that they were competitive in comparison with other suppliers.

After the first re-organisation in the summer of 1997, the responsibility of all the regional branches was moved from the production and finance department to the business centre. After that the business centre had all the contact with regional branches of the Post Office Administration, but did not actually visit any of them. It worked out the orders and gave them to the composition rooms and the printing shops. Thereafter, it monitored the production and dealt with all the complaints. It registered both incoming and outgoing orders, prepared invoices and received the payments.

The business centre was located on the ground floor beside the retail shop and had its entrance from the street. The premises were refurbished during the summer of 1997 and Zinaida Prokofyeva, the former shop manager, was appointed head of the business centre. Altogether, there were five employees working in the business centre. Three of them worked with the receiving the orders from customers. One managed orders that required quick execution (for instance, making copies on the newly acquired copy machine), and the last one forwarded the order from the stock room, which was also attached to the business centre as were the production of stamps and seals. After the second re-organisation in 1998, the business centre was still responsible for the forms and all the uncomplicated products and orders. Almost everything but the four-colour printing was processed in the business centre. From 1993 to 1998 some of the regional branches decided to discontinue buying from Tipografiya and in other cases the sold volumes decreased significantly. Throughout the period, Tipografiya was afraid of losing these customers, for instance, the Yaroslavl district and the Penza district, but had poor knowledge of them (as had been the case with the Yekaterinburg and Lipetsk districts), and took no measures to keep them as customers.

> I have never met any representatives from Yaroslavl, Lipetsk, or Yekaterinburg. We did not know them at all. We are concerned about Yaroslavl. There is a printing house there, which is able to print all these forms. That is why we have decreased the prices and began to abandon the requirement of prepayment. We require only 50% prepayment from them since we know them so well. We have never had any conflicts with them. Not only Yaroslavl and Penza are not required to make full prepayment. The same went for Moscow, but they found a printing house closer to them and stopped buying from us. Earlier, everyone paid on time, but nowadays everyone is applying for postponement (Zinaida Prokofyeva).

Over the years, few changes took place in these relationships. The same contact pattern was used, which meant that all contacts were made by telephone and at each branch there was a special contact person with whom Tipografiya communicated. Containers sent by train were used to make the deliveries in the same way as during the planned economy, and on some occasions deliveries were made in packages sent by mail.

Other Customers

Tipografiya was already the dominating printing house in the Novgorod district during the planned economy. During the transition period, the firm's customer structure, besides the newspapers and the Post Office Administration, changed. Tipografiya's management had difficulties in picking some specific customer as more important than the others. In 1996, around ten customers were considered to be of equal importance (Table 7), but besides them, there was many customers which used to be important but who had stopped buying from Tipografiya. The 10 most important customers could be divided into four groups: industrial firms, public organisations, a bank, and a trading company.

The first change related to these customers took place in 1992, when the economic reforms were introduced and inflation appeared. Tipografiya reacted to the inflation by beginning to calculate prices on a prime cost principle.

Table 7: Tipografiya's sales to ten big and important customers 1993–1996.[a]

Customers	1993	1994	1995	1996
Kvant	9,908 (2.80%)	39,520 (3.10%)	12,088 (0.30%)	4,652 (0.10%)
Universal-Neva	5,230 (1.50%)	10,426 (0.80%)	25,986 (0.70%)	36,689 (0.70%)
Novgorodmebel	1,558 (0.40%)	8,994 (0.70%)	21,903 (0.60%)	2,681 (0.05%)
Elkon	1,104 (0.30%)	85 (0.00%)	6,881 (0.20%)	– (0.00%)
Start	632 (0.20%)	1,095 (0.10%)	1,307 (0.04%)	206 (0.00%)
District Administration	309 (0.10%)	2,243 (0.20%)	56,211 (1.60%)	34,501 (0.60%)
Akademiya Selskogo Khozyastva	363 (0.10%)	245 (0.00%)	5,722 (0.20%)	52,658 (0.90%)
Sberbank	202 (0.06%)	6,727 (0.50%)	17,668 (0.50%)	28,968 (0.50%)
The Regional Post Office	85 (0.02%)	8,628 (0.70%)	21,305 (0.60%)	43,758 (0.80%)
The Museum of Novgorod	143 (0.04%)	3,699 (0.30%)	7,638 (0.20%)	10,411 (0.20%)

Source: Author's own calculations based upon internal data from Tipografiya.

Note: Irina Kondratyeva considered these to be the ten biggest customers (other than the newspapers) in September 1996.

[a] Thousands of roubles (share of total sales in %).

> We began to change the prices in 1991, or maybe it was in 1992. There were changes of the prices in connection with the crisis. The price is fixed from two principles. I calculate the prime costs according to the consumables used, salaries, paper, etc. The price is the expenses plus profit. I study the competitors. I call them and tell them that I am a customer. I especially like the way Ludmila Yakovleva does this. We compare with the competitors. In Novgorod, on many products, for instance, the forms, the lion's share of our volumes, we dictate the prices. All the other printing houses wait for us to increase the prices and then they increase their prices. Concerning the colour production, we follow St. Petersburg and other competing printing houses. There are two price calculation principles. I think that the cost principle is the first one. The second principle is market orientation (Irina Kondratyeva).

Industrial Customers

Most of Tipografiya's big industrial customers were on the edge of bankruptcy and many of them were not operating during most of the transition period.

> Start and Kvant stand still. They were very important customers (Nikolay Yevlampiyev).

The majority of them belonged to the defence industrial complex. Consequently their biggest customer was the Ministry of Defence and, due to the cut in the defence budget, there had been no demand for their products since 1992.

> I do not know if they had military orders. Earlier, we could not buy Sony and Panasonic. We had to buy Sadko, which was produced by Kvant. When the borders were opened, imported television sets appeared in the market. They were not more expensive than our domestic TV-sets and people stopped buying those, since they are of worse quality (Irina Kondratyeva).

Kvant produced television sets and each television set required documentation, guarantee certificate, instructions, and technical specifications. Tipografiya printed all kinds of documentation for them, but not the boxes. In 1997, Kvant produced 1000 television sets and Tipografiya printed everything needed for them. After that, Kvant had a debt to Tipografiya for this specific order for a long time, but eventually it was paid to Tipografiya but with great difficulty. In 1998 Kvant did not order anything from Tipografiya. It was not operating as before since there was no demand from consumers for their television sets.

Elkon and Start were two firms that were in operation during the last few years of the period studied. Elkon, which stands for Elektrolampovy Zavod, produced kinescopes for television sets. During the autumn of 1998 Elkon was trying to sell its premises. Start produced radio electronic equipment and Tipografiya used to print instruction and labels for them, but not packages. Kvant, Elkon, and Start probably had large production orders for the Ministry of Defence, but at Tipografiya they did not know the details of what was ordered or the extent of the orders. A new industrial customer appeared from the ashes of Start and that was Splav, which had been an important customer for a few years. Tipografiya printed different types of documentation for Splav. Table 7 shows that these three firms became less important for Tipografiya during the period from 1993 to 1996. In the end they had a smaller piece of the shrinking volume than they had when the reforms began. Novgorodmebel was in operation throughout the whole period, but it was always late with payments, and in the end Tipografiya decided not to deliver to Novgorodmebel any more.

Food Industry

Besides the 10 biggest customers, there were other firms that bought constantly and quite extensively from Tipografiya. The local food industry had always been a loyal customer. They bought mostly labels from Tipografiya and, for various reasons, some of them satisfied their needs in other ways. The liqueur and vodka plant, *Alkon*, which was situated in the same block as Tipografiya, was a regular customer of four-colour products from 1992 until 1998. It ordered labels for its vodka bottles once or twice each quarter. However, it also bought a lot from other printing houses. Throughout the period, Alkon was buying the lion's share of the labels in the Czech Republic, but it also bought from various printing houses in Russia, among them Tipografiya. KLEM began to do barter trade with Alkon, and was instead of cash, paid with vodka, which it resold in the market, whereas Tipografiya was only paid cash. Usually, Alkon bought 300,000–500,000 labels each time. At the beginning of the period Alkon had to pay in advance, but by the end of the period, it began to pay when it fetched the labels at Tipografiya. At the beginning of the period Alkon also began to buy its new labels from a printing house in Moscow. It claimed that Tipografiya could not provide the printing quality that was needed on the labels that were attached to the bottles. Thereafter, it turned to a printing house in the Czech republic. Alkon required pure and sharp colours, which could only be done with equipment for colour separation. During the entire period Alkon was perceived to be a large, attractive and important customer since it had money.

> They are printing labels in the Czech republic. We got an order from them after a break of some years and now we are printing labels for small bottles, so they have partly returned to us (Irina Kondratyeva).

The local brewery *Deka* had never been a constant customer for four-colour products, but had sometimes bought labels. They turned to another supplier in St. Petersburg, because Tipografiya could not offer the quality they required — a higher quality even than Alkon. Around 1996, Deka bought a lot of labels, but it was not satisfied with the quality. Tipografiya only had the technology to print the labels on chalk paper, which was a constraint. Both Alkon and Deka required pure sharp colours, which could only be done with equipment for colour separation, which Tipografiya did not have until 1997. But there was also another reason:

> There were only rouptnd beer bottles and we did not have the necessary equipment. Therefore we did not print for them. Deka loves to pay their suppliers with beer and wants us to sell it further, but we do not want to do that. We want money from our customers. We have more or less never done any barter trade (Irina Kondratyeva).

They wanted to pay for the labels with their products, which Tipografiya refused. *Rybokombinat* (the Fish Kombinat) did the same. Tipografiya printed labels for Rybokombinat, but they were experiencing big financial problems during the period. In 1995, Rybokombinat stopped buying from Tipografiya as they had large debts, which they had not settled. Tipografiya refused to produce anything more for Rybokombinat unless they paid and Rybokombinat then turned to another printing house, which they paid with cans of their products.

> We always printed the long thin labels for fish and it was only recently that we stopped doing it. The reason was the Rybokombinat's debts over the years. It has severe financial problems. We trusted it as a constant customer, despite the hard times, and continued to print the labels. Then, the debts became huge, and the Rybokombinat was declared bankrupt. It still exists, but it is far from a prospering firm and it buys labels somewhere else and pays with tinned goods (Irina Kondratyeva).

The dairy *Laktus* was a permanent customer, but it bought seldom and irregularly. Tipografiya had printed stickers for mayonnaise, but Laktus changed its technology and began to use plastic instead of glass bottles. The brand was already printed on the plastic bottle and labels became unnecessary. Another problem was that Tipografiya did not have the equipment necessary to cut the labels, which were printed on a roll of self-adhesive paper. Furthermore, Laktus was not ready to pay Tipografiya's prices and because of that, turned to other printing houses.

Podberezhsky bakery produced flour and in 1998 it gave Tipografiya a big order to print on the packages. The parties agreed on a price, which was low for Tipografiya, as the packages were stuck together by hand. From 1992 it also constantly bought one-colour labels, forms, and paper for printers. It always paid cash and fetched the products itself. Sometimes Tipografiya printed advertising material for *Myasokombinat* (the Meat Kombinat).

> They did not produce tinned meat, and labels were not needed for sausages. Nowadays, they need labels, but they found a cheaper printing house. But, I cannot understand how the labels can be cheaper than the paper itself; this is called price dumping (Irina Kondratyeva).

Later Myasokombinat began to produce tinned meat and sometimes bought small batches of labels for the tinned meat for prices Tipografiya believed were low. However, Myasokombinat was not pleased with the quality of the paper cutting. They had imported gluing equipment, which was sensitive to the shifting quality in how the labels were cut. Tipografiya's cutting equipment could not provide the quality needed.

The Remaining Customers

Tipografiya printed forms, diplomas, brochures, and folders for the *District Administration*.

> In 1995 the biggest customer was the District Administration. They bought 1.6% of our production. We have so many customers, but most of them buy less than 1% of our production (Irina Kondratyeva).

Another large and traditional customer, *Akron*, a petrochemical firm mainly producing artificial fertiliser, decided some years ago to invest in its own printing shop.

> I have been to Akron, Novgorodles, and Kvant in order to convince
> them to invest in Tipografiya and thereby improve the quality
> of our production. Since then, all of them have started their own
> in-house printing shops (Nikolay Yevlampiyev).

Despite the fact that Akron had its own printing shop from 1997, it turned
to Tipografiya for more complicated products, for instance, annual reports in
four colours, business cards, or advertising material. Its printing shop could
not manage sharp, four-colour production. It seldom ordered anything from
Tipografiya, but had a printing shop in-house, which was managed by the former
managing director and the former chief engineer of Tipografiya. On the other
hand, the trade union at Akron, which was in conflict with the management and
therefore forbidden to use the printing shop, regularly printed posters and leaflets
at Tipografiya.

A new and rather small group of customers appeared after Tipografiya bought
its equipment for colour separation. Several other printing houses began to buy
colour separation services from Tipografiya, for instance, *Fond Kluba Yunikh
Moryakov*, and *Transvit's own printing house* bought this service almost every
week from Tipografiya. Previously, these customers, as Tipografiya had done,
bought colour separation in St. Petersburg. However, the investment in colour
separation equipment meant very few completely new customers, besides the
printing houses that exclusively bought colour separation.

Re-Organisation of the Market Departments

When the marketing and advertising department was founded in August 1997,
Ludmila Yakovleva was appointed head of the new department, which was
officially opened in August. Three new employees joined her. The marketing
and advertising department was responsible for promotion of the firm and
the intention was that it would work with the big and demanding customers.
They were assumed to require more attention and their orders were usually more
complex. The marketing and advertising department was created to concentrate on
four-colour products and the intention was that it should work more with design,
layout, and artistic work than the finance department and the business center.
The marketing and advertising department did all computer composition and
make-up itself and had its own photographer. It discussed the products with the
customers, details of the order were worked out by the business centre, and then
the marketing and advertising department controlled the production. In parallel,
the finance department also had contacts with the customers. Its task, besides

being responsible for the contacts with the newspapers, was to find new customers and establish contacts with them. Irina Kondratyeva viewed her work in the following way:

> I will visit customers without support. However, I have one accountant subordinated to me. We are the connection to society. I worked as salesman, a title that did not correspond to what I did. I met the big directors from the big enterprises for some time in order to provide us with orders. I went to Chudovo where there are a lot of firms with foreign capital and nowadays we work with many of them (Irina Kondratyeva).

In 1998 in the second re-organisation, the marketing and advertising department had its name changed to *the editorial and publishing department.*

> It is closer to the technology and more correct. Now, after two years, the customers know us and it is more convenient for everybody if the customer comes to us. But, our department is very mobile. We talk with the customer on the phone and come to an agreement (Ludmila Yakovleva).

The new department took over some of the tasks previously aimed at the finance department, that is, visiting firms and searching for new customers in the Novgorod district. Since it was difficult to do that, it was decided that the editorial and publishing department should take care of the customers and orders found by the new PR and advertising department. The editorial and publishing department should stay in-house. It was still headed by Ludmila Yakovleva and a photographer and art director worked under her. The art director only worked on computer graphics on the newly bought colour-separation equipment. Ludmila Yakovleva was responsible for marketing and the financial side. Tipografiya was the only firm employing a photographer. He visited the customers and took the photographs they required. The art director showed the customers on the computer how the order would look and discussed improvements to the product with the customer.

> A customer comes and I tell him about design, prices, and shades that affect prices and time. We agree about what he wants. This is the first way. The second way is that the customer comes prepared, with everything already thought out. Our thing is only to print. The next person is our AD; if they do not have photos, it is taken care of

> by our photographer. Sometimes it happens that the customer does
> not know what he wants. Then I explain the prices, if necessary
> our photographer takes photos and if necessary we edit the texts.
> From the moment when we opened we offered a new type of
> service — trips to other towns for photographing. We are busy
> with advertising, all kinds of colour printing, and marketing. But,
> the main thing is photographing, design, and colour separation
> (Ludmila Yakovleva).

The changes meant changes in the way of organising the production from the
moment the customer came until the products were delivered changed. When
the photos were made, the art director decided on the design as a whole and
produced samples. Ludmila Yakovleva went immediately to the proofreader when
the order was signed. If everything was in order, she then took the material for
colour separation. It also meant that the order was passed on to the production
department. The films were then taken to the montage. By tradition, an order to
the editorial and publishing department meant that it was responsible for it and
monitored it all the way to the storeroom.

Numbering of the invoices at Tipografiya was taken care of by the business
centre for the whole printing house. Ludmila Yakovleva wrote the invoice and
handed it to the customer. The money was then transferred to Tipografiya's account
in Slavenbank. When Tipografiya learned that the money had been transferred
it started the production. The accounting department had daily contacts with
the bank. The orders generated by the editorial and publishing department were
mainly printed on the Dominant 745. The printers printed and the cutters cut,
and after that they took the products to the storeroom, but if it was a booklet it
was stitched in the bookbindery. When the product got to the storeroom Ludmila
Yakovleva called the customer and told him that it was ready.

In 1997 and 1998, the editorial and publishing department still required
prepayment, but there were exceptions. It happened when the timetable was
very squeezed. The customers picked up virtually all the orders themselves.
The editorial and publishing department became more and more important
for Tipografiya and so did the products sold by the editorial and publishing
department. Ludmila Yakovleva kept records of all the orders:

> I keep a record of all production orders. The colour production
> accounts for approximately 20%–25%. One fourth of the orders
> go through our department, but it is not the same every month.
> This indicator grows each month. This indicator grows (Ludmila
> Yakovleva).

Purchasing

Bought Products and Paper Suppliers

The quantities that were bought varied a lot during the period, and according to those who were involved in the purchasing, Svetlana Klimenko, Nikolay Yevlampiyev, and Valery Polyanskiy, there were various reasons for that. Firstly, the production and the sales varied considerably, which influenced which products and which quantities Tipografiya purchased. Secondly, after Tipografiya had the freedom to buy from where it wanted, its explicit ambition was to pay a lot of attention to price. For instance, when choosing between two types of paper that could be used for the same purpose, the determining factor was the price and nothing else was considered. Moreover, a big stock was viewed as a strength, especially when Tipografiya found the paper for a low price. A big stock was a comfort if the times should become tough. Tipografiya preferred to buy large quantities and to keep them in stock for long periods. Nikolay Yevlampiyev and Svetlana Klimenko were the two persons most closely involved in the purchasing of the paper.

> Each time when we buy paper, we first conduct market research in order to identify the supplier who offers paper at the cheapest price. We do not want long-term agreements with our suppliers. Nowadays it is better to work without agreements. We follow price cuts on paper. Since the export of paper there has been a cut in prices and the demand for newsprint decreases (Nikolay Yevlampiyev).
>
> When we find cheap paper, we prefer to buy big amounts and keep them in stock. Therefore we buy paper just a few times per year. We buy paper for the labels, which we use over a very long period. It happens that we get an order, which is later cancelled, but we have the paper aimed for that order in stock (Svetlana Klimenko).

The overall most important product bought was paper. The costs of paper were approximately 75% of the current assets, which meant that the price of paper was extremely important for Tipografiya. At the same time, the quality of the paper determined to a great extent the quality of the end products. This importance meant that the managing director was closely involved in the purchasing of the paper.

> I want to have control over the purchasing of paper, since it makes up the biggest expense. When buying paper, we need quite big amounts of money. We buy wagons of paper. The banks give us

loans for purchasing paper. It gives us the biggest income (Nikolay Yevlampiyev).

The chief engineer, on the other hand, was responsible for the purchase of other consumable materials, but also for investment and maintenance of machines and equipment. The managing director estimated that the purchasing activities took approximately 10% of his and the chief engineer's time.

It is easier to work now, to find different goods. Earlier, we had to turn to KPI and it meant a centralised inquiry and we waited and waited, while we were asking ourselves: Do we ever get the material or not? This despite the fact that we had transferred money to them. Nowadays, I just call Moscow and tell them that I want ink for instance. I search for the cheapest. But, everything was more secure and stable and there was always some kind of help. Now we have to do everything ourselves (Valery Polyanskiy).

In 1992, Tipografiya began to purchase paper without the plan authorities interfering. The only exception was the Post Office Administration, where LSSK still provided paper, but in contrast to the planned economy, Tipografiya now had to pay for the paper. However, after some time Tipografiya decided to buy paper for the forms as well (Table 8).

All the traditional paper suppliers, who had supplied Tipografiya with paper for ages, still existed over the whole period, even though foreign firms had acquired some of them. Tipografiya bought wagons of paper and it was the task of the supplier to secure the transport of the paper, which was done by train. The expenses for transport were included in the price. Despite the newly gained freedom to buy from any supplier and the explicit focus on prices, in the beginning of the period, Tipografiya continued to buy from the same kombinats, which had already been supplying it in the planned economy. As pointed out previously, knowledge about suppliers was poor and the contacts and communication limited. In general, the character of the relationship with the paper and pulp kombinats was the same as it had been for a long time: no one from Tipografiya had ever been to them and the main issue discussed besides price was logistics. However, during the first years of the transition period, communication became a little more extensive.

Now I talk with them (DAO Bumaga) on the phone. We trust each other. We have never deceived them. I have never been to Syktyvkar (Nikolay Yevlampiyev).

Table 8: Tipografiya's biggest suppliers of paper 1993–1998.[a]

Suppliers	1993	1994	1995	1996	1997	1998	Product
DAO Bumaga Arkhangelsk	100,191	158,855	101,439	–	–	–	Writing paper
Syktyvkarskiy TsBK	–	141,212	46,811	45,605	90,189	–	Newsprint
							Offset paper
							Printing paper
							Writing paper
Okulovskiy TsBK	59,223	4,960	8,200	–	–	–	Printing paper
Solikomskiy TsBK	40,000	–	–	–	–	–	Newsprint
Novgorodsnab	23,432	–	–	–	–	–	Printing paper
Nevskaya Bumaga	–	–	–	69,310	41,516	71,518	All types of paper
AOZT SPB KPK	–	–	–	16,136	18,161	3,500	Board
AO Kondopoga	–	–	–	–	80,475	–	Newsprint
AOZT Bereg	–	–	–	15,200	46,000	2,800	All types of paper
ZAO Russkaya Bumaga	–	–	–	–	–	4,823	Paper
AO Feba	–	–	–	–	–	29,630	–

Source: Author's own calculations based upon statistics from Tipografiya.
[a]Tonnes of paper and types of paper supplied.

Intermediaries

Tipografiya changed its purchasing behaviour in the middle of the 1990s, which is evident in Table 5.5. Several intermediaries had entered the market and Tipografiya began to buy from them instead of buying directly from the producers. For instance, the intermediaries replaced the biggest supplier, *DAO Bumaga* in Arkhangelsk, which used to supply writing paper, which was used for, among other things, the production of forms. Svetlana Klimenko discussed this at a time when Tipografiya changed its strategy:

> Nowadays we sometimes buy direct from the kombinats and sometimes from intermediaries. We do not have one single supplier, but choose the one that is cheapest at the moment. We buy mostly from intermediaries since it is cheaper than buying from the producer. We are abandoning the kombinats. We are practically not buying from them anymore. They are only delivering big volumes (Svetlana Klimenko).

In 1996, the intermediaries had taken over almost everything from the paper and pulp kombinats. Tipografiya bought from *Nevskaya Bumaga*, which was situated in St. Petersburg and Nikolay Yevlampiyev continued with that to the end of the period. Nevskaya Bumaga was previously called Lensnabpechat and was a regional plan authority for the printing industry in the Leningrad region. It had no production and bought most paper from Kondopoga TsBK. Nevskaya Bumaga purchased much larger quantities than Tipografiya and was able to cut the costs and consequently the price. Nevskaya Bumaga became Tipografiya's biggest supplier during the second half of the period from 1992 to 1998. An additional big advantage was that Nevskaya Bumaga did not require prepayment. Despite the big volumes, no one from Tipografiya met anyone from Nevskaya Bumaga, but still:

> They trust us and we have never fooled them (Nikolay Yevlampiyev).

However, Tipografiya did not leave the traditional kombinats completely. The only newsprint Tipografiya bought was for the Vechevoy Tsentr, which was launched in 1995. Initially, Kondopoga supplied newsprint to the Vechevoy Tsentr. For instance, in 1996, Tipografiya concluded an annual agreement with Kondopoga. According to this, two wagons were to be sent once a month, but this required 100% prepayment. Similar agreement was made with Syktyvkarskiy TsBK. Other intermediaries, who appeared in the market in 1996 were *Petrobumaga* and *Bereg*. Nikolay Yevlampiyev first learned about Bereg when he was looking for Finnish paper. Bereg required prepayment and the Finnish paper was more expensive than Russian, but it was also of much higher quality. Tipografiya decided to buy the Finnish paper from Bereg. It bought rather small quantities of Finnish paper, but from that moment it always turned to Bereg for such paper. On one occasion in 1997, Tipografiya bought a big quantity of paper from DAO Bumaga through the intermediary *Baltiyskaya Tsellyuloza*, which did not require prepayment. Baltiyskaya Tsellyuloza offered all types of paper. During 1996–1998, Tipografiya bought board from *Sankt-Peterburgskiy KPK*.

In the beginning Nikolay Yevlampiyev was a little suspicious towards all these intermediaries, who were trading in paper rather than producing it (an activity which was perceived as close to "speculation" — a previously criminal activity). Moreover, Tipografiya did not know them, but in the end the low price convinced Nikolay Yevlampiyev. He concluded that the intermediaries had an additional advantage, as they had a much keener ear to Tipografiya's needs and desires, especially concerning the quality of the paper. This was important, since quality had become a great problem for Tipografiya. The quality of the paper from the Russian suppliers was seen as always being lower than the paper offered by foreign suppliers. Quality was not an explicit part of Tipografiya's strategy, but it became more and more important, as some of the customers required paper of higher quality. Earlier all the Russian kombinats produced in accordance with governmental standards, but most of them abandoned the standards during the 1990s.

> No one maintains Gost,[3] especially Syktyvkar, an extraordinarily bad kombinat. We have stopped buying from Okulovskiy (Nikolay Yevlampiyev).

In parallel with the appearance of the intermediaries, a change in contrast to the beginning of the 1990s was that Tipografiya was constantly offered paper from new suppliers. Tipografiya was not interested in buying from them despite the sometimes-low price. Nevertheless, offers from wood-cutting firms (so called Lespromkhozes) were rather common. They were paid with paper when they sold timber to the paper and pulp kombinats and had to find buyers for the paper.

> We get endless offers from far and near and not seldom with lower prices than the paper and pulp kombinat can offer (Nikolay Yevlampiyev).

---

[3] See discussion in Chapter 5.4.

> We buy the label paper from different intermediaries in St. Petersburg: Nevskaya Bumaga, Bereg, and Regent. It is imported, coated paper. We still buy offset paper and newsprint from the kombinats: Kondopoga, Arkhangelsk, and Syktyvkar. These kombinats have representation offices in St. Petersburg (Irina Kondratyeva).

Inks, Films, Matrices, and Plates

Besides paper, inks continued to be the biggest products in terms of volume. Throughout the period, Tipografiya bought all the inks for the relief printing from *Torzhorskiy Zavod Krasok*. A few times a year, Valery Polyanskiy went to the supplier and the inks were collected by Tipografiya's own van. The quantities of inks purchased from this supplier decreased during the period from 1993 to 1998 (see Table 9), due to the decrease in production, but also because Tipografiya printed more and more on the offset machines, which required inks produced abroad.

> We buy ink from Torzhorskiy. They are cheaper. We pick up the inks once every third month. We do not buy any batches of ink. We had already bought from them during the planned economy. Previously, KPI had a store for ink. It received ink for the printing houses in the district and distributed it to them. We also use imported ink for the offset printing and we buy it from Heidelberg in St. Petersburg. Before that we bought it from a firm called Ipris in St. Petersburg, which is a joint venture (Valery Polyanskiy).

Film was mainly bought from *Tasmy* in Kazan, also a traditional supplier, but during the second half of the period Tipografiya on some occasions used Kodak.

Table 9: Tipografiya's biggest suppliers of consumables 1993–1998.[a]

Suppliers	**1993**	**1994**	**1995**	**1996**	**1997**	**1998**
Torzhorskiy Zavod Krasok	8,828	3,015	3,268	3,604	4,731	3,244
Poligrafresursy	10	10	12	–	–	–

Source: Author's own calculations based upon internal data from Tipografiya.
[a] Kilograms.

Tipografiya continued to buy matrices from *Poligrafresursy* and sometimes from *Shadrinskiy Zavod Poligraficheskikh Mashin* in Kurgan, while the offset plates were bought from *Ipris* in St. Petersburg, which like Poligrafresursy was a trading firm. The plates were mainly of Bulgarian origins. Poligrafresursy had supplied all plates for a long period, but around 1995 was replaced by Ipris. They were both located in St. Petersburg. Ipris represented and sold some foreign firms' polygraph material in the Russian market.

> It is a rather well known Russian firm, which promotes its goods well. We buy plates and films from them. Ipris is new market-minded firm (Nikolay Yevlampiyev).

Tipografiya used to buy zinc from a company in Moscow called *Moskovskiy Zavod Offsetnykh Materialov*, which was privatised at the beginning of the period, and from Poligrafresursy. The zinc was usually from Poland. Tipografiya purchased large quantities of zinc in 1993–1995 and put them in stock. These were used in 1996 and 1997. When needed once more in 1997, Poligrafresursy did not supply zinc anymore and since there was no zinc in the country, Tipografiya began to use photo polymer plates. The last time Tipografiya bought zinc was in 1998.

The photo polymer plates were initially bought from Ipris in St. Petersburg, but in 1998 Tipografiya was searching for suppliers in Moscow, as there were rumours that they were cheaper there. Valery Polyanskiy knew that he had to find new suppliers and that the photo polymer would be imported. In 1997 and 1998 Tipografiya tried to find suppliers for the imported photo polymer.

> We buy the photo polymer plates in Moscow, from a firm called Ilmis. The plates are called Regilonpop. For a while we also bought the offset plates from them. Now we buy the offset plates from Paritet. It is a small firm in Leningrad, not far away from here, convenient and not far to transport. The photo polymer plates are imported — Japanese (Valery Polyanskiy).

Finding and buying spare parts was a big problem during the planned economy, which was the reason that the mechanical shop was such an important department. However, during the transition period it became easier to find spare parts.

> I have been to both the Ukraine and Rybinsk. Purchasing of smaller equipment is done through Nauchno-Issledovatelskiy Institut Problem Poligrafii, which is situated in the Ukrainian town

of Lvov. I have contact with them by telephone. When we need spare parts for the Czech equipment we turn to Moscow where the orders are still centrally gathered. There is a new organisation, but the way it is done is the same. It takes around three months. Earlier we had to wait much longer (Valery Polyanskiy).

Chapter 6

Change Processes in Tipografiya's Relationships

Network and Change Processes

The second part of the case shows that Tipografiya bought and sold from specific customers and suppliers during the period. It is also obvious that some customers and suppliers appeared and disappeared while others remained partners throughout the transition period. The purpose with this first section of the analysis is to pinpoint the critical events in the process of Tipografiya's developing network over the period from 1992 to 1998. Network implies a structure and a change process; thus the focus is on the dynamics of this structure over the period. This approach allows the critical events from the case to be placed on a time continuum as shown in Figures 6 and 7. Such an approach supports a view of the transition as a sequence of individual and collective events, actions, and activities, which develop over time in a context (Pettigrew 1997; Van de Ven 1992), that is, a process.

I have followed Halinen *et al.'s* thoughts (1999) in which critical events are seen as incidents that trigger or cause change in the network. The processes that follow the critical events might be gradual and incremental or revolutionary, while Håkansson & Snehota (1995) are referring to changes that are triggered by either exogenous or endogenous events. The network is embedded in an institutional setting (Johanson & Mattsson 1991), which means that the exogenous changes appear when the actors in the network receive, interpret, and transmit the change to other actors in the network (Easton & Lundgren 1992). These changes are thus very much exogenous to the network. In the case of Tipografiya, the institutional change of governance of the economy resulted in a liberalisation of prices, and the abandonment of the plan and the plan authorities — all of which were external to Tipografiya's network. The effects of these changes meant that there was much space for revolutionary and unexpected changes in the network.

In Figure 6, several events that dominated the period from 1992 to 1995 are illustrated. These changes were effects of the facts that Tipografiya was privatised,

The official price list used in relationships with the newspapers was abolished

LSSK began to play a new role as an inter-mediary

Tipografiya's employees acquired all the assets from the state

Tipografiya dissolved the relationships with LSSK

The retail trade shop was founded

Tipografiya began to buy paper from intermediaries

The first issue of Vechevoy Tsentr appeared 13 September

1992   1993   1994   1995

Tipografiya began to require 50% prepayment

Tipografiya decided to start production only when the customer made 100 % prepayment

The rotary press was acquired

Tsirkon 66 was bought

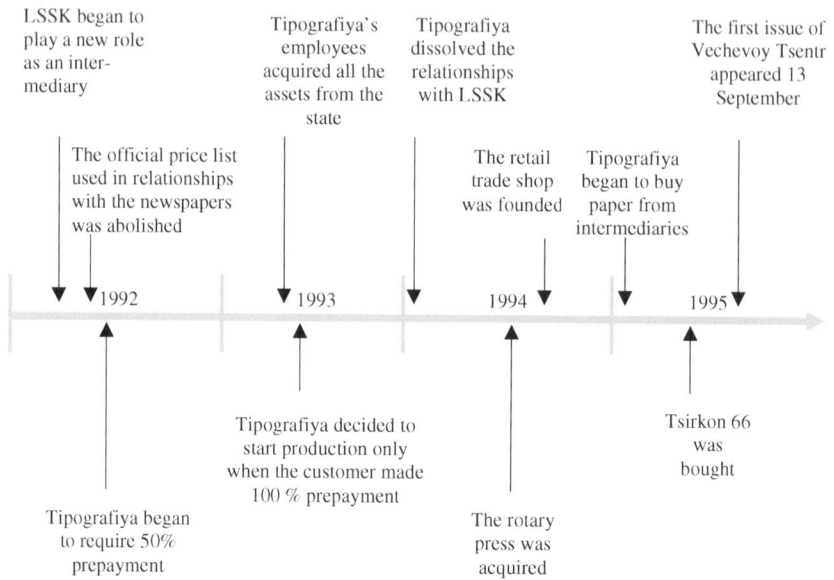

Figure 6: Events in Tipografiya's network 1992–1995.

the plan authority, LSSK, disappeared in two steps from the network and, as a consequence of the price liberalisation, Tipografiya began to manage its own pricing. Thus these events were based on exogenous factors. Not until 1994–1995 did changes that had a more endogenous character take place in the network, that is, they had both their causes and effects within the boundaries of the same network. It was then that Tipografiya founded the retail shop Delovoy Mir and the newspaper The Vechevoy Tsentr. It bought both a rotary press for production of newspapers and the Tsirkon, which aimed to improve the quality of the printed products. However, during those two years several customers piled up big debts as a consequence of the price liberalisation.

The following years, from 1996 to 1998, were a period when endogenous, but not so extensive, incremental changes in relation to the network seemed to be predominant. Tipografiya carried out two re-organisations in order to handle the relationships with customers better. The relationships with the Leningrad district and the newspapers changed. This was also the period when Tipografiya tried to find new customers and to produce more four-colour products. Thus, there was a lead-time between exogenous and endogenous changes and the first endogenous changes were very much an answer to the exogenous changes. These lead-times might be caused by the structure of the relationships in the network. After the

Tipografiya began to transport the forms to St. Petersburg

The regional branches of the Post Office Administration in Komi bought forms for the last time

The regional branches of the Post Office Administration in Vladivostok and Kemorovo bought forms for the last time

First re-organisation

Adept-Les bought newsprint for the newspapers

The Vechevoy Tsentr's circulation was 85,000 and it came out two–three times per week

1996

1997

1998

The production of the Vechevoy Tsentr was moved to the

Irina Kondratieva went to the Leningrad district

The second re-organisation

Three newspapers: the Chto? Gde? Kogda?, the Novgorodskiy Universitet, and the Shimskiye Vesty stopped buying from Tipografiya after conflicts about debts and payment

Tipografiya began to print the Novgorod by using photo polymer instead of zinc

The Novgorodskiye Vedomosty began to pay by not letting Tipografiya pay its taxes

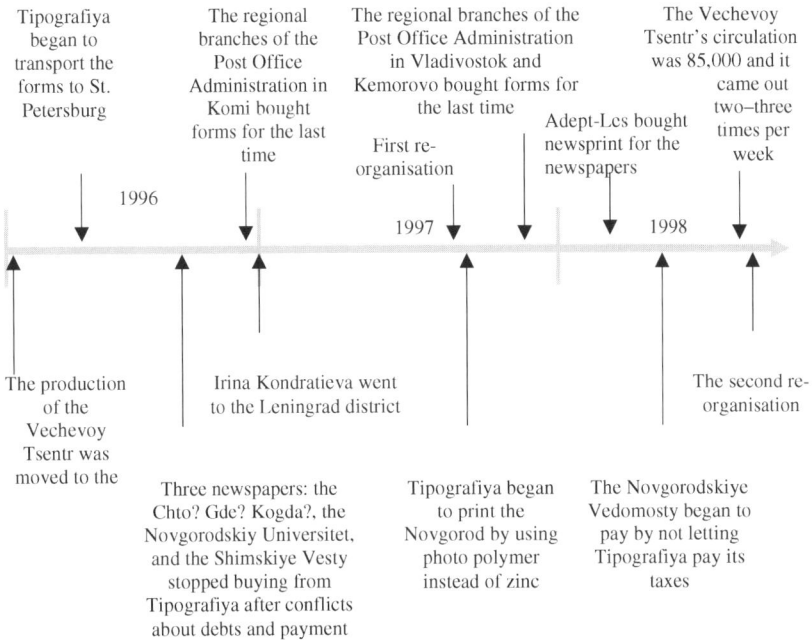

Figure 7: Events in Tipografiya's network 1996–1998.

ends and the means in the economy had been re-shuffled, the period from 1996 to 1998 was a time when Tipografiya's network tried to make sense of and adapt to the institutional changes. This means that the transition was characterised by some kind of inertia, which made it meaningful to proceed with a processual analysis of the network.

The discussion around the critical events in Tipografiya's network during the period from 1992 to 1998 implies that the changes can be divided into two types: changes *within* the network and changes *of* the network. One can say that they represent a typology of changes in networks. Changes of the network can, in turn, be divided into *dissolution* of relationships and *establishment* of relationships, and according to several researchers (see Chapter 1) they were a typical problem for Russian firms during the transition.

Dissolution can be defined as officially ending or breaking something up (Collins Cobuild 1987). Dissolution of relationships takes place when a customer who has frequently bought important products over a long period of time stops doing so for one reason or another. It is a process in which the relationship becomes weaker and finally disappears. The reverse concerns the establishment of a relationship, which can be described similarly. Establishment of an organisation or a system is the act of creating it for a particular purpose (Collins Cobuild 1987). By establishing a relationship a firm sets up or consolidates an exchange on a permanent basis.

Changes within the network mean that the relationships — the structure — remain the same even though the exchange of resources and use of resources in the network undergo changes. Changes that take place within the network are called *transformation* of relationships, and were discussed in Chapter 1. Transformation of a relationship occurs when its "appearance or function is completely changed" (Collins Cobuild 1987). The Concise Oxford Dictionary (1990) defines transformation "as an induced or spontaneous change of one element into another." In this case the element is the relationship. Due to the turbulent changes it is reasonable to believe that a number of existing relationships over the period have been changed and transformed. Change occurs when a new type of knowledge is created. Firms start to do things in new ways and use and exchange other products and equipment.

Types of Processes

The case study gives rise to several observations. The first is that Tipografiya's network underwent several changes during the period and the second is that experience from the network in the planned economy was a point of departure for these changes. The point of departure might be seen as the hierarchical structure, of which Tipografiya was a part, the static network, to which everyone was used, and the anonymity that prevailed in the economy. The latter is especially important because it shows that Russian firms had poor knowledge about customers and suppliers. By using and exchanging resources the firm gains experience, but in the planned economy experience was not related to other firms, because solutions were to be found either within the firm or in relations with the authorities.

Participating in the network process can be viewed as continuous interplay between *experience* and *expectation* (Lachmann 1986). Experience from the past and expectation of what could happen and what is desirable to happen is crucial in any change process (Hayek 1936). The experience the firm has makes up the plan, the mental map, or the frame for what the firm can imagine being able to achieve in the future. Expectation, on the other hand, makes up the frame for what is worth imagining. However, experience and expectation are also tied to each other and bounded to the network and are thereby the starting points for the change processes. Experience is something the firm acquires when it uses and exchanges resources and is an unavoidable consequence of doing. Hunt (1991) and Oliver

(1980) explained that expectations are the firm's defined probabilities of the occurrence of various events if firms engage or aim to engage in relationships with others in a market. According to Lachmann (1977) expectation is not a formalised calculation based on known history. It refers to anticipations, beliefs, wishes, and hopes about the unknown future (Cyert & March 1963; Lachmann 1977).

The definition of experience imposes a view of action in a time span or as a behaviour process, in the sense that firms learn from doing in order to undertake actions that will promote their activities in the future. This is the reason for the strong tie between experience and expectation. Penrose (1959: 77) viewed the search in the following way: "if we can assume businessmen believe there is more to know about the resources they are working with than they do know at any given time, and that more knowledge would be likely to improve the efficiency and profitability of their firm, then unknown and unused productive services immediately become of considerable importance, not only because the belief that they exist acts as an incentive to acquire knowledge, but also because they shape the scope and direction of the search for knowledge." Thereby where, when, how, and for what the firm searches is a result of its expectations, which is also in line with Hayek's (1945) and Cyert & March's (1963) ideas. Expectations are interpreted from each individual's experience (Lachmann 1977). This means that they usually are in balance and together design the firm's search. The balance between expectations and experience means that the firm tends to search locally (Cyert & March 1963), in its relationships (Uzzi 1997), and for phenomena similar to those that have generated a positive experience for the firm or other actors that the firm trusts. However, owing to the extensive institutional changes, a temporal imbalance, a tension, between the past and the future appears. With the change of governance of the economy, the experience of the network in the planned economy is questioned and the changed governance gives new meanings and contents to the expectations of the network.

Imbalance Between Expectation and Experience

The firm identifies the objectives, which is what it is searching for and how it intends to search for it. From this appears the first constraint. It seems if not impossible, at least extremely difficult, to identify an objective about which the firm has no knowledge. Thus, knowledge in the broad sense makes up the frame for the identification of what to search for. During the planned economy, expectation and experience used to be in balance, owing to the hierarchy and static network. What the firm knew from the past tended also to be valid for the future, and if that was not the case, there was a limited space to influence what was going to happen. This made changes and processes predictable and gave them a subordinated importance. However, it takes time to get rid of one's experience, whereas expectations can be more easily influenced. Owing to the richness and trustworthiness of one's own experience, it has been claimed to be an important source of input to the firm's expectations, which concern both the exchange and the use of resources.

The institutional change of governance of the economy gave a new content and a new role to the expectations, which questioned the value of the experience. The balance that until then had prevailed began to erode and turned into an imbalance between experience and expectation. Past experience, information, and objective knowledge, as well as gossip, rumours, and other types of non-experiential knowledge floating around, have an impact on the firm's expectations. When the picture described by the mass media, the authorities, actors in the illegal market, and the official documentation begins to dominate, it reduces the main role of experience in the formation of the expectation. Instead new expectations emerge, which contradict experience. But, the new expectations do not immediately change experience, which means that the firms are forced to rely on old experience from the network in order to realise the new expectations about the network in the market economy.

Four critical questions are crucial for the balance or imbalance of the experience and expectation. They are: *What to search for?*, *Where to search?*, *When to search?*, and *How to search?*. In a static network, there is a strong link between where, what, when and how. Experience provides the answers to these four questions, which are closely related to the firm's expectation of how, where, and when it will find something and what it will find.

In the planned economy, experience taught the value of a large stock of goods, low production goals, and control of both tangible and intangible resources. Achieving this was *what* the firm should search for and *where* to achieve it was within the boundaries of the firm. If this was not enough, the relationships with the authorities or in the illegal market were other places to search. The firm also gained experiential knowledge that shortage of resources, problems at the end of the plan period, when it was time to finish the plan, and negotiation of plan goals and opportunities to acquire products for the private life were matters that decided *when* it was time to begin to search. The experience of *how* to search was a consequence of the other three questions. Usually, the search took place within the firm and was in the form of giving and receiving orders, but the firms and their management learned to search hierarchically in relation to the authorities and the management of other firms.

As discussed above, institutional change dramatically changes the character of the firm's expectation and thus makes the experience partly obsolete. From that, an imbalance between experience and expectation appears, which can be viewed as the start for the change processes. The new governance opens up space and gives freedom for the firms to act and to change the way of exchanging and using resources. The new expectations are strong and say that the firms can and have to do something, whereas experience says that the firms do not have the knowledge and skills required to do what needs to be done. Low price, profit, and private fortune became new goals for which to search, and this search could now be conducted almost anywhere and all the time. The new expectation said that ownership, trade, and business were new ways to achieve the aims.

Firms learn in areas related to their prior knowledge and existing practice, because the experiential knowledge gained from exchanging and using resources is richer than non-experience-based knowledge (Cyert & March 1963; Kogut & Zander 1992). New knowledge is a product combining existing knowledge and new findings (Kogut & Zander 1992) or whether firms are able to absorb findings based on search or discovery in their knowledge structure. If and how the firm's process of finding is deployed in use or exchange has to do with its capacity to absorb the discovery (Cohen & Levinthal 1990; Lane & Lubatkin 1998). It is understood that prior knowledge related to the discovery enhances the ability to absorb the discovery. But that is not enough. Diversity of knowledge also plays an important role. Diverse knowledge offers a background to which the discovery could be related and compared.

The Search Process

Expectation affects search because if the firm does not believe that it will find what it is searching for, search turns out to be a meaningless activity. Changed expectation questions the value of the experience and stimulates the firm to search for changes, which correspond to the new expectation and not to the out-of date experience. But since the experience has lost its value the firm faces a dilemma. Either it can start the search, which is based on other types of knowledge than the firm's own experience (as that has been questioned to such an extent that it can be viewed as obsolete), or it can rely on its expectations, which usually contain less detail and are poorer than the experience. This is a starting point but also creates an ambivalence and uncertainty, which is going to follow the firm throughout the search process. By relying only on the expectation and neglecting the experience, it is likely that the perceived uncertainty will increase. However, since the firm initiated the search process, it is more certain and convinced that changes are necessary than the other way around.

That is the point of departure for the search process (the continuous line in Figure 8). The search process implies behaviour characterised by bounded or

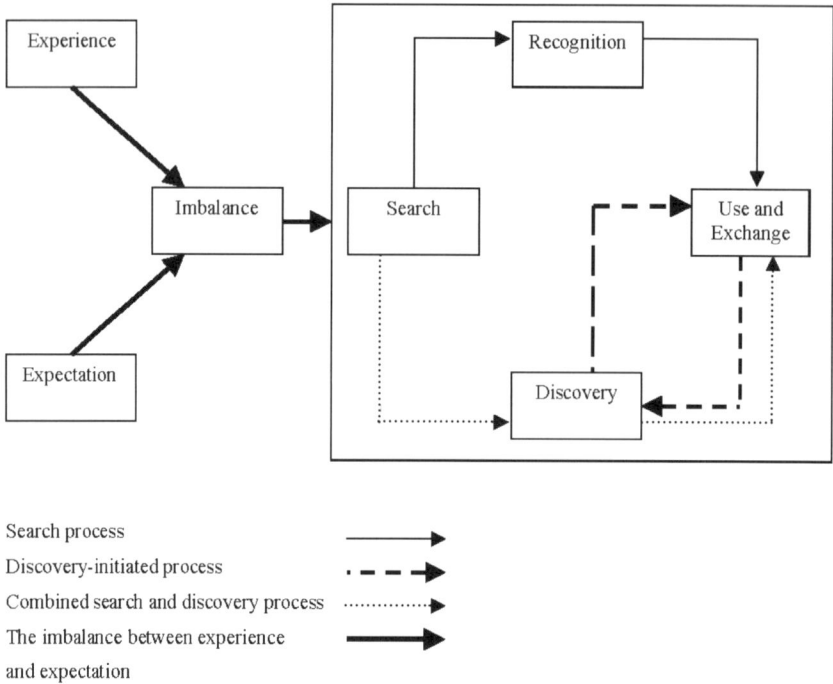

Figure 8: An extended model of the change processes in the network.

dispersed knowledge but still rational and very much common sense. Irrespective of the discussion above, until a new type of experience has been gained, experience from the past is a counterbalance to the expectation. Since the firm's knowledge consists of bounded and incomplete information, experience is a forceful input in all types of change processes. The firm's own experience is usually richer and trustworthier than the experience of others. Initially, the greater the firm's experience of finding what it is searching for in the past, the greater the possibility of working out a detailed search plan. However, this does not mean that the firm will be better able to codify its experience and plans, since these processes are often incremental and result in tacit knowledge that is difficult to codify.

The activities related to search embrace looking actively for something already identified, that is, a problem has occurred and the firm believes that it already knows the solution but it has to find it. However, analysing the network by collecting data and information gives some insight but cannot by itself give the firm unique insight into the network (Barney 1986). Since the where, what, how and where to search for require that they can be codified and moreover comparatively easy and cheap to distribute, it will be accessible to a larger number of firms. This is in line with Hayek's idea (1945) that crucial knowledge cannot be transformed into statistics.

However, codification of the knowledge becomes a problem first when the contents of the search process have to be communicated. In contrast to the plan authorities, which theoretically had to codify all knowledge, most firms and individuals search without ever codifying the knowledge, because codification takes time. The search process in a network involves more than two firms, which can be a reason for codification, but even if the search process is codified, conviction or enforcement might be necessary in order to conclude the search process. Even if these aspects go according to plan, search could still turn into discovery.

The identification of the objective and the way to find it are very closely tied to what the firm already knows. It is a way of achieving change by exploiting only the firm's existing knowledge. Consequently, but paradoxically, it might mean change without much new knowledge. Successful search processes in the past have tended to decrease the perceived uncertainty and confirm the existing structure, as the familiar is perceived as less uncertain. If one believes in the strength of experience it seems logical to propose that in following this process there is a strong tendency for the firm to repeat what has been done before in order to achieve what it is searching for during the transition. When facing a problem during the search, the firm will evaluate an already existing solution in trying to find an approach that has been proven to work. As one can see, the search process is very much an attempt to repeat the past. However, there is one type of search process that is more uncertain and that is when how, where, and what are combined in a new way. By starting to search for something known, but in a way that has been used only when searching for other things, the firm exposes itself to uncertainty. It seems that search processes suit situations where the network is static, as it was in the planned economy. As long as the search process concerns internal issues and is not affected by the surrounding network, the probability of success in the search process will be relatively high.

The Discovery-Initiated Process

The *discovery process* (the thick dotted line in Figure 8) is almost the opposite of the search process. Discoveries sometimes lead to failures, but they can also produce knowledge, provided that they are recognised as such. Learning by doing is the expression most suitable both for describing this process and for the result of this process. Doing, that is using the resources, precedes learning. It happens both on the use level and on the exchange level and occurs when the firm runs the daily operations. Discovery is viewed as an important feature when firms develop new products (von Hippel & Tyre 1995). Learning by doing or by using implies that both the problems and the solution are discovered (von Hippel & Tyre 1995). Both the problem and the solutions are discovered when running the daily operations and it is not uncommon that the problems are vague and ill-structured and that the solutions are unknown and uncertain.

Acquisition of knowledge through participation in the network can be viewed as an adjustment and revision of expectation due to new experience (Kirzner 1973). Thus some discoveries might thereby be input in the search process. Discovery processes are not the result of lack of experience or wrong expectations, but rather the other way around — a firm that has gained a lot of experience from expectation realises that it has to expect and face discoveries. Since discoveries are not intended, it is likely that many discoveries are not turned into new ways of exchanging or using resources. Often, discoveries do not fit into the discovering firm's current business or are perceived as having a negative impact on the use and exchange in the relationship. This type of process is initiated by a discovery, which interrupts the continuity that characterises the relationships in static networks. The firms can in this case try to ignore or neglect discoveries and if that does not work out, try to transmit the discoveries or their effects to other actors in the network. Usually, this happens because the discovery is perceived as having no value or because the discovering firm does not understand or is not able to evaluate the discovery.

The logic of the network in the planned economy supports the idea that discovery processes are common during the transition to a market economy. The static Soviet network meant the firms were not used to searching for change, but instead applied already existing knowledge in the use of the resources, which strengthened the structure.

The Combined Process of Search and Discovery

While search implies an ambition to change, discoveries cannot be viewed as results of a purposeful and intentional search process (meaning that the firm searches in a specific way to achieve expected results). The *combined process* (the thin dotted line in Figure 8) springs from the imbalance between experience and expectation of how, where, and what to search for, and takes place both on the exchange and use level. When the firm begins to search for something it discovers something that it did not know or had not searched for. It is a change process, which is initiated by search. But while the search for the specific objectives takes place, events occur that are beyond the boundaries of the firm's knowledge. The firm or firms make discoveries, which, in turn, end up changing how the resources are exchanged and used in the network.

Most network studies dealing with change are implicitly to be found here. Change is usually a path-dependent process, which makes a firm's discovery dependent on specific relationships. These processes are usually difficult to understand for outsiders and tricky to imitate, owing to the mixture of search and discovery. The firms search for new products and new versions of existing products or for new ways of using the resources in order to produce the products. The firms try and fail. The failures are partial or complete, but failure in the search process sometimes means finding not only what was within what was planned, but also, often, going beyond what could be planned for. Another expression used for this combined process is trial and error, which implies that the firm anticipates that a change is going to occur. Since a combined process contains a search for change, but results in discovering something not intended, it means that the firm is ready for change. This is basically the same argument as in the previous section, which suggests that firms that have experienced discoveries are better prepared to handle new discoveries.

In changing and turbulent networks the search process has a tendency to be interrupted by discoveries, which force the firms to get used to change. Since it is impossible to know all changes in advance, the firms learn to be ready for change. As in the search process, the imbalance between the just-appeared discovery and the obsolete experience, on the one hand, and the discovery and the valid expectation on the other, follows the process, but it also influences how the network receives the discovery.

Many combined processes seem to have their roots in the change of governance of the economy, which creates space and freedom and a necessity to change the way resources are used and exchanged in the relationships. However, since it is likely that such processes, which are not always compatible, take place simultaneously and that all this starts from a state where anonymity reigns in the network, search often ends in discovery. Moreover, although one knows what to search for it might be that it cannot be found, because it takes time for alternatives and new solutions, corresponding with the expectations, to emerge in the network.

Matrix of Change Processes

The purpose of this study is to investigate the change processes of a firm and its context during the transition from planned economy to market economy. On the one hand, there are the changes which the relationships undergo. When firms

	The Search Process	The Discovery-initiated Process	The Combined Process of Search and Discovery
Establishment of relationships	1	4	7
Transformation of relationships	2	5	8
Dissolution of relationships	3	6	9

Figure 9: Matrix of change processes.

establish relationships they develop dependence on each other; this interdependence erodes during the dissolution of the relationships. Transformation contains an element where interdependence changes, in terms of symmetry as well as strength. On the other hand, there are the processes which the firms in the relationships are experiencing when they search, recognise and discover new ways of exchanging and using resources. By combining the changes and the processes discussed in this chapter, a three-by-three matrix (see Figure 9) can be outlined. This matrix illustrates nine types of change processes, which can be applied to Tipografiya and its relationships.

Search Processes

Cell 1 — Search Process and Establishment of Relationships

The first search process concerns searching and finding specific firms in order to establish relationships. The retail shop was a new way of building relationships with some of the existing customers and attracting final consumers. In 1994, Tipografiya had experienced a drastic production decrease but also a greater freedom. Tipografiya strove to find a new way of exchanging resources when Russia was suffering a financial crisis. The reason for founding the shop was twofold: to give existing customers better service and to use waste from the production process to make new products, which could be sold in the shop. The shop became a success and a main source of income. The successful search process at the exchange level influenced the use of resources at Tipografiya. Tipografiya searched for a specific solution to a problem. After it found a new way of doing business with old and new customers; the search process turned into one of use.

In times of financial crisis and decrease in production, Tipografiya identified its needs. By buying new equipment and re-organising the firm, changes began on the use level. From around 1995 until 1997 Tipografiya searched for a way to reorient the firm's production in order to find new customers. The management considered that equipment for colour separation was necessary for this re-orientation. This would also mean abandoning the relief technology and exclusively using offset. Moreover, composition would in that case be done only on computers. However, during these years, Tipografiya simultaneously lost the customers that would have been the buyers of these products. Tipografiya knew what it wanted but an extensive *search* was necessary, since everything was new for the firm. Tipografiya had to find the technological solutions, including the new products, and new customers. In addition, very much tied to the aim to reorient, in 1997 Tipografiya changed its organisation in order to handle the new production technology and the new customers more effectively. It is striking that a year after the first re-organisation, the change at the exchange level forced the firm once more to re-organise, which was a result of discovering that it was not able to produce according to schedule. It seems to have been an intentional process, which started on the use level and only after some time influenced the exchange level, where the change meant new products and new customers. The production and sales of the products grew.

Typically for the hierarchical network in the planned economy, the firm had not had any possibility and consequently no experience, of establishing relationships with customers and suppliers. Although the change of governance meant freedom to search for, find, and establish relationships, it did not by itself provide experience. This was, therefore, not enough to make the firm search for establishing new relationships. The expectations that the firm would gain something by establishing relationships have to be stronger than the lack of experience. In this case, the expected gain was not supposed to come from finding and establishing customers for existing products, which they had experience in producing and exchanging; nor did Tipografiya believe it would gain anything from finding new customers for its existing products. A change in the use of resources preceded the search for new customers and new products, and expectations were strong that the firm had to search for both new products and new customers. This is evidence that the experience lost its value. Moreover, the intended search for new counterparts is a reaction to the dissolution of other relationships. Change processes are connected that is, a change process in one relationship tends to cause and influence change processes in other relationships as well.

Cell 2 — Search Process and Transformation of Relationships

The *second cell* illustrates the combination of search process and transformation. Transformation of the resources used and exchanged means that the relationships remain intact. The network does not change at first glance, and for those who are outside the network. It has already been discussed that the imbalance between experience and expectation tends to stimulate the firms to identify new aims and to try to achieve them. However, imbalance between experience and expectation is not enough, since transformation of a relationship implies that both parties are affected by the change. From that follows that a search process, aimed at transforming the relationship, is encouraged by each party having knowledge about the other's past and each one's thoughts about the future. It seems likely that the anonymity prevailing in the network in the planned economy makes this process difficult to realise. As the firms had no experience of a mutual search it is also tricky to match the search plans to the relationship. This problem can be handled if the firm either initiates a closer interaction, which might result in a richer and deeper experience from the relationship, or if the search is kept within the boundaries of the firm. The imbalance between experience and expectation is the starting point for searching for transformation, but simultaneously, the lack of experience of the counterpart, that is, the anonymity, makes this process difficult to realise.

However, although relationships are sometimes transformed as a result of a search process it does not mean that this takes place in isolation. The change of governance of the economy increases space and freedom to change in a previously static and hierarchical network. It concerns not only the relationship, but also the whole network, which consists of a set of relationships that are multilaterally dependent on each other. This means that the network influences the search process in the relationship. The network provides diversity and time to interpret, to capture and to begin to utilise the diversity, which enhances change. However, when not only a relationship but also the network begins to change, search processes are problematic. It then becomes crucial whether the firms in the relationship are resistant to surprises, arising from the connected relationships, or are able to reflect them back. The more changing network, the more difficult it is to keep the search process within the relationship.

Cell 3 — Search Process and Dissolution of Relationships

In *cell 3*, the search process ends up in a change of the network, which means that a relationship is dissolved while the process follows the route of *search-recognition-change in use and exchange*. This change process takes place when the firm identifies what it is looking for and what it wants to achieve in order to reach dissolution. The change process and its outcome are thus intentional, desirable, and expected. In the planned economy, the hierarchy meant that the firms were not allowed to terminate their relationships neither with neither customers nor with suppliers. Having the aim and the reason to terminate a relationship was meaningless, and consequently the firm had no experience from defining the aim to terminate a relationship. Moreover, as a consequence the firms seldom gained experience in how to terminate a relationship during the planned economy. This process requires that the aim for the change is easy to identify and codify, and price is such an aim. The expectation of institutional change of the governance of the economy meant that price came into focus in the network. The freedom to pay a low price or being paid a high price were strong incentives for dissolving relationships. However, this was not enough; the expectation has to be stronger than the experience, that is, the firm must believe that it is more beneficial to rely on the new expectation than on the experience for its search.

A constraint for dissolving relationships based on the price can be found in the multilateral dependence often prevailing on the use level, since it ties the firm not only to the counterpart and the relationship, but also to a set of relationships surrounding the relationship. Terminating a relationship therefore had consequences for other relationships. The changed governance of the economy meant reconsideration of the firm's ends and new expectations. It is likely that these new expectations were not compatible with the experience from operating in a shortage economy, which meant that firms instead of relying on suppliers preferred to produce resources themselves. Nevertheless, the case does not give us any example of intended termination of a relationship. It might be a consequence of the lack of experience of terminating relationships, but it could also be a result of the firms expecting to be paid a high price or to pay a low price, and that terminating relationships with customers or suppliers was viewed as not being beneficial. Terminating relationships means that the firm will not continue to exchange resources with a counterpart. Moreover, the dissolution of a relationship often has the effect that the firm has to find another business partner, which means that an intentional dissolution of a relationship tends to have effects on other already established relationships or on searching for a new partner.

Discovery-Initiated Process

Cell 4 — Discovery-Initiated Process and Establishment of Relationships

Cell 4 represents a discovery process, which results in the establishment of a relationship. This change process is not planned, but in the end, due to a discovery while running the operations, relationships are established. An example of this process can be seen in the paper and pulp kombinats. In 1992, when Tipografiya was buying some of its paper on its own behalf and had remaining the traditional way, Tipografiya was allowed to buy paper from where it wanted and at prices determined through negotiations between customer and supplier. The new expectation implied that it was best to find a low price, while their experience implied that one should buy large quantities of paper. A constant search for the lowest prices started. Tipografiya did not develop close relationships with the paper and pulp kombinats and because of that the use level in these relationships was never characterised by high interdependence. This weakness made the relationships fragile and they did not last long. After a few years several intermediaries appeared in the market.

Tipografiya did not find the intermediaries through conscious search. The firm made an unexpected discovery, while still purchasing paper from the paper and pulp kombinats. The focus at that time was on the traditional producers of paper and in the beginning, Tipografiya was suspicious and reluctant to rely on other firms. Both the intermediary function and the firms themselves were new for Tipografiya, but a price lower than the one offered by the paper and pulp kombinats corresponded with the new expectations and was impossible to resist. The intermediaries bought big volumes from the kombinats and could thus offer lower prices. They also offered a wider range of products and had a keener ear for Tipografiya's needs. It seems that quality, which was standardised during the planned economy, was not a driving force for establishment of these relationships initially, but the quality aspect became something that Tipografiya discovered and began to appreciate. Still in 1998, a big stock bought at a low price was the main aim and Tipografiya was prepared to terminate these new relationships if someone else offered a lower price.

Neither Tipografiya nor the intermediaries made any adaptations regarding the use of resources. So, the exchange did not influence the use and the interdependence did not increase. It seems likely that often two or more discovery processes were connected; for instance, the supply of paper underwent these types of change processes. A process was initiated by a discovery, which caused discoveries in other relationships. Discoveries have a tendency to give birth to other discoveries, which, in turn, means that the general turbulence escalates in the network.

Cell 5 — Discovery-Initiated Process and Transformation of Relationships

When the overall network structure remains the same, but changes, take place within the relationships, be they gradual and incremental or revolutionary, then one can claim that a transformation of relationships is happening. It sometimes coincides with the discovery process. It is not based on incentives to search for transformation, but it starts with a discovery, when using and exchanging resources in the relationship. In the case of Tipografiya, transformation was evident in the relationship between Tipografiya and the Novgordskiye Vedomosti. Around 1991, the Novgordskiye Vedomosti had a circulation of 50,000–60,000 per issue. Two years later, it had decreased to 25,000. The readers of the Novgordskiye Vedomosti suffered economic hardships at the time and did not buy newspapers to the same extent as before. Combined with the appearance of a free newspaper, the Novgorod, this resulted in a decrease in circulation. These discoveries on the exchange level were followed by conflicts, which forced the firms to interact in order to find solutions to these disputes — a new experience for them.

Almost all changes took place on the exchange level between the firms, but some of them also had a small effect on the use level. In 1997, the relationship was the target for two additional discoveries, which had their roots in connected relationships. Adept-Les began to sell the newsprint for the Novgordskiye Vedomosti, however, without doing any business with Tipografiya. This had no effects on the use level, because the newsprint and the producers were the same and the way the newsprint was transported and stored did not change. When zinc became unavailable, neither Tipografiya nor the Novgordskiye Vedomosti searched for changes. The transformation was a consequence of a change in connected relationships and appeared between Tipografiya and the Novgordskiye Vedomosti as various discoveries, through which mutual experience emerged. The two firms searched for solutions, but the transformation did not reach the use level. Instead, the main reason that this relationship was maintained was probably the pressure from the District Administration.

Tipografiya's relationship with the Novgorod had some commonalities with the relationship between Tipografiya and the Novgordskiye Vedomosti. However, in contrast to the Novgordskiye Vedomosti, the Novgorod was not late with its payment. The circulation was the same in 1998 as in 1992, and storing and purchasing of newsprint as well as distribution and the financial aspects of the relationships remained the same throughout the period. The change began when Tipografiya *discovered* that there was no zinc available in Russia, which caused the firm to search for, and begin to use, alternative technologies. Tipografiya was forced to begin to use a new material — photo polymer. This meant that the Novgorod would be printed on the offset presses, which gave a better quality and that Tipografiya began to compose on computers. For Tipografiya the change brought a higher profit. The re-organisation carried out in 1997 made the responsibility for the relationships clearer and was the final change that affected the relationships with the Novgorod.

The firms making discoveries when running their daily operations drove these processes. The trigger was often to be found beyond the customer-supplier relationships. Most of the causes had their origins in the connected relationships, but the discoveries made forced the firms to handle the findings. For an outsider the processes followed were difficult to see and almost impossible to reconstruct. The interdependence was strong, which forced the firms to carry out various adaptations and in the processes that followed the firms began to search for solutions in the relationships. For instance, when zinc was nowhere to be bought, Tipografiya and the Novgorod began to solve the problem jointly and to use a new technology. Thus, the discovery with its roots in the connected relationships forced the firms to resort to learning by doing within the boundaries of the relationship. There are functional discoveries and dysfunctional discoveries, which might lead to conflicts, but if solved, in the end they often strengthen the relationship.

Cell 6 — Discovery-Initiated Process and Dissolution of Relationships

The origin of the discovery processes is not to be found in the imbalance between experience and expectation. No changes are intended. Instead, the relationships are assumed to exist in the same way as they have existed for a long time. Still, the case gives at least four examples where Tipografiya discovered new things, which, in turn resulted in dissolved relationships. In the *first group of relationships*, customers such as Start, Elkon, and Kvant can be found. These firms were operating in the electronic industry and when foreign trade was liberalised they were not competitive. A second reason could be that they were part of the defence industry and when the Ministry of Defence heavily reduced its orders the suppliers suffered, which came as a surprise for Tipografiya. The discovery did not affect the use level, but on the exchange level the discovery was triggered by events taking place in connected relationships. When it happened, Tipografiya, having been used to operating in a static and anonymous network, was not able to deal with the changes and tried not to search for a solution on the exchange or the use level. The dissolution of these relationships was a reason for the management in 1996–1997 trying to re-orient the business towards four-colour products.

The *second group* consists of some of the regional branches of the Russian Post Office Administration. The plan-governance of the relationships resulted in low interdependence on the use level. When the plan and the plan authorities were dismantled and the prices liberalised the low interdependence made the relationships fragile. For instance, three of the biggest customers, Kemorovo, Komi and Primorskiy Kray, representing more than 50% of the regional branches, turned to suppliers other than Tipografiya. For Tipografiya this development was not expected, but understandable. Through the planning system, standardised products had been distributed over the country. The transportation costs, which were already considerable in the planned economy, increased heavily and constituted the lion's share of the price. Thus, many of the regional branches, which had printing houses located close to them, could buy more cheaply from one of them. One of the reasons for expecting this was that the product was easy to produce. More or less any printing house could print these forms and either relief or offset technology could be used. Despite the risk of losing these customers, Tipografiya took no measures to transform the relationships. The only changes were that Tipografiya on some occasions printed small volumes on the relief printing presses instead of the offset presses and that it began to print the forms on a lower quality paper in order to lower the price.

Three newspapers, the Shimsky Vesti, the Chto? Gde? Kogda?, and the Novgordskiy Universitet constituted the *third group*. These newspapers had a small circulation and were produced and distributed in the same way as the two big newspapers. Like the Novgordskiye Vedomosti, they built up big debts to Tipografiya. In 1996, the relationships became characterised by conflict. Tipografiya sued the Shimskiye Vesty and the Chto? Gde? Kogda? for unpaid bills. In the end, both of them paid, but the relationships were dissolved and the Shimskiye Vesty and the Novgordskiy Universitet turned to other printing houses, while the local TV and radio company decided to print the Chto? Gde? Kogda? itself.

Discoveries on the exchange level initiated these processes. For around two years the firms tried to find a solution on the same level. The low interdependence on the use level made the dissolution relatively easy.

The *fourth group* concerned two suppliers of zinc, Moskovsky Zavod Offsetnykh Materialov and Poligrafresursy. Zinc was not purchased in big volumes, but it was used to print photos in the newspapers. Tipografiya bought high volumes advantageously at the beginning of the 1990s. The company knew that sooner or later it would have to stop using zinc, but while it was *using* the stock of zinc daily, it suddenly discovered in 1997 that Moskovsky Zavod Offsetnykh Materialov and Poligrafresursy could not supply any more. The technology had become obsolete. The high dependence on the zinc suppliers meant that the dissolution of the relationships had major effects. A *search* for new suppliers found nothing and this forced Tipografiya to change the way of printing the Novgorod and to *search* for a new technology and new material, namely photo polymer. Tipografiya knew that the photo polymer would be imported and it had just started to search for new suppliers.

There is no imbalance between experience and expectation in these cases. Old truths are still valid, which means that the firms have no intention of dissolving or transforming these relationships. As evidence for that, the balance seemed to remain and no attempts were made to handle the dysfunctional discoveries mutually. After a few years, around 1995, the firm made some harsh discoveries, which resulted in a dissolution of the relationships. The customers' customers did not demand the products anymore, because of transportation costs the prices were too high, and the firms' debts to Tipografiya grew.

The change of governance caused dissolution of these relationships, but it was not a search for change, based on imbalance between experience and expectation, that drove these processes. Instead, the causes were externally derived and to be found in connected relationships. The reason that they appeared as surprising discoveries is probably a result of the anonymity. The firms had poor knowledge about their customers and their knowledge about connected firms was usually almost non-existent. Changes triggered beyond the exchange were probably perceived as discoveries. Despite the fact that the firms might have aimed at keeping the relationship intact, it did not mean that both the customer and the supplier were against change. Since new exchange and new use are often in conflict with the network's structure, this often results in the dissolution of old relationships and the establishment of new ones.

Combined Search and Discovery Processes

Cell 7 — Combined Search and Discovery Process and Establishment of Relationships

When it comes to establishment of a relationship through a combined process of search and discovery, the Vechevoy Tsentr provides an illustrative example. The relationship with the Vechevoy Tsentr became the most important one from a financial point of view. In the middle of the 1990s, Tipografiya experienced criticism from the two big newspapers, which claimed that the company had unfairly used its monopoly and increased prices. The Novgordskiye Vedomosti sued Tipografiya and complained to the district administration. So, the reason for establishing the Vechevoy Tsentr could be found in other relationships and as a response to this from Tipografiya. However, the search process originated in the imbalance between experience and expectation. Tipografiya's expectation of finding something that could solve the problems that had occurred was stronger than experience, which instead told Tipografiya that the network was hierarchical and static, that is, establishment of new relationships was out of question.

Tipografiya searched for solutions and several ideas existed, but on a business trip to Sweden, the managing director discovered that advertisers could finance newspapers. So, Tipografiya found a solution to the problem in an unexpected context and the discovery resulted in a new way of using the resources. Tipografiya then began to search for the people needed. It returned to the Novgorod, where three journalists, who had experience in running a free newspaper, were identified. The strategy to orient towards small- and medium-sized firms was a success. The readers appreciated the quality, while the relatively low prices; the printing quality and the efficient distribution attracted the advertisers. The quality derived from the Vechevoy Tsentr being printed on the offset presses, while the other newspapers were printed on the relief presses. This difference disappeared in 1998, when the Novgorod was also printed on the offset presses. During the period from 1995 to 1998 changes took place continuously, most of which concerned the use level.

The management identified an aim, a solution to a problem, and began to search for it. However, since an aim seldom stands alone, firms usually having a set of aims. More than one search run over a specific period is needed. The search for something in Sweden meant that Tipografiya discovered the solution to another problem. Moreover, the differences between the aims of the search and what the firm actually discovers are also critical. Since discovery creates new knowledge for the firm, while search means finding already existing knowledge, it does not always correspond with the firm's ambition. The firm's ability, flexibility, and willingness to exploit the discovery determine if a relationship is established.

Cell 8 — Combined Search and Discovery Process and Transformation of Relationships

The failure or success of a discovery depends on whether it fits into the current relationship. Sometimes it does not, and then it may result in the dissolution of an existing relationship or the establishment of a new one. It does happen, however, that discoveries made during the search for specific aims instead contribute to the transformation of a relationship. The relationship between Tipografiya and the Leningrad district was one that underwent such a transformation. The changes began on the exchange level and had an influence on the use level only after a few years. In 1992, LSSK began to play a role as an intermediary, but, in 1994, Tipografiya's expectation of what it could achieve without LSSK's presence in the relationship had became stronger than the experience that it fulfilled a function. Tipografiya terminated the contacts with LSSK and began to do business directly with the Leningrad district, which caused considerable changes in the exchange. When Russia ended up in the financial crisis, Tipografiya discovered that the Leningrad district did not pay as it used to and Tipografiya required prepayment. Furthermore, the product exchanged was transformed. The quality of the paper was originally standardised, but Tipografiya was given the possibility of deciding the quality and printing the forms on cheaper paper of lower quality, which decreased the price and was welcomed by the customers. Tipografiya also started to print more types of forms than during the planned economy, but the forms were still standardised.

In 1996, Tipografiya gave up the requirement of prepayment from the Leningrad district. For a long time it was the only customer that was granted such a concession. The transformation reached the use level only in 1996, when changes in the communication and the transportation of the forms gradually took place. For a long time, the only direct contact Tipografiya had with the Leningrad district was through the driver. But, at the end of 1996 a representative went to the Leningrad district for the first time, and from that moment on the volume and quality of the information exchanged increased. During the period, production was moved from the relief printing shop to the offset equipment, owing to decreasing total volumes to the regional branches, while both the sales and the volumes produced for the Leningrad district increased. By setting up the business centre in 1997, the management searched for a more efficient way to manage the relationships with the regional branches.

Discoveries played a crucial role in the transformation of this relationship. While searching for a specific aim it is evident that the events, which caused the changes, were external to the relationships. The dismantling of the plan-governance first caused changes on the exchange level and thereafter resulted in changes significantly falling behind on the use level. This difference in time was because of the anonymity, which until then had prevailed in the relationship. The changes first on the exchange level and after that on both the use and exchange levels, resulted in a higher level of trust, increased sales, and a high interdependence. Trust in the relationship increased the possibility of adapting and managing unpleasant discoveries. Combined processes, which result in transformation of relationships, obviously tend to mean more specialised and more complex relationships with a high interdependence.

Cell 9 — Combined Search and Discovery Process and Dissolution of Relationships

Cell 9 represents a change process where search and discovery are combined, but it is the discovery that is the reason for why and how the network's structure is changed. In the case described, dissolution took place in the relationship with the traditional paper suppliers. They both supplied Tipografiya with paper and partly sold to Tipografiya's customers, who stored their paper at Tipografiya. Over the period the relationships with the paper suppliers changed on several occasions, one could even say that initially they were established, but in the end dissolved. In 1992, owing to the change of governance, Tipografiya was suddenly given a free hand to buy the paper itself and from wherever it chose. Tipografiya had the experience of living in a shortage economy but also of finding large volumes of paper at a low price. The liberalised prices gave Tipografiya the possibility of buying cheaply. When this was accomplished, the management thought they had achieved something good. This imbalance triggered the firm to search for as low a price as possible. On each occasion, when it was time to purchase paper a new search process began and the aim was clear: low price.

When Tipografiya perceived that it had found the lowest price, it bought a large quantity and kept it in stock, which meant no changes of suppliers. Neither the exchange level nor the use level changed. It was perceived as less important when to use and from whom to buy the paper. There was low interdependence, as few adaptations were made. When Tipografiya discovered the existence of intermediaries, it combined something known and identified, low price and big volumes, with something until then completely unknown, which in turn convinced it to reconsider existing searches and relationships. It dissolved the relationships with the paper and pulp kombinats. The intermediaries offered lower prices, and since the interdependence on the use level was low, Tipografiya turned to them.

Dissolution of relationships can be viewed as a process, where sequences follow each other. It is not uncommon for something to disturb and disrupt the firm's search. It might be that the counterpart does not behave as expected, perhaps because it is searching for something that is incompatible with the firm's search. A second scenario could be that the connected relationships are not compatible. Relationships do not exist in isolation but in a network setting, which provides several relationships. Neither the aim nor the search take place in singular forms in isolation, but rather in plural forms in the network, and by combining them over a specific period, a search in some relationships can result in a finding in other relationships.

Discussion

The transition starts from a state where the firms have experience of networks as hierarchical, static and anonymous. When the governance of the economy is changed, when the prices are liberalised and the plan and the plan authorities are dismantled, the firms' expectation of what will happen in the network also changes. Imbalance between previous experience and new expectations always exists, but when such dramatic change as a change of governance takes place, it is likely that the imbalance will become considerable. However, a considerable imbalance does not in itself mean change. It is when the expectations become stronger than the experience that the firm begins to search for new ways of exchanging and using resources.

The empirical discussion shows that discovery is as common as search in the change processes taking place in the Russian transitional economy. Hierarchy in the network in the planned economy did not enhance changes based on discovering and finding new ways of exchanging and using resources. In a hierarchical network, an actor can coerce other actors to be subjected to its search. When the room for manoeuvre to use and exchange resources was decentralised to the firms in the network, it meant not only freedom to act, but also a necessity to do something in relation to other actors, which led firms to making discoveries. *Consequently, discoveries in the transition economy are partly a result of the experience of hierarchy in the planned economy.*

At start of the transition there is a balance between experience and expectation. Anonymity still prevails, there are few experiences from discoveries, and the firms do not expect discoveries to appear in the future. Instead, the first years are probably characterised by the firm's expectation that the exchange and use of resources will continue in the same way as before. When the firm slowly begins to move in the direction of stronger relationships with other firms, issues related to exchange with other firms (owing to anonymity) would be more characterised by discoveries than the pure internal use of resources, despite the fact that the firm is not looking for a change. Consequently, *discovery is a result of the experience of anonymity.* The static nature of the network surely contributes positively to the search process, since any type of interference or change in connected relationships might easily turn the search into discovery. *Turbulence* in the network might lead to re-definition of the ends and re-allocation of means. The consequences of this for the search process are often difficult to grasp. Facing a changing network is something completely new for the firm. A firm whose experience says that the network is static does not realise that it has to expect discoveries in the network. Discoveries come partly from expecting that the network is going to be static, thus, *discovery is a consequence of the experience of the network being static.* When the transition begins, the static network fades away and the firms have to deal with discovering new things.

Initially, the experience is in balance with the expectation of the search process, but gradually the balance is turned into an imbalance. It emerges, *firstly*, when the new expectations become stronger than the previous experience and, *secondly*, when several attempts to search turn into unexpected discoveries, or unintentional discoveries are made. Thus, discoveries initially enhance the imbalance between experience and expectation. Still, the predominant experience had been gained in the planned economy, but owing to discoveries the balance is overthrown. There are strong expectations that the firm can and should act in relation to others; however, they have little idea of where, how, and what to do. And keeping the balance between experience and expectation is problematic, as the connected relationships are also going through this phase. Thus, experiencing discoveries is the same as realising the imbalance between experience from the planned economy and expectation in the market economy.

The transition economy inherited a division of use and exchange in the network, which was characterised by a multilateral dependence on the use level, which became especially evident when relationships changed. Any type of change, be it on the exchange level or on the use level, had an effect on connected relationships due to the multilateral dependence. Owing to the anonymity in the network, the discoveries are sometimes connected, that is, what one firm discovers is a result of another firm finding what it is searching for. However, there can be a time delay between these two change processes.

By participating in the network processes, the firms make discoveries. Acting during the transition from a planned economy to a market economy can be viewed as a journey of discovery into the unknown, an attempt to discover new ways to do things better than they have been done before (Hayek 1936). The discoveries are not only important in themselves, but also because they support the movement to a new type of balance between experience and expectation.

The experience acquired through discoveries gives new answers to the questions where, what, and how, which means that discovery is a main input in new search processes. The firms have initially to rely on their old experience, which told them to search within their boundaries. Other possibilities were almost unknown for the firms, but the relationships, which had been governed by the authorities and where all knowledge needed was codified in the plan, got a new role. After the plan was abandoned and as the price did not always give the firms enough information, how to search and what to search for were given new answers. The lack of experience in realising the mutuality in the network meant that for a long time the discoveries were unilateral. But while unique experience is acquired not only within the boundaries, but also in the collision of firms in the network, firms realise the need to mutually match their search and discoveries. By discovering and recognising, the firms acquire experience of what, where, how, and when to search jointly in the relationships.

Chapter 7

Connected Change Processes in Tipografiya's Network

Development of Networks of Integrated Relationships

Up to this point, Tipografiya's network was discussed as a set of relationships, that is, several relationships independent of each other. One of the observations made in Chapter 6 is that change processes in various relationships are interrelated and tend to influence each other. For instance, a search process in one relationship may initiate a discovery process in another. Halinen *et al*. (1999) argued that changes in networks can be connected. To that, I would add that the processes preceding such changes are also often connected and tend to influence each other. In the case of Tipografiya, the background to the connected change processes is to be found in the network structure that evolved during the planned economy. The observations made in Chapter 4 indicate that the planned economy tended to produce networks where the exchange was strictly planned, while a somewhat bigger space for action was left for the firm on the use level. The result was that the two levels partly lived their own lives, separated from each other. The case provides several examples not only of independent relationships, but also of inter-connected relationships on the use level, which influence each other and where the use level and exchange level in various relationships are linked to each other in a complex pattern. The structural imbalance between the levels in the network might be viewed as a point of departure for the processes that characterised the network between 1992 and 1998 and in order to analyse these processes, this chapter advances three concepts, which might help to explain the connected change processes.

Multilateral Dependence

On the use level in the network, resources are used in combinations. When exchanged between firms, the features of a specific resource then become blended together with a large number of different resource features. In a network, resources are deployed and combined over the firms' boundaries and beyond the exchange between firms. The use level is more tacit and more difficult to completely codify than the exchange level. On this level, resources are combined and activated by a set of actors that, partly, but not completely, share knowledge. They have a common past. The knowledge is tied to the resources in each specific network. It is often implicitly assumed that the two levels follow each other. Investments and commitment are made towards the exchange partners and trust emerges when resources are exchanged. In networks the use levels do not only follow the exchange levels. In the case of technology, for example, the exchange is not slavishly followed; resources are invested in the network and not only in the exchange relationships.

Over time, in a dynamic and interactive process, the result is a *multilateral dependence* between resources controlled by three or more firms. The multilateral dependence in the network is a result of the fact that the use level is more complex and extensive than the exchange level. Due to the complexity, firms at the use level have to make adaptations (Hallén *et al.* 1991), which achieve a fit in the resources combined at that level. This means that the adaptations are not only directed towards the counterparts, but also affect the counterpart's customers and the suppliers' use of resources. Richardson (1972, 1995) argued that the relationship is dominated by the use of different kinds of resources. The counterparts provide various types of knowledge, equipment, and so on to the interface, but it is through the activities performed by the parties that the resources are adapted and devoted to the relationship (Heide & John 1990). Adaptation can be referred to as the ways in which mutual fit is brought about between firms' resources (Hallén *et al.* 1991) and they become complementary. Owing to the mutually adapted and rather unique collection of resources combined in the network, it is often difficult to *substitute* for one of the firm's resources and moreover, *transferring* from one network to another network might be costly and result in a loss of value of the resources (Dierickx & Cool 1989; Peteraf 1993).

The multilateral dependence on the use level affects the exchange level and is a constraint for changes in the network, which tends to cause inertia in the change processes. The multilateral dependence limits the room for manoeuvring when it comes to establishing and terminating relationships. However, multilateral dependence also has a structural implication. In 1985, Granovetter argued that economic action is embedded in a network of social relations. After that, the notion of embeddedness was also exploited in other areas (e.g. Dacin *et al.* 1999; Halinen & Törnroos 1998). Granovetter's thoughts have been applied here in order to deconstruct this network complexity. In a Granovetterian way, the idea that the economic action, in my terminology the exchange level, is embedded in the use level is introduced. These lines of argument are supported by Penrose (1959: 78) who claimed that the "services that the resources will yield depend on the capacities of the men using them." However she also realised that the interaction between the human and the physical resource affected those handling the resource: "but the development of the capacities of men is partly shaped by the resources men deal with." Therefore, the knowledge about a resource and how well developed that knowledge is in relation to the resource exchanged is crucial in order to realise the full potential value of a resource at a given moment.

One can find different schools supporting this. For instance, Astley & Zajac (1993) showed that in relationships the dependence caused by the division of labour, called "workflow interdependence" — that is, what everyone is actually doing — is more difficult to terminate than interdependence, which is a result of the exchange of resources. This argumentation is also in line with findings made by historians of technology (e.g. Hounshell 1995; Hughes 1989), who claimed that physical and non-physical artefacts are organised in technological systems. Hughes (1987: 51) says that "Technological systems contain messy, complex, problem-solving components. They are both socially constructed and society shaping," which implies that technological development takes place and functions in a specific context. Disharmonies and imbalances between the system's components (Hughes 1987; Hughes 1989) are the source for change in the network. The machines in use and the people operating them not only influence the exchange; they make up the frame in which exchanges are possible, but they are also a point of departure and cause for change in the network.

Integrated Relationships and Partial Relationships

Viewing the network as a structure having two levels means that there are two types of relationships. The *integrated relationship* contains an exchange level as well as a use level. The *partial relationship*, on the other hand, lacks one of the levels. This is illustrated in the lower part of Figure 10, where there are three partial relationships, one on the use level between the focal actor's suppliers and one of the customers, one on the exchange level between the actor and the same customer, and finally, one on the use level between two of the customers. These relationships contain knowledge, in the partial relationship either about how to use the resources in relation to the counterpart's use of resources or about how to exchange resources with the counterpart. Besides these two dimensions, the integrated relationship has an additional dimension, namely knowledge about how to combine and link them in relation to the counterpart.

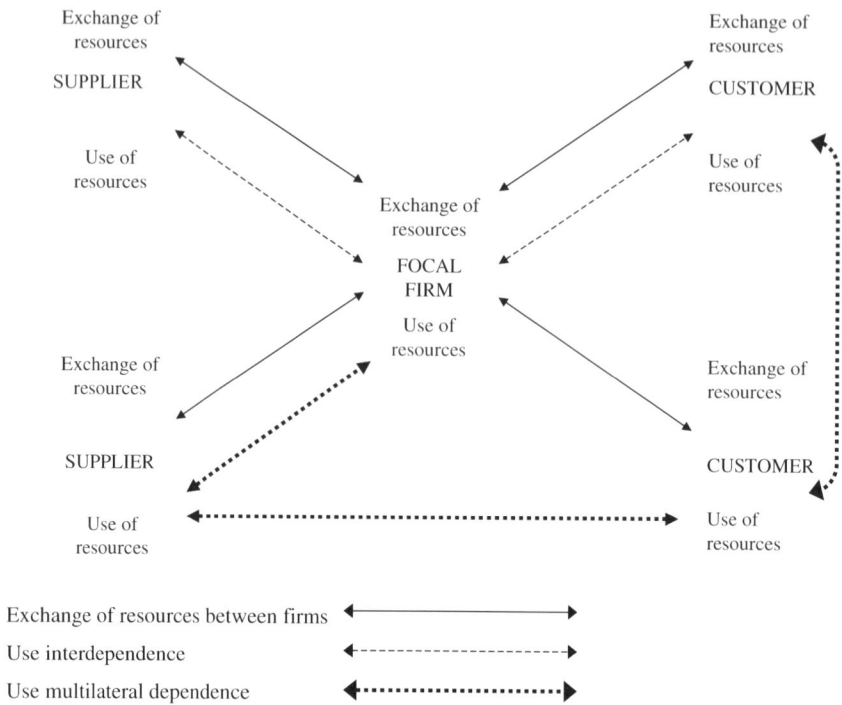

Figure 10: Relationships between the firms.

Knowledge about how to relate and link these two levels in an integrated relationship has, in turn, another implication. The integrated relationships offer greater possibilities of relating the use and exchange of resources not only towards the counterparts, but also to the surrounding network. Consequently, a network with integrated relationships can mobilise more resources and more expertise than a network with a bigger share of partial relationships. A network with integrated relationships has more potential alternatives and solutions than a network with partial relationships or a single firm can provide. It follows then that the latter type of network has greater limitations when firms try to find solutions to problems, whereas the network with integrated relationships can handle both positive and negative discoveries more effectively than those with partial relationships. If it is perceived as negative the effects can be shared among the firms, but there are also cases when negative discoveries for one firm can be perceived as positive for another firm.

As in so many other network studies, Johanson & Mattsson (1992) suggested that stability is the natural state of the network. Consequently networks exist in periods of stability and the network's structure is a manifestation of the stability in the exchange and the use of resources. This means that the point of departure for change can either be found at the exchange level or at the use level and correspondingly, their effects can be observed on either the exchange or the use level. In the transition economy, by the institutional changes of the governance of the economy the conditions at the exchange level changed, but the objective was to have an effect on the efficiency on the use level. They were assumed to affect the exchange level only indirectly, but this does not mean that the resources controlled on the use level do not have any impact on the pace and extension of the transition. A high degree of multilateral dependence on the use level between two firms would cause inertia in the transition process.

A Model for Development of Integrated Relationships

The notions of partial and integrated relationships describe the network in terms of whether the relationships are on either an exchange level or a use level, or in the case of an integrated relationship, both levels. In Chapter 4, it was observed that the planned network, owing to plan governance of the economy, generated relationships that tended to be partial. In the light of these two notions, multilateral dependence on the use level was put forward as a concept that could encompass the effects of the extensive plan governance of the exchange level. It seems that the planned network, with its partial relationships, tended to have a positive influence on the emergence of multilateral dependence in the network. As shown in Figure 10, the partial relationships and the multilateral dependence can be viewed as some kind of point of departure for the connected change processes observed in Chapters 5 and 7, with one large difference, however. Multilateral dependence slows down the processes and makes them more complex, as most changes have consequences for connected relationships. The changes have to be assimilated and absorbed in the connected relationships, which takes time and often requires new ways of using resources. The partial character of the existing relationships, on the other hand, tend to stimulate and even accelerate the change processes. During the transition, it is likely that there would be a movement from a network of partial relationships towards integrated relationships, since the integrated relationships provide a more robust basis for development of new knowledge and for higher efficiency compared with the partial relationships. To sum up, the partial relationships start the change processes because of their weakness compared with integrated relationships, and multilateral dependence tends to connect these change processes and slow down their pace.

From a theoretical point of view, three reasons for the movement might be singled out. First and most evident is that the development of new knowledge about how to use resources and how to exchange resources in the relationship is enhanced. A integrated relationship provides a more extensive interface than a partial relationship because more activities are performed and more people, who provide different types of expertise and experience, are involved. This also means that it is necessary to co-ordinate and to match the exchange and the use in the relationship. This more extensive interface not only deploys more resources, but also encourages the acquisition of experience.

Second, the economic consequences of the use of resources are more difficult to evaluate and grasp if they are not related to revenues, that is, to exchange. Resources used in the relationship acquire a value when they are tied to exchange, which is possible in a integrated but not in a partial relationship. Furthermore, the partial relationship does not offer the same possibility for relating expenses to revenues, as one of the levels is missing. For instance, a partial relationship, operating only on a use level, does not provide opportunities for the development of the conditions needed for evaluating how efficiently resources are used, as there are no revenues related to that use. Moreover, partial relationships make development of knowledge more difficult, for only a relationship that includes both levels gives space for an interplay between use and exchange, which could, for instance, be a strength in the development of new ways of using and exchanging resources. An integrated relationship offers the possibility of breaking the linearity that exists when the firm first develops the resources and then begins to exchange those resources with various counterparts. Such a relationship can promote an interaction between the two levels and more easily involve the counterpart in the process, which among other benefits offers possibilities for mobilising more expertise than a partial relationship.

Third, a network with integrated relationships offers an opportunity to relate and combine these two levels in one relationship to other connected relationships in the network. In a network with integrated relationships, more knowledge can be mobilised and combined in order to develop ways of exchanging and using resources. Thus, the change of governance of the economy initiates a movement towards a network of integrated relationships, which, in turn, means evolution of a closer relationship between knowledge and performance in the network. This discussion gives rise to a deeper discussion about the change processes in Tipografiya's network. Two parts of Tipografiya's network where these observations are visible have been chosen as illustrations of the movement reproduced in Figure 11. They concern production of forms for the Post Office Administration and the production of the big newspapers in Novgorod.

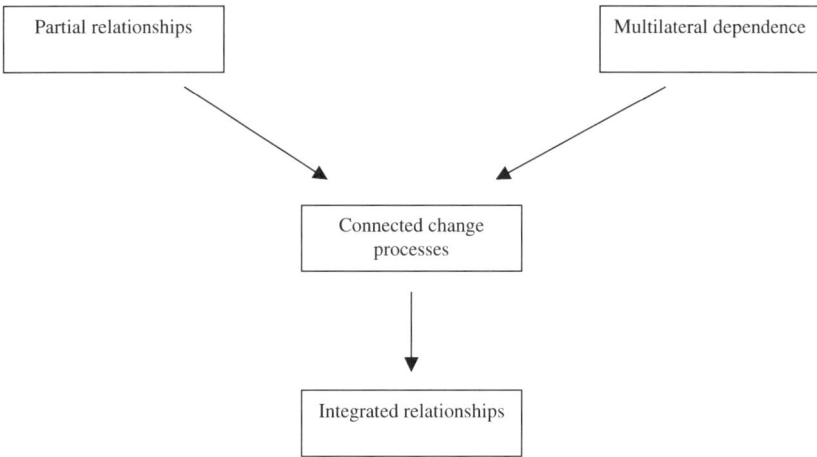

Figure 11: Movement towards a network of integrated relationships.

The Form Network

The Form Network in the 1980s

Figure 12 reflects a part of Tipografiya's network in the 1980s that was concerned with the production of forms for the regional branches of the Soviet Post Office

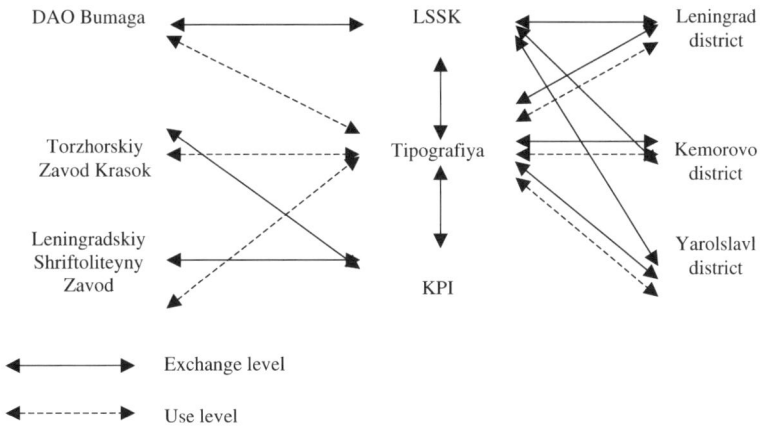

Figure 12: The structure of the form network in the 1980s.

Administration. It was valid until the beginning of the 1990s. Some of these relationships are worth discussing. The first three are to be found in the upper left corner of the figure and illustrate the supply of paper to Tipografiya for the production of forms. They create a triad between the paper supplier (DAO Bumaga), Tipografiya, and LSSK. Interesting here is that the triad was made up of two exchanges, where LSSK served the function of some kind of intermediary between DAO Bumaga and Tipografiya. LSSK governed the two exchanges and DAO Bumaga and Tipografiya were unilaterally dependent on LSSK. However, this unilateral dependence concerned only the exchange level. The use level was almost completely absent in these two relationships.

On the other hand, there was also a third relationship, which in contrast was characterised by the interdependence between DAO Bumaga and Tipografiya on the use level. It was certainly a partial and rather weak relationship as the representatives from the firms had never met and there was no exchange other than an extremely limited exchange of information. Still, one could not say that the relationship on the use level was completely absent. The case provides evidence that the employees knew from where the paper came, they learned how it differed from other paper, when it should be delivered, and they made some small adaptations depending on the specific supplier.

Not unimportant in this network were the suppliers of ink (Torzhorskiy Zavod Krasok) and lead (Leningradskiy Shriftoliteyny Zavod). The two consumables were centrally purchased by KPI, but delivered directly from the producer. This meant that Tipografiya had only partial relationships with these two firms on the exchange level. However, on the use level over time some interdependence emerged between the three firms, as Tipografiya learned to receive and combine the products from the suppliers of paper, ink, and lead in order to produce forms, which resulted in multilateral dependence in this part of the network.

The right-hand side of the figure, which contains Tipografiya, LSSK, the Leningrad district, the Kemorovo district, and the Yaroslavl district, is similar to the relationships just discussed. The latter two symbolise here the vast range of regional branches of the Post Office Administration. LSSK's role as governor of the network is evident in this figure. LSSK has relationships with Tipografiya, the Leningrad district, the Kemorovo district, and the Yaroslavl district on the exchange level, however without any interdependence on the use level. Over the years, Tipografiya, on the other hand, developed some kind of interdependence, albeit weak, on the use level with all three districts. The structure in Figure 12 shows that several relationships were only partial, lacking either the exchange level or the use level, which, in turn, means that the network was characterised by weak multilateral dependence. Actually, only the relationships with the three districts can be described as integrated, although, these relationships far from fully carried the economic consequences of the use of paper, lead, and inks in the production of the forms.

The Form Network at the Beginning of the 1990s

An event at the beginning of the 1990s may not have changed the structure radically to the naked eye — as illustrated in Figure 13 only one firm has been added — but in fact, it did make a difference. That event was the beginning of the erosion of plan governance. LSSK had just started to play a new role, this time as an intermediary taking commission for its service. Consequently, the arrow illustrating the exchange level between LSSK and Tipografiya now indicates business instead of plan commands with some economic implications, and the balance of the dependence on this level is more symmetric. The new role of LSSK also meant that it did not have any relation to the purchasing of paper. However, Tipografiya continued to be supplied from the same kombinats, here exemplified by DAO Bumaga. However, in this structure, the relationship between DAO Bumaga and Tipografiya was not only established on the use, but also on the exchange level. This means that the interdependence grew. Tipografiya began to buy paper from the supplier from which it had previously received paper, but now the focus was on price.

A third difference compared with the previous figure is that Tipografiya printed the forms partly on the offset machines. This meant that Tipografiya initially was supplied the offset plates for the forms by Poligrafresursy, which had for

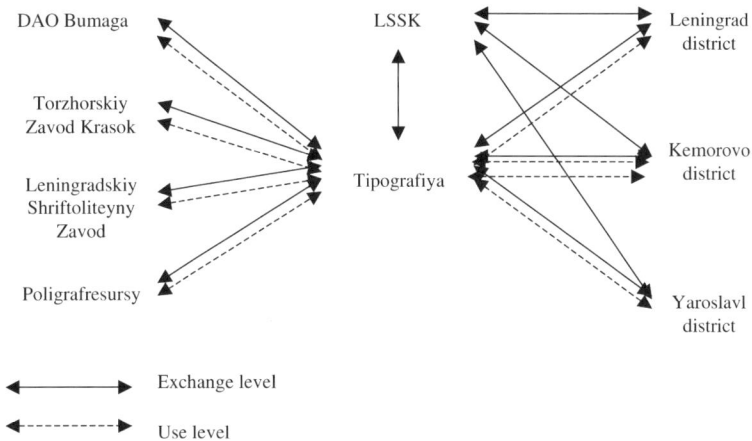

Figure 13: The structure of the form network in the beginning of the 1990s.

several years been supplying the plates for products other than forms. However, now Tipografiya began to buy the plates directly from Poligrafresursy and use them for the forms. The multilateral dependence here is both weaker and less extensive than in the previous structure, although it is likely that the multilateral dependence was the reason that the suppliers continued to supply Tipografiya. From Figures 12 to 13, there was a movement from multilateral dependence to interdependence on the use levels in the relationship. A fourth difference was that KPI disappeared, which enhanced the emergence of more integrated relationships. Also in this case, the strong multilateral dependence on the use level meant that the exchange level was embedded in the use level, which, in turn meant that Tipografiya continued to buy from Torzhorskiy Zavod Krasok and Leningradskiy Shriftoliteyny Zavod.

The Form Network in the Middle of the 1990s

Figure 14 advances to the middle of the 1990s. After a few years of the transition process, the structure has changed. At this point, the relationship with LSSK had dissolved, and the Leningrad and Yaroslavl districts were buying directly from Tipografiya. With the case in mind, it seems natural to claim that the interdependence on the use level in both these relationships increased. The firms, but especially Tipografiya, made several adaptations to the counterparts and this contributed to the increase. It is also striking that these two relationships were connected and that this connection influenced their transformation. After Tipografiya had successfully granted credit to the Leningrad district, it began to do the same in the relationship with the Yaroslavl district. Gradually, but when no problems occurred, as in the case with the Leningrad district, Tipografiya increased the size of the credits to the Yaroslavl district. Granting credit was a new experience for Tipografiya. In the beginning the expectation was that they would not be paid, which had been the case in relationships with some customers, but the experience from the relationship with the Leningrad district carried over to the new expectation in the relationship with the Yaroslavl district. LSSK's disappearance also had another effect. Several of the regional branches, in Figures 12 and 13 illustrated by the Kemorovo district, terminated the relationship with Tipografiya and turned to other printing houses. This was a new experience for Tipografiya and in the beginning, unexpected, but was, nevertheless, a fact of life with which they had to learn to live.

A second big structural change was the establishment of integrated relationships with intermediaries like Nevskaya Bumaga. They were not producing the paper, but were fulfilling a function as some kind of broker between the producer of

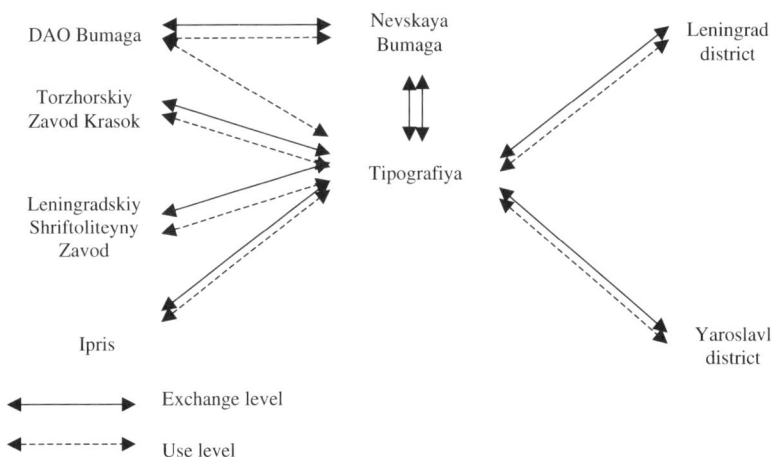

Figure 14: The structure of the form network in the middle of the 1990s.

the paper and the user. This meant that Nevskaya Bumaga had an exchange with both DAO Bumaga and Tipografiya, and that there was a relationship on the use level. Tipografiya's experience from this relationship existed, but was eroding, since Nevskaya Bumaga bought paper for Tipografiya from other producers as well. When it came to inks, stereotypes, and plates, little happened. Ipris replaced Poligrafresursy as a supplier of offset plates and the relationship with Leningradskiy Shriftoliteyny Zavod became much weaker as the relief technology was used less and less and by the end of the period was hardly used at all.

Connected Change Processes in the Form Network

In comparing the three figures, one can observe a change in movement from multilateral dependence and partial relationships to a network with less partial relationships. In Figure 13, LSSK still fulfils a function that prevents the emergence of a structure of only integrated relationships, but in Figure 14 LSSK has disappeared. By definition, partial relationships separate use from exchange, whereas in integrated relationships, the use of resources, technology and production is connected to the exchange of resources, which represents the economic consequences of using the resources. The most thorough experience is from using or exchanging resources in relation to a specific counterpart, and partial relationships are thus less efficient than integrated relationships.

There is also a dynamic consequence of this structure, since learning about how to use the resources is separated from the costs and benefits of putting the results of learning into use. It does not mean that learning is absent in a partial relationship based only on the use level, but the economic consequences of learning are small, which means that it is more difficult for the firm to find out whether a change is viable or not. The partial relationship offers a limited space for personal interaction over the firms' boundaries and since interaction is instrumental for learning, a partial relationship is a structural obstacle to learning.

Finally, the imbalance between experience (gained in the network structure in Figure 14) and the expectation produced by the change in governance of the economy partly led to the combined process of search and discovery in the relationships with various suppliers of the paper needed for the forms. The combined process also characterised the transformation of the relationships with the Leningrad and the Yaroslavl districts and the fact that several relationships with other regional branches were dissolved through a "sour" discovery process. The dominance of discoveries in these processes was instrumental for the reappearance of a balance between experience and expectation.

The Newspaper Network

The Newspaper Network in the 1980s

The Novgorodskaya Pravda was the predominant newspaper in the region during the planned economy. Tipografiya had quite a close relationship with the newspaper, on both the exchange level and the use level. The fact that the Novgorodskaya Pravda bought the newsprint and stored it in Tipografiya's premises made the relationship rather unusual. The Novgorodskaya Pravda had nothing to do with the physical handling of the newsprint. That was done between Tipografiya and Solikomskiy TsBK or one of the other two producers. Even though there was no exchange between Solikomskiy TsBK and Tipografiya and the interaction between them on the use level was limited, Tipografiya had to handle the newsprint: to receive and store it, and use it in production. KPI's role is typical. The financial transactions between the suppliers of metal, inks, and zinc and Tipografiya were channelled through KPI, which resulted in a structure where there was no exchange between the supplier and the customer. However, on the use level, there were relationships between Tipografiya and the three suppliers, similar to the multilateral dependence in the form network. Tipografiya learned to receive and combine the product in the production of newspapers. Thereby, the four suppliers were connected through the interdependence on the use level.

When it came to distribution, Tipografiya had relationships with both Gazetno-Zhurnalnaya Ekspeditsiya and Soyuzpechat on the use level, and although the Novgorodskaya Pravda paid for it, it had nothing to do with the actual physical distribution. Moreover, there was a relationship on the use level between Gazetno-Zhurnalnaya Ekspeditsiya and Soyuzpechat, as they fulfilled different functions in the distribution of the newspapers. In this case, partial relationships seemed to dominate the network. The only integrated relationship existed between Tipografiya and the Novgorodskaya Pravda. This meant, that Tipografiya did not fully experience the economic consequences of using products such as newsprint, inks, and zinc and other types of metals. Moreover, learning through search and discovery how to combine them with the firm's own resources, also had no economic consequence.

The Newspaper Network at the Beginning of the 1990s

Figure 16 illustrates the structure at the beginning of the 1990s. Following a political decision, the Novgordskiye Vedomosti replaced the Novgorodskaya Pravda and the Novgorod entered the market and established relationships with Tipografiya. Furthermore, KPI had disappeared, and Tipografiya was now buying directly from the producers without interference from any authorities. However, as in the form network, Tipografiya turned to suppliers with which it already had a relationship on the use level. Tipografiya's relationships with the Novgordskiye Vedomosti and the Novgorod were partly similar to the relationship established with the Novgorodskaya Pravda. The newspapers bought the newsprint themselves although Tipografiya carried out all the physical handling of the paper. It was also the same suppliers of newsprint as during the planned economy. A big difference, though, was that the official price list was abandoned and Tipografiya increased the prices on the exchange level in both relationships.

The distribution of the Novgordskiye Vedomosti was more or less the same as it had been with the Novgorodskaya Pravda. The Novgorod distributed the newspapers itself but Gazetno-Zhurnalnaya Ekspeditsiya packed them before they were distributed. This meant that this relationship operated on both the exchange and use levels. However, Rospechat, which had previously been called Soyuzpechat, had no relationship with the Novgorod. The development from the situation depicted in Figure 15 to the one in Figure 16 was characterised by rapidly emerging imbalance between old experience, which lost its value, and the expectations caused by the change of governance. New firms appeared, old firms disappeared, and the governance of the network changed completely.

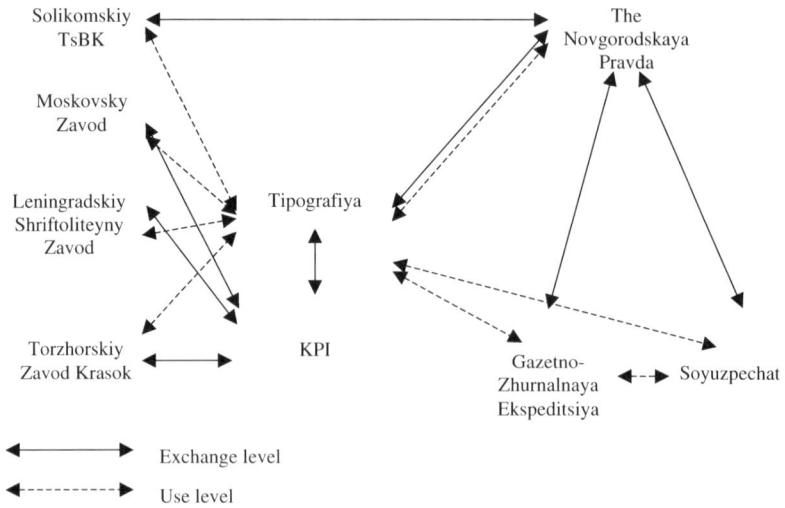

Figure 15: The structure of the newspaper network in the 1980s.

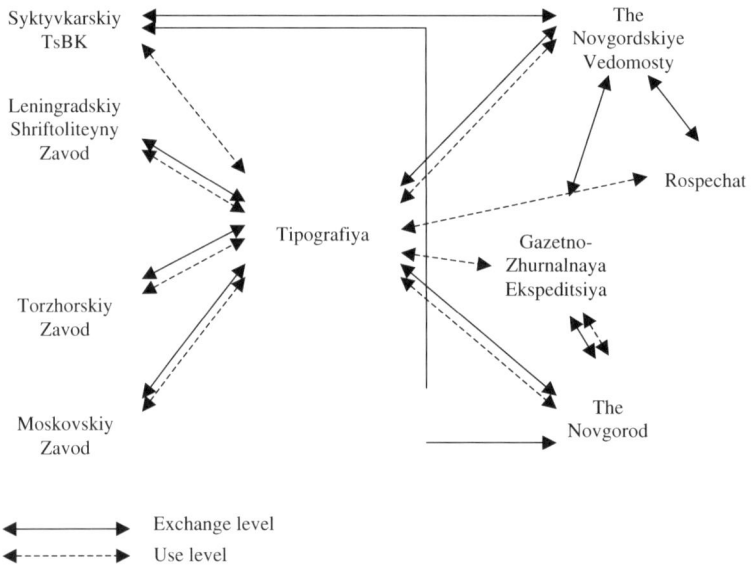

Figure 16: The structure of the newspaper network at the beginning of the 1990s.

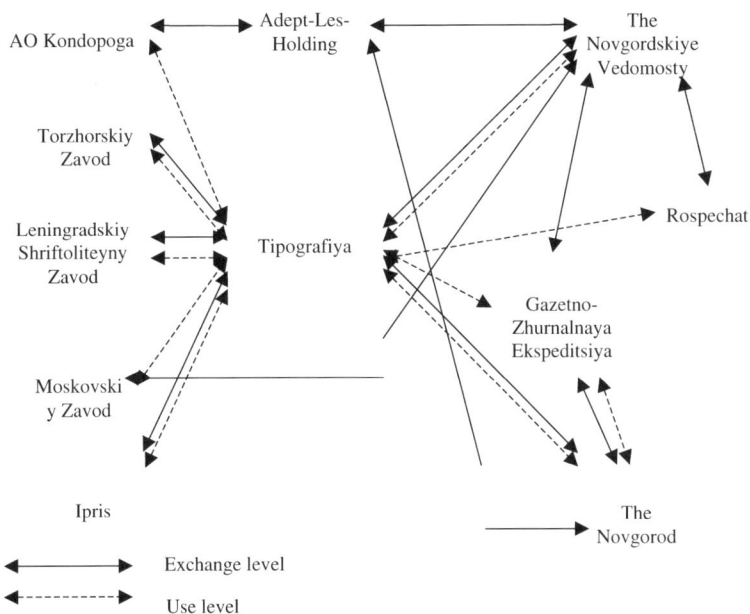

Figure 17: The structure of the newspaper network in the middle of the 1990s.

The Newspaper Network in the Middle of the 1990s

Figure 17 illustrating the network structure in the middle of the 1990s shows two big differences compared with the previous one. The first concerns the appearance of Adept-Les-Holding. It took a position on the exchange level as an intermediary between the two newspapers and the suppliers of newsprint (from the middle of the 1990s this was usually AO Kondopoga). Adept-Les-Holding's intermediating role was a result of a political decision by the District Administration, and certainly appeared close to the function of LSSK and KPI during the planned economy. It had no relationships on the use level with AO Kondopoga, the Novgordskiye Vedomosti, or the Novgorod. On the use level, Tipografiya was the intermediating firm. In 1997, this network underwent another change, when suddenly there was no zinc to buy. Ipris then began to supply Tipografiya with photo polymer plates for the printing of the Novgorod, while the Novgordskiye Vedomosti was forced by Tipografiya to find and buy zinc itself (represented in this figure by Moskovskiy Zavod). Once more Tipografiya had a relationship with a supplier on the use, but not on the exchange level.

Connected Change Processes in the Newspaper Network

Two movements can be observed in the newspaper network. Although not as evident but still in the same way as in the form network, the partial relationships are replaced by integrated relationships. During the planned economy the newspaper network was already more complex than the form network, and this tendency seems to have been strengthened. Taken together these two movements, although the network is becoming more complex it is accompanied by a development where it might be possible for partial relationships to be transformed into integrated relationships. Such a network structure assists in a higher level of efficiency and learning that is more appropriate for the firms in the network. The complex network made both multilateral searches, as well as a multilateral combined processes, but in this case, after the firm has made several discoveries. Discovery took place frequently in Tipografiya's relationships with the suppliers of newsprint, the suppliers of zinc, the Novgordskiye Vedomosti, the Novgorod, and the other newspapers. From Tipografiya's perspective the movement was from unilateral learning via mutual learning to multilateral learning, where Tipografiya through several discoveries gained a new type of experience, which was better balanced with the expectations.

In its relationships in the planned economy, Tipografiya had experience either use or exchange, but not of both. These were partial experiences and consequently, anonymity prevailed. A few years later, both the networks discussed had undergone several changes, which resulted in networks with more frequent integrated than partial relationships. When the governance of the economy changed, there was a decentralisation of where, how, when, and what resources to use and exchange among the firms. This resulted in a movement from partial to integrated relationships, which seems to have characterised the network during the transition. Consequently, the network can be viewed as moving from anonymity towards the development of an identity for each firm.

Chapter 8

Towards a New Network Logic

Movement Towards a New Network Logic

The end approaches. I started by assuming that the transition from a planned to a market economy implies that the means in the economy were re-allocated in order to reach the reconsidered and redefined ends. The institutional changes were discussed in terms of dismantling of the plan and the plan authorities and price liberalisation, and they were also referred to as the triggers in the time-consuming and turbulent transition process. In order to analyse these processes two models were launched.

The first was the network model, where it was argued that the relationship consisted of two levels that did not necessarily follow each other. The second advanced search, recognition and discovery as factors influencing change of the exchange and use of resources. The first model was later applied to the planned economy and I concluded that the network during that period was characterised by hierarchy, static networks, and anonymity. After that, the three types of processes based on the second model were combined with establishment, dissolution, and transformation of relationships in order to grasp the change processes in the network during the transition to a market economy. Finally, the first model was used to explain how the network changed during the transition.

The results of the various change processes in the network can be viewed as movement from one type of network logic towards another, new, network logic (see Figure 18). This is not a terminal point, but rather a movement, and many of the old characteristics still remain.

From Hierarchy to Mutuality

The transition started from a situation characterised by hierarchy, which, in turn, had produced relationships where the interdependence on the exchange

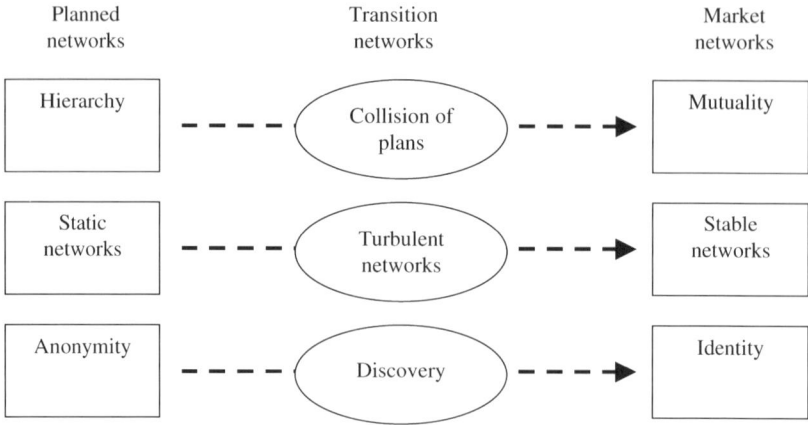

Figure 18: Movement towards a new network logic.

level was almost completely planned, while there was some freedom for the firms on the use level. Going from a system with hierarchy of plans to a system where the plans and the plan authorities are dismantled can be discussed from two aspects.

Firstly, going from a centralised plan to decentralised plans is in itself a *process*, and *secondly*, it is the *relationship* that undergoes the change of governance. In a system with decentralised planning and plans, firm A's plan is always related to firm B's plan. What A produces, which machines and equipment it uses, how it stores and transports goods, is never autonomous but related to how firm B deals with these and how much it pays for them. Moreover, it is also related to B's production, storage, transportation, and so forth. The knowledge needed for these activities was assumed to be codified in a central plan. The firms' limited experience of planning their operations was a constraint, when the transition started. Moreover, they lacked experience of jointly planning the exchange and use of resources in relationships with other firms and from that follows that the centralised planning was replaced by a decentralised planning where the firms made up the plans independently of the authorities, but also independently of their customers and suppliers.

This meant that even though they were able to plan their operations, the planning was made in isolation from other actors' plans, which, in turn, implied the fit or matching of the firms' plans was probably to a considerable extent a result of luck. Very often, the plans simply did not fit with each other. This tended initially to lead to collision between plans. Collision of plans causes turbulence, at least in the beginning. However, there is also an opposite force in this process, where fit is brought about in the plans so they begin to match each other, and matching causes stability.

Richardson (1972: 68) says that the matching of plans is typical for a relationship in a market economy: "This co-ordination cannot be left entirely to direction within firms because the activities are dissimilar, and cannot be left to the market forces in that it requires not the balancing of the aggregate supply of something with the aggregate demand for it but rather the matching, both qualitative and quantitative, of individual enterprise plans." In the planned economy, the matching of plans was done by uniting the individual firms' plans into one big centralised plan, whereas a decentralised system requires interaction between firms. It takes at least two to plan, and since plans can be viewed as codified knowledge, firms have to learn from each other. Interaction enhances this. The fact that it takes two to plan means that unilateral dependence on the plan authority and its knowledge is gradually transformed into mutuality between the firms in the network. However, this change does not take place in a vacuum. Poor matching and the collision of plans may result in dissolution of some relationships and establishment of others.

The second aspect concerns two matters: the type of knowledge and the strength of the relationships. In general, the planned economy produced partial, but static relationships. Partial relationships are less efficient when it comes to joint learning, since they are less reciprocal and mutual and, moreover, they are less embedded, as one level is missing. Thus, the consequences if they are dissolved are less severe. It also means that firms with partial relationships have to be more open to finding solutions outside the relationships. On the other hand, a firm with integrated relationships with a high degree of embeddedness searches for solutions within the relationships, where the problems have occurred, rather than across the relationships or beyond the boundaries of the network (Uzzi 1997).

In the market networks planning is also a decentralised activity, which seldom is interrupted or interfered by the authorities, but the collision of plans made by firms lacking experience about how to match plans, is gradually transformed into mutual planning where firms strive to match their plans to each other, but as the hierarchical planning is transformed into mutual planning the tautness and inflexibility of the plans in the planned networks disappear the plans will be more flexble so that they can cope with unexpected disturbances.

From Static Networks to Stable Networks

A related movement accompanies the process from hierarchy to mutuality. The transition provides excellent evidence that change is not unproblematic. It seems to be characterised by the paradoxical co-existence of on the one hand, inertia (that is, everything takes a long time), and on the other, turbulence (that is, lack of steadiness, too many, too fast and too unpredictable changes). In the previous section the argument was that the transition process is, owing to network anonymity, where firms are ignorant both about their customers and suppliers and how to jointly plan the operations in the relationships, initially characterised by a collision of plans. Two firms in a relationship are very lucky if their attempts to make the first joint plans succeed. Instead, it is rather likely that they will fail. The lack of experience in the relationship thus causes turbulence, which spreads throughout in the network.

The turbulence is a result of the decentralisation just discussed. The transition economies in Eastern Europe are often viewed as turbulent (Czaban & Whitley 2000; Salmi 2000). This is also the case in Russia. McCarthy *et al.* (2000) argue that the Russian market has undergone various stages since the late 1980s to the end of the 1990s, sometimes characterised by turmoil and crisis. Turbulence means that the changes in the market are frequent and unexpected. Due to the turbulence, it is difficult to predict the outcome of the firms' behaviour. Turbulence is partly a consequence of the institutional changes, since they lead to re-consideration of the ends for the firms at the micro level and re-allocation of the means controlled and used in the economy. Since both ends and means are given new meanings, they also recurrently force the firm to question its experience of the network. But the turbulence is also a result of changed behaviour. Firms interpret the changes in different ways and, therefore, form their expectations differently. Consequently, it is likely that the behaviour of the firms as a result of the movement away from plan governance will be unpredictable, which makes planning difficult. Moreover, behaviour of firms will also change over time, since some firms react quickly, sometimes almost instantly, while others do not change their behaviour until much later.

The turbulence in the network means that that dissolved business relationships were a widespread outcome of the change of governance (Davis *et al.* 1996; Gurkov 1996). Insufficient supplies have remained a big problem for Russian firms during the transition period (Blanchard & Kremer 1997; Shama 1992), and the relations to the suppliers have often deteriorated (Filatotchev *et al.* 1996). In parallel, a lot of existing products quickly became obsolete, while new products and technologies appeared (Golden *et al.* 1995), in many cases of foreign origins.

The privatisation of state-owned firms increased the turbulence in the network. The privatisation took place in a chaotic context (Potts 1999) and was closely tied to the political development, and since the political situation has been chaotic, the privatisation was neither been stable nor predictable. The privatisation produced alliances between the directors of the former state-owned firms and the employees.

While the managers sought to retain control over the firms, rejecting outside owners and capital, the employees' goal was to avoid lay-offs (Krivogorsky 2000). Under these conditions, the top-management applied short-term tactics with the aim to survive and where status quo was maintained. Because of such a conservative tactics, privatised firms tended to be passive in reconstructing their firms (Potts 1999), for instance, by way of establishing business with foreign firms (Filatotochev *et al.* 2001) or implementing new technologies and products (Krivogorsky 2000).

Further, entry barriers for new firms were abolished (Eliasson 1998), which meant that new customers and suppliers entered the network, which both increased the degree of competition, but also expanded the range of potential sources of supply. A huge number of small and medium-sized firms were established in the beginning of the 1990s (Kontorovich 1999). However, the number of firms registered recently has fluctuated over the years and even stagnated now and then. The small and medium-sized firms do not make a homogeneous group, since they have different backgrounds and act differently (Peng 2001; Smallbone & Welter 2001). Thus, it seems that the formation of small and medium-sized firms tends to contribute to the turbulence, but it has also been argued that complexity and turbulence per se stimulate and foster entrepreneurial activity (Peng 2001; Puffer & McCarthy 2001). Finally, the number of foreign firms operating in Russia increased. This produced a more complex network structure with greater competition, since foreign firms tended to change customers as a result of the change during the transition (Salmi & Möller 1994).

However, the turbulence will not remain forever, but is leading to a more stable network, implying that turbulence is a phase that is likely to precede a phase of *stability*. When network of integrated relationships gradually evolve and firms begin to match their plans, instead of letting them collide, a more stable structure will replace the turbulence, which prevails in the transition economy. However, it is important that there is a big difference between a static network and a stable network as the later allows changes, but they will take place within existing integrated relationships and have an incremental character. Moreover, in opposite to the static network, changes will not come as plan orders from the authorities, but be a result of the interaction, which the firms perform in the relationships, but also linked to the surrounding network.

The movements pictured in Figures 12–17 imply that the number of relationships Tipografiya had in the middle of the 1990s exceeds the number of relationships it had in the middle of the 1980s. An explanation of this change might be that the firm has gradually turned into a node of co-ordination. The increased number of relationships has also been viewed as a source of technological change (Ahuja 2000; Powell *et al.* 1996). More integrated relationships give access to more sources of information, but since the relationships serve the function of transmitter of information, the total flow of information can also increase. Uzzi (1997) also suggests that relationships, where the exchange is deeply embedded in social relations, enhance joint problem solving and transfers of fine-grained information. In order to create and use complex and non-codified knowledge in the Soviet Union, whole networks were designed; they were not self-organised through various connected change processes. This can be seen in the priority industries such as the space industry or the military industrial complex. Consequently, one would not expect the transition process to contain the transfer of fine-grained information and joint problem-solving, but rather novel knowledge and discoveries.

A paradox with networks in market economies is that at the same time as they are stable they enhance change (see e.g. Easton & Lundgren 1992; Håkansson 1987, 1989; Halinen *et al.* 1999). Stable networks provide two important preconditions for learning. First, firms usually tend to learn more about that of which they already have knowledge (Cohen & Levinthal 1990). Obviously, new knowledge is dependent on old knowledge and there is a path the firm has to walk. Furthermore, since learning is often a process, firms need time to repeat the experience, as do individuals, which means that the stability positively effects joint learning between the firms in the network.

From Anonymity to Identity

Anonymity prevailed in the Soviet network. Partial relationships with low interaction were typical. Ignorance and knowledge are antonyms and having a name, or rather, an identity can consequently be viewed as the opposite of anonymity. Identity has lately emerged as a way for how those inside and outside the organisation perceive the organisation (e.g. Dutton & Dukerich 1991; Gioia, Schultz & Corley 2000). However, the link between a clear identity and improved co-ordination in a market economy has also recently been examined (Kogut & Zander 1996). The emphasis has so far been on management's role in creating the identity and how the public and the media perceive the created picture. Moreover, it seems that the type of identity has been in focus, while the interaction in the identity-building process has been of subordinate interest.

However, the present approach has a somewhat different point of departure, since it views identity as relative concept. The word identity derives from Latin *idem*, the same (Concise Oxford Dictionary 1990). This "sameness" implies that something or someone is the same for those inside as for those outside. For instance, an identity card has a photo, an image, which should correspond to the face of the holder of the card. However, an identity card is not forever. It can by some accident lose its sharpness and clarity and since all our faces get older, older cards lose their validity. From that it follows that identity also grasps the "sameness" over time. Clarity and correspondence between the inside and the outside and some kind of consistency compose the firm's identity.

These three dimensions mean that identity is something changeable and formable and it seems that it is interaction that builds identities. The firm's identity develops when it fulfils specific tasks, not just any thing or the same as everyone else is doing, in the relationships with specific actors. "Identities are constituted out of the process of interaction. To shift among interactions is to shift among definitions of the self" (Weick 1995: 20). The firm has an identity, which is not the same as everyone else's and it is a result of an interaction with other firms, which implies a heterogeneity and diversity among the firms. The firms' identity is who it is and being someone also means not being someone else (Håkansson & Snehota 1995). It also means using and exchanging resources in a way that could be identified by other firms.

Identity seems to have two input components: *experience* and *reputation*. Experience is gained from doing things in relation to others. Interaction gives the firm experience and in a relationship, it consists of the firms jointly solving various problems (Uzzi 1997) or alternatively, failing to solve problems related to, for instance, transportation, payment, storing, production, negotiations, and so forth. Interaction takes place between different people in the relationship. The relationship is thus a vehicle for gaining experience, since experience is based in action and context.

The transition tends to mean movement from partial relationships to integrated relationships. The latter ones force firms to interact more extensively, not with everyone, but with some. By adding new activities or increasing the number and the quality of activities performed, the possibility of gaining experience increases. Consequently, the fewer the number of issues that have to be managed in the relationship, the less experience gained by the firms. Partial relationships tend to mean strong anonymity, whereas an integrated relationship with a more extensive interaction gives the firm a clearer and sharper identity. A firm's identity is thus constituted after a period of both exchange and use. The transition process thereby tends to give firms a deeper and richer type of identity, but it also diversifies the identity, since one cannot have a relationship with everyone. The heterogeneity of the identities increases (Figure 19).

However, the network identity constitutes of one additional component, the connected actors' way of perceiving the focal firm. By moving the focus from the relationship to the network, the issue of the transmission of experience to connected actors follows. Reputation is the mechanism that transmits the

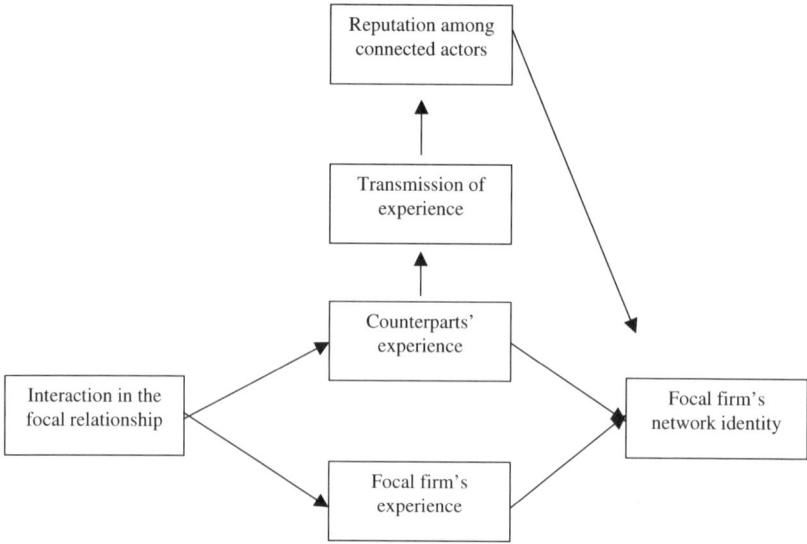

Figure 19: Components of the network identity.

experience of firms in the network, which makes it essential as a component of the network identity. Reputation is experience or other types of non-experiential knowledge that is transformed into opinions, ideas, and information about specific actors and then transmitted between the firms. Thereby, firms learn about other firms beyond the exchange. In the Russian context, Blanchard & Kremer (1997) suggest that the lack of reputation as a mechanism to transmit experience is a reason for the still existing shortage of input, and indirectly, for the production decline. If experience is gained from doing things in relation to others, reputation can be defined as the information actors in the network get about an actor without doing business or having any real direct contact with him. The interaction gives firms answers to the saying: "Tell me who your friends are, and I will tell you who you are," but it does not only concern the exchange partner.

Anderson & Weitz (1992) observe that a firm's reputation of fairness is instrumental when firms establish relationships. Relationships thereby fulfil a function both as vehicles for the acquisition of experience and as transmitters of reputation. An excellent example of the role the transmission of experience plays within a network is Granovetter's (1973) discussion of the strength of weak ties. He suggested that weak ties, which are distant and involve a low interaction, are efficient in providing the firms with novel knowledge and discoveries. But the codified and more objective knowledge about a firm, which is diffused in the network, is less important, compared to the experience. The codified and objective knowledge is available for all and lacks an element of trust. This means that no one stands behind it.

However, there are firms that do not interact with the focal firm, but gain knowledge about the focal firm through other firms. Two questions appear immediately. The first concerns the number of connections of the connected actors, or the density of the network. These aspects are important, because together they determine from how many directions experience can be acquired. They also open up possibilities for comparisons. Firms hear from different sources about other firms. Various aspects and details from various directions can be put together and give both a deep and wide picture of the firm's identity. The number of connections is also a control mechanism. The network can be utilised as a way of diffusing negative opinions and information about a firm.

The second aspect is how distant the connected actor is from the focal firm. Its importance is based on the assumption that the strongest input in the identity is interaction and therefore, the longer the experience travels in the network, the more it tends to lose richness and trustworthiness. The details become fewer and it will be perceived as less reliable. The conclusion is that the interaction between the firms in the relationships becomes more extensive and intensive and that the connected relationships also increase in quantity, which together mean that the firm's identity in the network becomes clearer and sharper during the transition process.

The three change processes discussed follow the decentralisation and are instrumental in the movement from anonymity to identity. While search either represents the transfer of knowledge existing somewhere else or re-creation of knowledge already possessed by the firm, discovery implies not only new knowledge, but also something that was unknowable for the firm. There is nothing the firm could do when it came to discovery; the firm cannot avoid it. Discovery is essential in the transition economy, because of the anonymity that prevailed in the planned network and the turbulence caused by the change of governance. When the economy is governed through an endless set of decentralised plans instead of one centralised plan, it means that the plans cannot always correspond. The firms realise that their plans will collide and they find things of which they had no prior knowledge. The transition means that the ends and the means are recurrently redefined and re-allocated and no one has complete knowledge about what is going to happen. This unpredictability means that it is impossible to have knowledge about even a very limited range of possible developments. All this, results in that an expanded interaction with customers and suppliers becomes necessary. In this phase the interaction itself and the customers, the suppliers and their characteristics are something new and unknown for the firm. In the interaction, the firms discover things that until then has been unknown.

Partial, thin and weak relationships tend to be a good soil for novel knowledge (Hansen 1999), thus, when the network moves from anonymity to identity, discoveries are important and this development is strengthened by the turbulence. When expanding the interaction firms often have to face situations that were impossible to plan and to predict beforehand. They are unknowable for the firm and from that follows that searching after the beforehand known often turns into discovering the unknowable or as Tsoukas (1996: 22) put it: "Firms are faced with *radical uncertainty*: they do not know, they cannot, know what they need to know." Thus, discovery is an important factor of the movement towards new network logic.

Concluding Remarks

The analysis of Tipografiya does not only increase our understanding of a firm and its context, in the light of the change of governance of the Russian economy, from a planned to a market economy. It also provides insight into the nature of networks in three different economic systems. Table 10 highlights six aspects of networks in three types of economic systems. These aspects are interrelated and they describe how the networks go from simple, centralised, and tautly planned to a system of decentralised planning, where the firms' individual plans are isolated from each other, which tends to cause them to collide. Moreover, in the planned networks, the interaction in the relationships has narrow range and low intensity, that is, few of the firms' activities are actually adapted to specific counterparts.

However, the planning affects not only the interaction in the relationships, but also the dynamics and changes that take place in the planned networks. Chapter 4 observed that, in planned networks, change and interaction are often separated in time and space. The reason for this is that the firms in the relationships interact while change usually is initiated from authorities that are remote from the relationships. This means that changes that strongly effect the firms are often made by authorities that are distant from the firm's daily operations. The firms, on the other hand, do not have any incentive to change the interaction, because they are not rewarded if the interaction becomes more efficient. As the centralised and taut planning of the networks are replaced by decentralised planning, the collision of plans tends first to mean radical changes, and later that the interaction and change begin to merge and become more integrated. Changes will then spring from the interaction within the relationships rather than coming as a result of initiatives from the authorities.

Table 10: Characteristics of three types of networks.

	Planning	Interaction	Change	Use of Knowledge	Relationships and Networks	Identity
Planned networks	Simple, centralised and taut planning.	Narrow range and low intensity.	Interaction and change are separated, either small or huge changes.	Knowledge is used to preserve the current structure.	Partial relationships in static networks.	Poor and one-dimensional.
Transition networks	Decentralised and isolated planning. Chaotic collision of plans.	Expanding range and irregular performance of interaction.	Interaction and change begin to merge. Radical changes.	Knowledge is used to extensively reconstruct the network, to defend old structures or to break down old structures.	Turbulent relationships in turbulent networks, which undergoes an integration process.	Emerging and contra-dictory.
Market networks	Decentralised and mutual planning. Matching of flexible plans.	Wide range and high intensity.	Interaction and change are integrated. Incremental changes.	Knowledge is used to cause change, but within a stable structure.	Integrated relationships in stable networks.	Multi-dimensional and rich in details.

As the transition ends, it is likely that the firms begin to match their plans. The planning is still decentralised, but no longer performed in isolation; rather it is conducted as a mutual activity. Typically, the planning is also slack, and the plans provide a flexibility that the taut planning does not inhibit. The flexibility is necessary as it makes the relationships less vulnerable to disturbing elements from the surrounding network. The flexibility is also necessary as the plans now concern and integrate a much wider interaction that is usually performed with a higher intensity than in the planned and transition networks. Altogether, this development is characterised by a movement from partial relationships and static networks via turbulent relationships and networks during the transition period to integrated relationships in stable networks. Owing to the integration and stability and to the decentralised planning, change separated from interaction is difficult to make. Instead, market networks tend to be dominated by incremental and gradual changes, which often arise from the interaction and which have to fit into the interaction in the relationship.

This slow development implies a new way of using knowledge in the network. While the planned networks are static and the relationship partial, the knowledge is mostly used to preserve the current network structure, but also to keep the narrow interaction intact. This means that new knowledge is not needed and instead the planned networks are to a large extent characterised by firms using already existing and old knowledge. The situation in the transition network is likely to be almost the opposite. As the firms learn about their customers and suppliers, and as the structure inherited from the planned networks is challenged, new knowledge is widely created and used. The new knowledge created in the market networks must be balanced with the old knowledge, which results in a combination of new and old knowledge.

As there are no reasons to interact more closely or to change the interaction, the firm's identity in the network is likely to be poor and one-dimensional, or, as was argued in Chapter 4, anonymity usually prevails in planned networks. But first, firms develop rich and multi-dimensional identities in the market networks; their identities emerge as contradictory in the process where knowledge often is used in order to break down the relationships inherited from the planned networks. In a chaotic situation, where plans are colliding and radical changes tend to dominate, firms often have to discover previously unknown details about the counterparts — details that in the market network make up the firm's identity. Returning to the initial quotation, it is question of seeing customers and suppliers with new eyes.

References

Ahuja, G. (2000). Collaboration networks, structural holes, and innovation: A longitudinal study. *Administrative Science Quarterly*, *45*(3), 425, 455.

Alchian, A. A., & Allen, W. R. (1964). *Exchange and production: Theory in use*. Belmont, CA: Wadsworth.

Alchian, A. A., & Demsetz, H. (1972). Production, information cost and economic organization. *American Economic Review*, *62*(5), 777–795.

Anderson, E., & Weitz, B. (1992). The use of pledges to build and sustain commitment in distribution channels. *Journal of Marketing Research*, *29*(1), 18–34.

Anderson, J., Håkansson, H., & Johanson, J. (1994). Dyadic business relationships within a business network context. *Journal of Marketing*, *58*(4), 1–15.

Astley, W. G., & Zajac, E. J. (1990). Beyond dyadic exchange: Functional interdependence and sub-unit power. *Organization Studies*, *11*(4), 481–490.

Aukutsionek, S. (1998). Industrial barter in Russia. *Communist Economies and Economic Transformation*, *10*(2), 179–188.

Barney, J. B. (1986). Strategic factor markets: Expectations, luck and business strategy. *Management Science*, *17*(1), 99–120.

Berliner, J. S. (1952). The informal organization of the Soviet firm. *Quarterly Journal of Economics*, *66*(3), 342–365.

Berliner, J. S. (1957). *Factory and manager in the USSR*. Cambridge: Harvard University Press.

Berliner, J. S. (1976). *The innovation decision in Soviet industry*. Cambridge, MA and London, England: MIT Press.

Blanchard, O., & Kremer, M. (1997). Disorganization. *The Quarterly Journal of Economics*, *112*(4), 1091–1126.

Blankenburg-Holm, D., Eriksson, K., & Johanson, J. (1999). Creating value through mutual commitment to business network relationships. *Strategic Management Journal*, *20*(5), 467–486.

Boettke, P. J. (1993). *Why Perestroika failed: The politics and economics of socialist transformation*. London: Routledge.

Bradach, J. L., & Eccles, R. G. (1989). Price, authority and trust: From ideal types to plural forms. *Annual Review of Sociology*, *15*, 97–118.

Bridgewater, S. (1999). Network and internationalisation: The case of multinational corporations entering Ukraine. *International Business Review*, *8*(1), 99–118.

Buck, T., Filatotchev, I., & Wright, M. (1998). Agents, stakeholders and corporate governance in Russian firms. *Journal of Management Studies, 35*(1), 81–104.

Burt, R. S. (1992). *Structural holes: The social structure of competition.* Cambridge, MA: Harvard University Press.

Caldwell, B. (1997). Hayek and socialism. *Journal of Economic Literature, 35*(4), 1856–1890.

Coffey, A., & Atkinson, P. (1996). *Making sense of qualitative data: Complementary research strategies.* Thousand Oaks: Sage.

Cohen, W. M., & Levinthal, D. A. (1990). Absorptive capacity: A new perspective on learning and innovation. *Administrative Science Quarterly, 35*(1), 128–152.

Collins Cobuild English Language Dictionary (1987). London and Glasgow: Peter Collin Publishing.

Commander, S., Dolinskaya, I., & Mumssen, C. (2002). Determinants of barter in Russia: An empirical analysis. *Journal of Development Economics, 67*(2), 275–307.

Concise Oxford Dictionary of Current English (1990). (8th ed.). Oxford: Oxford University Press.

Cook, K. S., & Emerson, R. M. (1978). Power, equity and commitment in exchange networks. *American Sociological Review, 43*(5), 721–739.

Cook, K. S., Emerson, R. M., Gillmore, M. R., & Yamagishi, T. (1983). The distribution of power in exchange networks: Theory and experimental results. *American Journal of Sociology, 89*(2), 275–305.

Cyert, R. M., & March, J. G. (1963). *The behavioral theory of the firm.* Cambridge, MA: Blackwell.

Czaban, L., & Whitley, R. (2000). Incremental organizational change in a transforming society: Managing turbulence in Hungary in the 1990s. *Journal of Management Studies, 37*(3), 371–393.

Dacin, M. T., Ventrasca, M. J., & Beal, B. B. (1999). The embeddedness of organizations: Dialogue and directions. *Journal of Management, 25*(3), 317–356.

Davis, J. H., Patterson, J. D., & Grazin, I. (1996). The collapse and remergence of networks within and between republics of the former Soviet Union. *International Business Review, 5*(1), 1–21.

Dictionary of Printing and Publishing (1989). (2nd ed.). Teddington: Peter Collin Publishing.

Dierickx, I., & Cool, K. (1989). Asset stock accumulation and sustainability of competitive advantage. *Management Science, 35*(12), 1504–1511.

Dubini, P. (1990). Doing business with the Soviet Union: Understanding management practices in Soviet companies. Paper presented at the 6th IMP-conference in Milano.

Dutton, J. E., & Dukerich, J. M. (1991). Keeping an eye on the mirror: Image and identity in organizational adaptation. *Academy of Management Journal, 34*(3), 517–554.

Easton, G., & Lundgren, A. (1992). Changes in industrial networks as flow through nodes. In: B. Axelsson, & G. Easton (Eds), *Industrial networks: A new view of reality* (pp. 89–104). London: Routledge.

Eisenhardt, K. M. (1989). Building theories from case study research. *Academy of Management Review, 14*(4), 532–550.

Eliasson, G. (1998). From plan to markets. *Journal of Economic Behavior & Organization, 34*(1), 49–68.

Emerson, R. M. (1981). Social exchange theory. In: M. Rosenberg, & R. Turner (Eds), *Social psychology: Sociological perspectives* (pp. 2–65). New York: Basic Books.

Ericson, R. (1991). The classical Soviet-type economy: Nature of the system and implications for reform. *Journal of Economic Perspective, 5*(4), 11–27.

Filatotchev, I., Dyomina, N., Wright, M., & Buck, T. (2001). Effect of post-privatization governance and strategies on export intensity in the former Soviet Union. *Journal of International Business Studies, 32*(4), 858–871.

Filatotchev, I., Hoskisson, R. E., Buck, T., & Wright, M. (1996). Corporate restructuring in Russian privatizations: Implications for U.S. investors. *California Management Review, 38*(2), 87–109.

Fischer, S., & Gelb, A. (1991). The process of socialist economic transformation. *Journal of Economic Perspective, 5*(4), 91–105.

Ford, D. (Ed.) (1990). *Understanding business markets: Interaction, relationships and networks.* London: Academic Press.

Gioia, D. A., Schultz, M., & Corley, K. G. (2000). Organizational identity, image, and adaptive instability. *Academy of Management Review, 25*(1), 63–81.

Golden, P. A., Doney, P. M., Johnson, D. M., & Smith, J. R. (1995). The dynamics of a marketing orientation in transition economics: A study of Russian firms. *Journal of International Marketing, 3*(2), 24–49.

Granovetter, M. (1985). Economic action and social structure: The problem of embeddedness. *American Journal of Sociology, 91*(3), 481–510.

Granovetter, M. S. (1973). The strength of weak ties. *American Journal of Sociology, 78*(6), 1360–1380.

Grossman, G. (1977). The second economy. *Problems of Communism, 5*, 25–40.

Gurdon, M. A., & Savitt, R. (2000). Exit/voice behaviors in the Czech Republic: A longitudinal study of consumer response to market dissatisfaction. *Competition and Change, 4*(4), 401–421.

Gurdon, M. A., Savitt, R., & Pribova, M. (1999). Consumer activism in the Czech Republic: The role of exit and voice in a changing economy. *Journal of Socio-Economics, 28*(1), 3–19.

Gurkov, I. (1996). Changes of control and business re-engineering in Russian privatized companies. *The International Executive, 38*(3), 359–388.

Hägg, I., & Johanson, J. (Eds) (1982). *Företag i nätverk.* Stockholm: Studieförbundet Näringsliv och Samhälle.

Håkansson, H. (Ed.) (1982). *International marketing and purchasing: An interaction approach.* Chichester: Wiley.

Håkansson, H. (Ed.) (1987). *Industrial technological development: A network approach.* London: Croom Helm.

Håkansson, H. (1989). *Corporate technological behaviour: Cooperation and networks.* London: Routledge.

Håkansson, H. (1992). Evolution processes in industrial networks. In: B. Axelsson, & G. Easton (Eds), *Industrial networks: A new view of reality* (pp. 129–143). London: Routledge.

Håkansson, H. (1993). Networks as a mechanism to develop resources. In: P. Beije, J. Groenewegen, & O. Nuys (Eds), *Networking in Dutch industries* (pp. 207–223). Leven-Apeldorn: Garant.

Håkansson, H., & Johanson, J. (1992). A model of industrial networks. In: B. Axelsson, & G. Easton (Eds), *Industrial networks: A new view of reality* (pp. 28–34). London: Routledge.

Håkansson, H., & Johanson, J. (1993a). Industrial functions of business relationships. In: D. D. Sharma (Ed.), *Industrial networks: Advances in international marketing* (Vol. 5, pp. 13–29). Connecticut: JAI Press.

Håkansson, H., & Johanson, J. (1993b). Network as a governance structure. In: G. Grabher (Ed.), *The embedded firm: Socio-economics of industrial networks* (pp. 33–51). London: Routledge.

Håkansson, H., & Snehota, I. (1989). No business is an island. *Scandinavian Journal of Management*, *5*(3), 187–200.

Håkansson, H., & Snehota, I. (1995). *Developing relationships in business networks*. London: Routledge.

Halinen, A., Salmi, A., & Havila, V. (1999). From dyadic change to changing business networks: An analytical framework. *Journal of Management Studies*, *36*(6), 779–794.

Halinen, A., & Törnroos, J.-Å. (1998). The role of embeddedness in the evolution of business networks. *Scandinavian Journal of Management*, *14*(3), 187–205.

Hallén, L. (1986). A comparison of strategic marketing approaches. In: P. Turnbull, & J.-P. Valla (Eds), *Strategies for international industrial marketing* (pp. 235–263). London: Croom Helm.

Hallén, L., Johanson, J., & Seyed-Mohamed, N. (1991). Interfirm adaptation in business relationships. *Journal of Marketing*, *55*(2), 29–37.

Hansen, M. T. (1999). The search-transfer problem: The role of weak ties in sharing knowledge across organization subunits. *Administrative Science Quarterly*, *44*(1), 82–111.

Hayek, F. A. (1936). Economics and knowledge. *Economica*, *n.s.*(4), 33–56.

Hayek, F. A. (1945). The use of knowledge in society. *American Economic Review*, *35*(4), 519–530.

Heide, J. B., & John, G. (1990). Alliances in industrial purchasing: The determinants of joint action in buyer-supplier relationships. *Journal of Marketing Research*, *27*(1), 24–36.

Hendley, K. (1997). Legal development in post-Soviet Russia. *Post-Soviet Affairs*, *13*(3), 228–251.

Hendley, K., Ickes, B. W., Murrell, P., & Ryterman, R. (1997). Observations in the use of law by Russian enterprises. *Post-Soviet Affairs*, *13*(1), 19–41.

Holt, D. H., Ralston, D. A., & Terpstra, R. H. (1994). Constraints on capitalism in Russia: The managerial psyche, social infrastructure, and ideology. *Californian Management Review*, *36*(3), 124–141.

Hounshell, D. (1995). Hughesian history of technology and chandlerian business history: Parallels, departures, and critics. *History and Technology: An International Journal, 12,* 205–224.

Huber, P., & Wörgötter, A. (1998). Observations on Russian business networks. *Post-Soviet Affairs, 14*(1), 81–91.

Hughes, T. P. (1987). The evolution of large technological systems. In: W. E. Bijker, T. P. Hughes, & T. J. Pinch (Eds), *The social construction of technological systems: New directions in the sociology and history of technology* (pp. 51–82). Cambridge, MA: MIT Press.

Hughes, T. P. (1989). *American genesis: A century of invention and technological enthusiasm, 1870–1970.* New York, NY: Viking.

Hunt, S. D. (1991). *Modern marketing theory: Critical issues in the philosophy of marketing science.* Cincinnati: South-Western.

Johanson, J. (1966). *Svenskt kvalitetstål på utländska marknader.* Licentiate thesis, Department of Business Administration, Uppsala University, Uppsala.

Johanson, J., & Mattsson, L.-G. (1991). Strategic adaptation of firms to the European single market: A network approach. In: L.-G. Mattsson, & B. Stymne (Eds), *Corporate & industry strategies for Europe* (pp. 263–281). Amsterdam: Elsevier Science.

Johanson, J., & Mattsson, L.-G. (1992). Network position and strategic action: An analytical framework. In: B. Axelsson, & G. Easton (Eds), *Industrial networks: A new view of reality* (pp. 205–217). London: Routledge.

Johanson, J., & Vahlne, J.-E. (1990). The mechanism of internationalization. *International Marketing Review, 7*(4), 11–24.

Kirzner, I. M. (1973). *Competition and entrepreneurship.* Chicago and London: University of Chicago Press.

Kirzner, I. M. (1992). *The meaning of market process: Essays in the development of modern Austrian economics.* London: Routledge.

Kirzner, I. M. (1997). Entrepreneurial discovery and the competitive market process: An Austrian approach. *Journal of Economic Literature, 35*(1), 60–85.

Kogut, B., & Zander, U. (1992). Knowledge of the firm, combinative capabilities, and the replication of technology. *Organization Science, 3*(3), 383–397.

Kogut, B., & Zander, U. (1996). What firms do? Coordination, identity, and learning. *Organization Science, 7*(5), 502–518.

Kontorovich, V. (1999). Has new business in Russia come to halt. *Journal of Business Venturing, 14*(5/6), 451–460.

Krivogorsky, V. (2000). Corporate ownership and governance in Russia. *The International Journal of Accounting, 35*(3), 331–353.

Kumar, N., Scheer, L. K., & Steenkamp, J.-B. E. M. (1995). The effects of perceived interdependence on dealer attitudes. *Journal of Marketing Research, 32*(3), 348–356.

Kvale, S. (1997). *Den kvalitativa forskningsintervjun.* Lund: Studentlitteratur.

Lachmann, L. M. (1977). *Capital, expectations and the market process.* Kansas City: Sheed Andrews and McMeel.

Lachmann, L. M. (1986). *The market as an economic process.* Oxford: Basil Blackwell.

Lane, P. J., & Lubatkin, M. (1998). Relative absorptive capacity and interorganizational learning. *Strategic Management Journal, 19*(5), 461–477.

Ledeneva, A. (1998). *Russia's economy of favours: Blat, networking and informal exchange.* Cambridge: Cambridge University Press.

Lundgren, A. (1991). *Technological innovation and industrial evolution – The emergence of industrial networks.* Doctoral dissertation, The Economic Research Institute, Stockholm School of Economics, Stockholm.

Luthans, F., Welsh, D. H. B., & Rosenkrantz, S. A. (1993). What do Russian managers really do? An observational study with comparisons to U.S. managers. *Journal of International Business Studies, 24*(4), 741–761.

Mahoney, J. T., & Pandian, J. R. (1992). The resource-based view within conversation of strategic management. *Strategic Management Journal, 13*(5), 363–380.

March, J. G. (1991). Exploration and exploitation in organizational learning. *Organization Science, 2*(1), 71–87.

Mattsson, L.-G. (1993). The role of marketing for the transformation of a centrally planned economy to a market economy. In: H. C. Blomqvist, C. Grönroos, & L. Lindqvist (Eds), *Economics and marketing eassays in honour of Gösta Mickwitz* (pp. 181–196). Helsinki: Svenska handelshögskolan.

McCarthy, D. J., & Puffer, S. M. (1995). 'Diamonds and rust' on Russia's road to privatization: The profits and pitfalls for western managers. *Columbia Journal of World Business, 30*(3), 56–69.

McCarthy, D. J., Puffer, S., & Naumov, A. I. (2000). Russia's retreat to statization and the implication for business. *Journal of World Business, 35*(3), 256–274.

Moran, P., & Ghoshal, S. (1999). Markets, firms and the process of economic development. *Academy of Management Review, 24*(3), 390–412.

Nove, A. (1984). *The Soviet economic system* (2nd ed.). London: George Allen & Unwin.

Oliver, R. L. (1980). A cognitive model of the antecedents and consequences of satisfaction decisions. *Journal of Marketing Research, 17*(4), 460–469.

Peng, M. W. (2001). How entrepreneurs create wealth in transition economies. *Academy of Management Executive, 15*(1), 95–108.

Peng, M. W., & Heath, P. S. (1996). The growth of the firm in planned economies in transition: Institutions, organizations, and strategic choice. *Academy of Management Review, 21*(2), 492–528.

Penrose, E. (1959). *The theory of the growth of the firm.* London: Basil Blackwell.

Peteraf, M. (1993). The cornerstones of competitive advantage: A resource-based view. *Strategic Management Journal, 14*(3), 179–191.

Pettigrew, A. M. (1987). Context and action in the transformation of the firm. *Journal of Management Studies, 24*(6), 649–670.

Pettigrew, A. M. (1990). Longitudinal field research on change theory and practice. *Organization Science, 1*(3), 267–291.

Pettigrew, A. M. (1992). The character and significance of strategy process research. *Strategic Management Journal, 13*(8), 5–16.

Pettigrew, A. M. (1997). What is a processual analysis? *Scandinavian Journal of Management, 13*(4), 337–348.

Poser, J. (1998). Monetary disruptions and the emergence of barter in FSU economies. *Communist Economies and Economic Transformation, 10*(2), 157–177.

Potts, N. (1999). Privatisation: A false hope. *The International Journal of Public Sector Management, 12*(5), 388–409.

Powell, W. W. (1990). Neither market nor hierarchy: Network forms of organization. In: L. L. Cummings, & B. M. Staw (Eds), *Research in organizational behaviour* (Vol. 12, pp. 295–336). Greenwich: JAI Press.

Powell, W. W., Koput, K. W., & Smith-Doerr, L. (1996). Interorganizational collaboration and the locus of innovation: Network of learning in biotechnology. *Administrative Science Quarterly, 41*(1), 116–145.

Puffer, M. S., & McCarthy, D. J. (1995). Finding the common ground in Russian and American business ethics. *Californian Management Review, 37*(2), 29–46.

Puffer, S. M., & McCarthy, D. J. (2001). Navigating the hostile maze: A framework for Russian entrepreneurship. *Academy of Management Executive, 15*(4), 24–36.

Richardson, G. B. (1972). The organisation of industry. *The Economic Journal, 82*(327), 883–896.

Richardson, G. B. (1995). The theory of the market economy. *Revue Economique, 6*, 1487–1496.

Ruble, B. A., & Popson, N. (1998). The Westernization of a Russian province: The case of Novgorod. *Post-Soviet Geography and Economics, 39*(8), 433–446.

Salmi, A. (1996). Russian networks in transition: Implications for managers. *Industrial Marketing Management, 25*(1), 37–45.

Salmi, A. (2000). Entry into turbulent business networks: The case of a Western company on the Estonian market. *European Journal of Marketing, 34*(11/12), 1374–1390.

Salmi, A., & Mattsson, L.-G. (1998). Overlapping social and business networks and dynamics of transformation in Russia. Paper presented at the 14th IMP-conference in Turku.

Salmi, A., & Möller, K. (1994). Business strategy during dramatic environmental change: A network approach for analysing firm-level adaptation to the Soviet economic reform. In: P. J. Buckley, & P. N. Ghauri (Eds), *The economics of change in East and Central Europe: Its impact on international business* (pp. 105–130). London: Academic Press.

Sedaitis, J. B. (1997). Networks in market transitions: Managerial constraints in post-Soviet commodity markets. *International Studies of Management and Organization, 27*(1), 61–83.

Seidel, J. P., & Kelle, U. (1995). Different functions of coding in the analysis of textual data. In: U. Kelle (Ed.), *Computer-aided qualitative data analysis: Theory, methods and practise* (pp. 113–128). London: Sage.

Shama, A. (1992). The transformation of Russian management: A qualitative and theory building approach. *International Business Review, 9*(5), 43–59.

Smallbone, D., & Welter, F. (2001). The distinctiveness of entrepreneurship in transition economies. *Small Business Economics, 16*(4), 249–262.

Snehota, I. (1990). *Notes on a theory of a business enterprise.* Doctoral dissertation, Department of Business Administration, Uppsala University, Uppsala.

Snehota, I. (1993). Market as network and the nature of the market process. In: D. D. Sharma (Ed.), *Industrial networks: Advances in international marketing* (Vol. 5, pp. 31–41). Connecticut: JAI Press.

Törnroos, J.-Å., & Nieminen, J. (1999). *Business entry in eastern Europe: A network and learning approach.* Helsinki: Kikimora Publications.

Tsoukas, H. (1996). The firm as a distributed knowledge system: A constructionist approach. *Strategic Management Journal*, 11–25.

Turnbull, P., & Valla, J. P. (Eds) (1986). *Strategies for international industrial marketing.* London: Croom Helm.

Uzzi, B. (1997). Social structure and competition in interfirm networks: The paradox of embeddedness. *Administrative Science Quarterly*, 42(1), 35–67.

Van de Ven, A. H. (1992). Suggestions for studying strategy processes: A research note. *Strategic Management Journal*, 13(8), 169–188.

Vlachoutsicos, C., & Lawrence, P. (1990a). *Behind the factory walls: Decision making in Soviet and U.S. enterprises.* Boston, MA: Harvard Business School Press.

Vlachoutsicos, C., & Lawrence, P. (1990b). What we don't know about Soviet management. *Harvard Business Review*, 68(6), 50–63.

von Hippel, E. (1988). *The sources of innovation.* New York: Oxford University Press.

von Hippel, E. (1998, May). Economics of product development by users: The impact of "sticky" local information. *Management Science*, 44(5), 629–644.

von Hippel, E., & Tyre, M. J. (1995). How learning by doing is done: Problem identification in novel process equipment. *Research Policy*, 24(1), 1–12.

Weick, K. (1995). *Sensemaking in organizations.* Thousand Oaks, CA: Sage.

Williamson, O. E. (1975). *Market and hierarchies: Analysis and antitrust implications.* New York: Free Press.

Williamson, O. E. (1985). *The economic institutions of capitalism.* New York: Free Press.

Yin, R. K. (1994). *Case study research: Design and methods.* Thousand Oaks, CA: Sage.

Appendix A: Key Words

Block	Piece of metal with a design in relief of the surface, used for printing an illustration by letterpress.
Colour separation	Separating the various colours from a design into the process colours to make a series of four films for printing.
Composition	Creating typeset text, either by using metal type or by keyboarding on a computer typesetter.
Cylinder press	Printer where the paper is carried on a fixed cylinder which presses it onto the flat forms containing the inked type.
Low resolution	Ability to display pre-set shapes on the screen rather than individual pixels.
Matrix	Copper mould used to cast a piece of metal type or mould made from a page of standing metal type.
Offset printing	Printing method that transfers the ink to image via a second cylinder.
Photo polymer plate	Printing plate which has a layer of photosensitive plastic bonded to a flexible metal plate.
Plate	Printing surface with an image on it, that conveys the ink to the paper.
Relief printing	Printing process in which the ink is held on a raised image such as the metal character in letterpress printing or on a woodcut block.
Repro	Finished artwork or camera-ready copy, ready for filming and printing, process of achieving this by camerawork or scanning.
Rotary press	Printing press whose printing plate is curved and attached to a cylinder.
Screen process printing	The design is inked through a fine screen parts, of which are covered by printing a stencil to prevent the ink passing through.
Setting	Action of composing text into typeset characters.
Sheet fed press	Printing press which takes single sheets of paper, as opposed to a web press which takes reels of papers.
Stereotype	Duplicate printing plate, cast in metal or plastic from a mould taken from metal type.
Type	A single metal letter or character; metal slugs with raised characters used for printing.

Source: Dictionary of Printing and Publishing, Peter Collin Publishing, 2nd edition, 1989.

Appendix B: Question Guide

INTERNATIONAL BUSINESS OBSERVATORY
Data Collection Format:
Parts:
1. The Business Unit
2. Customer Base
3. Key Customer/3
4. Supplier Base
5. Key Supplier/3
6. Network couplings?

The Company or Business Unit

Products   What are the five major products (product groups) of the company; their relative importance in sales (% of sales last year); how has the composition of sales changed over the last two years?

Product (Product Group)	% of Sales	Change?
1	....	
2	....	
3	....	
4	....	
5	....	
	100	

Technologies   Number of production sites? Location of the production sites: (% abroad?). What are the five main (major?) "technologies" in the production process of the company? (in terms of % of cost and value of investments?).

Technology	% of Total Costs	Value of Investments
a............................. ..	. ... ..	. ...
b............................. ..	. ... ..	. ...
c..........................	. ... ..	. ...
d.......................... . ..	. ... ..	. ...
e.............................	. ... ..	. ...

In what technology have major investments been made in the last three years? Type of production process: unit, small batch, process, series?

Product/technology matrix   Critical dependencies expressed as dominant technology element for product performance or for the costs of the product . . .?

Products		Technologies				
		a……..	b……..	c……..	d……..	e……..
1						
2						
3						
4						
5						
% of costs						

Organisation   What is the number of employees and split per functions ("categories"): Support, procurement, production, sales? How many of each function (category) have "regular" contact with customers, suppliers?

Total number of employees	Total number	Technicians in contact with	
		Customers	Suppliers
Of which			
"production"	………….…	…………. ..	…………. ..
"sales"	………….…	…………. ..	…………. ..
"procurement"	………….…	…………. ..	…………. ..
"support"	………….…	…………. ..	…………. ..
Employees abroad			

External organisation   Is the company (unit) part of a group? How big a part? How much sold/bought from the group? Do sales, purchasing or technical coordination exist at group level? HQ location? Are there other relationships of importance to the overall development of the company (e.g. cooperation agreements, joint-ventures etc.)?

Size and performance   Three years including the current year, or two years last year and the year before, alternatively now and three years ago?

Number of employees

. . ..

Sales development $

. . ..

Gross profit development $ (before tax)

. . ..

Investments

. . ..

Value of assets

. . ..

Sales and Customer Base

General

Total number of customers   Change
          –100   100–500   500–1000   1000–
How many customers account for 86% of the total sales?

0–10   11–20   21–30   31–50   51–100   100–
(Change in the concentration?)

What % of sales to new customers? (less than two years) . . . .%

Composition of sales: (sold locally within 100 km from the company's location? domestic, close foreign (e.g. Europe), overseas).

Area	Sales	+/–
Local		
Domestic		
Foreign		
Overseas		

Top 10 customers   % share of total sales . . . . . .

Customer	Sales $	Change	Products	Age	Size	Position	Location
1							
2							
3							
4							
5							
6							
7							
8							
9							
10							

Change: In invoiced sales, −10%, 5/10%, −0/5%, +/−0%, + 0/5%, +5/10%, +10−%.

Products: How many of the main products (product groups)?

Age: –3, 3–6, 6– years.

Size: Turnover: −10 ml$, 10–50 ml$, 50–200 ml$, 200–1000 ml$, 1006 ml$.

Status: Sole, main, one of the main, second?

Location: Total, national, European, other foreign?

Key Customer

Background

Name:
Type: (Independent company, division, part of a group . . .?).
Location: (HQ or the site where deliveries are made?).
Country. . . . .
Customers main product type. . . . . .and type of production technology
. . . .

Size (estimated turn-over last years).

–10ml$	10–50ml$	50–200ml$	200–1000ml$	1000–ml$

(or estimated number of employees?)

. . . .

The overall development of the company last three years?
   –growth?
   –profitability? (closed alternatives).
Degree of internationalisation? (sales).
Do ownership links exist between the company and the customer?
Formalization (of the contract)?

Nature of the relationship

How long has the Company been a customer?
. . . . .years

What are the main products sold to this customer? (same terms as the main product/product groups in Part 1). How did the composition of the sales change over the last two years?

Product	%	Change
. . . .	. . . .	. . . .
. . . .	. . . .	. . . .
. . . .	. . . .	. . . .
. . . .	. . . .	. . . .
. . . .	. . . .	. . . .

How do they enter the production process of the customer:?

material   component   equipment   "resold"

Degree of standardisation for the main product (product group):
Standard. . . . . .customers' own design
Does the customer use other suppliers for this product (substitutes)?
If yes, what is the "status" of the company as supplier?
Sole supplier   main supplier   one of the main suppliers   minor supplier
(share of the need)
How many other "suitable" suppliers of the same or substitute product to this customer exist?
Where are these located?
% of sales of the main product this customer account for?. . . . .

Change in the total of sales to this customer last two years

−10	−2–10	−0–2	+2–10	+10–

Volume change? Relative price level change?

Contact pattern Frequency of deliveries? Order cycle? (Length?)

How many persons from the following functions have regular contact with this customer

	Number of Persons
Sales	. . . .
Production	. . . .
Procurement	. . . .
Support	. . . .
Technicians	. . . .

Content of the relationship

Products				
1				
2				
3				
4				
5				

Relationship effects

What technology is critical for the product performance (product quality) for this customer?

What technology is critical for the cost performance for this customer?

Purchasing and the Supplier Base

General

Total purchase last year: .... $ (excluding investments)

of which
  goods   ....
  services   ....

value of investments last year? ....$

Total number of suppliers:

−100   100–200   200–500   500–1000   1000–

How many suppliers account for 80% of the total purchases?

0–10	11–20	21–30	31–50	51–100	100–500	500–

How much of the total purchasing accounts for new suppliers (less than two years)? ....%

How much bought locally? Direct imports?

The 10 major suppliers

Supplier	Purchase $	Change	Products	Age	Size	Position	Location
1							
2							
3							
4							
5							
6							
7							
8							
9							
10							

Change: In invoiced sales, −10%, −5/10%, −0/5%, +/−0, +5/10%, +5/10%, +10%

Products: How many of the main products (product groups)?

Age: –3, 3–6, 6– years

Size: Turnover –10ml$, 10–50ml$, 50–200ml$, 200–1000ml$,1000–ml$

Status: Sole, main, one of the main, second?

Location: Local, national, European, other foreign?

Key Supplier

Background

Name:
Type: Independent company, division, part of a group. . ...?
Location: The site where supplied products are produced ? country. . . . .
Main product . . . .and type of production technology . . . .
. ...?
Size: Or estimated turnover of employees?

–10ml$	10–50ml$	50–200ml$	200–1000ml$	1000–ml$

The overall development of the company last three years?
    – growth?
    – profitability? (closed alternatives)
Degree of internationalisation (sales)? Do ownership links to the supplier exist?
Formalisation? (of the contract?) How long has the company been supplier?
. . ...years

Content of the relationship   What are the main products bought from this supplier? (How did the composition of supplies change during the last two years?)

Product	%	Change
. . . .	. . . .	. . . .
. . . .	. . . .	. . . .
. . . .	. . . .	. . . .
. . . .	. . . .	. . . .
. . . .	. . . .	. . . .

Degree of standardisation for the main product (product group): standard
. . . . our own specification and design

How does the main product (s?) enter the production process of the customer?:

material   component   equipment   "resold"

Which of the company's technologies is primarily affected by products supplied by this customer? Which of the company's products does the supplier product affect? (and how does it enter the products production process: material, component, equipment, supplies?)

Technologies

products					
1					
2					
3					
4					
5					

Nature of the relationship   Are other suppliers used for the main product (substitutes)? If yes, what is the "status" of the suppliers?

sole supplier	main supplier	one of the main suppliers	minor supplier (share of the need?)

How many other "suitable" suppliers exist? (Where are these located?)
% of suppliers sales we account for?. . . . .
Change in the total of purchases from this supplier last two years
1–10 1–2–10 1–0–2 1+0–2 1+2–10 1 +10– 1
Volume change? Relative price level change?

Contact pattern   Frequency of deliveries? Order cycle? (length?) How many persons from the following functions have regular contact with this supplier: Number of persons

Procurement   . . . .
Production   . . . .
Sales   . . . .
Support   . . . .

Interdependence (Couplings)

Author Index

Subject Index

New Multinational
Network Sharing

Volume 5 in

LMX Leadership: The Series

Series Editor:
George B. Graen
University of Illinois, C-U

LMX Leadership: The Series

George B. Graen, Series Editor

Volume 1: Dealing with Diversity (2003)
edited by George B. Graen

Volume 2: New Frontiers of Leadership (2004)
edited by George B. Graen

Volume 3: Global Organizing Designs (2005)
edited by George B. Graen and Joan A. Graen

Volume 4: Sharing Network Leadership (2006)
edited by George B. Graen and Joan A. Graen

Volume 5: New Multinational Network Sharing (2007)
edited by George B. Graen and Joan A. Graen

New Multinational Network Sharing

edited by

George B. Graen

Emeritus, University of Illinois, C-U

and

Joni A. Graen

Graen & Associates

≡IAP

Information Age Publishing, Inc.
Charlotte, North Carolina • www.infoagepub.com

Library of Congress Cataloging-in-Publication Data

New multinational network sharing / edited by George B. Graen and Joni A.
Graen.
p. cm. — (LMX leadership)
Includes bibliographical references.
ISBN 978-1-59311-771-9 (pbk.) — ISBN 978-1-59311-772-6 (hardcover)
1. Leadership. 2. Business networks. 3. Interorganizational relations.
I. Graen, George B. II. Graen, Joni A.
HD57.7.N4894 2007
658.4'092—dc22

2007023796

ISBN 13: 978-1-59311-771-9 (pbk.)
ISBN 13: 978-1-59311-772-6 (hardcover)
ISBN 10:　　1-59311-771-X (pbk.)
ISBN 10:　　1-59311-772-8 (hardcover)

LIST OF CONTRIBUTORS

Yi Feng Chen	Lingnan University, Hong Kong
Ziguang Chen	City University of Hong Kong
Jennifer M. Ferreter	Baruch College, City University of New York
Yitzhak Fried	Whitman School of Management, Syracuse
George B. Graen	University of Illinois, C-U, Emeritus
Michael R. Graen	Procter & Gamble, Fayetteville
Wing Lam	The Hong Kong Polytechnic University
Gregory Laurence	Whitman School of Management, Syracuse
Kenneth S. Law	The Chinese University of Hong Kong
Ariel S. Levi	Wayne State University, Detroit
Xuefeng Liu	Guanghua School of Management, Beijing
Loren J. Naidoo	Baruch College, City University of New York
Chunyan Peng	Lingnan University, Hong Kong
Charles A. Scherbaum	Baruch College, City University of New York
Dean Tjosvold	Lingnan University, Hong Kong
Hui Wang	Guanghua School of Management, Beijing

CONTENTS

FOREWORD

This book employs a network-centric approach to the new field of multinational leadership and network sharing. Networks go beyond teams but may include teams of various types from homogeneous project teams to multinational strategy teams and every type of team between. Conventional wisdom was that nothing larger than a relatively small team could be led effectively because the number of relationships between people is about one half of the square of the size of the team. For a team in which every member depends on every other member, the number of interdependent relationships becomes overwhelming with relatively small team sizes. Fortunately recent technical advances in network analysis and multicultural cooperation have been developed to rescue us from mind boggling bombardments of everyone trying to communicate over all others at once. Merely thinking about such a Kafkaesque situation hurts our heads. Armed with these two breakthroughs fairly large networks, both national and multinational, can be led effectively with appropriate selection and training. This book furthers our attempts to make functional networks perform their promise of becoming "superteams."

New Multinational Network Sharing
p. ix
Copyright © 2007 by Information Age Publishing
All rights of reproduction in any form reserved.

PREFACE

Our small globe is shrinking at an accelerating rate due to new technology. Thanks to new satellites we can see and communicate over the whole world in real time, we can send money around the world with a few taps of a keyboard, and people jet around the globe in hours. We increasingly understand that China will be our giant unknown neighbor but potentially our largest trading partner within a few years. On the dark side, we are forced by often shocking events to admit that other nations have deeply embedded cultures for which they willingly die. These cultures must be acknowledged and understood as different than our own or we will continue to insult them or worse. Unfortunately, we cannot empathize with our Chinese friends for example because we Americans are "multinationally challenged." We learn only English and we expect all others to learn and use our language. Perhaps, we don't feel the need to understand and deal with other cultures in that we have not yet developed a true classical culture of our mere 231 years of existence beyond our internationally admired unifying constitution and legal system. Historically, immigrants from other nations acquired our language and legal system or paid the economic price. We expect the world to deal with us similarly. These dysfunctional practices of our upbringing should be put aside in favor of our acknowledgement that national cultures can be extremely important to our foreign friend's and our well-being. With the world shrinking, we must learn how to cooperate with colleagues from other countries in third culture ways. We can do it now or hide behind our great

New Multinational Network Sharing
pp. xi–xii
Copyright © 2007 by Information Age Publishing

walls as did China. This book is dedicated to our getting on with it without fear.

We would like to thank the contributors to title for their great work, patience, and dedication to the completion of this volume. Also, we thank George Johnson, publisher of Information Age Publishing for his guidance, patience, and production assistance.

On behalf of the contributors to this project, we respectfully dedicate this volume to George's parents and siblings, Clarence, Mary, Jim, Betty, John, and Richard Graen. We also dedicate the volume to Joni's siblings, Barbara Melchior and in memory of Scuss and her twin sister Jane Melchior.

CHAPTER 1

NEW GENOTYPE FOR ENHANCING SHARED NETWORK LEADERSHIP

George B. Graen

New approaches for cultivating and leading communications networks take a more human interaction approach to the effective transmission of needed knowledge than do traditional approaches. New approaches emphasize the building and maintenance of what are called "leadership sharing communications networks," whereas, traditional approaches emphasized noise and other transmission distorting factors. The following quote from a communication consultant makes our point.

> In business and innovation, communications have one primary, overriding purpose—to build relationships. Not to inform or persuade, not to plan or contract, not to document or account, not to direct or report, not to buy or sell, but to build lasting relationships. Hard to accept, isn't it? That means that product brochures are not really about products. Business plans not about businesses. Project reviews not about projects. Sales calls not about sales. (G. Lunquest, personal communication, December 21, 2006)

New Multinational Network Sharing
pp. 1–22
Copyright © 2007 by Information Age Publishing

INTRODUCTION

Most employers of college graduates look for at least two critical skills in new hires, communications and dependability. Unfortunately, some of the more technically competent in terms of grade point average (GPA) are passed over because of a weakness on either of these two critical skills. In addition and equally important, this chapter is about how a college student with an average grade point can become a person that employers will hire for the better jobs. This chapter is about both communications and dependability in an organization. It goes beyond the fundamental skills of speaking, writing, and informational technology to constructing and maintaining high speed, ego-based communications networks from your first job until retirement.

We documented the critical need for participation in informal communication networks in an early investigation of the effectiveness of top management pyramid of 75 managers and executives including the CEO (Graen, 1989). This corporation had experienced a slow but steady atrophy of its informal communications networks until many were confused and expressed frustration in not getting a clear sense of job mastery. Over the years with a succession of distant and autocratic CEOs, the lower managers followed the model set by the CEOs. Consequently, superiors did not communicate informally very often with their teams, peers within the same unit did not cooperate informally, and people in mission-interdependent positions did not communicate fully about their common interests.

The pyramid could be split into several categories in terms of sharing network leadership. Those who did share felt a sense of both position and mission achievement, were embedded in a number of informal mission-oriented networks, and were seen by others as influential and "together."

What we discovered while interviewing them was that the more they shared mission-oriented networks, the more influential they were seen by others who knew them. Managers who shared very few networks were seen by those who admitted knowing them as ruling their fiefdoms but being mainly outside of the informal communications networks. Many of the managers reporting directly to these managers also showed the same characteristics. What distinguished these managers was their participation in informal mission-oriented communications networks.

These findings alerted us to the vital process of informal, mission-oriented communication networks to what we call leadership in organizations. Those who can readily plug their "human computers" into all needed networks will be seen as informal leaders at times. In contrast, those who are unplugged from the networks remain "out of the loop" on needed mission information. These findings also brought home to us the power of informal human relationships in communications network acceptance or rejection. How do you get plugged into the needed mission-oriented, informal communications networks? This clearly may be one process that separates the fast-track managers and the high performance teams. This chapter and indeed this book are about this question for both domestic and multinational ventures. Based on our experience teaching this emergent process, we expect some readers to respond that they have done this successfully and others to respond that they do not do well at developing informal, mission-oriented relationships. Consequently, they never get plugged into enough of these communications networks. We also find that one can learn these interpersonal skills well enough to improve both one's career prospects and one's team contributions.

Graens and their colleagues (Graen & Graen, 2006) have shown that the proper communication networks are contributors to both job and career success and to overall team effectiveness. But, what are the proper networks? Before we discuss this key question, let us put together a straightforward framework for conceptualizing communications networks.

COMMUNICATIONS FRAMEWORK

Human organizational communications are messages sent and received containing both information and tone. A base communication requires a sender, a communications link, and a receiver. Lacking any one of these three components is not complete communications. As shown in Figure 1.1, communications within and between organizational members are divided into those formally specified often in writing and those that informally emerge through human interaction about the work of the organization (unwritten). Furthermore, both formal and informal communications can be divided into instrumental and expressive. Instrumental refers to doing some work and expressive means to add a personal touch. For our purposes, this is detailed enough for the formal, but we shall precede one division more for the informal. The informal instrumental and expressive can be divided further into offers or requests for work advice, for work assistance, for advice on personal problems, and for friendship. At this point, communications can create reputations and relationships of dependability. Those individuals who understand how to develop an authentic and trustworthy collegial relationship can use informal instrumental communications to offer and request both work assistance and work advice. In contrast, most individuals can offer or request both personal advice and friendship. We will focus this chapter first on the two

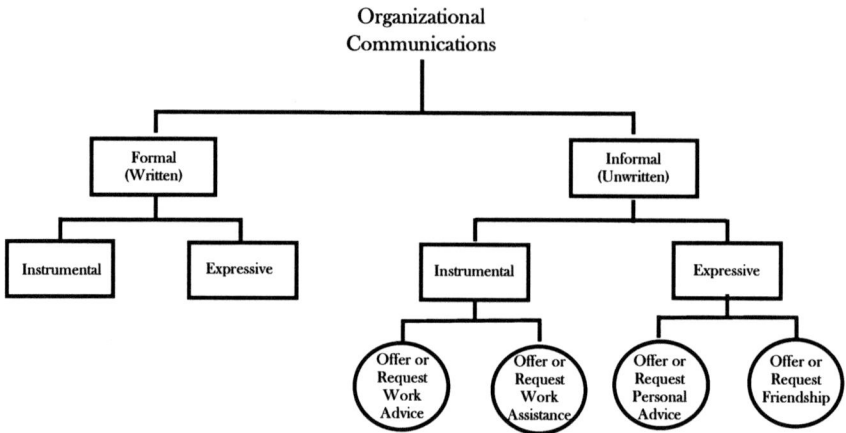

Figure 1.1.   Comminications framework.

instrumental activities. Before we do this, we need to discuss communications networks.

Networks

Eighty-five percent of all researched decisions in organizations involve getting advice from other people rather than searching relevant data bases (Doz, Santos, & Wilkamson, 2001). For this reason, networks are constructed carefully one link at a time in an organization involving a sender, a link, and a receiver. Beginning with the first day on the job network opportunities emerge. Only the foolish new employees would commit to any network until they understand the nature of the various networks. Membership in some networks may be detrimental to one's career by aligning one with a discredited network. Before any link is forged with a colleague the wise new employee assesses the attached network for hidden costs and if an error is made, it can be pruned quickly.

As shown in Figure 1.2, an ego network represents the focal person and those people who are directly connected in the network of communications. An extended ego network includes all those people who are connected to the ego by at least two lengths. In the example, Mike is linked to the leader via the link with Marcus (two links) and the leader, Marty and Marcus represent a tirade. Note that no links directly connect Mike with Marty, or the two with Jessie, or connect Jessie, Marty, Mike, or Marcus. These missing links are called network holes. The leader and Marcus are

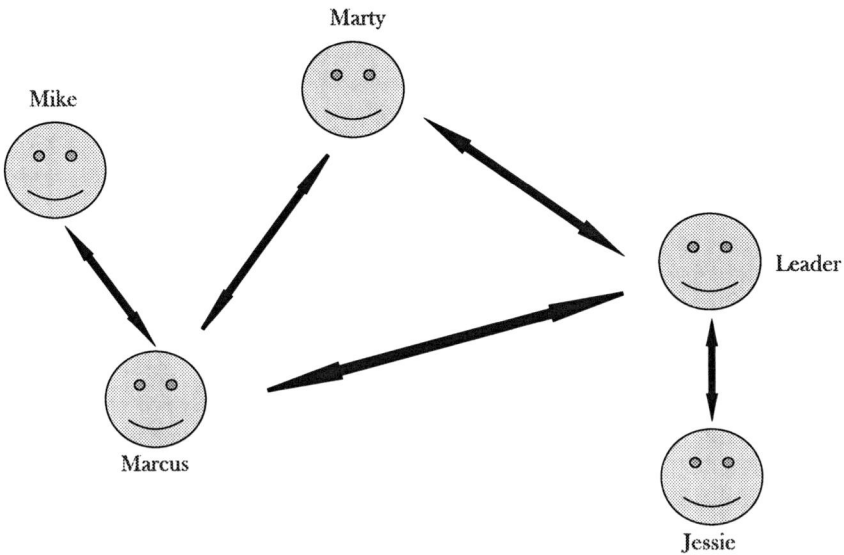

Figure 1.2.   Dyads, triads, and indirect relationships.

most central with the most links and Jessie and Mike are isolates with only one link to the core. These networks can be analyzed easily by available computer programs (Krackhardt & Hanson, 1993). Thus, employee's managers and executives must learn to think in terms of networks of different kinds and the overlap between and among them (Gibbons & Grover, 2006).

Leadership Sharing Networks

Now that we understand how networks are described in terms of links or relationships, we shall focus on the critical informal instrumental communication links. These links may become the web that leads into competence networks. A competence network is an informal communications network of people who get the impossible done and keeps the organization functioning. It is comprised of real doers who know how to successfully bypass formal deadends and accomplish things in extra organizational manners. These networks are difficult to join because new candidates must prove themselves worthy under fire, and the tests are unannounced and often unfair.

Competence networks are constructed from informal, instrumental communications links by sharing leadership on a project or a job problem. This is begun by offering to or requesting work assistance or work advice of a colleague and his or her acceptance. Such offers or requests may grow into a shared leadership relationship over repeated exchanges through offering work assistance or advice on a job problem to a colleague and having it accepted and their reciprocating your kindness. This informally accepted interdependence usually starts with specific small problems and can successively grow to include much larger activities. As the exchanges become increasingly more complex, mutual respect and trust expand until the morphing of the exchanges from mutually instrumental to mutually expressive. At this point, the leadership sharing is between close friends. Such relationships once established may last over the entire lives of the two people.

At the extreme of this process are networks of dyads (two-person links) that depend on each other for their very lives, such as surgical teams, soldiers, fire rescue workers, and police. These jobs put people in harm's way and leadership sharing at the highest level is demanded. Below this are highly competitive units of organizations in turbulent environments. Lower still are the situations of career cooperation and competition in our life. Below this are professional sports. We are educated to the fact that our careers are a series of progressively more difficult competitions with our peers and yet we must cooperate with them. The answer to this conundrum is that we cooperate within our leadership sharing networks and compete with our peers outside them. Our studies of entire careers of college graduates who joined the same large, multinational corporation in 1962 and retired in 2002 showed that those who most effectively practiced leadership sharing networking were most successful throughout their careers in terms of speed of promotion and compensation (Graen, Dharwadkar, Grewal, & Wakabayashi 2006).

Leadership sharing should begin with the most significant others to an employee and this usually includes the direct report (supervisor). It should proceed to the next most significant other and then the next and so on. Periodically new relationships will be added as needed until one's leadership networks cover all relevant functions inside and outside the employing organization. One way to look at your leadership sharing networks is that these are the people who will help you when you need them most. Those outside of your networks likely will turn you and your problems away with "sorry that's not my job," but those inside will assure you that "your problem is my problem and we'll get it solved somehow."

In this way, leadership sharing relationships in which the parties agree to share who leads and who follows on various parts of projects augment the power of the formal organization to get things done. In these leadership sharing exchanges, who leads and who follows to support frequently are based on who has needed appropriate skills and information, and influence resources. In these networks, all get to lead some of the time. A network of these is called *Leadership Sharing Networks*. These networks are the keys to understanding emergent events, because when organizations are faced with new opportunities, whether positive or negative, the relevant leadership sharing networks are activated to cope. These networks, once activated, can be monitored to identify and map the organization's reaction. The wise employee can enhance his or her career progress by identifying, monitoring, and joining local networks.

The earliest links will be with a new employee's direct supervisor, unit peers, and those whose work is interdependent. Choices of links must be made quickly, but the offers should be carefully assessed for the long term. How can a new employee make such career relevant decisions quickly. Below are some things that may help.

Supervisor Strategies

Supervisor can be categorized into three strategies for communication relationship development and employees reporting to supervisors also can be categorized into three categories according to Graen (2006) as shown in Figure 1.3. Supervisor's strategies for leadership sharing communications relations with his or her team are (a) Team Maker, who makes initial offers to all team members, (b) Cherry Picker, who makes offers only to the chosen few, (c) Isolate, who makes no offer to any team member. The first strategy is the most work for both the supervisor and the team members who accept. The second strategy is less work but returns less benefit. Finally, the no offer strategy is no work and no benefits. In contrast, when the supervisor focuses on his or her nonteam members in the organization, the strategy of choice may be different. For many situations the supervisor should use strategy *a* for the team and strategy *b* for outside the team, because we find supervisors should be seen as fair beyond a doubt with his or her team but selective outside the team (Graen, Hui, & Taylor, 2004).

Follower's Strategies

Employees who report directly to a supervisor should make offers to selective people including the supervisor and use the cherry picker strategy. The shotgun strategy of offering to all is to risk in that poor choices of network members have negative consequences on better choices. Therefore, the cherry picker strategy implies that one picks carefully based on respect of capabilities and trust in dependability. Those colleagues who do

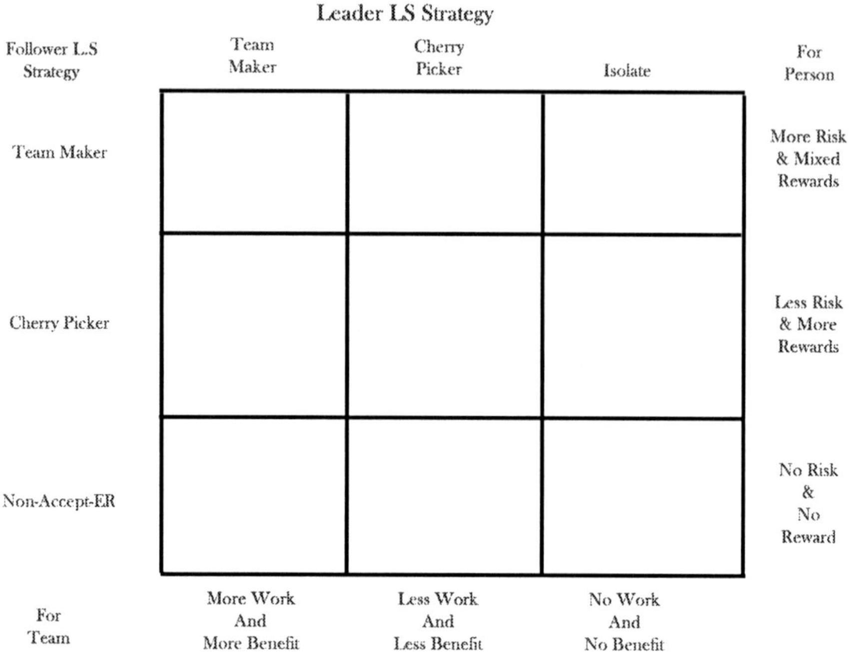

Leader LS Strategy

Follower L.S Strategy	Team Maker	Cherry Picker	Isolate	For Person
Team Maker				More Risk & Mixed Rewards
Cherry Picker				Less Risk & More Rewards
Non-Accept-ER				No Risk & No Reward
For Team	More Work And More Benefit	Less Work And Less Benefit	No Work And No Benefit	

Figure 1.3.   Leadership sharing strategies of leader and follower.

not pass the tests at any point are dropped from one's network. Clearly, the process needs to be discussed and should not be attempted by the nonserious employee. Next we turn to some dos and don'ts.

Some dos and don'ts for the newcomers are as follows.

1. Do join the correct leadership sharing (LS) networks as soon as feasible and choose wisely.
2. Don't join the wrong LS networks, because some links can be poison to your effectiveness.
3. Do commit to chosen LS network links until proven faulty and then cut ties quickly and publicly.
4. Do nurture valuable LS network links to grow them to maturity.
5. Do maintain mature links by paying dues regularly.
6. Don't forget to forge triads and teams within your networks.
7. Do grow ever larger and more diverse LS networks inside and outside of your organization.
8. Do understand that LS networks keep the entire organization functioning and they change over time.

9. Don't forget that this is a well-researched communications theory, but it must be applied carefully and everyone makes mistakes.

Bottom Line

The research is clear, people use other people much more than data bases for making decisions at work and the people that they consult are key member of the LS network. Why should this be the case? Databases supply more valid facts than experts, but they cannot make the necessary value judgments to back up a critical decision in a turbulent situation.

In addition to decision support, your LS network can supply other valuable resources such as:

1. Helping hands from others on your job problems.
2. Inside information about the organization.
3. Influence beyond your job.
4. Latitude in your use of resources.
5. Access to other's resources.
6. Opportunities to make a difference.
7. Support by others.

WHAT OTHERS SEEK OF YOU AND YOU SHOULD SEEK OF OTHERS

We asked over one thousand managers in five leading manufacturing companies how they attempted to demonstrate their leadership sharing potential to select their colleagues (Graen 1989). Thirteen actions distinguished between effective employees and others.

1. Demonstrate initiative to get things moving (Self-starter).
2. Attempt to exercise leadership to make the things more effective (Show the way).
3. Show a willingness to take risks to accomplish assignments (Be bold).
4. Strive to add to the value of assignments (Go beyond).
5. Actively seek out new assignments for self-improvement (Volunteer).
6. Persist on a valuable project after others give up (Stay the course).
7. Build elaborate leadership sharing networks to extend capability (Push the envelope).

8.   Influence others by doing something extra (Set an example).

9.   Deal constructively to resolve ambiguity (Think it out).

10.   Seek wider exposure to people outside the home division (Get outside).

11.   Apply technical training on the job, and build on that training to develop broader expertise (Stay current).

12.   Work to build and maintain a close working relationship with the immediate supervisor and colleagues (Seek leadership sharing links).

13.   Work to get the members of the leadership sharing networks promoted (Boost your network members).

The following examples illustrate how each of these actions enabled these followers to become key players.

1.   *Demonstrate Initiative.* By demonstrating initiative, followers make their boss and colleagues aware that they are eager to outgrow their jobs. For example, they may demonstrate initiative by identifying problem areas in their job, and then act to correct the problems. Thus, when you see a problem with a customer order, and handle the problem the way you have seen your manager handle it before (even though this is not part of your job description), you are indicating to your boss that you are capable of and willing to take on added responsibilities.

2.   *Exercise Leadership.* An important characteristic of key players is that they are able to exercise leadership when necessary. You show this by helping your colleagues perform their jobs more efficiently, and by providing direction when they are not certain as to the best method to use. In addition, you attempt to exercise leadership by offering to take charge of special projects, such as interdepartmental task forces, which will help to develop your leadership sharing network.

3.   *Take Risks.* The need to take risks increases as you reach higher levels in the organization. Similarly, those managers who are going to be successful in the organization are willing to take calculated risks in their dealings with their boss and colleagues. One way managers may do this is by communicating to their superior's and colleagues' hidden problems in the work process or soliciting advice or added resources as needed even though pressure in the work group dictates that this is not done. Similarly, they may take risks by supporting issues that they believe are correct, even though others in the work unit may not support the issue. In

addition, they are not afraid to talk about their mistakes. Rather, they use past follies to their advantage by indicating to others what they have learned from their mistakes.

4. *Add Value.* They are constantly looking for opportunities to grow in their jobs. They find that one of the best ways to do this is to make their work more challenging and meaningful. For example, in his job as a supervisor of a market research department, Bill Atsuta found that unless he added value to his work, his job became boring and repetitive and didn't allow him to develop his skills. Thus, rather than just monitoring the performance of the telephone interviewers, as his job description suggested, he added value to his job by offering his managers input as to how interviews could be conducted more effectively, and he wrote unsolicited reports to those network members in charge of the development of the interviews that identified problem areas and made suggestions for improvement. As a result of his extra effort, Bill found himself promoted to department head and on his way to the fast track.

5. *Self-Improvement Assignment.* Rather than waiting for others to offer them opportunities, they seek opportunities on their own to make the most out of not only their jobs but also themselves. Thus, they look for opportunities that will allow them to develop their skills and to grow on the job. They may request special training or take on assignments that require them to use new skills. They may also ask others in their networks to indicate their strengths and weaknesses so that they may improve in their areas of weakness.

6. *Persist on a Project.* If an assignment appears to be going nowhere, pause a moment in order to ask your network to help you to view the assignment in a new way. If even this strategy leads to failure, which in some cases it does, assess the situation to find out what went wrong, and use the mistake as an opportunity for learning. Perhaps most important, learn never to make the same mistake twice.

7. *Build Networks.* Getting ahead means making as many strong contacts as possible in your field, and, in particular, contacts with those in competence networks. Find out what is going on in the organization and who is responsible for getting work problems solved. Then, initiate relationships with these people, which involves helping them or providing them with information that would help them in their positions. By building credits with the people in this network you are thus able to obtain resources and

accomplish things that would not have been possible without the help of others.

8. **Influence Others.** Influencing others is not as easy as it may appear. It involves building credibility, as well as adjusting your interpersonal style to match those of others. As you build your leadership sharing networks, you learn to be authentic even when it hurts.

9. **Resolve Ambiguity.** One of the most difficult problems for employees and managers in organizations is learning how to deal with ambiguity because ambiguity characterizes many of the difficult situations people face in the work place. Frequently, it's unclear what's not working, why it's not working, or what's needed in order to make things work. Also, people in the workplace may present ambiguous requests or offer ambiguous rationales. Those people who learn how to handle these ambiguous situations most effectively find themselves on the fast track. When you find yourself working with a boss who is always very ambiguous in his requests, take several steps to deal with the ambiguity rather than simply becoming frustrated and not completing the assignments. Perhaps most importantly, take the initiative to gather as much information and assistance as possible from your network of supervisors, peers, and others. When necessary, make educated assumptions that allow you to continue the task. Throughout the process, approach your network for brief feedback on whether you are performing the assignment properly. By using your network knowledge and best judgment, complete ambiguous tasks while requiring very little of your supervisor's time.

10. **Seek Wider Exposure.** Because information is such a powerful resource in organizations, employees who aspire to get ahead actively seek ways to gather more information through forming networks. One way to do this is by associating with people outside the home division. By interacting with outside managers, you gain a better understanding of your organization and its operations, as well as the different problems faced by members of other departments.

11. **Build on Existing Skills.** When new employees enter organizations, they have a certain amount of knowledge and technical skills that make them desirable to the organization. Often, however, this technical training is limited, and within a relatively short period of time, it may become obsolete. Thus, managers

must continually work to keep their technical skills current through interactions within their networks.

12. ***Develop a Good Working Relationship With Your Boss and Other Network Members.*** One of the most powerful influences in your career progress is your immediate boss. Your boss controls the types of opportunities and resources, as well as the types of rewards, you will receive from the organization. It is vital that you strive to develop the best working relationships possible with your boss and other network members.

13. ***Promote Your Boss and Network Members.*** One of the best ways to get accepted to the leadership sharing network may be to work toward promoting your boss and your network members: Do your job the best you can so that you help make them look good. Then, when they advance through the organization, they may help you along.

These activities all require employees to grow out of the narrow confines of their job by constructing a network which provides opportunities to assume greater personal responsibility by taking larger risks, and by growing more quickly professionally. Those upstairs will notice these activities and make a difference to your career. Participation in these activities communicates readiness for network investment. Once noticed as a person with a powerful network, you become a candidate for investment, and additional opportunities to show your stuff likely will be forthcoming.

GETTING PICKED

Before you can hope to establish a leadership sharing link with another, you must pass his or her entrance test and convince him or her that you can be trusted to deliver on your promises and that you have something of value to offer. Convincing your potential partner of the former is more difficult than the latter; however, both require some thought. Even a great "pick up" line only gets momentary attention. Then, you must follow through with your proof.

Some people trust you, or not, based on rumors about you. True, some basis for trust can be found in this way, although it is too unreliable. This is open to stereotyping and biases. What is recommended is a more direct approach called the "growth need interview." This interview is designed to suggest to others that you are interested in furthering your career by describing your interests and ambitions. This attempt to show your growth needs as an individual can go a long way toward passing the entrance test. Through such conversations, which may stretch out over several weeks, you tell your selected others what you want now and what you hope for in long term. Also, you ask your selected others to share the same information with you. It may be uncomfortable at first, but it becomes routine after a conversation.

After this interview, the next step is to achieve an initial challenge to begin growing out of one's job in the form of some small request which is somewhat outside of the selected other's expectations. This offer should make clear that this request is authentic and requires no exchange of like kind. If you require special information or other resources, ask for them. In addition, if you get into trouble, your colleague will be obliged to help you out. Once the request is fulfilled, you should receive your colleague's thanks. The early "grabber" rewards are material and the later "sustaining" rewards are more social and self-fulfilling.

Graen and his associates (Graen, Hui, & Taylor, 2006) have developed a measure that taps into the magnitude of Sharing Leadership Expectation (SLX) with six sensitive questions you ask yourself about each and every member of your personal network at work. The higher your score when you are brutally honest the greater your chance of developing a shared leadership relationship. Start with your immediate supervisor; next do each of those who report to you; and continue with all those people who depend on you or who you depend on at work. For each of the six questions, the responses are *Strongly Disagree = 1, Disagree = 2, Don't know = 3, Agree = 4, and Strongly Agree = 5*. The six questions are as follows.

1. My (colleague, supervisor, or subordinate) is satisfied with my work?

2. My (colleague, supervisor, or subordinate) would help me with my job problem?

3. My (colleague, supervisor, or subordinate) has confidence in my ideas?

4. My (colleague, supervisor, or subordinate) has trust that I would carry my workload?

5. My (colleague, supervisor, or subordinate) has respect for my capabilities?

6. I have an excellent working relationship with my (colleague, supervisor, or subordinate).

When you add your six scores, the range of scores is 6 to 36, and the higher your score, the greater your chance of developing a leadership sharing link. If your score with, say your supervisor, is low (24 or below), you should act quickly to correct this unfavorable situation. Clearly, the six questions should help you identify the areas that need your immediate attention. When you first start your job, your score should be about 24, because you don't know about any of the six areas. Test yourself at appropriate intervals and act to improve the problem areas. You have these tools to help you in your quest to become a key communicator in your organization and make a difference.

If you pass this initial test, you seek another larger project. After a few of these exchanges, your selected colleague will begin to trust your promises. But, never make a promise that you cannot keep. When your selected colleague offers the challenges, seek more and explain the developmental process in terms of mutual benefit. If your other demurs, keep working until all hope is lost. If you reject your leader's offers, they will cease being offered. You cannot rightly complain after you reject an offer, so be careful. You may opt back into the process later when you see the growth and achievements of your peers who completed the process from the first offer.

Through these informal episodes of seeking and achieving appropriate challenges based on current work flows and the developing needs, getting support for your projects, and rewards after the projects are completed, mutual trust, respect, and commitment grow. Over this process, the challenging projects become more responsible and the corresponding rewards become more significant. The process of building leadership sharing networks flows smoothly once the initial tests are passed and both parties continue to construct ever-stronger bonds of mutual trust, respect, and commitment.

Our research investigations have shown that leaders and followers who complete this process gain the advantages of performance beyond expectations, satisfaction with their jobs and their careers, mutual trust, respect, and commitment, and optimism about the future. Over their careers, they consistently develop these agreements with their leaders, followers, and peers, as they move up the hierarchy of their companies until they find their dream job. Finally, they move up higher and faster than their peers do over their careers and arrive home earlier.

Research suggests that its not nice to attempt to fool your boss (Lam, Huang, & Snape, 2007). Those who were seen by their superiors as being self-serving actors were not permitted leadership sharing status. Only those viewed as authentic were granted such status for their role making attempts. Clearly, both appropriate values (motivation) and performance are necessary but not sufficient for leadership sharing status. These attributes are difficult to judge, but can be made clear over repeated assignments. Clearly, being authentic is the better way to achieve leadership sharing status.

WHAT IS THE ADVANTAGE?

From a network member's viewpoint, because a potential partner grows from a supporter to a partner through the process, he or she and the focal person have created strategic human assets (Uhl-Bien, Graen, & Scandura, 2000). When one partner has a problem that he or she cannot solve, the other partner will help even though it may cost him or her personally or professionally. As one network member goes beyond his or her job, the other reciprocates in kind. All parties share information openly and honestly, even when it may be painful. Both create their own network language based upon shared experiences (Fairhurst, 1993). This language allows one member to talk to the other in their coded language in the presence of others without their comprehending.

Network structures also contribute to team performance and morale according to a meta-analytic investigation (Bakundi & Harrison, in press). This study found that analyzing 17 studies showed that the density of "advice ties" in a team was predicted by population correlation of team performance (ρ. 15) and team morale (ρ. 15). Moreover, team leader centrality on advice ties within team was predictive of team performance (ρ. 29) as was team centrality in their intergroup network (ρ. 13). As predicted the contribution of "advice ties" disappeared with experience in the team. When the newcomers learn the ropes they probably use the advice network less. It was unfortunate that LMX and MMX networks were not available to many of these early network investigations, because LMX was found to be highly predictive of performance as well as sharing the same networks as one's leader (Sparrowe & Liden, 2005). In another set of three longitudinal studies (Graen et al., 2006) both LMX and MMX were predictive of both team performance and team process. A model of how this may work to augment team process effectiveness and subsequent team performance would be: team leader and members work to establish many strong and elaborate expert (people who seek their advice) networks both (1) within their team (team density of experts) and (2) within networks outside of their team (internetwork centrality), team members would establish many strong LMX and MMX conditions for sharing network leadership (3) within their team and (4) internetwork, team leader would have high centrality as experts in both (5) team and (6) internetwork, and (7) team leader and many team members would share the same advice networks outside of the team. Add these outcroppings of the emergent processes proposed by Gibbons and Grover (2006) and the result is a highly recommended, strong inference model with many testable hypotheses.

CONTINGENT COMMUNICATIONS STRATEGIES

Strategies for different structural linkages in the formal organization require different strategies to develop leadership sharing communication relations. As shown in Figure 1.4, vertical (or direct authority flows) rela-

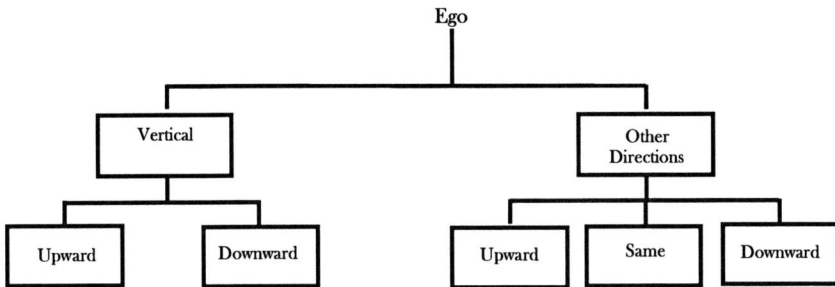

Figure 1.4.   Communication strategies.

tions should have different strategies than other (or no direct authority flows) relations. This is due to the complications that one party has superior control of the other's formal organizational outcomes such as promotion and dismissals. Clearly, career outcomes are influenced by one's superior. This should be divided further into upward and downward, because upward is constrained by concerns for showing respect for the office, being seen authentic and career outcome concerns and downward is constrained by concerns about being seen as fair to all group members and achieving group goals.

In situations where the other potential communications relations have no direct authority flows to the ego, different strategies should be applied for those above the ego's level (Upward), those at the same level (Same), and those below (Downward). The differences in strategies among those three directions on the organization's chart differ contingent upon slightly different constraints on actions of ego. Upward is constrained by the needs to be seen as both respectful of the superior status, authentic as a person, and not be seen as going over someone's head. At the same level, ego's communications strategy is constrained by the need to balance cooperation with career competition. Finally, downward relations are constrained by respect of formal communications and authority flows and the need to not be seen as going behind someone's back.

OVERCOMING FEARS

With all of these benefits of leadership sharing, why do so many leaders of creative teams fail to fully engage the process? As was described by Kramer (2006), one communication strategy to initiate team leadership sharing is for the leader to admit that he or she doesn't have all of the answers and ask for suggestions from team members. Those who readily offer suggestions are encouraged and recognized for good ideas but are protected from criticism for poor ideas. Those team members who resist offering suggestions can be asked again and again. This process is self correcting as the team will help sort out the more useful from the less useful ideas when given the opportunity. One question that arises from this is: What factors inhibit the easy acceptance of this promising method of building a creative team of leadership sharing teammates?

We find that managers we have trained to become leaders usually have several doubts about entering a process of leadership sharing. First, they fear a loss of control by giving team members too much latitude in decision making and coordination of the team may become too difficult and make them look bad. Second, they fear that team members will ask for personal favors and create embarrassing obligations for leaders. Third, they fear that team members will find out that they do not have all of the answers and lose respect for them. Finally, although many more fears have been expressed, the last resort is that their teammates do not want to share leadership with them. These fears must be addressed and worked through before leaders will test the unknown of leadership sharing. Fortunately, these fears can be overcome with proper training in the strategies of leadership sharing. Trainees come to understand that the process of sharing leadership is a successive approximation process in which successively more significant opportunities are reinforced when successful with progressively more meaningful recognition and resources. Also, they learn that followers must be made to succeed especially early in the development.

As the process unfolds, followers who share leadership grow into leaders within the team and share equitably in the success of the team. They grow out of their old roles and into new roles within the team. They come to understand that team leadership can be multiplied by following appropriate strategies. Team leaders come to recognize that sharing too much leadership too soon is a strategic mistake. They learn that until a follower is prepared to respect and enact a leadership sharing opportunity, it should not be given. After they are given, opportunities need to be supported as necessary to ensure success, because success invigorates the growth of shared leadership. Clearly, the benefits out weigh the risks in building a creative leadership sharing team. Even when a leader develops only one member into a leadership sharing partner, the benefits are worth the effort.

RESEARCH FINDINGS

New approaches for cultivating and nourishing communications have highlighted a number of generalizations about organizational behavior.

1. Most of communication behavior of humans in organizations is overdetermined by the rules and procedures of the formal organization enforced by legal contracts and agreements. That being stated, the most interesting and beneficial behavior is underdetermined and is called informal communication. Both are necessary for an organization's survival. Informal organization is governed by the nature of humans as self-aware, need satisfying, social creatures with limited rationality, imperfect information, creative imaginations, and deep-seated hopes and fears.

2. Informal communications can be mapped in terms of networks of expertise, information, influence, and social capital at any point in time and overtime in terms of flows sensing relevant events, sense making, and implementation throughout the organization and its environments. As Orton and Dhillon (2006) described the flows of strategy, formulation goes from microactions (low levels) to meso-options (middle levels) to macrostrategy (top levels of organization) for the purpose of continuously improving the organization's future. One key to this mapping process is the rigorous measurement of relationships between formal and informal influences on individual, team and network flows of behavior.

3. Informal communication relations are granted between employees in exchange and in proportion for shared leadership. Thus, for a person to grow his or her leadership influence to get the right things done the right way with others, he or she must find a way to share leadership with those ready and willing to invest it properly. As shown in Figure 1.5, peo-

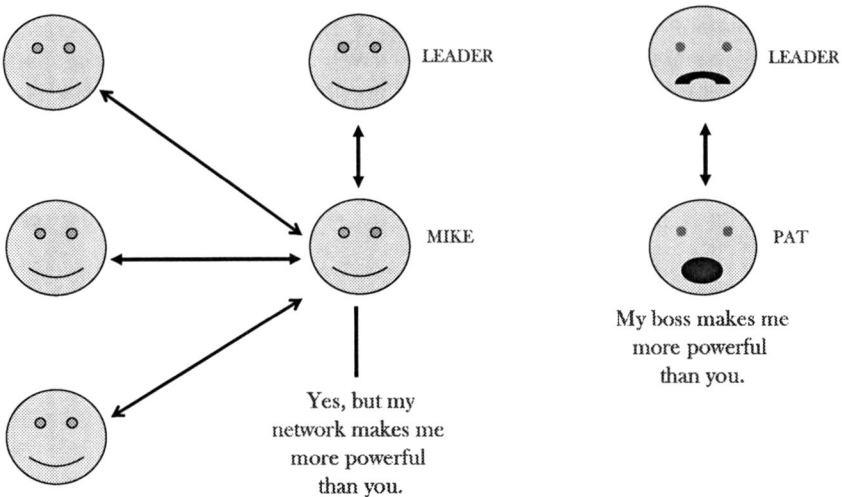

Figure 1.5.   It takes a network.

ple who understand this multiplier effect are those who are most successful over their entire careers.

4.   Those who understand that leadership sharing among members creates social capital throughout networks should encourage their associates and followers to do so for the good of their organization and their careers.

5.   They can destroy their social capital if they are not careful. Those who understand this and respect their followers will benefit from social capital.

6.   Those who successfully grow influence in their networks also agree that those in their networks can in turn influence them.

7.   Certain people in organizations can form a competence network for a focal person. This is an influence network made up of people with abundant social capital that get "impossible" things done in bureaucracies (Graen, 1989).

8.   We support the marriage of communications theory and network analysis theory and hope that the new theory of leadership sharing in teams and networks is a step in that direction. We expected the goal to be reached soon after our early research showed that one's leader's relationship with his or her boss limited the influence and social capital of a focal person (Graen, Cashman, Ginsburg, & Schiemann, 1977). The communications network up the chain of command made a difference for lower participants.

9.   The impact of what a leader says to his or her follower depends on the particular leadership sharing link between the two (Wang, Law, Hackett, Wang, & Chen, 2004). A leader may use any of a number of transformation leadership styles, but the proof of the pudding is in the critical sharing of leadership. We shouldn't be fooled by the ease of training leaders to talk the transformation talk to followers and forget about the critical process of using authentic leadership sharing to grow leadership and other social capital (Bass & Avolio, 1997). Clearly, it doesn't matter what the leader says about vision, if followers do not really listen and buy in. We need to let a million flowers bloom to understanding more authentic leadership.

RECOMMENDATIONS

As we enter the information age, communications become even more critical to effectiveness of individual, dyads, triads, teams, silos, organizations, industries, and so on. Communications relations both motivate and direct activities at all levels in our increasingly turbulent environments. Those networks that supply the needed information and resources will determine the future of people and their organizations in the 21st century.

For those who aspire to make a difference and share in the success of modern organizations in this information age, we recommend that they do their homework and cultivate and nourish their communication networks. Herein lay the keys to success for those who choose wisely.

REFERENCES

Bakundi, P., & Harrison, D. A. (in press). Ties, leaders, and time in teams: Strong inference about network structure's effects on team validity and performance. *Academy of Management Journal.*

Bass, B. M., & Avolio, B. J. (1997). *Full range leadership development: Manual for the multifactor leadership questionnaire.* Palo Alto, CA: Mind Garden.

Doz, Y., Santos, J., & Williamson, P. (2001). *From global to metanational.* Boston: Harvard Business School Press.

Fairhurst, G. T. (1993). The leader-member exchange patterns of women leaders in industry: A discourse analysis. *Communication Monographs, 60,* 312-351.

Gibbons, D. E., & Grover, S. L. (2006). Network factors in leader-member relationships. In G. B. Graen & J. A. Graen (Eds.), *LMX leadership: The series: Vol. 4. Sharing network leadership* (pp. 63-93). Greenwich, CT: Information Age.

Graen, G. B. (1989). *Unwritten rules for your career: 15 secrets for fast-track success.* New York: Wiley.

Graen, G. B. (2006). Post Simon, March, Weick, and Graen. In G. B. Graen (Ed.), *LMX leadership: The series: Vol. 4. Sharing network leadership* (pp. 269-278). Greenwich, CT: Information Age.

Graen, G. B., Cashman, J. F., Ginsburg, S., & Schiemann, W. (1977). Effects of linking-pin on the quality of working life of lower participants. *Administrative Science Quarterly, 22,* 491-504.

Graen, G. B., Dharwadkar, R. Grewal, R., & Wakabayashi, M. (2006). Japanese career progress over the long haul: An empirical examination. *Journal of International Business Studies, 37,* 148-161.

Graen, G. B., & Graen, J. A. (2006). *LMX leadership: The series: Vol. 4. Sharing network leadership.* Greenwich, CT: Information Age.

Graen, G. B., Hui, C., & Taylor, E. T. (2004). A new approach to team leadership: Upward, downward, and horizontal differentiation. In G. B. Graen (Ed.), *LMX leadership: The series: Vol. 2. New Frontiers of leadership* (pp. 33-66). Greenwich, CT: Information Age.

Graen, G. B., Hui, C., & Taylor, E. (2006). Experience-based learning about LMX leadership and fairness in project teams: A dyadic directional approach. *Academy of Management Learning and Education, 5*(4), 448-460.

Krackhardt, D., & Hanson, J. (1993, July-August). Informal networks: The company behind the chart. *Harvard Business Review,* 104-111.

Kramer, M. W. (2006). Communication strategies for sharing leadership within a creative team: LMX in theater groups. In G. B. Graen & J. A. Graen (Eds.),

LMX leadership: The series: Vol. 4. Sharing network leadership (pp. 1-24). Greenwich, CT: Information Age.

Lam, W., Huang, X., & Snape, E. (2007). Feedback-seeking behavior and leader-member exchange: Do supervisor-attributed motives matter? *Academy of Management Journal, 50,* 348-363.

Orton, J. D., & Dhillon, G. (2006). Macrostrategic, mesostrategic, and microstrategic leadership processes in loosely coupled networks. In G. B. Graen & J. A. Graen (Eds.), *LMX leadership: The series: Vol. 4. Sharing network leadership* (pp. 137-167). Greenwich, CT: Information Age.

Sparrowe, R. T., & Liden, R. C. (2005). Two routes to influence: Integrating leader-member exchange and network perspectives. *Administrative Science Quarterly, 50,* 4.

Uhl-Bien, M., Graen, G. B., & Scandura, T. A. (2000). Leader-member exchange (LMX) for strategic human resource management systems: Relationships as social capital for competitive advantage. *Research in Personnel and Human Resources Management, 18,* 137-185.

Wang, H., Law, K. S., Hackett, R. D., Wang, D., & Chen, Z. X. (2004). Leader-member exchange as a mediator of the relationship between transformational leadership and followers' performance and organizational citizenship behavior. *Academy of Management Journal, 48*(3), 420-432.

CHAPTER 2

PHENOTYPE FOR ENHANCING MULTINATIONAL NETWORK LEADERSHIP

George B. Graen

Taking China and the United States as our target nations, we propose to explore the differences in national experience regarding sharing network leadership between the 2 countries. We consider postmodern China compared to the United States in terms of several deep-level differences in past history and current circumstance. The underlying process (genotype) of sharing network leadership appears similar for postmodern China and America; however, the particular behavior involved in this processes (phenotype) is learned and hence influenced by socialization and learning. American managers in China should take the time to learn about their true Chinese coworker. This chapter is a brief introduction to "true cultural bonding" (TCB) through cooperative conflict resolution research on American managers and their Chinese business associates in mainland China.

INTRODUCTION

Although I am neither Asian nor European but American, I was educated cross-culturally in Japan during my formative years as a scholar (1970-

New Multinational Network Sharing
pp. 23–42
Copyright © 2007 by Information Age Publishing

1986). The dramatic experiences of being allowed "inside" the culture of Japan drove home to me the many fundamental differences in national strategies, operations, and tactics between "Nippon" and "American."

Similar differences make extremely difficult and often impossible the task of adequately translating Western leadership concepts into Chinese thoughts and vice versa. What Buddha, Jesus, Mohammed, or your chosen moral leader would do in a given situation does not help because each leader's thoughts have been filtered by these cultural differences. The words may be translated the same, but the connotative meanings are different between East and West. Before this East-West transfer of connotative isomorphic meaning can take place cross-culturally experts on both sides must be trained for this task (Graen, Hui, Wakabayashi, & Wang, 1997). Some of my coauthors on multinational networking in the present book are at the level of expertise in leadership that is called "Sino-American transculturalist" which indicates that they understand their Chinese and American cultural and history well enough to offer their understanding of Chinese leadership to the West. As the deep-level reader can see, they do wonderful work.

Of course, I have been an eager student of Chinese history and thought, since as a child reading my first adult novel: Pearl Buck's *The Good Earth* and my study of leadership in China has benefited enormously from my cross-cultural studies with my Japanese mentors, Professors Katsuo Sano and Mitsuru Wakabayashi at Keio and Nagoya Universities during the 1970s and 1980s. From them I learned the difference between surface-level behavior and deep-level behavior. Surface-level behavior is the stuff of cultural stereotypes and caricatures such as those of (Hofstede, 1984, 2001; House, Hanges, Jaridan, Dorfman, & Gupta, 2004)

Although some people believe that these surface-level, cultural stereotypes contain some introductory useful information, I believe that such cultural stereotypes and caricatures are, on balance, dysfunctional for any meaningful cross-cultural relationship (Graen, 2006). For example, I have never owned a cow yet I am stereotyped as an American "cowboy." I reject that image and object to anyone treating me as a John Wayne clone.

Chinese leadership history differs from the West in many respects, but a few of the more noteworthy are the absence of a Magna Carta in 1215 in which the King of England agreed to be judged under the laws and the early decline of the feudal system and the rise of the industrial revolution with its steam engine and industrial machines. These events fostered colonialism and the rise of dominant corporations in the West. Instead, China became a giant country early in its history and was ruled by emperors who were above the law. It continues this experience and only the emperors have changed by forces of different kinds until the present day.

I was told by my Chinese mentors early in my studies that "the Chinese are pragmatic and the emperor is far away." This meant that because the emperor and his representatives have always been above the law, Chinese business must use the "backdoor." Many Chinese told me that "it is better to go to hell than go to a Chinese court." The English "Star Chamber" was the same before the Magna Carta of 1215. Fortunately, the Chinese legal system recently has made advances toward the transparent rule of law for everyone.

Leadership in China is to be found at all levels of society and profits enormously from the past Chinese scholars' works on the theories and practices of convincing people to follow toward righteous opportunities, while maintaining the overall cost to benefit ratios and keeping faith with those who would sacrifice all for the good of the many.

The impact of Chinese theories of leadership can be found wherever Han Chinese people live, and these theories are adapted to their local situation. Strains of Chinese leadership theories can be found on every continent and many islands around the globe. Confucianism can be found in its stronger forms in Taiwan and to a lesser degree in Hong Kong. It was turned upside-down in mainland China during the 10 years of the "cultural revolution" by Chairman Mao, but it has recovered somewhat under Deng's "open door revolution." However, under Deng's revolution, the old values of the ancestral village, for many young Chinese entrepreneurs, has been replaced by personal self-interest, wealth, and power, all free of family responsibility. For these business people, Confucianism is an old superstition held by their ancestors with little relevance to them. In sum, mainland China is searching for a moral philosophy to bring order and unity to a turbulent nation.

Chinese business is in search of a leadership theory for the twenty-first century that must be useful in developing leadership networks that include people from other Eastern and Western countries. This theory must help find the "true middle ground" between people from vastly different cultures, so that, they can truly bond culturally. Thousands of years of Chinese isolation to remain "unstained" by the unclean outsiders have not prepared China's children to deal with offers from many different foreigners. Hunkering-down in one's small, Chinese family business may serve the Confucian family, but it is not the answer needed to compete with large, multinational corporations because large fish eat small fish when hungry that cannot hide and the traditional Chinese family business with some notable exceptions has been severely restricted in terms of growth by its inherent risk aversion. No head of a Chinese family business wants to be the one that bankrupts the family. Chinese business must learn to blend the effective business technology of the West with the cultural forces of China to find a workable leadership theory. In addition,

China is growing at such a rate that she will be the largest economy on the globe and she will need an effective theory of international leadership to avoid becoming the world's greatest factory and largest resource spoiler without attendant leadership on the global stage.

China and America must find the "third way" (Graen & Wakabayashi, 1994) and leap-frog the process of becoming sophisticated in international business partnership networks. The first step is to be knowledgeable regarding the lessons of Chinese leadership from the ancients to the present (Chen & Lee, in press). The next step is to integrate this understanding with that of foreign leadership to be capable of true cultural bonding with foreigners.

TRUE CULTURAL BONDING

If you seek to understand Chinese leadership thought from a modern Chinese perspective you must become a serious student of deep-level China and understand the Han people's genetic endowment, past history and current circumstance. The reader should try to interpret theories of Chinese leadership within the proper context and seek the deeper meaning (Chen & Lee, in press). The skill is to learn to withhold Western value judgments until you achieve a nontrivial level of Sino-Western understanding when foreigner's behavior shocks your sensibilities.

An Example of Conflicting Norms

My Chinese students in the United States tell me that one hurdle for them to overcome was the practice in China of choosing friends based on social attraction and building trust, respect and commitment to the relationship first and later seeing its instrumentalities. In contrast, Americans in the United States reverse the selection criteria and seek instrumentalities first and later social attraction. This becomes a problem for my Chinese students, who often select and develop the less instrumental relationships, in competitive situations where strong communications links are advantageous. In these situations, my Chinese students receive greater friendship support (cheerleading) and less instrumental support (task-relevant resources) from their networks.

In our Shanghai study, our Chinese MBA students also had difficulties in developing strong relationships with Western peers and superiors but not with Chinese coworkers. In addition, to getting beyond the cultural, history, and current circumstance differences, this fundamental practice of selecting friends can be disadvantageous for Chinese employees of

Western corporations in China. Where the Chinese managers seek social support and harmonious comradeship, the Western managers look for potential instrumentalities first and friendship later. In fact, Western managers will choose to develop strong ties with coworkers that they do not like or barely tolerate for the sake of achieving the forthcoming instrumentalities. More, such relationships may never develop into friendship. Although my Chinese students see this as social prostitution or worse, Western managers see this as "business as usual" and recommend it to those who aspire to promotions.

What was a functional social norm for choosing friends in a bucolic feudal system becomes a dysfunction norm in a highly competitive information age. Instrumentalities of relationships take on more importance than expressive factors. The social norm becomes not hedonism of the present, but hedonism of the future: Sacrifice now for a better life in the future.

For a Sino-Western venture in China, what is the proper course to a system that disadvantages neither and both groups can endorse? This is the question that this book seeks to answer. But before we can consider the new research findings on this question, we consider the relevant history of the Middle Kingdom.

BRIEF HISTORICAL BACKGROUND

The understanding of leadership models in China calls for a context. The reader needs to know that before Confucius and Mencius theory was the systems of feudalism by which the society was structured and functioned. At the top were the emperor and his court, followed by in descending order lords, their vassals, their peasants and slaves. Members of the court discovered that the Confucian system could reinforce the feudal system and managed its adoption throughout the empire. It worked tolerably well for each succeeding dynasty until it was destroyed by the Cultural Revolution of 1966-1976. It was planned to be replaced by the leadership of emerging peasants through hard work and suffering. This plan failed and the value system of Deng was a return to pragmatism and the postmodern individuality of capitalism. Although traditional Confucian values are alive and well in Taiwan, and Singapore, Coastal China and Hong Kong values have become more pragmatic.

Networks in Feudal China

China discovered the value of networks of human relationships very early in her history for ordering family affairs, village commence and interactions with the state. These networks were transformed into systems of owing obligations to superiors and responsibility for welfare to subordinates by the Confucian system. On the surface, this system was based on ancestry of family and virtue of all including government. Later it was revised by Xenzi—to recognize the dual nature of man. Confucius and Mencius saw only the god-man side of humans and designed a structure for their society. However, they overlooked the animal-man side of humans that Xenzi proposed needed to be socialized by education beginning in the family and extending throughout the networks. Xenzi also recognized individual differences in people. These things were discovered by psychology in the West during the twentieth century. Later, Han Fei made his contributions to refining a theory of bureaucracy by which a large population can be governed.

Hwang (in press), outlined the history of leadership thought from a modern Taiwan perspective focusing on Han Fei's theory of leadership. Hwang contends that Han Fei's theory of legalism can be reorganized to be applicable to both a feudal state and modern organizations in Taiwan. Hwang outlines how legalism rationalized the Confucian order to become a kin to Weber's bureaucracy and replacing the old aristocracy with bureaucrats. Unfortunately, the competitive knowledge economy has made the classic bureaucratic organization obsolete and replaced it with overlapping team organization (Orton &Dhillon, 2006; Seers, 2004).

Many other theories of leadership originated in China including Daoistic leadership that turns leadership into the mystical concept of "like water" and reminds us that leaders often appeal to mythical values to attract dedicated followers. Humans need their myths to give them something of value beyond their short and otherwise animal existence. Leaders of the way need a higher calling to become a saint.

Another theory popular and misinterpreted in the West is Sun Zi's *Art of War*, a handbook for Western leaders in competition that counsels leaders to think twice before they act, to understand that strategy is all important, the battle not fought and the prize achieved is the best, and that you should know your enemy better than you know yourself and use his strengths against him.

Networks of lasting relationships have characterized the Han people throughout their history and any leadership theory that denies this facet will thereby suffer. Leadership theory for the Han people must include sharing networks of such relationships. To get anything out of the ordinary accomplished that a Chinese leader cannot do alone requires some trusted relationships. This is one way pragmatism emerges in Chinese Society.

The implications for this leadership in Sino-American dyads should be clear. In contrast to Chinese history of reliance on networks of relationships, American history describes rugged individuals and self-reliance. Both of these myths contain a grain of truth, but clearly both the Chinese and American relied on both individual and network activities to survive and prosper. It has been a mistake for scholars to call Americans "individualistic" and young Chinese in Coastal China "collectivistic" in the twenty-first century where even the family networks are breaking down, not to mention the village networks, and the state networks. The pendulum of network to individual has swung from one extreme pole to the other for both peoples from one generation to the next, but both require leadership theory that speaks to both individual and collective networking. Such a theory is available and has been tested empirically in both China and America (Graen & Graen, 2006).

Leaders must be the best of the network and dependent on the network over time. The network must grant leadership and can reclaim it. American organizations have recently accepted the power of teams and are beginning to discover that leadership cannot be contained by teams but requires networks (that may include numerous teams).

Competing Social Structures

A brief outline of the major social structures used by mainland China from its early development as a feudal system to the present is presented in Table 2.1. As shown, the stages of development begin with the Confucian (about 600 B.C.) dual system (A1 and A2) under which the people served the hierarchy up to and including the emperor and the nine classes of nobles served both the emperor and the people. In addition, the value systems of A1 and A2 differed in that A1 values were directed at harmony in interpersonal hierarchical relationships and A2 values were directed at scholarly pursuits. Equity struggles between people and nobles were frequent based on the two-class system of privileged. Leaders emerged under the two classes differently with seniority, birth order, gender and guanzi for family and testing and seniority for nobles. The dark side (B) of the heavenly system of Confucius and Mancius was proposed as a missing component of the complete social system by Xen Zi (about 285 B.C.). His system of legalism moved the favored nobles back under a common law and introduced the struggle with (A2). The emperor was still above the law. The value system was based on social contracts and violations of these were punished according to judgments handed down by legal courts. Legal positions of leaders were filled by the emperor's authority.

This three-part system was the framework in China until the last emperor. Even the many invasions of China failed to change the China

Table 2.1. Chronology of Competing Social Structures in China

Characteristic	Confucian-I	Confucian-II	Legalism	Maoism	Dengism	USA Legalism
Final Say ...	Emperor	Emperor	Court	Chairman	Chairman	Court
Some Say ...	People	Nobles	People	Party	Party	People
System ...	A1	A2	B	C	D	E
Values ...	Workers	Elite	Social Contracts	Peasant Values	International Business Values	Due Process
Prime Mover ...	Serve Family	Serve Society via NINE Classes	Protect Society	Punish Enemies of Revolution	Open Door & Suspend Legalism	Constitution World Court
Leader ...	Seniority	Testing and Seniority	Appointment	Long March with Mao	Party Bureaucrats	Master Networks
Struggles ...		A1 vs A2	A2 vs B	C vs A1, A2, B	D vs C	E vs D
Time Line ...	500 B.C.	500 B.C.	285 B.C.	A.D. 1950	A.D. 1976	A.D. 2000

way. However, the fall of the emperor and the replacement by Chairman Mao and his party spelled the tragic end of the Chinese system. Maoism (1950) replaced the emperor with the Chairman of the party, replaced intellectual merit with party loyalty during the "long march," elevated peasant values to the highest level, and sought to punish all enemies of the revolution. Leaders were appointed by the Chairman and favored those who made the "long march." Mao's 10-year culture revolution was successful in destroying the Confucian system for a generation of Chinese, but the Confucian system still remains strong in Taiwan and other places outside China.

After Mao's death, Deng became Chairman and opened the door for trade with the world (D). The final say was by the party although a weak legal system remained. The party was above the law and used selective enforcement to attract foreign funds and modern manufacturing technology. China was open for international business and privatization was encouraged for all state-owned enterprises. All of the necessary conditions for capitalization were put in place except the economic transparence and legal due process required by the American legal system. Dengism struggles to find a China way to achieve these two missing components.

Today Taiwan's system is a mixture of Confucism and American legalism that makes it very different from mainland China. What may work nicely in Taiwan such as the paternalistic model (Farh, Liang, Chou, & Cheng, 2007) may not work so well in mainland China. Entrepreneurs in China must deal with resource systems that are controlled by state. Clearly Taiwan has developed a system that works in international trade based on a postmodern mix of Confucian values and Western legalism. Progress on this in China is encouraging as portrayed in a recent incident involving human rights. November 29, 2006, in China, people were outraged by the local police parading in the street citizens accused of being or visiting prostitutes. They saw this as a violation of their legal rights. Moreover, they complained that prostitution was a violation of the social order and was punishable by administrative detention rather than a criminal conviction. The parade was promoted by the party official as a way to discourage prostitution. The struggle between party and legal authority continues.

CURRENT CIRCUMSTANCE

New China ventures are evolving to challenge the best of the global corporations. China as an economy caught fire when Chairman Deng opened the door to the world. In terms of share of global gross domestic product, China's share grew from 3.2% in 1980 to 13.0% in 2004 and is projected to reach 20.37% by 2015. This will be accomplished by a merging of older style Chinese leadership and new style adoptability in global technology and marketing, global alliances, and global rapidly adaptable organizational networks. At the present time, China is dominating manufacturing based on price competition using foreign marketing and distribution networks, such as Wal-Mart with 5,000 plus stores in China and growing. Consequently, China's products do not need to spend on developing the marketing and distribution networks that held back the Japanese products in the sixties and seventies.

China products are threatening the old Japanese order by "shock and awe" entry into new global markets at both the low end and the high end of technology. The old Japanese order was to enter at the low end only and gradually move up to high end technology. This is the order Japan imposed on other Southeast Asia countries. China's new order is speed, breath of products, technology range, broad competitive variety of supplies, alliances through foreign investment, economies of scale, access through retail giants like Wal-Mart, and World Trade Organization membership.

The China price advantage is derived by many sacrifices compared to Western practices. China is paying its dues and is beginning to reap its rewards. But the next step demands a new kind of organization. A new set of rules for surviving in economic organizations is emerging that are different from the old rules of organization. China is looking to the future for economic prosperity and the west must prepare for China's century of economic leadership.

Control of hierarchies throughout the industrialized world in the last century made leading people relatively straightforward in that it could rely on the top-down flow of legal authority. The evolution in organizational forms such as downsizing, outsourcing, joint ventures and alliances, contingent employment, lean management, network organization, and the very frequency of organizational restructuring all make this use of power no longer effective. A key functional objective for the last century organizational design was that of operating efficiency, through minimizing costs associated with wasteful variation. Reinforcing predictability and stability in hierarchical structures was quite appropriate. But the battleground of the fight for survival in the twenty-first century has shifted to the terrain of innovation and design flexibility rather than stabilizing efficient operations, because China has defined the race with the dominant "China Price" (*BW*, 2004). The China price is 30% to 50% lower than the lowest Western supplier including shipping.

The twentieth century was a period of unprecedented economic and technological development. Markets and hierarchies have been the two organizational mechanisms for that development, and the information costs of transactions necessary to that development determined which mechanism was preferable for various transaction types. Hierarchies were elaborated as information-processing mechanisms, requiring large numbers of managers. As the need grew for employees whose productive contribution centered on directing and coordinating the productive contributions of other employees, so did the search for ways to identify prospective managers who could be expected to perform well as leaders of other employees.

Early observers in America, such as Chester Barnard, recognized that the motivation of employees also was influenced by the behavior of organizational superiors dispersed across work units and organizational levels. This was called "leadership." As the mass production era grew the human relations school of thought gained dominance in America. The mobilization of effort necessary for World War II production in America encouraged the growth of research directed toward the possibility of better recognizing leadership potential and of optimal development of leadership potential among military officers and civilian supervisors. After World War II, American business firms sought to apply the lessons of organization and leadership learned in the war effort. At this time, the postwar U.S. economic landscape was dominated by large, vertically and horizontally integrated mass producers, concentrating employment and economic power disproportionately in a few hundred major corporations.

Right Sizing

The prototypical organizational form in the industrialized countries of the mid-twentieth century tended to be tall rather than flat, and endeavored to consolidate and integrate related production activities within a clearly bounded, single large corporation rather than develop amorphous networks of small specialist firms. Clearly distinct organizational roles were preferred, which helped minimize ambiguity in the development of working relationships. Vendor-customer relationships could operate in accord with the norms of economic exchange, while supervisor-subordinate relationships could operate in accord with the norms of hierarchical bureaucracy.

In transition from the last century's relatively stable manufacturing economy to today's knowledge economy, corporations have experimented with nontraditional employment relationships and organizational forms, such as contingent employment, joint ventures and alliances, and network organization. The rapid advance of information technology has lowered costs of access to information and made reliance on human information processors (in the form of tall management hierarchies) a relatively expensive business practice. As decentralized computers have taken on the more routinized aspects of information processing, corporations have found it too expensive to maintain relatively large supervisory hierarchies. Some research has addressed the implications for change in the roles of managers attributable to the resulting structural experimentation. Such changes have typically broadened spans of control and job definitions and required more cross-boundary management and negotiation. The development of flexible forms of work has brought to managers a good bit of the instability and insecurity once characteristic of only the lowest levels of the labor market. The effect of these trends is exacerbated by continued acceleration in the pace of change.

Leap-Froging by China's Innovators

As a consequence of this global information economy, China's private organizations have anticipated the super-fast development of their markets by establishing powerful brands of products and services that can compete successfully at home and overseas. Global organizations, based in China, must be large enough to reach out and prosper abroad. Early examples are Haier Group (U.S.$10 billion) Lenovo Group, Ltd. (U.S.$13 billion), TCL (U.S.$3.5 billion), Wahaha (U.S.$1.2 billion), GOME (U.S.$2.1 billion), Bird (U.S.$1.3 billion), Greely (U.S.$484 million), TsingTao Beer (U.S.$907 million), Li-Ning (U.S.$121 million), and Yonghi King (U.S.$36 million), based on 2003 figures.

Although Chinese ventures both large and small have taken over much of global manufacturing, they have much to learn about global marketing networks. Knowledge is the currency of this next challenge. Those ventures that can generate new products and services and learn to market them globally on a regular schedule will dominate the knowledge economy. Examples of this trend in China are Lenovo's becoming the first Chinese company to be a top sponsor of Olympic Games (2008), Haier entering the U.S. market, TCL's new joint venture in Europe, and Geely Auto entering the Middle East market, according to *Business Week Online* (2004).

What this should mean to Chinese CEOs about the information economy are five rules of organizing.

1. Private organizations must become more organic (active learners) and less mechanical (passive responders).
2. In private organizations work must be shifted away from contexts with rigid foundations of hierarchical accountability.

3. Rapid adaptations of private organizations through flexible structures will be demanded by super-fast market changes.

4. Company teams at all levels must have the mission to properly adapt rapidly the social structures that guide and motivate action.

5. Private organization's failure to adapt rapidly and appropriately will lead to obsolescence and death.

These modern organizations will demand more of associates, managers, and executives in terms of (1) problem finding, (2) solution solving, (3) solution implementation, and (4) organizational impact. This means that a successfully implemented solution to a problem is not the end of the responsibility. It requires that the implication of this incident be stored appropriately in operating organization memory.

People who can contribute to this organizing via organizational learning will be highly valued. This means that employees who develop elaborate networks of instrumental human relationships throughout the organization and its relevant environments will be seen as more valuable in terms of human capital than those who have simple friendship networks. The name of the game for postmodern organizations in both China and the American networking is for enhanced human capital appreciation. This book is about methods of building elaborate networks of instrumental human work relationships both within and between Chinese and American enterprises to benefit company and family.

COST OF WESTERN ETHNOCENTRIC LEADERSHIP IN CHINA

Although the cost of ethnocentric leadership in Sino-Western enterprises in China is not captured by the accounting process, it is a drag on Sino-Western and Sino-Japanese enterprise profits. This is the cost of failed true cultural bonding (Graen & Graen, 2007). Those companies who can match the successes in combining traditional Chinese values with Japanese and Westerns ways of doing business will likely be the survivor in the China market in the coming shake outs.

Shanghai 150

Let's consider for example postgraduate young Chinese in Sino-Western enterprises in China. What do young MBA students seek in their Sino-Western or Sino-Japanese enterprise positions? They seek opportunities to be developed professionally and to be promoted for their performance about expectations by a competent and personally interested leader. They seek to be understood at some deeper than surface-level and be listened to when making important suggestions. Although they are heavily recruited by search agents for more attractive positions with other companies, they would prefer not to leave. But they do leave when they lose hope for improvement. Based on our five years of research on Chinese MBAs in Sino-Western corporations doing business in Shanghai economic areas, the companies are wasting valuable Chinese managerial resources by failing consistently to train and control their middle-level Western managers so that they lead by combining traditional Chinese values with Japanese and Western ways of doing business.

Our MBA students made it clear that their Western boss was expected by subordinates to "take care" of them in both their professional and personal lives. In addition, they expected their boss to respect their "face" and show interest in their work. This meant that they expected any boss to develop a strong communications and caring bond with them individually and as part of the collectivity in the office. They were prepared to tolerate some tensions in the beginning of the relationship development with their boss, but they were not prepared for the Western technical boss who treated subordinates as ignorant hired hands who could not understand Western slang, had difficulty communicating in the boss' native language, never complained enough to get the boss' attention, needed long and detailed assignments, and acted like a humble servant. Our Chinese managers could not understand how a Sino-Western venture could come to China and bring Western bosses who acted as though they were still back home dealing with Chinese hired hands who were expected to get up to speed quickly within the boss' culture or get fired. In sum, many Western bosses continued to act as they did on their jobs back home. Many were technical people who had little interest in foreign things. In contrast, many other bosses were more transcultural and studied the Chinese way of working with bosses, peers, and subordinates and of treating people in general. These bosses met the above expectations of their Chinese subordinate managers and were admired for this. This treatment by Western transcultural bosses led to harmony with their offices. The clear and expected result was that those Chinese managers with culturally ignorant bosses resigned within 18 months (48%) while those with more transcultural bosses tend to resign much less (24%).

This book should be required reading for all Western and Japanese managers posted in Sino-Western or Sino-Japanese enterprises in China. The simple act of discussing this book with their Chinese subordinate managers should open the doors to better communications. To convince young Chinese managers that they are interested in understanding traditional Chinese values, Western superior and peer managers should avoid the many cultural stereotypes and caricatures of the Chinese value by Hofstede and his followers. Young Chinese managers reject such surface-level descriptions. Remember that the turnover cost is larger than the cost of replacement by a warm body. It also includes the loss of production during the learning curve interval and during the network rebuilding interval. This can become a significant figure after it is multiplied by the number of talented young managers lost per year. In our five-year study, the figures for those most valued by the company 48% of those with poor bosses quit their companies but only 24% of those with good leaders did so after 18 months (Graen, Hui, & Taylor, 2004). In 5 years the project turnover rates would be 24% and 80%. The future of these Sino-Western ventures depends on the development of these young Chinese managers and the future is bleak for those with a majority of these unfortunate bosses.

My colleagues at Procter and Gamble (P&G) are amazed at these numbers, because they were training Chinese managers very early in Deng's open-door period and claimed to have lost not one young Chinese manager who they really wanted to keep. It can be done. Western, college-educated bosses can be trained to do true cultural bonding with their followers Chinese managers. Wal-Mart with the assistance of P&G trainers are currently in the process of learning true cultural bonding in China (Graen, 2006).

TCB RULES FOR SINO-WESTERN OR SINO-JAPANESE LEADERS

1. Develop a serious interest in understand the background of the postmodern Chinese people you work with and around. Read about their history and current circumstance. Ask questions and ask for help in understanding

2. Show a cooperative interest in confronting and resolving value conflicts with your Chinese associates.

3. Learn to communicate at a deep-level by sharing understanding of values to avoid surface-level stereotypes that get in the way and that are displeasing to you.

4. Build the required level of cross-cultural trust by showing that you can be an "outsider" who can be treated as an "insider." Treat your Chinese associates as unique individuals who have their own personalities.

5. Attempt to share network leadership with your Chinese colleagues using the Shared Network Leadership (SNL) practices.

6. Learn the difference in leadership expectations between your and by your Chinese subordinates and associates.

7. When in China try to do things that are compatible with the modern China way.

Clearly, three research-based leadership models dominate the post-modern scientific literature in China and America: Paternalistic Leadership (PL), Charismatic-Transformational Leader Style (CTLS), and Sharing Network Leadership (SNL). All have been researched in both Chinese and American organizations as well as many organizations in different countries. For summaries of research see Graen and Graen's, *Sharing Network Leadership* (2006), Northhouse (2001), Farh and Cheng (2000), and Chen, Tjosvold, and Peng (in press).

In Chinese organizations, research has shown that the American transformational leader style does not work without first achieving the conditions for sharing network leadership (Wang, Law, Hackett, Wang, & Chen, 2005) and that Graen's *SNL* predicts organizational citizen behavior (OCB) in both China and the United States (Hackett, Farh, Song, & Lapierre, 2003).

The well-known, career-long, longitudinal investigation of the entire careers of Japanese managers (Graen, Dharwadkar, Grewal, & Wakabayashi, 2006) demonstrates the power of the SNL model in Japanese corporate society. This investigation documented that career progress in a Japanese corporation is predictable using the SNL model. Recent studies in China suggest that this SNL model works well to predict job performance citizenship and job satisfaction of Chinese employees in both Sino-Western ventures and Chinese corporations in coastal China (Graen & Graen, 2007). The SNL model also was shown to be helpful in highlighting the cross-cultural leader and member communications problems in Sino-Western ventures and suggest remedies (Graen, Hui, & Gu, 2004).

Farh and Cheng (2000) propose a three-factor theory of paternalistic leadership that they claim is thriving in Taiwan's large companies and small. We may contrast this leadership model with those of the modern bureaucratic organization and the postmodern true cultural bonding (TCB) organization as shown in Table 2.2. As shown, the three leadership facets are (a) Moral leadership, projects a activating mission of service beyond self, (b) Authority leadership, offers direction with respect and trust, and (c) Servant leadership seek mutual commitment to collective. These three are seen as legs of a stool and all three must be strong or leadership collapses.

Farh and Cheng's (2000) model was based on the traditional Chinese family business that has successfully merged Chinese Confucian values with modern technology. It may require a population with a complete socialization in a Confucian society like Taiwan. Weber's bureaucratic theory was based on the same three legs, however, it relied on more legal basis for moral, authority, and servant functions. It worked well during the modern industrial times, but may not be appropriate to nongovernmental organizations in the postmodern, information age.

Table 2.2.   Leadership in Mainland China

Leadership Facet	Traditional Chinese Paternalistic	Modern Corporate Economic	True Cultural Bonding
Moral	Obligation to enhance and preserve reputation of family as demanding respect and esteem (Face Enhancing)	Obligation to enhance and preserve health of company for all stakeholders, equitably (Create Wealth)	Achieve profit, be a good citizen and ensure welfare of for all by managing efficiency, risk and adaptation (Fairness)
Authority	Clear lines of authority and trust according to family ties (Confucian Values)	Bureaucratic structures supported by legal system (Legitimate)	Network organization characterized by sharing network leadership at all levels and in all functions (Functional)
Servant	Treat all employees as extended family or family by patriarch or his representatives (Father's Duty)	Standardized and group consideration of all employees needs by bureau (Personnel Department)	Bicultural servant and mentor of employees as needed for both inside and outside work issues (Brother's Duty)

Note: Graen's modification of Farh and Cheng (2000).

True cultural bonding is more appropriate for the challenges of the information age with it's emphasis on stable human relationships with rapidly changing network activity throughout the organization's internal and external webs. With challenges originating from unpredictable location in the webs, strong, flexible networks will be required to make sense of noises and behave appropriately to adjust the systems. Leadership with networks is shared in the name of service beyond self (morale), getting the mission accomplished (authority), and keeping the networks in proper condition (servant). This true cross-national organization requires that organizational policies and practices from strategies to operations to tactics be designed to be cross-nationally friendly. For American organizations to live long and prosper in China, a new postmodern organization such as described herein is needed. We Americans may be at a distinct disadvantage to design and operate such an organization because of our socialization to be insensitive to national differences spanned by our "melting pot" myths. We need cooperatively to overcome our lack of appreciation for other's national history and give them their due respect and admiration. As Newt Gingrich once said, America's common culture is its legal system and little else. This cannot be said validly about China because the Chinese people are proud of their culture and history. As well they should be.

Table 2.3.   Third Culture Management Conflicts

Performance Appraisal	
American Way:	Prepare your case with documents and sell it hard by pushing the envelope to make yourself look the best.
PRC Way:	Prepare your Zen to be judged by your superior and be humble and understate your achievements.
Leadership/Followership	
American Way:	Be a team player but seek to grow out of your job by excelling at special assignments from your boss (self actualize). Expects technical bosses to be self-absorbed and distinct
PRC Way:	Be a super team player and maintain group harmony (selflessness). Expect all bosses to take care of both professional and personal welfare of subordinates.
Participation in Decision Making	
American Way:	Seek to contribute to your Boss' decision through brain storming suggestions, background work, consultations, and playing devil's advocate (all when appropriate).
PRC Way:	Seek to do your own job and not involve yourself in your Boss' job by only doing what is specifically requested by your boss.
Teamwork	
American Way:	Be a team player but push the team to excel by going beyond your assigned tasks and helping your teammates when appropriate.
PRC Way:	Be a team player and maintain harmony by not becoming too invisible (the nail that sticks up gets hammered).

In the next chapter, the research base is presented for using a cooperative as opposed to a competitive conflict resolution method when dealing with cross-national conflicts (Chen, Tjosvold, & Peng, this volume). Conflicts for this cooperative process in Sino-Western ventures in China were identified by Graen, Hui, and Gu's (2004) five year investigation of Chinese college graduate managers reporting to Western bosses in China. These conflicts can be reduced by the methods discussed by Chen and his associates, but too many multinations in China have taken the easy avoidance path of turning a blind eye to these conflicts. This cooperative approach to conflicts must be undertaken if the venture is to survive in China without becoming completely nationalized by the parent corporation.

RECOMMENDATIONS

The first chapter of this book was written to outline in simple terms the recently discovered underlying process (genotype) of building ego networks to enhance the sharing of network leadership in organizations. It was based on research in America, China, and Japan. This underlying process works the same in all three nations at the genotype level however, the behaviors involved are nationally determined at the phenotype level. The basic conditions necessary for the sharing of network leadership, mutual trust, respect, and commitment to the informal bonds are the same, but the interactions generating these dyadic dimensions are different. For example, drinking in bars after work with your boss is a strong indicant in SNL in Japanese and Chinese organizations, but only a weak indicant for Americans. In this chapter, we focused on informing American managers in China how to begin the process of network cooperatively approaching cultural conflicts and misunderstandings before sharing with their Chinese business associates. Chinese can be understood well enough for cross-national bonding with authentic cooperative effort. Let us begin to look at our Chinese fellow employees with respect and trust, and for cooperative conflict resolution and eventual true cultural bonding and network leadership sharing.

REFERENCES

Business Week. (2004). China's multinational.

Chen, C. C., & Lee, Y. -T. (in press). *Business leadership in China: Philosophies, theories & practices*. London: Cambridge University Press.

Farh, J. -L., & Cheng, B. -S. (2000). A cultural analysis of paternalistic leadership in Chinese organizations. In J. T. Li, A. S. Tsui, & Z. Wedlon (Eds.), *Management and organization in the Chinese context* (pp. 94-127). London: Mcmillian

Farh, J. -L., Liang, J., Chou, L. -F., & Cheng, B. -S. (2007). Paternalistic leadership in Chinese organizations. In C. C. Chen & Y. -T. Lee (Eds.), *Businesses leadership in China: Philosophies, theories & practices*. London: Cambridge University Press.

Graen, G. B. (2006). In the eye of the beholder: Cross-cultural lesson in leadership from Project GLOBE. *Academy of Management Perspectives, 20*(4), 95-101.

Graen, G. B., Dharwadkar, R. Grewal, R., & Wakabayashi, M. (2006). Japanese career progress over the long haul: An empirical examination. *Journal of International Business Studies, 37*, 148-161.

Graen, G. B., & Graen, J. A. (Eds.). (2006). *LMX leadership: The series: Vol. 4. Sharing network leadership*. Greenwich, CT: Information Age.

Graen, G. B., & Graen, J. A. (Eds.). (2007). *LMX leadership: The series: Vol. 5. New multinational network sharing*. Charlotte NC: Information Age.

Graen, G. B., Hui, C., & Gu, Q. L. (2004). A new approach to intercultural cooperation. In G. B. Graen (Ed.), *LMX leadership: The series: Vol. 2. New frontiers of leadership* (pp. 225-246). Greenwich, CT: Information Age.

Graen, G. B., Hui, C., & Taylor, E. T. (2004). A new approach to team leadership: Upward, downward, and horizontal differentiation. In G. B. Graen (Ed.),

LMX leadership: The series: Vol. 2. New frontiers of leadership (pp. 33-66). Greenwich, CT: Information Age.

Graen, G. B., Hui, C., Wakabayashi, M., & Wang, Z. M. (1997). Cross-cultural research alliances in organizational research: Cross-cultural partnership-making in action. In C. Earley & M. Erez (Eds.), *Cross-cultural research in industrial organizational psychology* (pp. 160-189). San Francisco: Jossey Bass.

Graen, G. B., & Wakabayashi, M. (1994). Cross-cultural leadership making: Bridging American and Japanese diversity for team advantage. In H. C. Triandis, M. D. Dunnette, & L. M. Hough (Eds.), *Handbook of industrial and organizational psychology* (pp. 415-446). Chicago: Rand-McNally.

Hackett, R. D., Farh, J. -L., Song, L. J., & Lapierre, L. M. (2003). LMX and organizational citizenship behavior: Examining the links within and across Western and Chinese samples. In G. Graen (Ed.), *LMX leadership: The series: Vol. 1. Dealing with diversity* (pp. 219-263). Greenwich, CT: Information Age.

Hofstede, G. (1984). *Culture's consequences: International differences in work-related values* (Abridged ed.). Beverly Hills, CA: Sage.

Hofstede, G. (2001). *Culture's consequences: Comparing values, behaviors, institutions, and organizations across nations* (2nd ed.). Thousand Oaks, CA: Sage.

House, R. J., Hanges, P. J., Jaridan, M., Dorfman, P., & Gupta, V. (Eds.) (2004). *Leadership, cultures, and organizations: The Globe Study.* CA: Sage.

Hwang, K. -K. (2007). Han Fei's theory of leadership and its function in Confucian society. In C. C. Chen & Y. -T. Lee (in press). *Businesses leadership in China: Philosophies, theories & practices.* London: Cambridge University Press.

Northhouse, R. G. (2001). *Leadership: Theory and practice* (2nd ed.). Thousand Oaks: Sage.

Orton, J. D., & Dhillon, G. (2006). Macrostrategic, mesostrategic, and microstrategic leadership processes in loosely coupled networks. In G. B. Graen (Ed.), *LMX leadership: The series: Vol. 4. Sharing network leadership* (pp. 137-167). Greenwich, CT: Information Age.

Seers, A. (2004). Interpersonal workplace theory at a crossroads. In G. B. Graen (Ed.), *LMX leadership: The series: Vol. 2. New frontiers of leadership* (pp. 1-31). Greenwich, CT: Information Age.

Wang, H., Law, K. S., Hackett, R. D., Wang, D., & Chen, Z. X. (2005). Leader-member exchange as a mediator of the relationship between transformational leadership and followers' performance and organizational citizenship behavior. *Academy of Management Journal, 48*(3), 420-432.

CHAPTER 3

CONFLICT AND HARMONY IN FOREIGN-SINO VENTURES IN CHINA

Yi Feng Chen, Dean Tjosvold, and Chunyan Peng

Leadership has traditionally been defined as the ability to influence, motivate and enable employees to contribute to the effectiveness of organizations (House, Javidan, Hanges, & Dorfman, 2002). But this ability is complex and difficult to master. Indeed, in a survey, only 8% of executives believed that their organization had sufficient leadership (Groves, 2005). Fortunately, considerable recent research has emphasized that leaders who develop high-quality relationships are able to empower employees to perform both in-role and extra-role responsibilities (Brower, Schoorman, & Tan, 2000; Graen & Uhl-Bien, 1995; House, Wright & Aditya, 1997; Hui & Law, 1999). But developing these relationships is also challenging, especially when leaders and employees are from different cultures. This chapter proposes programs of that cooperative conflict management helps leaders and employees, especially when they have different national/cultural backgrounds and values, develop leader-member exchange (LMX) high-quality relationships and take advantage of them.

New Multinational Network Sharing
pp. 43–63

INTRODUCTION

Globalization has intensified the reality that leaders and employees who are culturally diverse must work together effectively on a daily basis. Our research has focused on foreign leaders in China. China has become the world's third largest recipient of foreign direct investment, after the United States and Britain (UNCTAD [United Nations Conference on Trade and Development], 2006). Foreign firms are attracted to China's growing, potentially huge market but also by its production capabilities. Originally, most firms had to export their products but they came because they could produce high-quality goods at reasonable cost. They found a large population of able, motivated manufacturing workers in a penny economy and large segments with research and development potential.

To capture these advantages, foreign firms have established subsidiaries and joint ventures (Buvik & Gronhaug, 2000; Charman, 2000; Cyr, 1995; Doz & Hamel, 1998; Hitt, Harrison, & Ireland, 2001; Hitt, Lee, & Yucel, 2002; Inkpen & Beamish, 1997; Lane, Salk, & Lyles, 2001). However to lower costs, improve quality, and participate in China's growing marketplace, these subsidiaries and ventures must recruit and retain Chinese employees and in other ways be well led.

This chapter addresses the confusions with our understanding the relationship between energized cooperation, specifically from high-quality leader relationships LMX, and interpersonal conflict. Conflict is assumed to be the opposite of cooperation in the West and to harm harmony and *guanxi* ego networks in China. The Chinese value of *harmony* is often considered literally as the need to avoid conflict (Bond & Lee, 1981; Cocroft & Ting-Toomey, 1994; Gudykunst, Ting-Toomey, & Chua, 1988; Ting-Toomey, 1988). Chinese are thought to be collectivists whose identity is embedded in their relationships and who have a strong sense of their connections with others. As a consequence, they are highly sensitive to the possibility of losing social face in public; they avoid conflict so that they and their conflict partners need not fear disrespect and alienation. But recent studies suggest that managing conflict cooperatively very much contributes to effective LMX relationships between foreign managers and Chinese employees.

This chapter makes several contributions by bringing conflict research and practice to bear on the study of LMX and leadership more generally. The chapter reviews theory and findings on the conditions and dynamics by which foreign managers and Chinese employees work together productively and, in particular, how they use cooperative conflict to develop their high-quality LMX relationships. High-quality leader relationships are useful because they are the basis upon which leaders and employees can make effective use of information and energy of conflict and thereby contribute to their organizations. The chapter also integrates Western theory and some Chinese values. Researchers have emphasized that guanxi, personal network connections, are critical for doing business in Asia but tend to assume that these relationships are based on conflict avoidance (Hui, & Law, 1999; Tung, 1991). This chapter reviews research showing that conflict handling methods very much contribute to developing and sustaining genuine network harmony in China. It also describes practical implications of this research for how leaders can have an enduring constructive impact by developing a cooperative framework for conflict as a useful approach for nationally/culturally diverse people to use to develop quality LMX leadership relationships and networks.

THE ROLE OF
LEADER RELATIONSHIPS IN NETWORK HARMONY

One of the critical factors leading to network harmony in China is to build and maintain good relationships (guanxi). High-quality LMX relationships are essential for developing and sustaining genuine harmony in Chinese organizations. It is extremely hard for Chinese employees to work in an organization without broad, far-reaching positive personal interaction with their leaders and coworkers (Wang, Law, Chen, & Wang, 2001).

Guanxi not only plays a significant role in Chinese society, but also has serious implications for foreign-Sino ventures (Hui & Graen, 1997). To effectively lead with (deleted?) their Chinese subordinates to accomplish their missions, foreign managers must be able to develop meaningful leader relationships in a way that is acceptable to all parties (Hui & Graen, 1997).

Although research has documented that close working relationships can help diverse people reduce their initial suspicions and prejudice, developing the required high-quality LMX relationships requires more active interventions (Stephen, 1986). Studies indicated that people from diverse cultures are able to develop trusting relationships when they are made more aware of their own perspectives when managing conflicts (Lam, 2000; Matveev & Nelson, 2004; Triandis & Singelis, 1998; Wheelan, Buzalo, & Tsumura, 1998). More cross-cultural research is nevertheless needed to help foreign managers overcome barriers and develop genuine harmony in foreign-Sino ventures (Earley & Mosakowski, 2000; Smith, 2003).

UNDERSTANDING CONFLICT

Traditionally, conflict has been defined of opposing interests arising from scarce resources, goal divergence, frustration and the like (Mack & Snyder, 1957; Pondy, 1967; Schmidt & Kochan, 1972). More recent studies have carried on this tradition (Barki & Hartwick, 2004; Lewicki, Saunders, & Minton, 1997; Rubin, Pruitt, & Kim, 1994). One problem with the traditional approach is that defining conflict as opposing interests confounds conflict with competition defined as incompatible goals or zero-sum situations.

This chapter uses Deutsch's (1973) definition of conflict as apparently incompatible activities; one person's actions interfere, obstruct or in some way get in the way of another's. Conflict occurs when one person's ideas, information, expectations, and preferences are apparently incompatible with those of another as they seek an agreement.

Conflict can and often does occur when people have cooperative, highly compatible goals; they debate the most effective way of pursuing their common task as well as the most efficient and fair way to divide the burdens and benefits of their joint work. Previous research has documented that this confusion very much frustrates our understanding and managing of conflict. When conflicts arise between people with compatible goals, the joint problem processing can be divided neatly into three processes: (1) Identify the problems underlying the conflict, (2) Find the solutions(s) to the problem, and (3) Implement the proper solution (Graen, 1989). When people with conflicting paths, work on these issues in a cooperative framework, they often find ways to resolve their conflict and re-establish harmony.

Conflict should be clearly distinguished from competition defined as incompatible goals. Otherwise it is unclear whether theorized effects of conflict are due to competition or to conflict. In addition, as research summarized in the next section indicates, taking a competitive approach to conflict makes it difficult to develop constructive dynamics and outcomes.

MANAGING CONFLICT TO
BUILD QUALITY LEADER RELATIONSHIPS

Although conflict is part of working cooperatively, the good news is that the conflict can be very useful. When well managed, conflict, is a highly constructive force in organizations (De Dreu & Van de Vliert, 1997). Although conflict has traditionally been considered disruptive, researchers have argued that it is how conflicts are managed, not conflict itself that affects the outcome (Edmondson, Roberto, & Watkins, 2001; Lovelace, Shapiro, & Weingart, 2001). When discussed directly and open-mindedly, conflict can be useful for solving problems and developing relationship (Aldag & Fuller, 1993; Amason, 1996; Chen, Su, & Tjosvold, 2003). It is not conflict itself that affects relationships, but the inability to cope with it directly and constructively. This section reviews research indicating that managing conflict cooperatively can strengthen leader relationships.

Ways to Manage Conflict

Our studies have used Deutsch's (1980, 1973) theory of cooperation and competition to identify major approaches to managing conflict. As people deal with their incompatible activities, they can emphasize their cooperative goals; they believe that their goal attainment facilitates each other's goal achievement. Recognizing that the success of one promotes the success of the other, they tend to solve the problem for mutual benefit. They view conflict as a mutually solvable problem and try to develop a common solution. They discuss opposing positions open-mindedly, try to integrate their ideas, and work for a mutually acceptable solution, that in turn results in high-quality solutions to problems and effective implementation (Deutsch, 1973; Tjosvold, 1989).

People in conflict can also emphasize their competitive interests. They believe as one succeeds, the other moves away from goal attainment (zero-sum); they tend to view the conflict as a win-lose struggle. In the belief that their goals are incompatible, that is, if the other wins, they lose, they try to "beat" the "competitor" and win. The emphasis on competitive interests leads to tough, closed-minded arguments that undermine quality solutions and relationships. Consequently, people fail to use their conflicts to solve difficulties and improve their join work. Social psychological research has documented that whether protagonists emphasize cooperative or competitive goals alters the dynamics and outcomes of conflict (Deutsch, 1980, 1990).

Besides confronting conflict directly, people can choose to avoid it. Smoothing over conflicts and withdrawing from discussion communicate the intention that problems should not be openly considered. Researchers have documented that Asians tend to use avoiding and other accommodative approaches to deal with conflicts whereas Westerners tend to confront conflict directly (Graham, Kim, Lin, & Robinson, 1988; Kirkbride, Tang, & Westwood, 1991; Leung & Tjosvold, 1998; Triandis, 1990; Triandis, Mccusker, & Hui, 1990; Tse, Francis, & Walls, 1994; Weldon, Jehn, Doucet, Chen, & Wang, 1998).

EFFECTS OF APPROACHES TO DEAL WITH CONFLICT IN CHINA

Until recently, there was not much research on the effects of different conflict approaches, especially avoiding conflict in China (Leung, 1996, 1997; Leung, Koch, & Lu, 2002). Building upon considerable evidence in the West, we have used experimental, survey, and interview methods to test the idea that cooperative conflict captures many benefits of conflict in China. Our studies have found that a cooperative approach to conflict enhances constructive conflict resolution; whereas, assuming that goals are incompatible (competitive) interferes with it.

In an experiment (Tjosvold & Sun, 2001), Chinese participants with cooperative goals were committed to mutual benefit, were interested in learning more about the opposing views, considered these views useful, came to agree with them, and tended to integrate them into their own decisions. They were more positively attracted to their protagonists and had greater confidence in working together in the future with them than participants in the competitive condition. More surprisingly, Chinese participants in the cooperative condition used and responded favorably to open discussion itself than those in the competitive condition. They also showed more direct disagreement, compared to smoothing over the opposing views, strengthened cooperative relationships, and induced curiosity, explored opposing views, demonstrated knowledge, and worked to integrate views (Tjosvold & Sun, 2003). Indicating that they found open discussion valuable, participants characterized protagonists who disagreed directly and openly as strong persons and competent negotiators whereas avoiding protagonists were considered weak and ineffectual.

Field studies provide evidence that the experimental findings apply to various kinds of issues and organizational settings in China. For example, a cooperative conflict discussion helped Hong Kong accountants and managers dig into and resolve budget issues, strengthen their relationships, and improve budget quality so that limited financial resources were used wisely (Poon, Pike, & Tjosvold, 2001). Over 100 teams working in Chinese organizations that discussed issues cooperatively and openly were able to deal with biases and took risks effectively (Tjosvold & Yu, in press). According to their managers, these risk-taking groups were able both to innovate and to recover from their mistakes. Studies have also shown that cooperative conflict approach contributes to effective collaboration across organizations. Supply network partners in China that relied on a cooperative approach to conflict, rather than the competitive or avoiding approaches, felt that they had developed a strong sense of justice in their relationships and this in turn resulted in strategic advantage and innovation (Tjosvold, Wong, & Chen, 2005).

Cooperative conflict management can very much contribute to effective top management teams in China. Executives from 105 high technology firms around Beijing who indicated that they relied on cooperative rather than competitive or and avoiding conflict were rated by their CEOs as very effective and their organizations as innovative (Chen, Liu, & Tjosvold, 2005).

Field and experimental studies in North America and Asia provide strong internal and external validity to central hypotheses of cooperative and competitive conflict. Whether protagonists emphasize cooperative or competitive frame drastically affects the dynamics and outcomes of their conflict management. Surprisingly, Chinese participants appear to appreciate others who speak their minds directly and cooperatively.

MANAGING CONFLICT TO DEVELOP
CROSS-CULTURAL LMX RELATIONSHIPS IN CHINA

As managing conflict cooperatively has been found to be useful in China as well as in the West, it might be a basis on which foreign managers and Chinese employees can strengthen their relationships and joint work. A series of studies confirms this hypothesis.

Cooperative, open conflict helped Hong Kong senior accounting managers effectively lead employees in mainland China (Tjosvold & Moy, 1998) and Chinese employees work with their American and Japanese managers (Chen, Tjosvold, & Su, in press). Managers in the Hong Kong parent company and new product specialists in Canada who developed cooperative links and openly discussed their opposing views were able to develop strong, trusting relationships despite their cultural differences and geographic separation (Tjosvold, 1999). Cooperative, constructive controversy interactions were also found critical for Chinese staff to work productively and developed relationships with Japanese managers, outcomes that in turn built commitment to their Japanese companies (Tjosvold, Sasaki, & Moy, 1998). Cooperative conflict was found to help Chinese employees develop effective relationships with their Western managers (Chen, Su, & Tjosvold, in press). More than 200 Chinese employees from various industries in Beijing, Shanghai, Fujian, and Shandong indicated that cooperative, but not competitive or independent, goals helped them and their foreign managers develop a quality leader-member exchange relationship and improve leader effectiveness, employee commitment, and future collaboration (Chen & Tjosvold, in press).

Previous research has emphasized the value of relationships between managers and employees for leadership and the difficulties of forming such relationships, especially across cultural boundaries (Brower et al., 2000; Graen & Uhl-Bien, 1995; House, Wright, & Aditya, 1997; Hui & Law, 1999). Results of our studies support the theorizing that cooperative conflict management is an important way to develop and strengthen the leader relationships even in China and in such cross-cultural settings as subsidiaries and ventures with foreign companies operating in China.

THE ROLE OF VALUES

Results documenting that conflict management can be highly constructive in China challenges traditional theorizing that Chinese values on relationships make open discussion of differences very difficult and culturally inappropriate. More fundamentally, findings challenge traditional assumptions about the role of cultural values. Cultural values are thought to have direct and pervasive effects on people's actions: Collectivism leads to the tendency to avoid conflict. But our studies underline that people have choices to make about how values are to affect them, namely, they can select among a range of values and they can then decide how to express these values.

CHOOSING VALUES

Traditional, Confucian, and collectivist values are often thought to induce Chinese people to try to avoid conflict and seek harmony. Some studies support this reasoning in that evidence has been developed that Chinese compared to Western people prefer to avoid easily open discussion of their differences (Adler, 1983; Chiao, 1981; Herbig & Gulbro, 1997; Hofstede, 1980; Swierczek & Hirsch, 1994; Tang & Kirkbridge, 1986). But Chinese values also allow conflict to be engaged when necessary.

Certainly more modern Chinese values have embraced diversity and conflict. Communist ideology extols the value of class conflict for social change. Mao wanted "to let a hundred flower bloom" and "a hundred school of thoughts contend." During the Cultural Revolution, Lin Biao compelled the Red Guards to "eradicate the four olds" of customs, ideas, habits, and culture. But even traditional values are not uniformly conflict-negative. Confucius himself argued that the "the small man echoes without being in agreement" whereas "the gentleman agrees with others without being an echo." He also wrote, "If it becomes necessary to oppose a ruler, withstand him to his face, and don't try roundabout methods." Confucius scholars had to argue, debate, and fight against those advocating more militant ways to organize society. The influential

Confucian scholar, Mencius, argued, "Indeed, I am not fond of disputing, but I am compelled to do it … I also wish to rectify men's hearts, and to put an end to those perverse doctrines, to oppose their expressions."

Modern Chinese people have a great variety of values from which to choose. The ideals and reasoning of socialism, communism, social welfare, nationalism, and the free market, openness to the West as well as Confucianism, Buddhism, and Daoism all have their proponents in Modern China (Chen & Lee, 2007). Chinese people are not restricted to one set of values that they are obliged to follow. China's long history may have made it possible to strengthen and extend a philosophy over the centuries but it has also made possible the development of many worldviews.

APPLYING VALUES

"By blending the breath of the sun and the shade,
true harmony comes into the world."

Tao Te Ching (poem 42)

The reasoning that traditional values lead to conflict avoidance not only assumes that these values are uniformly conflict-negative but also that there is one way to express these values. But values are general guides and people develop their own ways to interpret and to apply them. Harmony is an important, general Chinese traditional value, but it may not be expressed simply as avoiding conflict. Leung, Koch, and Lu (2002) have recently proposed that harmony has two distinct motives in Chinese society. Disintegration avoidance is instrumental in nature in that the maintenance of harmony is a means to other ends. With this motive, people avoid conflict as a way to further their self-interest and avoid potential interpersonal problems. Harmony can also refer to the desire to engage in behaviors that strengthen relationships, a motive called harmony enhancement. This motivation represents a genuine concern for harmony as a value in and of itself and involves feelings of intimacy, closeness, trust, and compatible and mutually beneficial behaviors. Valuing collectivist relationships then can lead to open conflict engagement, not conflict avoidance.

Consistent with Leung's argument, a study of 194 teams in three regions of China suggests the positive role of collectivist values on conflict (Tjosvold, Law, & Sun, 2003). Teams that had developed collectivist rather than individualistic frames were found to have cooperative goals. The analysis also indicated that these cooperative frames helped the teams discuss their opposing views openly and constructively that in turn resulted in strong relationships and productivity as rated by their managers.

A recent experiment supported the causal relationships that collectivist values heighten cooperative goals and open-minded controversy. Chinese protagonists with opposing views in organizations that valued collectivism, compared to individualism, were found to feel cooperatively interdependent (Tjosvold & Wu, 2005). They were also confident that they could work together and make decisions, sought to understand the opposing position by asking questions, demonstrated that they understood the opposing arguments, accepted these arguments as reasonable, and combined positions to create an integrated decision.

Social face concerns need not result in conflict avoidance and indeed can be a foundation upon which to develop constructive, cooperative conflict. Experimental studies indicate that social face concerns, when expressed by confirming the face of protagonists, promote cooperative conflict (Tjosvold, Hui & Sun, 2000; Tjosvold & Sun, 2001). Emphasizing their cooperative goals, protagonists demonstrated more curiosity in that they explored the opposing views and were interested in hearing more of the other's arguments. Protagonists, whose face was confirmed, compared to those affronted, were prepared to pressure the other and experienced more collaborative influence. They also learned from the discussion, considered the opposing views useful, and worked to integrate and accept them. Results from a field study also indicate that confirmation of social face helped Chinese people discuss their frustrations cooperatively and productively (Tjosvold, Law, & Sun, 2003).

Chinese people have been theorized to avoid conflict because they assume that conflict requires coercion and they prefer persuasion. However, conflict can give rise to either persuasion or coercion. Persuasive influence was found to result in feelings of respect, cooperative relationships, and openness to the other person and position (Tjosvold & Sun, 2001). Persuasion compared to coercion helped discussants seek mutual benefit, open-mindedly listen to each other, integrate their reasoning, and strengthen their relationship. Chinese culture has been characterized as a high-context society where implicit communication is influential (Gudykunst, Ting-Toomey, & Chua, 1988). Conflict is thought to be avoided because open conflict communicates interpersonal hostility. However, nonverbal communication can help develop a cooperative context for conflict discussion. Expressing warmth compared to coldness developed a cooperative, mutually beneficial relationship with the opposing discussant (Tjosvold & Sun, 2003). Protagonists who experienced warmth incorporated the opposing view and reasoning into their decision and thinking, and were confident they could work with the other in the future.

Chinese values are not only compatible with cooperative goals and conflict but they can be a valuable foundation for them. Feeling collective, sensitivity to social face and specifically to giving social face, using persuasive influence attempts, and expressing interpersonal warmth have been found to help Chinese managers, employees, partners deal with their differences openly and productively. Valuing relationships is not an impediment to conflict management; indeed, as the studies reviewed indicate, cooperative relationships are a foundation for open, constructive conflict.

POWER DISTANCE AND CONFLICT MANAGEMENT IN CHINA

High power distance is thought to be a basic value in China. Chinese leadership is assumed to be autocratic where followers quickly and automatically follow the wishes and decisions of leaders. Chinese employees have been found to accept unilateral decision-making and prefer their leaders be benevolent autocrats (Leung, 1997). However, Western leaders should recognize that this high power distance may not be expressed in dominating and authoritarian ways as leaders in China are expected to be supportive and nurturing (Spencer-Oatey, 1997).

Consistent with the LMX research in the West, our studies indicate that leaders in China must develop open, mutual relationships with employees (Chen & Tjosvold, in press; Liu, Tjosvold, & Yu, 2004; Tjosvold, Hui, & Su, 2004; Tjosvold, & Leung, 2004; Tjosvold, Wong, & Hui, 2004). Authority cannot be assumed but leaders must earn it by demonstrating a commitment to employees and openness to them. Strong cooperative goals were found to be critical for a high-quality leader relationship, and this relationship in turned led to employees being effective organizational citizens (Tjosvold, Law, & Hui, (1996). An open-minded discussion of opposing views between leaders and employees was highly crucial, resulting in productive work, strong work relationships, experiencing the leader as democratic, and believing that both the leader and employee are powerful (Tjosvold, Hui , & Law, 1998). These studies support the view that democratic, open-minded leadership is valued in China; Chinese employees want a relationship with their leaders and, although they may at times be hesitant to initiate conflictful discussions, expect their leaders to consider their needs and views. Western managers should not assume that they can lead in autocratic, coercive manner without developing relationships.

Cooperative conflict is a concrete way for managers in China to develop the leader relationship and demonstrate their openness. Despite power distance values, leaders and employees in China can benefit a great deal by managing their conflicts cooperatively. Cooperative conflict is an ideal that both managers and employees in China and in the West can aspire to.

Conflict Management for Genuine Harmony

In today's diverse and global marketplace, theories, especially about conflict, that can only be applied in one culture are increasingly irrelevant. If continued to be successfully demonstrated in various cultures (Tjosvold & De Dreu, 1997), the framework of cooperative, constructive conflict has the potential of acting as a common guide for how people from different cultures can develop their own ways of managing conflict. Diverse people together decide that they want to use a cooperative approach to conflict as the major way of handling their disputes and then put in place the incentives and procedures that support cooperative goals and conflict.

A RECOMMENDED APPROACH TO
LEADING MULTINATIONALLY USING CONFLICT

Recently, researchers have argued that culturally diverse people need theoretical frameworks for how to deal with barriers and obstacles and interact effectively (Bond, 2003; Smith, 2003). Diverse individuals, in addition to understanding general value differences that may impact their interaction, can use knowledge to form a common understanding and platform for how they can work together productively (Leung, in press; Tjosvold & Leung, 2003). Research supports that foreign managers and Chinese employees in subsidiaries and joint ventures of foreign companies in China can both value and engage in cooperative conflict management. However, results do not imply that they have highly similar ways of managing conflict (Tjosvold & Hu, 2005). While the "genotypes," the underlying conceptual structure of the theory of cooperation and competition, appears to be similar, the "phenotypes," how the theory is manifested in particular situations, often are not. In particular, the actions that develop cooperative goals and communicate an attempt to discuss conflicts openmindedly may be quite different in China than in North America, as may the general levels of cooperative goals and conflict.

The theory of cooperation and competition may be a basis for diverse managers and employees to develop a common approach to managing their conflicts and strengthening their relationships. In particular, foreign managers and local employees who are motivated and skilled in managing their conflicts cooperatively appear to have a strong basis for productive mutual work in China and perhaps in other societies as well. Using a cooperative approach to conflict contributes to effective relationships between foreign managers and Chinese employees that in turn helped employees feel trusting and committed to their job.

Without a common framework, organizations are apt to impose the procedures of one culture on another, such as, insisting that everyone conform to the head office's ways. Or they may use trial-and-error in hope that they develop new procedures. However, these approaches are apt to result in organizations characterized by destructive conflict and conflict avoidance.

Developing a Multinational Approach Together

Foreign managers and Chinese employees can agree to use cooperative conflict as common framework for how they are going to disagree to strengthen their relationships and improve their performance. Together they commit themselves and learn how to communicate the intention to cooperate, maintain a quality relationship, and develop mutually beneficial solutions. They trained together to confront their differences directly and to speak their mind freely; they stop defending their own views long enough to ask each other for more information and arguments. They show their intention to maintain their cooperative relationship and understand each other by putting themselves into each other's shoes. They recognize that they want to resolve the conflict for mutual benefit. They realize that their goal is to strengthen cooperative relationship and help each other get what each other really needs and values, and not to try to win and outdo each other.

Foreign managers and Chinese employees can form small cooperative groups where they commit themselves and strengthen their cooperative conflict management skills together. These cooperative groups are themselves very facilitative of the goals of the training. Findings indicate that people in cooperative groups have higher achievement than those in competitive and independent settings (Johnson, Druckman, & Dansereau, 1994). Team members can become more knowledgeable and skilled in working cooperatively through team training and follow-up activities. The method of cooperative team training reinforces the message. Cooperative experiences can improve feedback processes that stimulate learning. Chinese people have been found to be more accepting, open, and respectful of feedback when they are working cooperatively rather than competitively (Tjosvold, Tang, & West, 2004). Foreign managers and Chinese employees can develop ways of managing conflict cooperatively that are appropriate and effective for them. Then they are able to express their diversity and use their conflicts to solve problems. Cooperative conflict management strengthens their relationships, appreciation of their diversity, and performance.

CONCLUSIONS

Personal connections are critical for doing business in China (Hui & Law, 1999; Tung, 1991). Studies have found that in Chinese organizations, compared to British and American enterprises, maintaining good relationships is essential for employee commitment (Easterby-Smith, Malina & Lu, 1995; Wang et al. 2001). Chinese employees are looking for managers who can communicate effectively and understand their concerns; they can be highly frustrated if they have to work in an organization without broad, far-reaching personal interaction (Hui & Graen, 1997). A key to leading in China is building and maintaining guanxi, which is a close interpersonal connections in a network. Guanxi has significant implications for foreign ventures as well as managing in Chinese firms (Graen, Hui, & Gu, 2004; Hui & Graen, 1997). Harmony and guanxi have traditionally been highly valued in China, but considering conflict as negative and avoiding conflict appear generally ineffective for promoting successful organizations in China. Chinese people want harmony but appear to recognize that managing conflict is needed to develop authentic harmony where frustrations are resolved and relationships maintained (Leung, et al, 2002).

Our studies in China suggest that conflict management is critical for modern development (Tjosvold, Leung, & Johnson, 2006). Chinese employees who use their conflicts cooperatively have been found to improve the quality of products and services and reduce costs. They have used cooperative conflict to strengthen their relationships within their groups and organizations but also with alliance partners. Participative management and democracy more generally requires that leaders be responsive and open; cooperative conflict contributes to open-minded, productive relationships between leaders and employees. Genuine harmony and conflict management are not opposites but are mutually reinforcing.

It is particularly fitting that a chapter on harmony and conflict is in the LMX book series. Constructive conflict is one reason high-quality leader relationships are so valuable; leaders and employees with strong relationships are able to use conflict to solve problems and get things done as well as strengthen their relationships. Effective leadership is also needed for constructive conflict in organizations. Managing conflict constructively takes two. Leaders can strengthen the understanding, values, procedures, and skills that help organizational members discuss their differences openly and successfully. The power of conflict management knowledge is realized when people, perhaps especially multinationally diverse ones, study and apply it together. Leaders can have a lasting influence to motivate and enable employees to contribute to the effectiveness of organizations by together with their employees strengthening their relationships through learning and applying cooperative conflict.

ACKNOWLEDGMENT

This study was supported by the RGC grant project No: LU3404/05H to the second author.

REFERENCES

Adler, N. J. (1983). Cross-cultural management research: The ostrich and the trend. *Academy of management Review, 8*, 266-232.

Aldag, R. J., & Fuller, S. R. (1993). Beyond fiasco: A reappraisal of the groupthink phenomenon and a new model of group decision processes. *Psychological Bulletin, 113*, 533-552.

Amason, A. C. (1996). Distinguishing the effects of functional and dysfunctional conflict on strategic decision making: Resolving a paradox for top management teams. *Academy of Management Journal, 39*, 123-148.

Barki, H., & Hartwick, J. (2004), Conceptualizing the Construct of Interpersonal Conflict. *International Journal of Conflict Management, 15*(3), 216-244.

Bond, M. H. (2003). Cross-cultural social psychology and the real world of culturally diverse teams and dyads. In D. Tjosvold & K. Leung (Eds.), *Cross-cultural foundations: Traditions for managing in a cross-cultural world.* Hampshire, United Kingdom: Ashgate.

Bond, M. H., & Lee, P. W. H. (1981). Face saving in Chinese culture: A discussion and experimental study of Hong Kong students. In A. Y. C. King & R. P. L. Lee (Eds.), *Social life and development in Hong Kong* (pp. 289–303). Hong Kong: The Chinese University Press, .

Brower, H. H., Schoorman, F. D., & Tan, H. H. (2000). A model of relational leadership: The integration of trust and leader-member exchange. *Leadership Quarterly, 11*, 227-250.

Buvik, A., & Gronhaug, K. (2000). Inter-firm dependence, environmental uncertainty and vertical co-ordination in industrial buyer-seller relationships. *Omega, 28*, 445-454.

Charman, C. D. (2000, May-June). A CEO roundtable on making mergers succeed. *Harvard Business Review*, 145-154.

Chen, C. C., & Lee, Y. T. (2007). *Businesses leadership in China: Philosophies, theories & practices.* London: Cambridge Press.

Chen, G., Liu, C. H., & Tjosvold, D. (2005). Conflict management for effective top management teams and innovation in China. *Journal of Management Studies, 42,* 277-300.

Chen, Y. F., Su, F, & Tjosvold, D. (2003, August). *Working with foreign managers: Conflict management for effective leader relationships in China.* Paper presented at the 5th Australia Industrial & Organisational Psychology Conference, Melbourne, Australia.

Chen, Y. F., Tjosvold, D., & Su, F. (2005). Working with foreign managers: Conflict management for effective leader relationships in China. *Journal of International Conflict Management, 16,* 265-286.

Chen, Y. F., & Tjosvold, D. (in press). Cross cultural leadership: Goal interdependence and leader-member relations in foreign ventures in China. *Journal of International Management.*

Chen, Y. F., Tjosvold, D., & Su, F. (in press). Goal interdependence for working across cultural boundaries: Chinese employees with foreign managers. *International Journal of Intercultural Relations.*

Chiao, C. (1981, November-December). *Chinese strategic behavior: Some general principles.* Paper presented at a conference in honor of Professor John M. Roberts, Claremont, CA.

Cocroft, B. A. K., & Ting-Toomey, S. (1994). Facework in Japan and in the United States. *International Journal of Intercultural Relations, 18,* 469–506.

Cyr, D. J. (1995). *The human resource challenge of international joint ventures.* Westport, CT: Quorum Books.

De Dreu, C., & Van de Vliert, E. (Eds.). (1997). *Using conflict in organizations.* Thousand Oaks, CA: Sage.

Deutsch, M. (1973). *The resolution of conflict.* New Haven, CT: Yale University Press.

Deutsch, M. (1980). Fifty years of conflict. In L. Festinger (Ed.), *Retrospections on social psychology* (pp. 46-77). New York: Oxford University Press.

Deutsch, M. (1990). Sixty years of conflict. *The International Journal of Conflict Management, 1,* 237-263.

Doz, Y. L., & Hamel, G. (1998). *Alliance advantage: The art of creating value through partnering.* Boston: Harvard Business School Press.

Easterby-Smith, M., Malina, D., & Lu, Y. (1995). How culture-sensitive Is HRM? *International Journal of Human Resource Management, 6*(1), 31–59.

Earley, P. C., & Mosakowski, E. (2000). Creating hybrid team cultures: An empirical test of transnational team functioning. *Academy of Management Journal, 43,* 26-49.

Edmondson, A. C., Roberto, M., & Watkins, M. (2001, August). *Negotiating asymmetry: A model of top management team effectiveness.* Paper presented at the Academy of Management Meetings, Washington, DC.

Graen, G. B. (1989). *Unwritten rules for your career: 15 secrets for fast-track success.* New York: Wiley.

Graen, G. B., Hui, C., & Gu, Q. L. (2004). A new approach to intercultural cooperation. In G B. Graen (Ed.), *LMX leadership: The series: Vol. 2. New frontiers of leadership* (pp. 225-246). Greenwich, CT: Information Age.

Graen, G. B., & Uhl-Bien, M. (1995). Relationship-based approach to leadership: development of leader-member exchange (LMX) theory of leadership over

25 years: Applying a multi-level multi-domain perspective. *Leadership Quarterly, 6,* 219-247.

Graham, J. L., Kim, D. K., Lin, C., & Robinson, M. (1988). Buyer-seller negotiations around the pacific rim: differences in fundamental exchange processes. *Journal of Consumer Research, 15,* 48-54.

Groves, K. S. (2005). Linking leader skills, follower attitudes, and contextual variables via an integrated model of charismatic leadership. *Journal of Management, 31,* 255-277.

Gudykunst, W. B., Ting-Toomey, S., & Chua, E. (1988). *Culture and interpersonal communication.* Thousands Oaks, CA: Sage.

Herbig, P., & Gulbro, R. (1997). External influences in the cross-cultural negotiation process. *Industrial Management and Data System, 97,* 158-170.

Hitt, M. A., Harrison, J. S., & Ireland, R. D. (2001). *Mergers & acquisitions: A guide to creating value for shareholders.* New York: Oxford University Press.

Hitt, M. A., Lee, H. U., & Yucel, E. (2002). The importance of social capital to the management of multinational enterprises: Relational networks among Asian and western firms. *Asia Pacific Journal of Management, 19,* 353-372.

Hofstede, G. (1980). *Culture's consequences: International differences in work-related values.* Thousand Oaks, CA: Sage.

House, R. J., Javidan, M., Hanges, P. J., & Dorfman, P. W. (2002). Understanding cultures and implicit leadership theories across the globe: An Introduction to Project GLOBE. *Journal of World Business, 37,* 3-10.

House, R. J., Wright, N. S., & Aditya, R. N. (1997). Cross-cultural research on organizational leadership: a critical analysis and a proposed theory. In P. C. Earley, & M. Erez (Eds.), *New perspectives on international industrial/organizational psychology* (pp. 535-625). San Francisco: The New Lexington Press.

Hui, C., & Graen, G. B. (1997). Guanxi and professional leadership in contemporary Sino-American joint ventures in Mainland China. *Leadership Quarterly, 8(4),* 451-465.

Hui, C., & Law, K. S. (1999). A structural equation model of the effects of negative affectivity, leader-member exchange, and perceived job mobility on in-role and extra-role performance: A Chinese case. *Organizational Behavior and Human Decision Processes, 77,* 3-21.

Inkpen, A. C., & Beamish, P. W. (1997). Knowledge, bargaining power, and the instability of international joint ventures. *Academy of Management Review, 22,* 177-202.

Johnson, D. W., Druckman, D., & Dansereau, D. (1994). Training in teams. In D. Druckman, & R. Bjork. (Eds.), *Learning, remembering, believing: Enhancing human performance* (pp. 140-170). Washington, DC: National Academy Press.

Kirkbride, P. S., Tang, S. F. Y., & Westwood, R. I. (1991). Chinese conflict preferences and negotiating behavior: cultural and psychological influences. *Organization Studies, 12,* 365-386.

Lam Y. L. (2000). Reconceptualizing problem-solving and conflict resolution in schools: A multi-disciplinary perspective. *The International Journal of Educational Management, 14(2),* 84-90.

Lane, P. J., Salk, J. E., & Lyles, M. A. (2001). Absorptive capacity, learning, and performance in international joint ventures. *Strategic Management Journal, 22,* 1139-1161.

Leung, K. (1996, June). *The role of harmony in conflict avoidance.* Paper presented in the Korean Psychological Association 50th Anniversary Conference, Seoul, Korea.

Leung, K. (1997). Negotiation and reward allocations across cultures. In P. C. Earley & M. Erez (Eds.), *New perspectives on international industrial/organizational psychology* (640-675). San Francisco: Jossey-Bass.

Leung, K. (in press). Effective conflict resolution for intercultural disputes. In T. Gärling, G. Backenroth-Ohsako, B. Ekehammar, & L. Jonsson (Eds.), *Diplomacy and psychology: Prevention of armed conflicts after the Cold War.* London: Marshall Cavendish.

Leung, K., Koch, P. T., & Lu, L. (2002). A dualisic model of harmony and is implications for conflict management in Asia. *Asia Pacific Journal of Management, 19,* 201-220.

Leung, K., & Tjosvold, D. (1998). Conflict fordoing business in the Pacific Rim. In K. Leung & D. W. Tjosvold (Eds.), *Conflict management in the Asia Pacific* (pp. 1-14). Singapore: Wiley.

Lewicki, R., Saunders, D. M., & Minton, J. M. (1997). *Essentials of negotiation.* Chicago: Irwin.

Liu, C. H., Tjosvold, D., & Yu, Z. Y. (2004). Traditional values for applying abilities and leader effectiveness in China. *Leadership & Organization Development Journal, 25,* 318-331.

Lovelace, K., Shapiro, D., & Weingart, L. R. (2001). Maximizing cross-functional new product team's innovativeness and constraint adherence: A conflict communications perspective. *Academy of Management Journal, 44,* 7798-7793.

Mack, R., & Snyder, R. (1957). An analysis of social conflict—Toward an overview and synthesis. *Journal of Conflict Resolution, 1,* 212-248.

Matveev, A. V., &. Nelson P. E. (2004). Cross cultural communication competence and multicultural team performance: Perceptions of American and Russian managers. *International Journal of Cross Cultural Management, 4*(2), 253-270.

Pondy, L. R. (1967). Organizational conflict: concepts and models. *Administrative Science Quarterly, 12,* 296-320.

Poon, M., Pike, R., & Tjosvold, D. (2001). Budget participation, goal interdependence and controversy: A study of a Chinese public utility. *Management Accounting Research, 12,* 101-118.

Rubin, J. Z., Pruitt, D. G., & Kim, S. H. (1994). *Social conflict: Escalation, stalemate and settlement* (2nd ed.). New York: McGraw Hill.

Schmidt, S. M., & Kochan, T. A. (1972). Conflict: towards conceptual clarity. *Administrative Science Quarterly, 17,* 359-370.

Smith, P. B. (2003). Meeting the challenge of cultural difference. In D. Tjosvold & K. Leung (Eds.), *Cross-cultural management: Foundation and future* (pp. 59-73). England: Ashgate.

Spencer-Oatey, H. (1997). Unequal relationships in high and low power distance societies: A comparative study of tutor-student role relations in Britain and China. *Journal of Cross-Cultural Psychology, 28,* 284-302.

Stephen, W. G. (1986). The contact hypothesis in intergroup relationship. In C. Hendrick (Ed.), *Group processes and intergroup relationships* (pp. 13-40). Newbury Park, CA: Sage.

Swierczek, F., & Hirsch, G. (1994). Joint ventures in Asia and multicultural management. *European Management Journal, 12*(2), 197-209.

Tang, S. F. Y., & Kirkbridge, P. S. (1986). Developing conflict managing skills in Hong Kong: An analysis of some cross-cultural implications. *Management Education and Development, 17,* 287-301.

Ting-Toomey, S. (1988). Intercultural conflict style: A face-negotiation theory. In Y. Y. Kim & W. B. Gudykunst (Eds.), *Theories in intercultural communication* (pp. 213-238). Newbury Park, CA: Sage

Tjosvold, D. (1989). Interdependence and power between managers and employees: A study of the leader relationship. *Journal of Management, 15,* 49-62.

Tjosvold, D. (1999). Bridging East and West to develop new products and trust: Interdependence and interaction between a Hong Kong parent and North American subsidiary. *International Journal of Innovation Management, 3,* 233-252.

Tjosvold, D., & De Dreu, C. (1997). Managing conflict in Dutch organizations: A test of the relevance of Deutsch's cooperation theory. *Journal of Applied Social Psychology, 27,* 2213-2227.

Tjosvold, D., & Hu, J. (2005). *Managing conflict in China* (in Chinese). Shanghai, China: Shanghai Far East.

Tjosvold, D., Hui, C. & Law, K. S. (1998). Empowerment in the leader relationship in Hong Kong: Interdependence and controversy. *Journal of Social Psychology, 138,* 624-636.

Tjosvold, D., Hui, C., & Su, F. (2004). *Leadership in Chinese enterprise* (in Chinese). Shanghai, China: Shanghai Far East.

Tjosvold, D., Hui, C. & Sun, H. (2000). Social face and open-mindedness: Constructive conflict in Asia. In C. M. Lau, K. S. Law, D. K. Tse, & C. S. Wong (Eds.), *Asian management matters: Regional relevance and global impact* (pp. 3-16). London: Imperial College Press.

Tjosvold, D., Law, K. S., & Hui, C. (1996). *Goal interdependence, leadership relationship, and citizenship behavior in China.* Paper presented at the International Association for Conflict Management, Ithaca, NY.

Tjosvold, D., Law, K. S., & Sun, H. F. (2003). Collectivistic and individualistic values: Their effects on group dynamics and productivity in china. *Group Decision and Negotiation, 12,* 243-263

Tjosvold, D., & Leung, K. (2003). *Cross-cultural foundations: traditions for managing in a cross-cultural world.* Hampshire, United Kingdom: Ashgate.

Tjosvold, D., & Leung, K. (Eds.) (2004). The leadership challenge in high growth Asia. In *Leading in high growth Asia: Managing relationships for teamwork and change* (pp. 1-12). London: World Scientific.

Tjosvold, D. Leung, K., & Johnson, D. W. (2006). Cooperative and competitive conflict in China. In M. Deutsch, P. T. Coleman, & E. Marcus (Eds.), *The handbook of conflict resolution: Theory and practice* (pp. 671-692). San Francisco: Jossey-Bass

Tjosvold, D., & Moy, J. (1998). Managing employees in China from Hong Kong: Interaction, relationships, and productivity as antecedents to motivation. *Leadership & Organization Development Journal, 19*, 147-156.

Tjosvold, D., Sasaki, S., & Moy, J. (1998). Developing commitment in Japanese organizations in Hong Kong: Interdependence, interaction, relationship and productivity. *Small Group Research, 29*, 560-582.

Tjosvold, D., & Sun, H. (2001). Effects of influence tactics and social contexts: An experiment on relationships in China. *International Journal of Conflict Management, 12*, 239-258.

Tjosvold, D., & Sun, H. (2003). Openness among Chinese in conflict: Effects of direct discussion and warmth on integrated decision making. *Journal of Applied Social Psychology, 33*, 1878-1897.

Tjosvold, D., & Tang, M. L., West, M. (2004). Reflexivity for team innovation in China: The contribution of goal interdependence. *Group & Organization Management, 29*, 540-559.

Tjosvold, D., Wong, S. H., & Chen, Y. F. (2005, August). *Conflict management for justice, and innovation and strategic advantage in organizational partnerships.* Paper presented at the Academy of Management Meetings, Hawaii.

Tjosvold, D., Wong, S. H., & Hui, C. (2004). Leadership research in Asia: Developing relationships. In K. Leung & S. White (Eds.), *Handbook of Asian management* (pp. 373-395). Netherlands: Kluwer Academic.

Tjosvold, D., & Wu, P., (2005, June). *Collectivist values for discussing and integrating opposing views: An experiment on goal interdependence in China.* Paper presented at the International Association for Conflict Management, Seville, Spain.

Tjosvold, D., & Yu, Z. Y. (in press). Group risk-taking: The constructive role of controversy in China. *Group & Organization Management.*

Triandis, H. C. (1990). Cross-cultural studies of individualism and collectivism. In J. J. Berman (Ed.), *Nebraska symposium on motivation*, (pp. 37, 41-133). Lincoln: University of Nebraska Press.

Triandis, H. C., McCusker, C., & Hui, C. H. (1990). Multimethod probes of individualism and collectivism. *Journal of Personality and Social Psychology, 59*, 1006-1020.

Triandis, H. C., & Singelis, T. M. (1998). Training to recognize individual differences in collectivism and individualism within culture. *International Journal of Intercultural Relations, 22*(1), 35-47.

Tse, D. K., Francis, J., & Walls, J. (1994). Cultural differences in conducting intra- and inter-cultural negotiations: A Sino-Canadian comparison. *Journal of International Business Studies, 24*, 537-555.

Tung, R. (1991). Handshakes across the sea: Cross-cultural negotiating for business success. *Organizational Dynamics, 14*, 30-40.

UNCTAD. (2006). Trade and Development Report 2006, released on August 31, 2006, from http://www.unctad.org/Templates/Page.asp?intItemID=3922&lang=1

Wang, H., Law, K. S., Chen, Z., & Wang, D. X. (2001, August). *Relationship between LMX and performance appraisal: The moderating effects of leadership style.* Paper presented at the Academy of Management Meeting, Washington DC.

Weldon, E., Jehn, K. A., Doucet, L., Chen, X., & Wang, Z. M. (1998, January). *Conflict management in US-Chinese joint ventures.* Paper presented at the research conference on China Management, Hong Kong University of Science and Technology, Hong Kong.

Wheelan, S. A., Buzalo, G., & Tsumura, E. (1998). Development assessment tools for cross-cultural research. *Small Group Research, 29*(3), 359-370.

CHAPTER 4

MAKING LMX LEADERSHIP WORK IN CHINA

Ziguang Chen and Wing Lam

The purpose of this chapter is to present the theoretical and empirical work on leader-member exchange (LMX) in China. The theoretical reception of LMX has generally the same meaning in the West and in China, but there are differences in these receptions due to vast cultural influences. These will be discussed in the current chapter. Empirically, LMX research in China shows that the predictive results of using validated Chinese LMX measures are similar to those in the West, particularly in the United States, indicating that establishing a high-quality LMX is helpful for employees to obtain career success in both the Chinese and the American work contexts. The results strongly suggest that LMX is a critical predictor of various work attitudes and outcomes such as high degree of job satisfaction, career success, increased work performance, and organizational citizenship behaviors in both China and the West. However, because of cultural differences between China and the West, there appears to be variance in values, norms, and actions that may make LMX work in different ways. We thus explain the issue of how to make LMX work in China by telling stories on growing up in mainland China and the learning of Chinese values.

New Multinational Network Sharing
pp. 65–77
Copyright © 2007 by Information Age Publishing
All rights of reproduction in any form reserved.

INTRODUCTION

While leader-member exchange (LMX) has long been of interest among researchers and practitioners in the West (e.g., Graen, in press; Graen, Novak, & Sommerkamp, 1982; Uhl-Bien & Maslyn, 2003) and Japan (Graen, Dharwadkar, Grewal, & Wakabayashi, 2006; Wakabayashi & Graen, 1984.), empirical research on it in China has started only recently (e.g., Chen, Lam, & Zhong, 2007; Lam, Huang, & Snape, 2007; Wang, Law, Hackett, Wang, & Chen, 2005). Therefore, much of the research on LMX in China is still in the infancy stage—in the process of obtaining the theoretical construct or meaning of LMX in the Chinese work context. Is generalizability a problem for the Western construct of LMX in China? To address this research question, we begin by discussing the LMX experience in the West and in China.

In lectures conducted in the West and in China, we asked students what were their expectations of our classes. Surprisingly, we did not receive instrumental responses such as getting an A grade as a final score. Instead, most of the students merely hoped that we might maintain a good relationship with each of them during the whole semester so that they would enjoy attending class. This experience immediately inspired us to believe that many employees in today's workplace might have similar hopes. In the current chapter, we therefore focused on two interesting research questions: Is there really a need for LMX, and what does the concept mean to employees in both the Western and Chinese work contexts?

WHAT DOES LMX TELL IN THE WEST?

Graen and his associates (Graen & Cashman, 1975; Graen, Orris, & Johnson, 1973; Johnson & Graen, 1973) acknowledged that in a work unit, leaders indeed develop different patterns of relationship with their subordinates. The authors therefore proposed the concept of LMX, which is a relationship-based approach to leadership. Moreover, this approach is based on the "upward dyad linkage" which focuses on the relationship between a supervisor and his or her subordinate. In the upward dyad linkage, the authors documented that supervisors do not only use an average leadership style within their work groups but also develop differentiated relationships with each of their directed subordinates. Early research suggested that due to limited resources and time, supervisors can profitably develop and maintain only a few high-quality exchange relationships with subordinates, whereas the rest would involve lower-quality exchanges and retaining formal authority relationships. However, later research recommended offering the opportunity for high-quality exchange relationships to all (Graen, 2003).

A high-quality LMX is a close working relationship characterized by interpersonal attraction (Graen & Cashman, 1975), trust and support (Liden & Graen, 1980), and mutual influence (Yukl, 2006). In a high-quality LMX, both supervisors and subordinates gain valued outcomes. Subordinates who share a high-quality exchange with their supervisors earn special benefits and opportunities including favorable performance appraisals, promotions, pay raises, support in career development, and feelings of empowerment (Graen, Wakabayashi, Graen, & Graen, 1990; Kacmar, Witt, Zivnuska, & Gully, 2003; Keller & Dansereau, 1995; Wakabayashi & Graen, 1984; Yukl, 2006). In return, supervisors benefit from working with committed, competent, satisfied, and hardworking subordinates (Graen, 2003; Liden & Graen, 1980; Podsakoff, MacKenzie, & Hui, 1993; Scandura, Graen, & Novak, 1986; Scott & Bruce, 1994; Stepina, Perrewe, Hassell, Harris, & Mayfield, 1991; Vecchio, Griffeth, & Hom, 1986). In contrast, a lower-quality LMX is associated with less mutual support and trust between supervisors and their subordinates. This relationship is characterized by unidirectional downward influence and the exercise of formal organizational authority. Therefore, supervisors who have a lower-quality LMX with their subordinates obtain subordinates' routine performance, and these subordinates in turn receive standard organizational benefits (Graen & Uhl-Bien, 1995; Yukl, 2006).

WHAT IS THE MEANING OF LMX AMONG THE CHINESE?

Many scholars (e.g. Butterfield, 1983; Hui & Graen, 1997) have noted that in comparison with Westerners, the Chinese have a much stronger tendency to divide people into categories and treat them accordingly. This tendency to treat people differently is based on one's relationship with them. Individuals would enjoy greater protection and reciprocation within the group if they have close relationships with others (Hwang, 1987). This concept is greatly built on the indigenous belief of *"who you know is more important than what you know"* in the Chinese socio-culture (Tsui, 2001). This belief clearly illustrates that in a relation-based society like China, having a good *"Guanxi,"* a form of interpersonal connection networks in all contexts of a person including his or her work unit, is a key for personal success (i.e., career success in the workplace) (Bae & Lawler, 2000; Hwang, 1987; Wall, 1990). *Guanxi* refers to "informal, personal, and particularistic relationships based on mutual obligations" (Peng, 2001, p. 55). *Guanxi* ties people together according to the specific relationship among these people; examples of this are being a relative (close or distant), *having the same ancestral origin, being a former neighbor, school-mate, supervisor, or subordinate, having the same interests, and so on* (Farh, Tsui, Xin, & Cheng, 1998; Hui & Graen, 1997). People in the same social network are obligated to fulfill mutual obligations within the group. This phenomenon can be explained by the traditional Confucian hierarchical notion of *wu-lun* (five cardinal relationships): relationship between the emperor and subject, father and son, husband and wife, elder and younger sibling, and friend to friend (Cheng & Farh, 2001; Farh et al., 1998; Hui & Graen, 1997; Luo, 2000). *Wu-lun* is the basis of the Chinese social network, requiring each actor to perform his or her positional role in such a way that he or she says precisely what he or she is supposed to say, and does not say what he or she is not supposed to say (Yang, 1993). *Violation of these social rules can bring a loss of face for both the individual and the family.* These five relationships give order and stability to the social system in the Chinese context. Applying the concept of *guanxi* in the Chinese work context, the role relation of a father to his son (supervisor-subordinate relationship in today's work context) seems to be similar to that espoused by the LMX theory. This is because subordinates who are highly involved in the role relation of emperor-subject tend to enjoy more protection and receive better resources and support from their immediate bosses. Bosses are expected to "take care of" each subordinate in a fatherly way both professionally and personally. Beyond the strong business only relations of the LMX theory in the United States, Chinese, employees who have a closer emperor-subject relation receive broader benefits and resources from their supervisors. Part of this difference is that American supervisors do not intervene in subordinates' personal life as Chinese supervisions do.

However, the underlying assumption of LMX in China is different from the social networks observed in the West (Chen, 2006; Wang, Niu, & Law, 2004). First, the supervisor-subordinate relationship in the Chinese work context focuses more on hierarchical role relations with large power differences between supervisors and subordinates, while Western interpersonal networks concern close power differences between dyadic members (Cheng & Rosett, 1991). Second, the Chinese supervisor-subordinate relationship is also maintained primarily by special obligations based on strong norms of fairness that are much more precise than in America. When a person gives a certain value of resource or a favor to another, he or she is expected to receive a fair repayment sometime in the future (Farh et al., 1998). However, Western social networks are less dependent on specific, tangible, and transactional reciprocity (Cheng & Rosett, 1991; Luo, 2000; Yeung & Tung, 1996). Third, past research conducted in the West suggested that subordinates perceive promotion as a key to build and maintain a higher-quality LMX with their leaders (Gerstner & Day,

1997; Graen & Uhl-Bien, 1995; Liden, Sparrowe, & Wayne, 1997). This is because based on the notion of reciprocity (cf., Uhl-Bien & Maslyn, 2003), supervisors perceive that those capable employees will reciprocate by performing better at their work. In comparison, in the Chinese work context, employee ties by social networks involve a strong and clear sense of role obligations, and an upholding of very high levels of trusts, loyalty, and altruism (Hui & Graen, 1997). This means that as compared to other colleagues, a subordinate who has an additional relationship (e.g., a relative of the leader) is more likely to be treated as a special member regardless of the competency he or she may have. Some researchers (Redding, 1990; Whitley, 1991) particularly found that having a closer personal relationship (including interpersonal trust) is more effective than using one's reputation in gaining work success in the Chinese society. However, this practice may be changing rapidly as new business entrepreneurs define what counts within their companies. Many Sino-Western ventures forbid using family connections for personal benefit.

EMPIRICAL RESEARCH ON LMX IN THE CHINESE WORK CONTEXT

In general, the LMX-7 instrument indicates good reliability in most research conducted in the Chinese work context (e.g., Chen et al., 2007; Hui et al., 1999; Lam et al., 2007; Schaubroeck & Lam, 2002). The authors validated the LMX-7 modified by Graen and Uhl-Bien (1995), and the results consistently showed high Cronbach's alphas for the instrument (larger than .75). In addition, the correlations of LMX-7 to the outcome variables are similar to those in the Western context. In particular, Chen et al. (2007) and Lam et al. (2007) found that LMX is positively related to in-role work performance, while Hui et al. (1999) and Aryee and Chen (2006) found that LMX is positively related to both in-role performance and organizational citizenship behavior. Wakabayashi and his colleagues did a series studies that showed that managers tend to use Western managerial skills more often under the condition of higher LMX quality both in Chinese state-owned corporations and in Sino-foreign joint venture corporations in China (Chen, 1996; Wakabayashi, Chen, & Kondo, 2001; Wakabayashi, Chen, & Graen, 2004; Wakabayashi, Takeuchi, & Chen, 2002).

A second instrument used to assess LMX is the LMX-MDM measurement developed by Liden and Maslyn (1998). This instrument was translated into Chinese (Wang & Liu, 2005; Wang & Ren, 2005; Wang et al., 2004). With the use of two studies in their research (Wang et al., 2004), the four dimensions of LMX-MDM (i.e., affect, loyalty, contribution, and professional respect) were confirmed to fit the Chinese work context, and only

one item in each dimension was added. The additional items were as follows: "I like to work with my supervisor" for affect, "When there is a conflict between others and me, my supervisor is on my side" for loyalty, "For
my supervisor, I do my best in in-role and extra-role works" for contribution, and "It is well known that my supervisor's knowledge and ability
relate with his/her job" for professional respect. In the first sample using
168 Chinese employees of a bank located in China, Wang et al. (2004)
found that the reliabilities of LMX-MDM were = .74 for affect, .85 for loyalty, .88 for contribution, and .81 for professional respect. In their second
study with a sample of 203 part-time Chinese MBA students, the authors
found the alpha coefficients of .87, .67, .86, and .89 for affect, loyalty, contribution, and professional respect, respectively. The results also showed a
high significant power on predicting the task performance and contextual
performance of the employees (Wang et al., 2004; Wu & Wu, 2006). These
findings are similar to the results obtained in the United States.

GROWING UP IN CHINA

Since the 1990s, more and more foreign companies have started to invest
in China. In relation to this, Yan (2004, p. 123) stated that foreign
companies must understand "the special situation in China" or "Chinese
characteristics" (*guo qing*) in order to deliver products with value, quality,
and convenience that will appeal to Chinese consumers." Confucian philosophy pervades Chinese culture and is a central part of Chinese
characteristics that foreign companies need to understand. It is therefore
interesting to see how a native mainland Chinese grows up, learns, and
absorbs the values of his origin.

Sit Well in Class

Once, I (the first author, a native mainland Chinese) told Wing (the second author, a Hong Kong Chinese) that when I was a primary school student, we were forced to sit straight by our teacher during class hours, and
he required that we lean forward on our elbows with our forearms criss-
crossed and each hand touching the opposite shoulder so as to avoid any
restless movement. Wing was very surprised and asked how teachers could
treat little kids like this. She said to me, "Why couldn't the little kids be
given any freedom in classrooms? This can be explained by the following:
"From as early as kindergarten, there is an emphasis on discipline and
learning rather than free play. Teachers are treated with respect, and
learning is teacher centered. Students are generally expected to speak

when spoken to and not otherwise" (Tang & Ward, 2003, p. 14), and "Children are expected to be seen but not heard in family gatherings at which the senior adults hold the floor. The good child is one who heeds what he or she is told (*ting hua*—"listens talk") and does not interrupt or talk back" (p. 17). I realized that then, I was being taught to *respect authority.*

To continue the above story, a little girl was sitting next to me, and she behaved well by sitting in the ways we were told to do so by our teacher. The teacher therefore praised the girl and gave her a little red flag as an award, which was then displayed on the back wall of the classroom with her name on it. In order to motivate us, our whole class was divided into several groups and then we were encouraged to compete by getting as many flags as we can. As I was an active boy in class, one time, I did not sit in a good manner; a red flag was immediately taken away from our group. As a result, I was blamed and treated isolatedly by my groupmates. This incident imparted to me the second message that each of the members of a group *has the obligation to behave in the ways commonly shared and accepted within the group.* This case clearly reflects Tang and Ward's (2003) description of the Chinese culture, that is, how an individual behaves often determines which group he/she will be classified into, which is either insiders (*zijiren*) or outsiders (*wairen*). Now, I agree and understand Bond and Hwang (1986) in their conclusion that collectivism has for many centuries been so central to life in China, in which there is promotion of the value of "harmony-in-hierarchy."

Read Between the Lines

The Chinese favor the reserved, the implicit, and the indirect. Let me narrate an example from a naughty boy (me again). One time, I fought with another boy, and my teacher immediately said "You are so brave! Shall I ask others to learn from you?" Clearly, she was sarcastically scolding me for my misbehavior.

Sometimes, the Chinese do not like to speak directly. They are constantly on the alert to "read between the lines" (Tang & Ward, 2003). When one can *understand others' true meanings "between the lines,"* this person is perceived as being sensitive to human relations, and it is more likely that he or she may easily establish good relationships with other Chinese. Otherwise, he or she finds it difficult to belong to a social group.

Make More Friends and Save Faces

Recently, I read an interesting article written by Wei (2005) that discussed social network and face saving in China. Wei (2005) used the case-study approach to explain the importance of *saving face among friends even amidst conflicts on a money issue.*

Case: Friends and Well-Known People Do not Turn in Sales

When company J just became a listed one, it did not have much money to advertise because it was a small company. The detrimental effect is that if its products do not have a market, the company will obviously not gain profit. The owner, old H, became very worried about it. Old H wanted to enter the market and to increase their market share as much as possible. Thus, he used the method of trial sales with the help of sales agents. The company distributed products to well-known people, friends, or sales persons, and let them sell the products. Although the sales were not bad, the problem was the collection of the proceeds. Many sales agents sold the products but did not return the money to the company. Among all the sales agents, those who were closest to him were the ones who did not return the money. Many of them felt that since old H owns the company, he does not need the money anymore. Thus, the returns came in very slowly, or the concerned people did not return the money at all. Faced with such situation, old H felt nothing could be done. He thought that as they were friends, there was no need to ask them to return such a little amount. Thus, in many cases, the money was never returned. As a result, old H said "As we did not receive the payment, we would not give them any products to sell anymore, and the friendship is over." Ironically, the agents who they did not know so well returned more money to the company. (Adopted from Wei, 2005)

A Tall Tree Catches the Wind

"A tall tree catches the wind" is a traditional Chinese idiom. It means that a person in a high position is prone to be the target of critical attacks. In order to prevent additional problems and uncertainty, it is therefore better *to be number two instead of number one.* Let us read a case supporting this idea by Tang and Ward (2003).

Case: Avoiding Trouble

"There are a lot of things missing, steel plates here, nuts and bolts there," the manager commented, pointing at the places where the missing parts should be. "The contractor deliberately omits quite a number of details from the design (drawn) by the architects. But no one wants to stir up trouble by bringing this out into the open."

"But what happens if it falls down?"

"If one brings these problems up for discussion, then they have to be solved, and the persons to be held responsible have to be found. This will be very painful. So it is much better not to bring the problems out into the open now; after the building is completed, everybody will have left the site, and the problems are discovered, then it will be much more difficult to find out whose fault it is. Usually, everybody will be blamed. And if everybody is blamed, then nobody will suffer much. So it is much better that way." (From an interview with one of the managers of a construction project in northern China during a tour of the site, 2001; source: adopted from Tang and Ward, 2003, p. 16)

CONCLUSION

With regard to the theoretical reception of LMX in China, it was found that a high-quality supervisor-subordinate relationship needs to be cultivated through intensive and proactive interactions initiated by subordinates instead of passively waiting for special offers provided by supervisors. The most important rationale behind this is the strong relational orientation that most Chinese employees have (Hwang, 1987; Wall, 1990). Scholars (e.g. Chiao, 1982; Yang, 1994) have identified four particular tactics to help Chinese employees establish, develop, maintain, and utilize a high-quality relationship with supervisors. These tactics include (1) *xi* (inheriting family connections) in which subordinates inherit the existing relational resources that were built by their *wu-lun* members such as grandparents and parents with the supervisors, (2) *zuan* (digging into or pushing up) in which subordinates approach somebody in authority by all possible means, (3) *lian* (expanding or networking) in which subordinates use intermediaries to strengthen their relationship with supervisors, and (4) *ren* in which subordinates strengthen to a previous association with the supervisors. Therefore, research on the cultural influences on the reception of the LMX concept and its outcomes in the Chinese work context helps us to understand how to sail across the Sino-American sea.

ACKNOWLEDGMENTS

We sincerely thank Jian An Zhong, Meng Xian Xiang, and Bin Wang for their assistance in searching for related literature and in conceptualizing the preliminary analysis. This chapter was supported by grants from the Research Grants Council of the Hong Kong Special Administrative Region, China (Project No. City U 1432/05H), City University of Hong Kong (Strategic Research Grant, project No. 7001671), and the Hong Kong Polytechnic University (the Departmental General Research Funds, Grant #U305).

REFERENCES

Aryee, S., & Chen, Z. X. (2006). Leader-member exchange in a Chinese context: Antecedents, the mediating role of psychological empowerment and outcomes. *Journal of Business Research, 59*, 793-801.

Bae, J., & Lawler, J. J. (2000). Organizational and HRM strategies in Korea: Impact on firm performance in an emerging economy. *Academy of Management Journal, 43*, 502-517.

Bond, M. H., & Hwang, K. K. (1986). The social psychology of the Chinese people. In M. H. Bond (Ed.), *The psychology of the Chinese people* (pp. 213-266). Oxford, England: Oxford University Press.

Butterfield, F. (1983). *China: Alive in the bitter sea.* London, UK: Coronet Books.

Chen, T. Y. (2006). Review on antecedents and outcomes of leader-member exchange quality. *Management Consulting, 4*, 49-50.

Chen, Z. (1996). Managerial skill formulation in Chinese state-owned corporations: Focusing on the leader-member exchange relation as a facilitator for skill learning. *Forum of International Development, 6*, 217-236.

Chen, Z., Lam, W., & Zhong, J. A. (2007). Leader-member exchange and member performance: A new look at individual-level negative feedback-seeking behavior and team-level empowerment climate. *Journal of Applied Psychology, 92*, 202-212.

Cheng, B. S., & Farh, J. L. (2001). Social orientation in Chinese societies: A comparison of employees from Taiwan and Chinese mainland. *Chinese Journal of Psychology, 43*, 207-221.

Cheng, L. Y., & Rosett, A. (1991). Contract with a Chinese face: Socially embedded factors in the transformation from hierarchy to market, 1979-1989. *Journal of Chinese Law, 5*, 143-244.

Chiao, C. (1982). Guanxi: A preliminary conceptualization [Guanxi: Chu Yi]. In K. S. Yang & C. I. Wen (Eds.), *The sinicization of social and behavioral science research in China* [She hui ji xing wei ke xue yan ji de zhong guo hua] (pp. 345-360). Taipei, China: Academia Sinica.

Farh, J. L., Tsui, A. S., Xin, K., & Cheng, B. -S. (1998). The influence of relational demography and guanxi: The Chinese case. *Organization Science, 9*, 471-488.

Gerstner, C. R., & Day, D. V. 1997. Meta-analytic review of leader-member exchange theory: Correlates and construct issues. *Journal of Applied Psychology, 82*, 827-844.

Graen, G. B. (Ed.). (2003). Interpersonal workplace theory at the crossroads. In *LMX leadership: The series: Vol. 1. Dealing with diversity* (pp. 145-182). Greenwich, CT: Information Age.

Graen, G. B. (in press). New approaches for cultivating and nourishing communications networks. In C. Wankel (Ed.), *Handbook of 21st century management* (pp. 1-32). Thousand Oaks, CA: Sage.

Graen, G. B., & Cashman, J. F. (1975). A role making model in formal organizations: A developmental approach. In J. G. Hunt & L. L. Larson (Eds.), *Leadership frontiers* (pp. 143-165). Kent, OH: Kent State Press.

Graen, G. B., Dharwadkar, R. Grewal, R., & Wakabayashi, M., (2006). Japanese career progress over the long haul: An empirical examination. *Journal of International Business Studies, 37,* 148-161.

Graen, G. B., Novak, M. A., & Sommerkamp, P. (1982). The effects of leader-member exchange and job design on productivity and satisfaction: Testing a dual attachment model. *Organizational behavior and human performance, 30,* 109-131.

Graen, G. B., Orris, D., & Johnson, T. (1973). Role assimilation processes in a complex organization. *Journal of Vocational Behavior, 3,* 395-420.

Graen, G. B., & Uhl-Bien, M. (1995). Relationship-based approach to leadership: Development of leader-member exchange (LMX) theory of leadership over 25 Years: Applying a multi-level multi-domain perspective. *Leadership Quarterly, 6,* 219-247.

Graen, G. B., Wakabayashi, M., Graen, M. R., & Graen, M. G. (1990). International generalizability of American hypothesis about Japanese management progress: A strong inference investigation. *Leadership Quarterly, 1,* 1-23.

Hui, C., & Graen, G. B. (1997). Guanxi and professional leadership in contemporary Sino-American joint ventures in mainland China. *The Leadership Quarterly, 8,* 451-465.

Hui, C., Law, K. S., & Chen, Z. X. (1999). A structural equation model of the effects of negative affectivity, leader-member exchange, and perceived job mobility on in-role and extra-role performance: A Chinese case. *Organizational Behavior and Human Decision Processes, 77,* 3-21.

Hwang, K. K. (1987). Face and favor: The Chinese power game. *American Journal of Sociology, 92,* 944-974.

Johnson, T., & Graen, G. B. (1973). Organizational assimilation and role rejection. *Organizational Behavior and Human Performance, 10,* 72-78.

Kacmar, K. M., Witt, L. A, Zivnuska, S., & Gully, S. M. (2003). The interactive effect of leader-member exchange and communication frequency on performance ratings. *Journal of Applied Psychology, 88,* 764-772.

Keller, T., & Dansereau, F. (1995). Leadership and empowerment: A social exchange perspective. *Human Relations, 48,* 127-146.

Lam, W., Huang, X., & Snape, E. (2007). Feedback-seeking behavior and leader-member exchange: Do supervisor-attributed motives matter? *Academy of Management Journal, 50,* 348-363.

Liden, R. C., & Graen, G. B. (1980). Generalizability of the vertical dyad linkage model of leadership. *Academy of Management Journal, 23,* 451-465.

Liden, R. C., & Maslyn, J. M. (1998). Multidimensionality of leader-member exchange: An empirical assessment through scale development. *Journal of Management, 24,* 43-72.

Liden, R. C., Sparrowe, R. T., & Wayne, S. J. (1997). Leader-member exchange theory: The past and potential for the future. *Research in personnel and human resources management, 15,* 47-119.

Luo, Y. (2000). *Guanxi and business.* Singapore: World Scientific.

Peng, S. (2001). Guanxi-management and legal approaches to establish and enhance interpersonal trust. *Journal of Psychology in Chinese Societies, 2,* 51-76.

Podsakoff, N. P., MacKenzie, S. B., & Hui, C. (1993). Organizational citizenship behaviors and managerial evaluations of employee performance: A review and suggestions for future research. In G. R. Ferris (Ed.), *Research in personnel and human resources management* (pp. 1-40). Greenwich, CT: JAI Press.

Redding, G. (1990). *The spirit of Chinese capitalism.* Berlin, Germany: Walter de Gruyter.

Scandura, T. A., Graen, G. B., & Novak, M. A. (1986). When managers decide not to decide autocratically: An investigation of leader-member exchange and decision influence. *Journal of Applied Psychology, 71,* 579-584.

Schaubroeck, J., & Lam, S. S. K. (2002). How similarity to peers and supervisors influences organizational advancement in different cultures. *Academy of Management Journal, 45,* 1120-1136.

Scott, S. G., & Bruce, R. A. (1994). Determinants of innovative behavior: A path model of individual innovation in the workplace. *Academy of Management Journal, 37,* 580-607.

Stepina, L. P., Perrewe, P. L., Hassell, B. L., Harris, J. R., & Mayfield, C. R. (1991). A comparative test of the independent effects of interpersonal, task, and reward domains on personal and organizational outcomes. *Journal of Social Behavior and Personality, 6,* 93-104.

Tang, J., & Ward, A. (2003). *The changing face of Chinese management.* London: Routledge.

Tsui, A. S. (2001). Book reviews: Guanxi and business. *Asia Pacific Journal of Management, 18,* 407-413.

Uhl-Bien, M., & Maslyn, J. (2003). Reciprocity in manager-subordinate relationships: components, configurations, and outcomes. *Journal of Management, 29,* 511-532.

Vecchio, R. P., Griffeth, R. W., & Hom, P. W. (1986). The predictive utility of the vertical dyad linkage approach. *Journal of Social Psychology, 126,* 617-625.

Wakabayashi, M., Chen, Z., & Graen, G. B. (2004). The global Asian way: Managerial efficacy profile (MEP) and LMX relationship in Asia. In G. B. Graen (Ed.), *LMX leadership: The series: Vol. 2. New frontiers of leadership* (pp. 121-137). Greenwich, CT: Information Age.

Wakabayashi M., Chen, Z., & Kondo, M. (2001). Comparative managerial skills: A study on Asian-styles of management based on managers from ten different area/nations. *Forum of International Development Studies, 17,* 1-27.

Wakabayashi, M., & Graen, G. B. (1984). The Japanese career progress study: A 7-year follow-up. *Journal of Applied Psychology, 69,* 603-614.

Wakabayashi, M., Takeuchi, N., & Chen, Z. (2002). Managerial skills for meeting challenges from globalization and market competition. *Japanese Journal of Administrative Science, 16*(2), 131-150.

Wall, J. J. A. (1990). Managers in the People's Republic of China. *Academy of Management Executive, 4,* 19-32.

Wang, H., Law, K. S., Hackett, R. D., Wang, D., & Chen, Z. X. (2005). Leader-member exchange as a mediator of the relationship between transformational leadership and followers' performance and organizational citizenship behavior. *Academy of Management Journal, 48,* 420-432.

Wang, H., & Liu, X. Y. (2005). The impact of leader-member exchange (LMX) on employees' performance and organizational commitment. *Economic Science, 2,* 94-101.

Wang, H., Niu, X. Y., & Law, K. S. (2004). Multi-dimensional leader-member exchange (LMX) and its impact on task performance and contextual performance of employees. *Acta Psychologica Sinica, 36,* 179-185.

Wang, H., & Ren, X. P. (2005). Leader-member exchange and its progress theory, measurement, antecedents and outcomes. *Advances in Psychological Science, 13:* 788-797.

Wei, J. W. (2005). *The strength of ties and entrepreneurs' behaviors: The perspective of embeddedness—Empirical study on the private entrepreneurs in Beijing.* Retreived March 2, 2007, from http://www.sachina.edu.cn/Htmldata/article/2005/11/520 .html

Whitley, R. D. (1991). The social construction of business systems in East Asia. *Organizational Studies, 12,* 1-28.

Wu, Z. M., & Wu, X. (2006). An empirical study on the impact of transformational leadership on organizational citizenship behavior in knowledge work teams. *Studies in Science of Science, 24,* 283-287.

Yan, R. (2004). To reach China's consumers, adapt to *guo qing*. *Harvard Business Review on Doing Business in China,* pp. 123-140.

Yang, K. S. (1993). Chinese social orientation: An integrative analysis. In L. Y. Cheng, F. M. C. Cheung, & C. Nie (Eds.), *Psychotherapy for the Chinese: Selected papers from the first international conference* (19-56). Hong Kong: The Chinese University of Hong Kong.

Yang, M. F. (1994). *Gifts, favors and banquets: The act of social relationships in China.* Ithaca, New York: Cornell University Press.

Yeung, I. Y. M., & Tung, R. L. (1996). Achieving business success in Confucian societies: The importance of guanxi (connections). *Organizational Dynamics, 25,* 54-65.

Yukl, G. (2006). *Leadership in organizations* (6th ed.) Upper Saddle River: NJ: Pearson Education.

CHAPTER 5

ATTRIBUTION THEORY
AND LMX THEORY

Wing Lam

According to the attribution theory (Davis & Gardner, 2004; Green & Mitchell, 1979; Kelley, 1967), we judge people differently depending on what motives, beliefs, or intentions we associate with an observed behavior. Therefore, it is predicted that the quality of leader-member exchange (LMX) should be dependent on how supervisors attribute the empowerment-seeking behavior of subordinates (Davis & Gardner, 2004; Steiner, 1997). In this chapter, I discuss how supervisors' attributions about subordinates' feedback-seeking behavior contribute to the strength of LMX ties. It is predicted that supervisors tend to reciprocate weak LMX for those subordinates whom they perceive to have weak performance-enhancement motives and strong impression management motives, and reciprocate the strong LMX (sharing network leadership) for those whom they perceive to have strong performance-enhancement but weak impression management motives. This is because supervisors tend to trust the motives of subordinates who strive for task improvement (performance-enhancement motives) but not for the enhancement and manipulation of impressions (impression management motives). Therefore, leaders should be careful in avoiding being "fooled" by ingratiators and should instead develop the authentic team players.

New Multinational Network Sharing
pp. 79–91

INTRODUCTION

Substantial research on leader-member exchange (LMX) has greatly enhanced our understanding of supervisor-subordinate relationships (Gerstner & Day, 1997; Graen, 2006, in press). Most LMX research has consistently shown the beneficial effects of building a high-quality LMX (e.g., Gerstner & Day, 1997; Liden, Sparrowe, & Wayne, 1997) but has yet to clarify the contributions of attributions toward the behavior and motivations of other parties. Therefore, the purpose of this chapter is to explore the consequences on LMX of how supervisors attribute the motives of their members' feedback-seeking behavior. Similar attribution processes are expected from the members' view of the supervisor's influence attempts in terms of being authentic and manipulative.

The primary focus of feedback exchange in past research has been on how a sender (usually a supervisor) conveys a message to a recipient (e.g., a subordinate) (Ilgen, Fisher, & Taylor, 1979). In a seminal article, Ashford and Cummings (1983) challenged this perspective by arguing that subordinates may proactively seek feedback rather than passively wait for it to be delivered, as they wish to know exactly how their work has been perceived and what they should do to manage their careers. In a more recent work, Morrison and Phelps (1999) echoed this view by suggesting that the success of organizations today depends on employees' initiative to continuously improve their work performance. Employees may want to gauge their work performance by taking the initiative to seek feedback from their supervisors (Ashford, 1986; Ashford, Blatt, & VandeWalle, 2003). This kind of behavior is referred to as feedback-seeking behavior. A dominant form of feedback-seeking behavior is the explicit verbal request for information on work behavior and work performance (Ashford & Cummings, 1983; Ashford & Tsui, 1991; VandeWalle, Ganesan, Challagalla, & Brown, 2000). Studies have indicated that the feedback-seeking behavior of subordinates may be positively related to the quality of LMX through the following: (1) clarification of role expectations from supervisors (e.g., Morrison, 1993) and (2) creation of positive impressions (e.g., Ashford & Tsui, 1991; Edwards, 1995). In two studies comprising of a sample of 499 supervisor-subordinate dyads, Lam, Huang, and Snape (2007) provided empirical support by finding the positive relationship between subordinates' feedback-seeking behavior and the quality of LMX. Their findings will be discussed in detail in this chapter later.

Subordinates' feedback-seeking behavior may not necessarily help in building a high-quality LMX because supervisors may interpret the behavior differently (Davis & Gardner, 2004; Green & Mitchell, 1979; Kelley, 1967). Hence, these interpretations explain how supervisors choose to build relationships ranging from high to low quality of exchanges with their subordinates. Researchers have suggested that two separate kinds of motives may be associated with feedback-seeking behavior: *performance-related motives* and *impression management motives* (Ashford & Cummings, 1983; Ashford & Tsui, 1991; Morrison & Bies, 1991). Ashford and Cummings (1983) argued that performance-related motives involve an authentic desire to obtain useful information in order to accomplish tasks effectively and enhance performance. This kind of motive includes an important element: information gathering about the work role (Ashford et al., 2003; Crant, 2000). Meanwhile, impression management motives refer to the desire to control how one appears to others. When supervisors attribute the feedback-seeking behavior of subordinates to performance-related motives, such behavior is likely to positively influence judgments on the subordinates, whereas behaviors attributed to impression management motives may be devalued or discounted (Eastman, 1994; Schlenker, 1980). The feedback-seeking behavior of subordinates can be attributed to being more (or less) driven by either performance-enhancement or impression management motives but less (or more) on another, or more or less on both. Figure 5.1 depicts a 2 × 2 matrix explaining the possibilities of how supervisor-attributed motives predict the quality of LMX. In particular, I only described the two extreme cases which respectively lead to the highest and lowest quality of LMX—one is when supervisors attribute the motives of subordinates' feedback-seeking behavior more to performance-enhancement and simultaneously less to impression management motives (Quadrant I), and the other is when supervisors attribute the behavior less to performance-

		I	II
	HIGH	Highest LMX	Moderate LMX
Supervisor-attributed performance-enhancement motives		IV	III
	LOW	Moderate LMX	Lowest LMX
		LOW	HIGH

Supervisor-attributed
Impression management motives

Figure 5.1.   Matrix describing how supervisor-attributed motives for subordinates' feedback-seeking behavior affect the quality of LMX.

enhancement motives and simultaneously more to impression management ones (Quadrant III).

Quadrant I: Strong Supervisor-Attributed Performance-Enhancement Motives and Weak Supervisor-Attributed Impression Management Motives

As shown in Quadrant I of Figure 5.1, supervisors attribute the motives for subordinates' feedback-seeking behavior more to performance-enhancement and simultaneously less to impression management. When a supervisor interprets the motivation behind the feedback-seeking behavior of a subordinate more to performance-enhancement motives, he/she tends to regard the subordinate as achievement focused or with the intention to accomplish work tasks to a high standard (Ashford et al., 2003; Crant, 2000). Recent research empirically demonstrated that an individual who pays close attention to his or her performance tends to use feedback-seeking behavior as a tool to set his or her personal improvement goals, with the aim of obtaining information to reduce uncertainty, to know how to meet performance expectations, and to understand how to improve both the quality and quantity of his or her performance (Renn & Fedor, 2001; Tuckey, Brewer, & Williamson, 2002). Supervisors tend to appreciate this type of performance-focused effort from subordinates (Day & Crain, 1992), and they are likely to reciprocate by offering support, special benefits, and opportunities for career development (Graen & Uhl-Bien, 1995; Graen, Wakabayashi, Graen, & Graen, 1990; Kacmar, Witt, Zivnuska, & Gully, 2003). In turn, this becomes conducive to a high-quality LMX.

Quadrant III: Weak Supervisor-Attributed Performance-Enhancement Motives and Strong Supervisor-Attributed Impression Management Motives

The case in Quadrant III reflects the situation in which supervisors attribute subordinates' feedback-seeking behavior less to performance-enhancement motives and simultaneously more to impression management ones. In such a situation, these subordinates are probably viewed as having the high desire to enhance their image in the eyes of their supervisors. Therefore, they purely focus on building good relations with their supervisors, but they have low motivation to accomplish their tasks well. People tend to affirm their self-concepts. In organizations, subordinates may thus strengthen their self-concepts through the use of impression management, in which there is an attempt to control or manage the impressions that their supervisors form about them (Bolino, 1999; Wayne & Liden, 1995). Prior research has particularly suggested that subordinates may engage in feedback-seeking behavior if they believe that such behavior is an instrumental tool to boost their personal image (Ashford et al., 2003; Ashford & Tsui, 1991; Bolino, 1999; Crant, 2000).

However, whether or not a supervisor seeks to build a high-quality LMX with a subordinate is often highly dependent on how the supervisor attributes the behavior of the subordinate and not on the true motivation or belief that is held by the subordinate. When a supervisor attributes feedback-seeking behavior as driven more by impression management motives or as tactics used by the subordinates to enhance their personal image, things are different. In relation to this, it is worthy to note Fodor's (1973, 1974) studies which found that employees who attempted to impress their supervisors received no greater rewards compared with those who made no such attempt. It is because individuals usually form negative attitudes about others whom they have identified as having attempted to manipulate their impressions (Eastman, 1994; Fodor, 1973, 1974). In a similar vein, Crant (1996) also pointed out that subordinates who engage in impression management may be perceived as untruthful, unreliable, and calculating. Their feedback-seeking behavior may similarly be perceived as manipulative and is aimed at gaining rewards (Crant, 2000). If supervisors attribute the motivations for subordinates' feedback-seeking behavior to impression management, such behavior is less likely to create a positive impression (Morrison & Bies, 1991). Therefore, they tend to provide less support to such subordinates, and a low-quality LMX results.

IMPLICATIONS FOR THOSE SEEKING TO SHARE NETWORK LEADERSHIP (HIGH-QUALITY LMX)

The balance of the positive effects of subordinates' feedback-seeking behavior may thus highly depend on how supervisors attribute the underlying motives to performance enhancement and/or impression management. Specifically, the quality of LMX should be lowest for strong supervisor-attributed impression management motives but weak supervisor-attributed performance-enhancement motives (Quadrant III), moderate for either strong or weak performance-enhancement and impression management motives (Quadrant II and Quadrant IV), and highest for strong performance-enhancement motives but weak impression management motives (Quadrant I).

There are two major implications for those seeking to share network leadership (high-quality LMX), which are as follows:

1. There is a need to communicate to subordinates about the supervisor's strong desire for "role making" (strong performance-enhancement motives) through feedback-seeking behavior, and

2. There is a need to communicate to subordinates about the supervisor's aversion to sucking up and maintaining overly positive images (impression management motive) through feedback-seeking behavior.

RECENT EVIDENCE FROM CHINA

Lam and her colleagues (2007) surveyed 209 supervisor-subordinate dyads from a telecommunication services company in Shandong province of China. The company was originally a state-owned enterprise, but it was transformed into a shareholding company and is now listed in the New York and Hong Kong stock exchange. It is currently the market leader in its field and has about 15,000 employees.

Measures

Feedback-seeking behavior scale, supervisor-attributed performance-enhancement motives scale, and supervisor-attributed impression management motives scale were rated by the supervisors, while the LMX7 scale was rated by the subordinates. Moreover, a five-item *feedback-seeking behavior* scale validated by VandeWalle et al. (2000) was rated by their supervisors. The scale items are shown in Table 5.1.

In a subsequent study, Lam and her associates (2007) surveyed 240 supervisor-subordinate dyads from two Chinese corporations, each with more than 1,500 workers. Both companies were from the vehicle component manufacturing industry in Hangzhou in Zhejiang province of China. The two companies used a piece-rate pay system in which workers received their monthly pay according to the quantity of their output. Therefore, the monthly piece-rate scores for all respondents were employed.

The results of the two studies showed that both the interaction of general (or negative) feedback-seeking behavior and supervisor-attributed performance-enhancement motives ($p < .05$), and the interaction of general (or negative) feedback-seeking behavior and supervisor-attributed impression management motives ($p < .05$) were significant on LMX. The

Table 5.1.   Scales Used

Items	Component 1	Component 2	Component 3
C1: Feedback-seeking behavior	$a = .92$		
How frequently the subordinate asks for your feedback regarding ...			
Whether you feel his or her values and attitudes are appropriate for the firm.	.89	−.03	.05
Your role expectations of him or her.	.89	−.05	.02
His or her technical performance on the job.	.88	.06	.10
His or her overall work performance.	.81	.06	.25
His or her social behaviors.	.75	.01	.33
C2: Supervisor-attributed impression management motives		$a = .81$	
Desire to create a good impression.	−.06	.78	.14
Desire to build up favors for a later exchange.	−.01	.73	−.16
Desire to enhance his or her image (e.g., to make me believe that he or she is a helpful employee.	.14	.72	.17
Desire to obtain recognition or other organizational rewards.	.00	.72	−.22
Desire to capture my attention on him or her.	−.09	.70	.01
Desire to "show-off" his or her expertise.	.09	.61	.29
C3: Supervisor-attributed task-enhancement motives			$a = .80$
Desire to seek exactly what is expected of him or her.	.13	.08	.81
Desire to seek what his or her responsibilities are.	.27	−.01	.75
% of variance explained	31.45	23.54	9.48

Note: $n = 209$ supervisor-subordinate dyads.

interactive effects (regarding negative feedback-seeking behavior) are plotted in Figure 5.2. Simple slope analyses showed that negative feedback-seeking behavior was more positively and significantly related to LMX when supervisors interpreted the behavior as being driven by strong performance-enhancement motives (simple slope test: $p < .05$) than when they interpreted the behavior as being driven by weak performance-enhancement motives (simple slope test: *n.s.*). In addition, the negative feedback-seeking behavior was more positively related to LMX when supervisors interpreted the behavior as being driven by weak impression

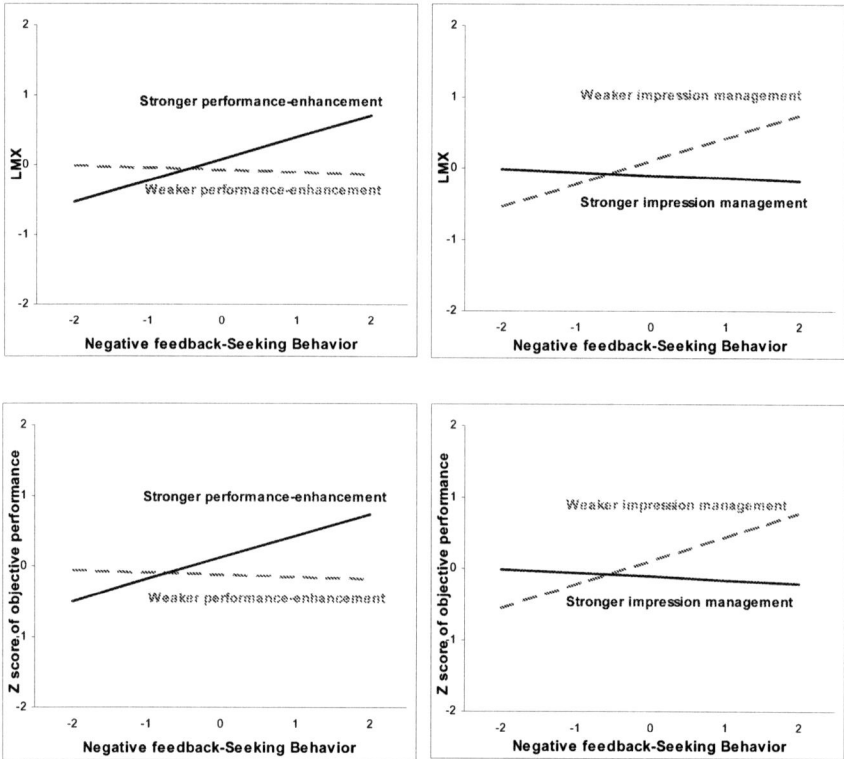

Figure 5.2. The moderating effects of supervisors' attributions of subordinates' negative feedback-seeking behavior to underlying motives.

management motives (simple slope test: $p < .01$) than when they interpreted the behavior as being driven by strong supervisor-attributed impression management motives (simple slope test: *n.s.*).

The results further revealed a significant effect of LMX when added on work performance ($< .001$), while the interactions of negative feedback-seeking behavior and supervisor-attributed performance-enhancement motives and supervisor-attributed impression management motives become no longer significant, meeting the third and fourth requirements for mediated moderation. As Figure 5.2 also shows, negative feedback-seeking behavior was more positively and significantly related to work performance when supervisors interpreted the negative feedback-seeking behavior as being driven by strong performance-enhancement motives (simple slope test: $= .17, p < .05$) than when they believed that the behavior was driven by weak performance-enhancement motives (simple slope test: = .09, *n.s.*). Additionally, we found that negative feedback-seeking behavior was more positively related to work performance when supervisors interpreted the behavior as being driven by weak impression management motives (simple slope test $p < .01$) than when they believed that the behavior was driven by strong impression management motives (simple slope test: *n.s.*). These results suggest that LMX completely mediated the interaction effects on subordinates' objective performance. In both studies, three-way interactions were null.

FUTURE RESEARCH DIRECTIONS

The findings of the current research and of most works in feedback-seeking behavior literature suggest an upward relational dyadic-focused relationship, in which subordinates may ask for feedback from their immediate supervisors. Widening our focus in considering relevant parties of an employee based on the sharing of network leadership (SNL) model (Graen, in press), an employee may ask for feedback from his/her immediate supervisors, bosses (leaders), subordinates, peers, or coworkers. Therefore, future studies may further explore the following research questions on relational dyad attributions in all directions of the role set:

1. What moderating (+) or (–) attributions do leaders make about their members' influence attempts?
2. What moderating (+) or (–) attributions do members make about their leaders' influence attempts?
3. What moderating (+) or (–) attributions do coworkers make about their peers' influence attempts and vice versa?
4. What moderating (+) or (–) attributions do network brokers make about their coworkers' influence attempts and vice versa?

The above questions can be asked with reference to any influence attempt in the upward, downward, diagonal, or horizontal directions. As shown in Figure 5.3, the leader trusts his member Jessie, (A), but Jessie does not trust her leader (B). Also, the leader trusts his peer Marcus (C), and Marcus reciprocates this trust (C). Finally, the leader trusts the network broker Marty (D), but Marty does not reciprocate this trust. Standard questions should therefore be asked by supervisors when a member of their unit or team requests additional negative feedback about their job performance: *Why do these people really want this criticism of their performance? Do they enjoy criticism? Do they want to use this feedback to correct their mistakes in the future? Do they want to ingratiate themselves into my good graces? Do they*

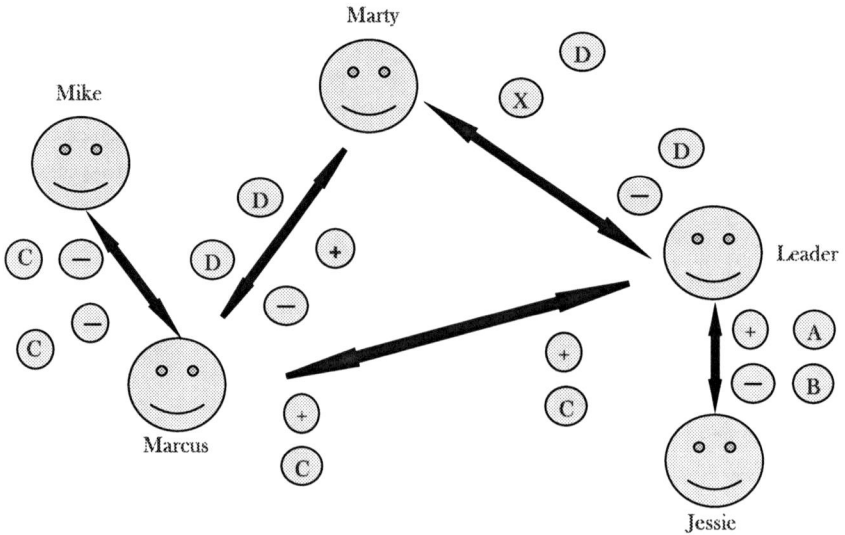

Figure 5.3.   Network attributions for influence attempts (+) or (−).

seek to make me look like a naive fool? Perhaps, the answer can be a combination of all of these motives, but the main question which supervisors should ask themselves is as follows: *Do I trust (+) or distrust (−) the influence attempt through this unusual request?* Each of the above motives requires an appropriate response. Supervisors who get fooled by dishonest requests for negative feedback do not obtain respect and instead weaken their leadership. In comparison, supervisors who are not fooled by such tactics are respected by their people and strengthen their leadership. With these, it is thus interesting to empirically examine the patterns of upward, downward, and horizontal dyadic relationships in terms of attributions to feedback-seeking motives.

We may also think broadly of the implications of not considering relevant attributions by leaders, members, coworkers, and network members. What would happen in such a situation? What are the corresponding consequences on concerned persons? Once a person is made a "fool" by another by playing a devious role, that person loses the respect of all network members who see through the trickery. Once one gains such a reputation of being easily fooled, that person's career progress is in jeopardy. Clearly, effective performers must consider attributions for any influence request from anyone (leaders, members, coworkers, and network members). This issue is another interesting research direction that can be dealt with in future studies.

CONCLUSION

Both interactions of impression management with feedback-seeking and performance enhancement with feedback-seeking behavior contributed to LMX in both studies examined in Lam et al.'s (2007) paper, but role playing's interaction contributed negatively and authentic's positively. Clearly, attributions made a difference in the established relationship. Nobody, regardless of being a supervisor, member, or coworker, would like to be fooled by a fellow employee. The same logic applies to members' attributions of their leader's and coworkers' respective influence seeking behaviors. Once these contributions were made and the LMX relation was established, it was strongly related $(r = .54)$ to objective, piece-rate performance. The implications of this attribution model for the Sharing Network Leadership (SNL) model (Graen, in press) are clear. Few coworkers willingly share network leadership with those whom they do not trust to be authentic when seeking sensitive information. Therefore, this should open a new area for both national and international leadership research on attribution's role in the influence process.

ACKNOWLEDGMENT

I gratefully acknowledge the insightful feedback and suggestions of George B. Graen (University of Illinois), Xu Huang, Ed Snape (The Hong Kong Polytechnic University), and Ziguang Chen (City University of Hong Kong) on this chapter. This work was supported by Grant #305 from Departmental General Research Funds of the Hong Kong Polytechnic University.

REFERENCES

Ashford, S. J. (1986). Feedback-seeking in individual adaptation: A resource perspective. *Academy of Management Journal, 29*, 465-487.

Ashford, S. J., Blatt, R., & VandeWalle, D. (2003). Reflections on the looking glass: A review of research on feedback-seeking behavior in organizations. *Journal of Management, 29*, 773-799.

Ashford, S. J., & Cummings, L. L. (1983). Feedback as an individual resource: Personal strategies of creating information. *Organizational Behavior and Human Performance, 32*, 370-98.

Ashford, S. J., & Tsui, A. S. (1991). Self-regulation for managerial effectiveness: The role of active feedback seeking. *Academy of Management Journal, 34*, 251-280.

Bolino, M. C. (1999). Citizenship and impression management: Good soldiers or good actors? *Academy of Management Review, 24,* 82-98.

Crant, J. M. (1996). Doing more harm than good: When is impression management likely to evoke a negative response? *Journal of Applied Social Psychology, 26,* 1454-1471.

Crant, J. M. (2000). Proactive behavior in organizations. *Journal of Management, 26,* 435-462.

Davis, W. D., & Gardner, W. L. (2004). Perceptions of politics and organizational cynicism: An attributional and leader-member exchange perspective. *The Leadership Quarterly, 15,* 439-465.

Day, D. V., & Crain, E. C. (1992). The role of affect and ability in initial exchange quality perceptions. *Group and Organization Management, 17,* 380-397.

Eastman, K. K. (1994). In the eyes of the beholder: An attributional approach to ingratiation and organizational citizenship behavior. *Academy of Management Journal, 37,* 1379-1391.

Edwards, J. R. (1995). Alternatives to difference scores as dependent variables in the study of congruence in organizational research. *Organizational Behavior and Human Decision Processes, 64,* 307-324.

Fodor, E. M. (1973). Disparagement by a subordinate, ingratiation, and the use of power. *Journal of Psychology, 84,* 181-186.

Fodor, E. M. (1974). Disparagement by a subordinate as an influence on the use of power. *Journal of Applied Psychology, 59,* 652-655.

Gerstner, C. R., & Day, D. V. (1997). Meta-analytic review of leader-member exchange theory: Correlates and construct issues. *Journal of Applied Psychology, 82,* 827-844.

Graen, G. B. (2006). To share or not to share leadership: New LMX-MMX network leadership or charismatic leadership on creative projects. In G. B. Graen, & J. A. Graen (Eds.), *LMX leadership: The series: Vol. 4. Sharing network leadership* (pp. 25-36). Greenwich, CT: Information Age.

Graen, G. B. (in press). New approaches for cultivating and nourishing communications networks. In C. Wankel (Ed.), *Handbook of 21st century management* (pp. 1-32. Thousand Oaks, CA: Sage.

Graen, G. B., & Uhl-Bien, M. (1995). Relationship-based approach to leadership: Development of leader-member exchange (LMX) theory of leadership over 25 years: Applying a multi-level multi-domain perspective. *Leadership Quarterly, 6,* 219-247.

Graen, G. B., Wakabayashi, M., Graen, M. R., & Graen, M. G. (1990). International generalizability of American hypothesis about Japanese management progress: A strong inference investigation. *Leadership Quarterly, 1,* 1-23.

Green, S. G., & Mitchell, T. R. (1979). Attributional processes of leaders in leader-member interactions. *Organizational Behavior and Human Performance, 23,* 429-458.

Ilgen, D. R., Fisher, C. D., & Taylor, M. S. (1979). Consequences of individual feedback on behavior in organizations. *Journal of Applied Psychology, 64,* 359-371.

Kacmar, K. M., Witt, L. A., Zivnuska, S., & Gully, S. M. (2003). The interactive effect of leader-member exchange and communication frequency on performance ratings. *Journal of Applied Psychology, 88,* 764-772.

Kelley, H. H. (1967). Attribution theory in social psychology. In D. Levine (Ed.), *Nebraska symposium on motivation* (pp. 192-238). Lincoln: University of Nebraska Press.

Lam, W., Huang, X., & Snape, E. (2007). Feedback-seeking behavior and leader-member exchange: Do supervisor-attributed motives matter? *Academy of Management Journal, 50,* 348-363.

Liden, R. C., Sparrowe, R. T., & Wayne, S. J. (1997). Leader-member exchange theory: The past and potential for the future. *Research in personnel and human resources management, 15,* 47-119.

Morrison, E. W. (1993). Newcomer information seeking: Exploring types, modes, sources, and outcomes. *Academy of Management Journal, 36,* 557-589.

Morrison, E. W., & Bies, R. J. (1991). Impression management in the feedback-seeking process: A literature review and research agenda. *Academy of Management Review, 16,* 522-541.

Morrison, E. W., & Phelps, C. C. (1999). Taking charge at work: Extrarole efforts to initiate workplace change. *Academy of Management Journal, 42,* 403-419.

Renn, R. W., & Fedor, D. B. (2001). Development and field test of a feedback seeking, self-efficacy, and goal setting model of work performance. *Journal of Management, 27,* 563-583.

Schlenker, B. R. (1980). *Impression management: The self-concept, social identity, and interpersonal relations.* Belmont, CA: Brooks/Cole.

Steiner, D. D. (1997). Attributions in leader-member exchanges: Implications for practice. *European Journal of Work and Organizational Psychology, 6,* 59-71.

Tuckey, M., Brewer, N., & Williamson, P. (2002). The influence of motives and goal orientation on feedback seeking. *Journal of Occupational and Organizational Psychology, 75,* 195-216.

VandeWalle, D., Ganesan, S., Challagalla, G. N., & Brown, S. P. (2000). An integrated model of feedback-seeking behavior: Disposition, context, and cognition. *Journal of Applied Psychology, 85,* 996-1003.

Wayne, S. J., & Liden, R. C. (1995). Effects of impression management on performance ratings: A longitudinal study. *Academy of Management Journal, 38,* 232-260.

CHAPTER 6

CREATION OF THE WAL-MART TEAM OF PROCTER & GAMBLE

Michael R. Graen

The role that information technology has played in the cultural changes over the last 10-20 years has been dramatic. The advent of the personal computer, communication networks, the Internet, cellular phones and pagers has changed the way we do business globally. Information is exchanged at a rapid pace leading to faster and better quality decisions. Technology's role in the evolving manufacturer and supplier relationship has been just as significant. Electronic integration of data and the automation of business practices has driven costs down and built sales by satisfying consumer needs. This chapter is about the role that technology of several kinds has played in the Wal-Mart and Procter & Gamble business relationship.

INTRODUCTION

In 1988 my boss and I met with Mr. Sam Walton in his office at Wal-Mart headquarters to discuss the business relationship between Wal-Mart and Procter & Gamble (P&G). We expected our meeting to be cordial because I had gathered the numbers on P&G sales to Wal-Mart and they looked very good. However, Sam Walton stated that Wal-Mart was losing money

New Multinational Network Sharing
pp. 93–104
Copyright © 2007 by Information Age Publishing

on P&G products and he wanted this turned around quickly. After checking our figures, we found that Sam Walton was correct. Mr. Walton told me to go to his data-handling office and arrange to share Wal-Mart's relevant data with P&G. Over the resistance of some Wal-Mart managers, we were able to agree on a data-sharing plan. I became the first "double" manager, with commitments to two separate corporations, but soon many employees of both Wal-Mart and Procter & Gamble also became double managers. In fact, our name is now the *Wal-Mart Team of Procter & Gamble*. We now have 200 employees on the P&G payroll in Fayetteville, Arkansas.

The business relationship in 1988 between Wal-Mart and Procter & Gamble was adversarial. The business itself was $375 million a year and growing. In spite of this, the business relationship between the two companies was dysfunctional. P&G had organized itself into 12 different internal product divisions. Each division had different strategies regarding customers, such as Wal-Mart and their respective sales managers would separately and independently call on Wal-Mart. These individuals were accountable for the sales results of each division and never came together and represented P&G as a whole. The relationship between Wal-Mart and P&G was characterized as: (A) Adversarial, Wal-Mart was apprehensive about doing business with P&G. P&G was too complicated and inflexible. (B) Transactional: Day-by-day selling; success was that you got the order today—failure was that you did not push for sales irrespective of what the customer needed, or was rewarded for; No testing or long term planning, (C) Relationship and activities were managed by the buying and selling function only, the selling function within P&G was responsible for all customer activity. They were responsible for selling to the customer. The role that P&G's information systems played in the relationship was nonexistent. P&G typically got involved only after phone calls down the chain informed us that a technology project such as electronic data interchange (EDI) was requested by the customer.

An outcome of all this was that in 1985, Sam Walton called Procter and Gamble's CEO to inform him that Wal-Mart had awarded P&G their prestigious "Vendor of the Year" Award. The sales organization dealt with customers and Mr. Sam's call to P&G's corporate office resulted in him being transferred five to six times. Having never reached P&G's CEO, Mr. Sam decided to give the award to another vendor.

P&G began to re-think the way it approached its customers. About the same time, our newly appointed vice president of sales met with Sam Walton and discussed the Wal-Mart/Procter & Gamble relationship. Sam indicated that it was a shame that two quality companies could not work together effectively. He commented that P&G had an extremely overcomplicated and inflexible sales organization. He stated that if we thought of Wal-Mart stores as an extension of the P&G company, we would treat

Wal-Mart differently. This challenge became the rallying cry for our two companies.

Great strides have been made since the 1988 start-up of the P&G dedicated Wal-Mart team. We have grown our joint businesses from $375 million in 1988 to over $10 billion dollars today. Moreover, Wal-Mart and P&G have improved the profitability of both companies by using multifunctional resources to drive out costs and improve sales. We use joint scorecards to review our business and make annual plans to drive category growth for both companies. We use technology as a method to drive out costs, and openly share data to better understand our joint customer—the consumer.

Wal-Mart and P&G Team Mission Statement

The mission of the Wal-Mart/P&G business team is to achieve the long-term business objectives of both companies by building a total system partnership that leads our respective companies and industries to better serve our mutual customer—the consumer.

Technology has played a key role with Wal-Mart in three areas:

1. Joint scorecards and measurements
2. Driving out costs through automation
3. Sharing data to better understand the consumer needs and drive sales

Joint Scorecard and Measurements

In 1988, P&G's corporate reporting system was developed based on the market and geographic structure used by the 12 product divisions. All sales reports were designed so P&G could track the amount of product (e.g., laundry detergent) sold in the western part of the country, however, they did not have a system capable of reporting total product sales by customer. A system needed to be developed to track sales by customer. Once this system was developed, tracking sales by customer was possible. P&G's shipment data proved helpful in understanding how much business was sold to Wal-Mart. Some of the questions Wal-Mart had were: (1) How much of the product was sold at stores last year? (2) How many customers bought P&G products? (3) What was the profitability of these products for both Wal-Mart and P&G? These questions needed to be answered. The infrastructure that was needed to link P&G's data with Wal-Mart's data proved to be a critical step in understanding the consumer's needs. Wal-

Mart was just coming online with a new data warehouse that allowed them to track sales of all products in each of their stores. P&G and Wal-Mart jointly developed a data highway that linked P&G data to data driving down costs and sharing information to meet the consumers' needs.

Data Highway Concept

The data highway concept was straightforward, Wal-Mart had scanners in all of their stores to track, measure and analyze their business. Wal-Mart collected its own data then analyzed the results. P&G also had data about the consumer which was used to make product decisions. Why did she/he prefer a certain product or go to a certain store to buy diapers for her/his children? Insights from P&G about the consumer were combined with information from Wal-Mart about what was happening inside the store thus creating an Information Data Highway.

These linkages allowed P&G to build "exit ramps" to support applications such as joint business scorecards, replenishment, EDI, customer table checking and category management. Each of these will be explained later.

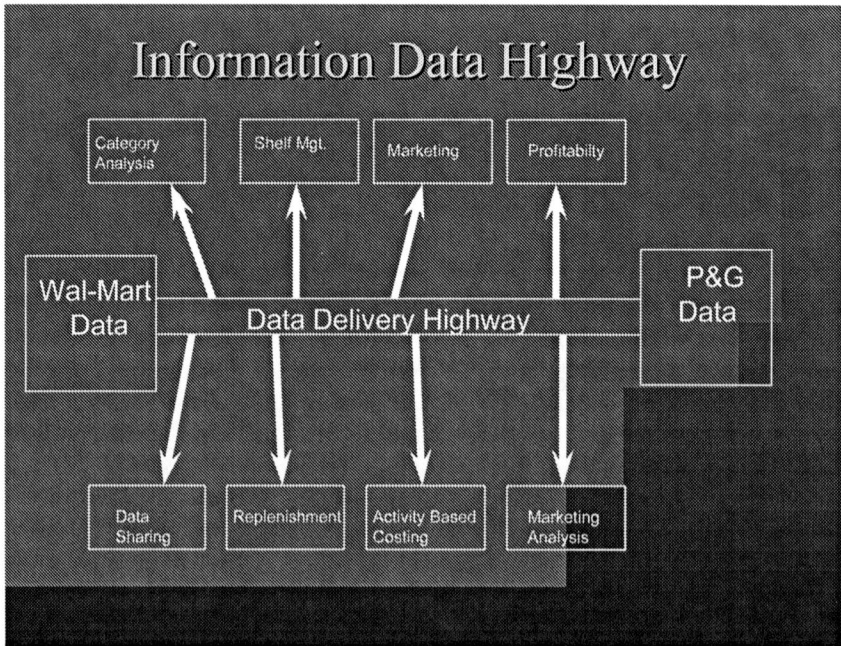

Figure 6.1.

Wal-Mart - Procter & Gamble U.S. Business
1998-99 Scorecard
Wal-Mart Fiscal Years - $ Millions

	Wal-Mart FYs		
	96/97	97/98	Index
Retail Sales (W-M POS Data)			
Wal-Mart Stores			
Gross Margin % (W-M POS Data)			
Wal-Mart, Inc.			
Inventory Management (Wal-Mart Stores)			
Store Inventory DOH			
Total DOH			
Service Levels (% Fill)			
In Stock Level			
On-Time Delivery to Whse			
Financial			
PO/Invoice Match Rate			
Deduction Rolling Balance			
Past Due Invoice Payment Rolling Balance			
Customer Pick-Up Revenue			

Figure 6.2.

Joint Business Scorecard

A joint, common scorecard was developed that reported: the sale of P&G products at Wal-Mart, margin and profit results, inventory turns, and other financial and logistics measurements. The integration of Wal-Mart and P&G data played a key role in delivering these scorecards. This common "language" allowed the partnership to focus on the end consumer and used combined data to measure joint progress.

Driving Out Costs Through Automation

Leveraging technology to drive costs out of the supply system is another important aspect of the information systems function. The delivery of products to the end consumer involves a series of steps including raw material delivery, conversion to a finished product, transportation to

Role of Technology

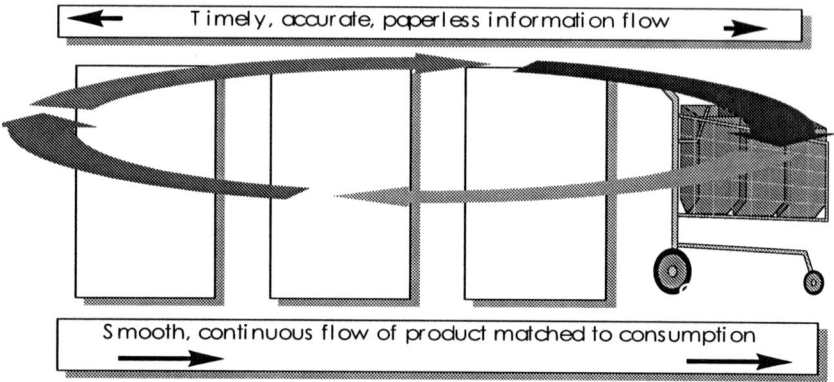

Figure 6.3.

a distributor or customer distribution center, transportation to the store and placement on the store shelf. The degree to which all parties involved can drive costs out of these systems result in savings that can be passed on to the consumer in the form of lower product costs.

In order to drive down costs, product information is needed to move from the retailer back through the supply system. As better consumer data flowed back from the consumer to the raw material supplier, better forecasts could be anticipated and the right material put in place for finished product manufacturing.

Replenishment

P&G replenished Wal-Mart's inventory based on inventory data received from Wal-Mart's distribution center. This data allowed P&G to manage the inventory levels to insure that P&G products were in stock at all times. P&G used their information data highway to fundamentally change the replenishment process. This was done by linking Wal-Mart's inventory data at their distribution centers and P&G's replenished inventory based on movement of product through their distribution center's. P&G reduced the order cycle time (amount of time from the order generation to delivery) by 3–4 days. This process also dramatically increased inventory turns which resulted in a reduction in the inventory of the entire system.

EDI

The role of technology was to link the supply chain by using industry standards Electronic Data Interchange (EDI) to communicate key business documents. Purchase orders, invoices, advanced shipment notification, and financial payment are just a few examples the electronic transmission of EDI. It was critical that EDI not be used to automate poor business practices. It was imperative that we streamline the business "handoffs" then use automation to drive the process. To understand the value of simplifying the business process then applying technology, the business situation below provides a concrete example.

Customer Table Checking

By 1990, P&G's business relationship with Wal-Mart was headed in a positive direction. Joint sales were up, standard scorecards to track the business were used, and both companies were proud of the progress of the partnership. However, there continued to be issues in the area of accounts payable/receivable.

For example, P&G had developed a billing accuracy system that was used to measure how accurate P&G's invoices were against Wal-Mart's purchase orders. P&G felt that Wal-Mart's accuracy was very good, exceeding 95%. During a meeting to discuss vendor performance, the accounts payable manager of Wal-Mart stated that P&G was one of their worst vendors with the lowest purchase order to invoice match rate. Of the purchase orders sent to Wal-Mart, 15% matched invoices. Something was wrong. All purchase orders were via EDI as were all invoices. If the invoices matched, they would be paid automatically. If they did not match, both companies manually handled them. P&G believed that 95% of the invoices were accurate, Wal-Mart believed it was 15% and deductions were at an all time high.

To address this problem P&G placed a person from their customer service organization into Wal-Mart's accounts payable group. The person's responsibility was to track each purchase order/invoice combination and attempt to identify the problem. After a 3-week assessment, P&G found that they had different definitions of billing accuracy. P&G defined billing accuracy as being billed for a certain number of cases that were shipped to Wal-Mart. However, Wal-Mart defined billing accuracy as both the number of cases and the dollar amount of each case. For example, if P&G had a box of detergent for $25 in their item file while Wal-Mart had the same product for $25.05, the invoice sent did not match the purchase order! P&G also discovered that most purchase orders and invoices that did not

Customer Table Checking

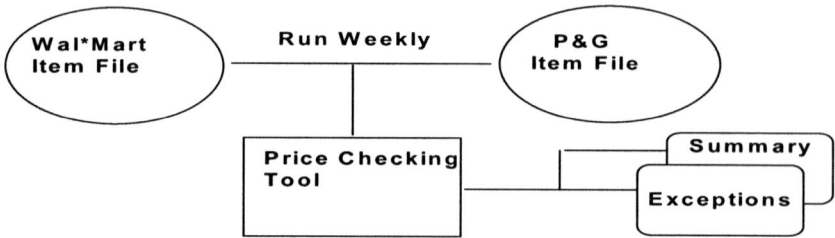

Figure 6.4.

match were due to different prices in the Wal-Mart and P&G system. The automation through EDI only moved bad data faster and resulted in re-working both systems. The cost of the mismatch was calculated at $50 per occurrence.

Technology played a role in identifying and correcting pricing errors. A tool was built called the Customer Table Checking Tool. Every Monday morning before any purchase orders were created, P&G linked into Wal-Mart's item file of P&G products and compared them to the pricing and product specifications in P&G's item file. If any of the items did not match, they were flagged as an exception and electronically corrected.

As a result, P&G's purchase order-invoice match rate went from 15% to 95%. This new system has resulted in P&G moving from one of Wal-Mart's worst vendors to one of the best. The customer service organization insured the data in both systems would be correct and EDI was used to drive down costs and improve the order cycle time. This tool has been used with P&G customers worldwide.

Category Management

Finally, using the design technology of data sharing allowed Wal-Mart and P&G's partnership to make better consumer-based decisions. The key decisions made by the retailers include:

1. What are you going to buy?
2. Where are you going to put it (shelf location)?
3. How are you going to price it?
4. When should it be promoted?

Key questions for retailers can be answered by integrating data from manufacturers' internal point-of-sale systems and third party market data providers such as Nielsen or IRI. Retailers point of sales data show the results of consumer's choices thus providing the answer. It provides the platform resulting in information on what is selling and the selling price. It does not explain why nor does it provide insight into the market dynamics.

In contrast, manufacturer's consumer data is helpful to understand why a product is being purchased. P&G is a Research and Development company first. Consumer needs are studied, products are then developed and manufactured to meet those needs. P&G studies consumer trends and understanding these trends provides insights that the retailer itself does not have.

Finally, third-party data providers help explain the market dynamics of a product. It provides insight into consumer trends and provides a perspective on growing consumer needs. Should a retailer be pleased with a 10% increase in sales versus last year in a particular category? If the retailer's competition is indexing at 5% the answer is yes, if the competition is indexing an increase at 18% then the buyer is losing share in a

Category Management

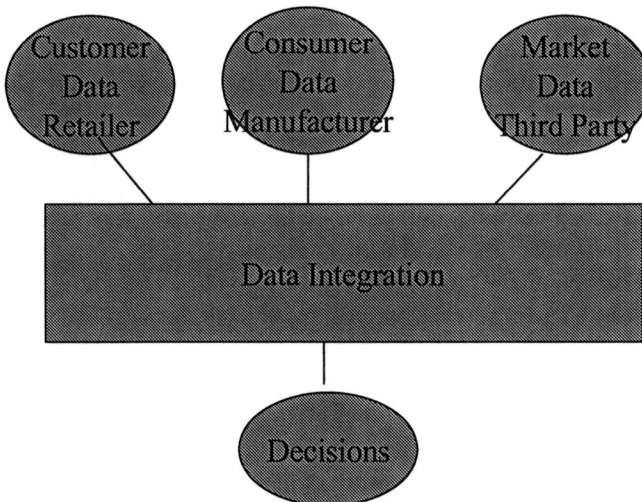

Figure 6.5.

growing category. This information is valuable in determining the markets key items not carried in their stores.

The key is the integration of these three data sources for making decisions. A joint manufacturer/retailer workstation should be used to share common data scorecards and allow for quick analysis by all parties.

Industry Standard

Each business application between a manufacturer and a retailer should be agreed on early if it is proprietary between the two companies or if it can be shared with other customers/suppliers. Wal-Mart, for example, now has a strategy to share data with their vendor partners. A tool has been developed called "Retail Link" that links Wal-Mart's data with their key vendor partners and carriers. P&G has reapplied their customer replenishment systems and the Customer Table Checking Tool to other customers. It is critical for both companies to come to a common point of view on the expansion of these systems. Ideally, most of the electronic linkages between manufacturers and retailers will be similar to the EDI standards that are in place today (UCS, VICS for U.S. and EANCOM globally).

Future—What Role Will Technology Play in the Future?

Technology continues to play a role between manufacturers and suppliers. On the supply side, we have moved from EDI purchase orders and invoices to looking at Collaborative Planning Forecasting and Replenishment (CPFR). This industry model provides a platform for the collaboration of a joint forecast between manufacturers and suppliers that will ultimately drive the replenishment process through the entire supply chain. This may eventually lead to the elimination of purchase orders and invoices as we know them today.

Second, watch for industry standard approaches to share the demand side data similar to the standards we have in place today for EDI. Developing an industry based approach for sharing point of sales data, market data, and consumer data for joint decision making will be a key to success. In addition, driving key third party data providers such as Nielson and IRI to provide quality data in agreed to industry standard hierarchies will lead to better integration between joint buyer/seller workstations. The Internet will provide the technical platform to exchange information between manufacturers, retailers and third-party data providers.

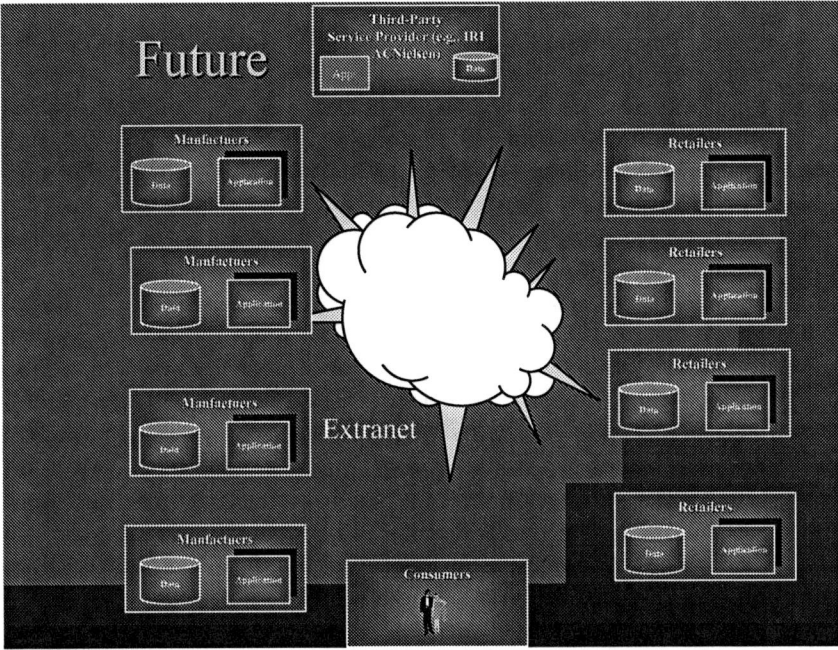

Figure 6.6.

INSIGHTS

Looking back over the 18-year period between Wal-Mart and P&G, information technology has created a common language, driven down costs, and provided an avenue for increased sales for the Wal-Mart and P&G partnership. Several key lessons may be helpful when understanding the role that information technology plays in the manufacturer/supplier relationship:

1. *Use information technology resources:* Information technology (IT) resources can play a key role in the business. IT can provide technology solutions to link suppliers and retailers. It can ensure proper staffing of these resources to drive volume and reduce costs.

2. *Teach them the business:* Take time to train your information technology team about the business. The days of the business ignorant programmers are fading. When I was first brought in to the P&G team, I was an information technology manager, now, as a business manager I use technology to drive sales and reduce costs.

3. *Focus on the consumer:* Use data and technology to better understand the consumers' needs. When a debate about which way to approach their needs occurs, ask yourself the question "What is right for the consumer, what are her/his needs?" This will help you approach the problem differently.

4. *Data can be information:* Retailer data is typically used for quick decision support, but P&G data is used for analytic decision support. When merged, these data create tremendous gains for both companies. Information technology can also be used to sift through large amounts of data and provide exceptions or out of range business parameters. Using IT to identify key outages such as low sales on a fast moving item, out of stock on a key sku, and so forth, will provide powerful business solutions for both companies.

5. *Employ industry standards:* Driving toward common methods of communicating business transactions and data sharing reduces cost for the entire supply chain. Just as we have standardized logistics such as pallet size and truck dimensions from a supply-chain perspective, automating business transactions will also drive down costs of the manufacturer/supplier relationship.

6. *Offer leadership sharing between corporations:* Take time to cooperate with your business partners and suggest data exchanges to make easier work of both sides of the boundaries. Remembering that dysfunctional supplier-retailer relationships can be threats to corporate profitability and eventual sustainability.

CHAPTER 7

LEADER-MEMBER EXCHANGE IN THE PEOPLE'S REPUBLIC OF CHINA

Preliminary Research on the Contents and Dimensions

Hui Wang, Xuefeng Liu, and Kenneth S. Law

Two data sets were used to generate measures of the domain of leader-member exchange in the Chinese organization context. In the first part, an inductive research method was employed to investigate the contents and categories of Chinese leader-member exchange quality. Based on 11 categories developed in the first part, a Chinese measure of LMX was developed and tested. Of the 5 dimensions in the new measure, 2 of them, loyalty and personal interaction, are emic dimensions which are rooted in Chinese culture, but are not predictive of leadership outcomes. The remaining 3 dimensions appear to be similar to Graen's dimensions (2003) underlying the American LMX-7: Contribution (commitment), Closeness (trust and respect), and Liking (liking). We also provided the reliability and validity information on the new measure.

New Multinational Network Sharing
pp. 105–127
Copyright © 2007 by Information Age Publishing

INTRODUCTION

Graen and his associates (Graen & Cashman, 1975) introduced leader-member exchange theory (LMX) to capture the variance of member perceived leadership behavior discarded by the average leadership style approach. Since then, LMX has attracted much interest in the Western management academy. LMX has become a hot topic in the research field of leadership. As noted by Graen and Uhl-Bien (1995), the majority of the early literature focused on the antecedents and consequence of LMX. For example, Graen, Liden and Hoel (1982) found that the level of LMX was a great indicator to predict employee turnover. In a more recent study, Wayne, Shore, and Liden (1997) proved that LMX had a significantly unique interpretation power on performance rating, organizational citizenship behavior and favor doing of employees. Along with them, Duarte, Goodson, and Klich (1994), Masterson, Levis, Goldman, and Taylor (2000), Dunegan, Duchon, Uhl-Bien (1992) showed similar evidence with different samples. Other studies explored the antecedents of LMX (e.g., Engle & Lord, 1997; LaGrace, 1990; Phillips & Bedeian, 1994). According to Engle and his colleagues, both subordinates' and supervisors' self-schemas, subordinates' negative affectivity and perceived similarity significantly predicted LMX ratings. Through an empirical study, Phillips and Bedeian (1994) also found that attitudinal similarity between a dyad and follower extraversion was positively related to LMX.

However, despite numerous research findings showing the relationship between LMX and many important work outcomes, there have been continuous criticisms on its ambiguity in definition and measurement. For example, Gerstner and Day (1997) once wrote, "Despite claims of an apparently robust phenomenon, there is surprisingly little agreement on what LMX is or how it should best be measured," although they found that LMX-7 works the best (p. 828). Liden and Maslyn (1998) also noted that there were at least seven different measures of LMX used by researchers but the gold standard is LMX-7. This may be one reason why some studies got inconsistent or even contradict results of the effects of LMX on some outcome variables.

The purpose of this project is to study the dimensionality and develop an indigenous measure of LMX in the People's Republic of China. As Liden and Maslyn (1998) suggested, there should be formal psychometric supports before a LMX scale could be used. Although it seems promising to apply LMX theory in the Chinese context, one should not use LMX measures developed in the West directly in China, because there are well-known, deep-level cultural differences between supervisor-subordinate interactions in the East and West. A clear and indigenous measure of

LMX in China would help the development of LMX research in this transformational economy.

Chinese Context of LMX

Hofstede (1980) claimed that people in different culture may have different values and different behavioral manner. Triandis (2001) also proposed that individualism-collectivism cultural syndrome is the most significant cultural difference among cultures, with China representing collectivism role, and Unite States as the representative of individualism culture (Bond, 1986; Hofstede, 1980; Hsu, 1981). According to Hofstede (1991, p. 12), "Individualism stands for a society in which the ties between individuals are loose; everyone is expected to look after himself or herself and his or her immediate family only.... Collectivism stands for a society in which people from birth onwards are integrated into strong, cohesive in-groups, which throughout people's lifetime continue to protect them in exchange for unquestioning loyalty." Therefore, it is reasonable to explore LMX within China. Beyond the dichotomy of one characteristic, we expect that due to the differences in modern history, culture and current circumstance may shape the different interaction pattern and quality between a leader and his/her subordinates in the People's Republic of China.

Specifically, the first character of Chinese culture is its relationship-orientation. Just as Kitayama, Markus, Matsumoto, and Norasakkunkit (1997, p. 1248) showed, "Western cultures are organized according to meanings and practices that promote the independence and autonomy of a self that is separate from others, in contrast, many Asian cultures do not highlight the explicit separation of each individual, and they are organized according to meanings and practices that promote the fundamental connectedness among individuals." Triandis (1995), Rhee, Uleman, and Lee (1996), Holtgraves (1997) also found that the distinct characteristic which differentiate the collectivist from the individualist is that the former makes a large relational investment in in-group (family) members. To maintain the close relationship with in-group members, supervisors in collectivism cultures would attend events in the personal life of subordinates (Hui, Eastman, & Yee, 1995; Hui & Luk, 1997). Farh and Cheng (2000) even identified one leadership style, namely benevolent leadership, which was regarded as a component of paternalistic leadership in the context of China. Benevolent leadership, which originated from the Confucian ideal that as a superior, one should be kind and gentle, implied a leader should treat his subordinates benevolently, such as demonstrating individualized, holistic concern for a subordinate's well-being both on and off the job. Farh and Cheng (2000) studied 1,025 employees from the PRC, 1,188 employees from the Taiwan, and 256 employees from Hong Kong, and the results of factor analysis and ANOVA showed that the factor, which was called expectation of leader's benevolence, was found for all three groups. Chinese employees had a strong expectation of leader benevolence. In light of such finding, we could expect that in the interactive process between a leader and a member in organizations, supervisors would take care of the personal lives of their subordinates.

The second character of Chinese culture is intergroup discrimination. People in collectivism culture emphasized the harmony of social relationship, but they do not treat all their social acquaintance in the same way. In an empirical study by Takahashi and colleague (2002), the authors found that the Japanese participants who were believed to embed in the collectivism culture, constructed hierarchical structures of affective relationships with a clear specification of who was the most significant figure for them. Though scholars reported the same social phenomena, namely ingroup favoritism in Western countries (Allen & Wilder, 1975; Billig & Tajfel, 1973), some cross-culture studies proved that Chinese subjects displayed favoritism to in-group members, while American subjects displayed favoritism to themselves, and treated their in-group members the same way as strangers. Some other scholars (Butterfield, 1983; Parsons, 1949) also found that Chinese always categorized people who had interaction with themselves into different groups and treated them differently based on the relationship with them.

Hwang (1997) proposed that traditional Chinese cherish hierarchical status in social relations. They usually adopt and display multiple standards of behavior for interacting with different persons around them. When the resource allocator is asked to distribute a social resource to benefit the petitioner, the potential allocator will first carefully consider: "What is the guanxi [connection] between us?" In addition, Triandis (2001) showed that people in collectivism cultures, compared with those in individualist cultures, are more likely to focus on context more than the content when making attributions. In a study on collectivism and individualism, Morris and Peng (1994) also found that collectivists and individualists explained behavior in different ways. Collectivists (e.g., Chinese) preferred "external attributions" whereas individualists (e.g., Americans) preferred "internal attributions." Bauer and Gaskell (1999), Kim and Markus (1999), Wagner (1998) all suggested that individualism and collectivism do manifest themselves in people's behavior, which is determined by the social context. The behaviors and the interpretations of these behaviors result from the interaction between individuals and their milieu. In another empirical study, Ng and Zhu (2001) proved that collectivists favor externality and individualists favor internality, by demonstrating the important intervening role of situations.

Therefore, it is a social norm to treat people in different categorizes differently in China (Yang, 1993). In the context of organizations in China, we expect that the exchange relationship between dyad would be different from its counterpart in Western countries in which the individualists are primarily concerned with achieving justice (Ohbuchi, Fukushima, & Tedeschi, 1999). As Graen, Hui ,and Gu (2004) found, managers in Chinese organizations put more emphasis on the process, less on the criterion of objective performance.

In summary, it is reasonable to expect that the phenotypic contents and dimensions of LMX in of China would be different from its Western counterpart. We hypothesize that Chinese managers would demonstrate more behaviors on taking care of the personal life of their subordinates, show large degree of in-group favoritism in the exchange process with their subordinates.

Present research included two studies. The first investigated the behaviors or activities which fall into the domain of LMX. We used an inductive approach to identify critical incidents of leader-member exchange in the Chinese organizations by employing the similar method used by Law, Lee, Farh and Pillutla (2001) and Xin, Tsui, Wang, Zhang and Chen (2002). This approach calls for gathering descriptions of concrete incidents from respondents and then by content analysis, classifying them into a number of categories with an agreement index constructed using multiple judges (Anderson & Gerbing, 1991; Kerlinger, 1986). This inductive approach is particularly important in cross-cultural research where construct and measurement equivalence cannot be taken for granted (Van de Vijver, & Leung, 1997). Based on the dimensions and behavioral incidents in the first study, the second study developed a scale to measure LMX in the Chinese context. The psychometrical information related to the indigenous measure will be provided.

STUDY 1: THE CONTENTS AND
CATEGORIES OF LMX IN THE CHINESE CONTEXT

Overview of Method

The purpose of the present study was to identify the domains and contents of LMX in the Chinese organizations. A structured questionnaire was adopted to collect incidents from employees. We asked responses to describe incidents which could describe the degree of exchange quality between leader and members. After generating a large item pool, we proceeded with a rigorous item sorting and classification process. During the coding process, graduate students majored in the management department were invited to classify these incidents into a number of mutually exclusive categories. These categories then were contrasted with the dimensionality of LMX in the West.

Sample

Data were collected from 77 middle-level managers who were MBA students of a prestigious university in north China. These MBA students worked in a various industries such as manufacturing, service, education, and others. The average age of the responses was 33.4 years, and the average organizational tenure was 7.7 years. And 67% of them are male, with a 5.9-years average education level after high school. The detail information on the sample is listed in the Table 7.1.

Procedure

Each respondent was asked to fill out a questionnaire containing two open-ended questions. The first one was: Please list at least five typical incidents to show that you have built a certain level of exchange relationship with your direct supervisor. The second one was: Please list at least five typical incidents to show that you had built a certain level of exchange relationship with your direct subordinate. Before distributing the questionnaire, we gave a brief instruction related to the leader-member exchange theory. Because there is no consistent and clear definition of LMX, we presented respondents with instructions based on the social exchange theory (Blau, 1964). We told them what was the social exchange (high level LMX) and what was the economic one (low level LMX). To avoid misleading of the respondents, we did not mention anything about the dimensions of LMX found by Western scholars. We also asked the respondents to report their demographic information as well as organizational characteristic.

The seventy-seven respondents generated a total of 778 items. The first two authors of this chapter screened these items first. If any of the incidents expressed two or more distinct meaning in one statement, we then split it into two or more statements accordingly. And we also deleted some incidents by two criteria: a) the item must have clear meaning in Chinese language; and b) the item must relate to the exchange relationship quality of a dyad. A total of 771 useable items were gotten after this procedure.

Table 7.1. Sample Characteristics (*N* = 77)

Characteristics	Percentage
Sex	
Male	68.4
Female	31.6
Age	
21-30	19.5
31-40	77.9
41-50	2.6
Tenure	
Less than 5 years	36.6
5–10 years	43.7
More than 10 years	19.7
Positions	
High-level managers	26.3
Middle- level managers	42.7
Low-level managers	23.3

Data Coding and Categories Identification: First Round

Three PhD students in the university were invited to sort the 771 incidents. Before the sorting, we gave them instructions as follows:

The purpose of this sorting task is to require you to categorize statements on leader-member exchange collected from a MBA class. Please sort these statements into different categories based on your understanding on the similarity of the contents of the statements. Different level of Leader-Member Exchange means that a supervisor would develop different relationships with different subordinates, such as a supervisor had a good working relationship with one of his key subordinate, while only having formal work relationship with others. In another word, high-level leader-member exchange means that the exchange relationship between a supervisor and a subordinate is the kind of social exchange, while low-level leader-member exchange means the kind of economic exchange. Some existing studies have identified that only the relationship of social exchange can lead to trust and the feeling of responsibility and reciprocity between the two parties in the exchange relationship, while the pure economic exchange can not do this.

The three PhD students sorted the first 200 statements and then had a discussion about the definition of every category identified by them. The three students generated 12, 12, and 20 categories respectively, and after discussion, they reached consistency on a scheme that included nine categories. The authors of the present study reviewed the results of first-round sorting and discussed the labels and definition of these nine categories. After the discussion, the authors and the coders agreed to make some modification to capture the substance of LMX better and make the categories clearer and neater. At last, a total of 11 categories and their definitions were identified.

Then the three coders sorted the remaining 571 statements with the new category system. Since each statement was classified by three students independently, there were three possible outcomes: (1) full agreements-all three students classified the statement into the same category; (2) two agreements—two of the three students classified the statement into the same dimension; (3) zero agreements—the three students classified the statement into three different dimensions. In order to test if the three coders have the consistency and reliability during the coding system, we calculated the agreement among the three coders as the reliability of the coding process. Table 7.2 showed the results of reliability test.

Data Coding and Categories Identification: Second Round

Although we developed a category system with 11 categories to code the 771 statements and the reliability test showed that it is stable and reliable, we still need a cross validation to test if the system could be used by others. Therefore, another three PhD students were invited as coders in the second round. The task for these new coders is a little simple. What they need to do is just to code all the 771 statements using the same instruction and system as that in the first round. We also calculate their inter-rater reliability as shown in Table 7.2.

The interrater reliability test in the two rounds showed that the coders could reach agreement when using the category system. In the first

Table 7.2.   Item Characteristics

Types	Items	Percentages
Total number of items	778	100
Usable items	771	99.1
Nonusable items	7	0.9
Results of inter-rater reliability test: first round		
Full (three) agreements	330	42.8
Two agreements	321	41.6
No agreement	120	15.6
Results of interrater reliability test: second round		
Full (three) agreements	672	87.26
Two agreements	60	7.78
No agreement	39	5.06

round, the three coders could reach to agreement on 42.8% of total statements, and two coders could reach to agreement on 41.6% of the statements. While in the second round of coding, 87.26% of the statements could be identified into the same category by three coders. These results showed that the 771 statements could be identified into different categories with the coding system by different coders. And the coding process is stable and reliable.

RESULTS

Categories of LMX in Chinese Context

Table 7.3 presents the 11 categories of LMX in the context of Chinese organizations, as well as their definitions and typical items. To get a comparative view, we also listed their corresponding dimensions in Western cultures if any of the categories have been found by Western literature and we called this kind of categories as common category.

Common Categories

The first common category is called **trust,** which refers to a positive and confident mental situation, believing that the other party would not do unfavorable things deliberately. This category is similar to trust (Graen & Scandura, 1987) and mutual influence (Yukl, 1981). A total of 92 statements, or 12.4% of the total, were identified into this category.

The second common category is called **loyalty,** which means the expression of public support of the other member in the leader-member dyad. This category is similar to loyalty (Dienesch & Liden, 1986; Liden & Maslyn, 1998). A total of 62 statements, or 8.4% of the total, fell into this category.

The third common category is called **liking,** which refers to the mutual affection that the members of the dyad have for each other based primarily on interpersonal attraction rather than work or professional values. This category was overlapped completely with affect dimension in the multi-dimension measure of LMX (Dienesch & Liden, 1986; Liden & Maslyn, 1998). This category included 15 statements, or 2% of the total.

The fourth common category is called **assiduity,** which refers to subordinate's acting properly for the completion of task or the benefit of the organization for maintaining high quality with the supervisor in a dyad. This category was similar to professional respect (Dienesch & Liden, 1986; Liden & Maslyn, 1998) and subordinate competence (Liden & Graen, 1980), because they all emphasized the job-related behavior. This category included 92 statements, or 12.4% of the total.

Table 7.3. LMX Dimensions in the PRC

Common Categories

Definition	Sample items	Corresponding Western LMX Dimension
Trust A positive and confident mental situation, believing that the other party would not do unfavorable things deliberately	• My supervisor does not abstain from letting me know some confidential information. • I tell something what should not be discussed publicly to my subordinate.	• Trust (Graen & Scandura, 1987) • Mutual influence (Yukl, 1981)
Loyalty The expression of public support for the goals and the personal character of the other member of the LMX dyad.	• I try to maintain my supervisor's authority everywhere, and rebut other's criticism to him. • When somebody criticized my subordinate's performance, I would give some explanation to excuse him.	• Loyalty (Dienesch & Liden, 1986; Liden & Maslyn, 1998)
Liking The mutual affection members of the dyad have for each other based primarily on interpersonal attraction rather than work or professional values.	• I appreciate my supervisor's management style what emphasizes trust and delegation. • I appreciated the ways by which my supervisor got things done.	• Affect (Dienesch & Liden, 1986; Liden & Maslyn, 1998)
Respect Subordinate's acting properly for the completion of task or the benefit of the organization for maintaining high quality with the supervisor in a dyad.	• I will do my best to finish all the work that are good to the organization. • It is my responsibility to finish the tasks that are good to our organization.	• Professional respect (Dienesch & Liden, 1986; Liden & Maslyn, 1998) • Respect for performance (Graen & Uhl-Bien, 1995)
Intimacy Having little worries in the interactive process with the other parts of the dyad or interact frequently, with little psychological distance with the other part.	• Getting together from time to time. • Having dinner or going to shopping together in the leisure time.	

Job-Related Support Providing proper help within one self's responsibility for the better completion of the other's task.	• Working hard to improve my supervisor's performance. • I gave my subordinate some suggest as he met difficulty in a negotiation.
Favoritism Providing extra favor or making one exempt for punishment, even doing so may lead to inequity.	• I provide more promotion opportunity for my subordinates. • I made efforts to keep an apartment for my subordinate during the decision making process of house allocation .
Personal Friendship Helping the other member in a dyad and considering his or her interesting initiatively in personal life.	• I provided material or psychological support when my subordinate meets difficulty in his or her personal life. • I am concerned about the personal matter of my supervisor, such as his birthday.
Performance Recognition Supervisor's recognition about the contribution a subordinate has made, and praises him or her accordingly.	• My boss spoke highly of my performance and gave me material encouragement. • After the successful accomplishment of one task, I would provide the opportunity of reward to my subordinates.
Obligation Assuming ones own responsibility for one job fail, or taking extra responsibility for the interest of the other side.	• When my subordinate was criticized by a manager with higher title, I would take the responsibility to defend for him or her.
Understanding Considering the intention and motivation of the other side with illustrating psychological acceptance and behavioral support.	• I could understand my supervisor's intention and cooperate with him smoothly. • I forgave the misunderstanding of my supervisor to me.

Extended Categories

The first extended category is called **intimacy**, which is defined as personal closeness for which two parties in a dyad have little worries in their interactive process or interact frequently with little psychological distance. It included 120 statements, or 16.2% of the total.

The second extended category is called **job-related support**, which refers to providing proper help within one self's responsibility for the better completion of the counter part's task. A total of 139 statements, or 18.8% of the total, were categorized into this category.

The third extended category is called **favoritism**, which refers to the behavior of providing extra favor or making one exempt for punishment, even such doing leading to inequity. It included 47 statements, or 6.3% of the total.

The fourth extended category is called **personal friendship**, which refers to helping the other members of the dyad and considering his or her interest initiatively in personal life. Ninety-five statements (12.8%) were classified into this category.

The fifth extended category is called **performance recognition**, which refers to that the supervisor could recognize the contribution a subordinate have made and praise him or her accordingly. It included 41 statements, or 5.5% of the total.

The sixth extended category is called **obligation**, which refers to responsibility-taking that each party in a dyad assumes his or her own responsibility for one job-related blame, or take extra responsibility for the interest of the other side. A total of 16 statements or 2.2% of the total were identified into this category.

The last category is called **considering**, which refers to understanding the intention and motivation of the other side, with psychological acceptance and behavioral support. Twenty-two statements, or 3.0% of the total were classified into this category.

STUDY 2: AN INDIGENOUS MEASURE OF LMX IN THE CHINESE CONTEXT

The purpose of Study 2 is to investigate the dimensionality and develop an indigenous measure of LMX in the People's Republic of China based on the results of inductive research in Study 1.

We developed a total of 11 dimensions in the study above to describe the exchange relationships between the supervisor-subordinate dyad in Chinese organizations (we refer to it as the Chinese LMX or CLMX measure later on for easy reference). In this study, we start by selecting five representative items for each of the eleven CLMX categories identified in

Study 1. A total of 55 items were selected. We then collect data using MBA students and test the reliability and validity of the final scale developed.

Sample and Procedures

Sample. The sample consists of a total of 165 part time MBA students who study in a major university in Beijing, PRC. These students have a mean age of 29.81, with 7.86 years of education after middle school and 7.5 years of job tenure on average. Seventy three percent of them are male.

Measure. The 55 items we selected constitute the pilot item pool for the indigenous CLMX measure in this study. To validate the newly developed scale, we also measured LMX-7 (Gerstner & Day, 1997), job satisfaction (Tsui, Egan, & O'Reilly, 1992), organizational commitment (Mowday, Steers & Porter, 1979), and intention to quit (Bluedorn, 1982.) in the same questionnaire. All questions are scored on a 7-point scale from *1 = disagree strongly* to *7 = agree strongly*.

Results

We started using exploratory factor analyses (EFA) to select items that converged into the expected CLMX dimensions. In each step of EFA, items with cross loadings larger than .3 were deleted, then the remaining items were subjected to another EFA, and the process was repeated until the items converged into factors with clear loadings. At the end, 17 items remained which loaded on five distinct factors. These five factors were named contribution, closeness, liking, loyalty, and personal interaction. The factors as well as the respective items loaded on each factor are shown in Table 7.4.

The first dimension is named *contribution*, which refers to the perception of the amount, direction, and quality as work-oriented activity each member of the dyads puts forth toward the mutual goals. Four items load heavily on this dimension. Coefficient alpha of this dimension is .86. The second dimension is *loyalty*, which refers to the extent to which both leader and follower publicly support other's actions and character. It consists of three items. Coefficient alpha is .69. The third dimension is called *liking*, which refers to the mutual affection members of the dyad have for each other based primarily on interpersonal attraction rather than work or professional values. Three items load on this factor, and the coefficient alpha is .86.

Table 7.4.   Results of Exploratory Factor Analysis

	Contribution	Closeness	Liking	Loyalty	Personal Interaction
If needed, I am willing to do any job for my direct supervisor.	.82	.28	.13	.16	.07
If my supervisor has difficulty to do his or her job, I will try to help.	.80	.33	.06	.24	.12
I am willing to make more effort for my supervisor's interest.	.74	.08	.31	.16	.13
For my supervisor, I am willing to sacrifice my own interest.	.72	.16	.31	.04	.16
I could communicate my viewpoint with my supervisor frankly.	.13	.79	.11	.11	−.09
I could understand my supervisor's intention.	.21	.77	.10	.00	.13
My supervisor always asks me for suggestions when facing important matters.	.09	.70	.24	.30	.19
I always propose my suggestions to my supervisor without any hesitation.	.24	.69	.02	.17	.11
I have very similar values with my supervisor.	.27	.23	.83	.10	.16
I have the same hobby with my supervisor.	.11	.07	.82	.24	.18
I appreciate my supervisor's personality very much.	.33	.11	.78	.15	.04
If I were in conflict with others, my supervisor would give me support.	.19	.08	.10	.84	.10
My supervisor would come to my defense if I were "attacked" by others.	.06	.18	.20	.80	.14
My supervisor never criticizes me for my misplay on public occasions.	.16	.14	.10	.64	.08
I have much personal interaction with my supervisor.	.10	.10	.18	.23	.80
I interact with the family members of my supervisor sometimes.	.17	−.01	−.02	.01	.79
My supervisor likes to chat with me on some job-unrelated things.	.07	.24	.31	.11	.67
Eigenvalue	6.39	1.67	1.44	1.28	1.17
Percentage of variance explained	37.60	9.83	8.48	7.52	6.88

The forth dimension is called *closeness*, which is defined as personal closeness for which two parties in a dyad could interact easily. Four items load on this factor, and the coefficient alpha of this dimension is .79. The fifth dimension is named personal interaction, which refers to the interaction of a dyad in their private lives. Three items load on this factor and the coefficient alpha is .72. Three out of the five dimensions, namely liking, loyalty and contribution, are exactly similar to what have been found by Liden and Maslyn (1998). They are considered as the etic LMX dimensions. The other two, closeness and personal interaction, are emic dimensions. They capture the specific influence of Confucianism on interpersonal relationship, especially those between supervisors and subordinates in the PRC.

Since the five factors are found using item selection based on factor analyses, one would need further evidence on their discriminant validity. We employed two indices, median correlation and difference in correlation (Finkelstein, 1992), to test that the five factors are distinct CLMX factors. The *median correlation index* is the median correlation of items within each dimension minus median correlation of items with other dimensions. A positive median correlation means that items within each dimension converge and are discriminated from items in other dimensions. The *difference in correlation index* refers to the correlation of each item with its own dimension *minus* the maximum correlation of this item with other dimensions. Again, a positive difference in correlation implies that this item is heavily correlated with this dimension and less correlated with other dimensions. Results of both indices are shown in Table 7.5, and we can see that there are strong evidences on discriminant validity of the five CLMX dimensions.

We checked the correlation of this construct with LMX-7 to investigate its convergent validity. While cultural characteristics may exist, this new CLMX scale should correlate reasonably with existing measures of LMX because they are measuring the same construct conceptually. As a result, we expect each dimension of this new CLMX measure to have significant correlation with LMX-7. Results in Table 7.6 confirm this hypothesis. The Pearson correlations between contribution, closeness, liking, loyalty, and personal interaction and LMX-7 are .66, .67, .64, .47 and .42 respectively (all $p < .01$).

To investigate the criteria-related validity of the new CLMX measure, we also correlate it with job satisfaction, organizational commitment and intention to quit. Table 6 shows that the Pearson correlation between each of the five CLMX dimensions all correlated significantly with the three criteria variables ($p < .05$), except that of loyalty with intention to quit. We conclude that evidence on criteria validity of this CLMX scale was found.

Table 7.5.   Discriminant Validity of the
Chinese Leader-Member Exchange Scale

	Correlation With the Subscale	Median Correlations[a]	Differences in Correlations[b]
Contribution Commitment		.29	
If needed, I am willing to do any job for my direct supervisor.	.86		.46
If my supervisor has difficulty to do his or her job, I will try to help.	.87		.46
I am willing to make more effort for my supervisor's interest.	.83		.48
For my supervisor, I am willing to sacrifice my own interest.	.83		.51
Closeness, Trust & Respect		.21	
I could communicate my viewpoint with my supervisor frankly.	.80		.53
I could understand my supervisor's intention.	.78		.49
My supervisor always asks me for suggestions when facing important matters.	.83		.43
I always propose my job suggestions to my supervisor.	.73		.42
Liking		.39	
I have very similar values to my supervisor.	.92		.52
I have the same hobby as my supervisor.	.86		.47
I appreciate my supervisor's personality very much.	.87		.51
Loyalty		.08	
If I were in conflict with others, my supervisor would give me support.	.82		.48
My supervisor would come to my defense if I were "attacked" by others.	.82		.46
My supervisor never criticizes me for my misplay on public occasions.	.74		.55
Personal Interaction		.21	
I have much personal interaction with my supervisor.	.86		.48
I interact with the family of my supervisor sometimes.	.79		.60
My supervisor likes to chat with me on some job-unrelated things.	.76		.42

Notes: [a]Median correlations refer to the differences between "the median correlation of each item making up the dimension and other items in the same dimension" and "the median correlation of each item making up the dimension and other items making up other dimensions." [b]Differences in correlations refer to the differences between "correlation of an item with its own dimension" and "the maximum correlation of an item with other dimensions."

Table 7.6. Descriptive Statistics and Correlations[a, b]

Variables	Mean	S.D.	1	2	3	4	5	6	7	8	9
Contribution (Commitment)	5.07	.98	(.86)								
Closeness (Trust & Respect)	5.18	.95	.49**	(.79)							
Liking	3.91	1.36	.55**	.40**	(.86)						
Loyalty	4.52	1.00	.41**	.41**	.42**	(.69)					
Personal interaction	3.85	1.34	.37**	.31**	.41**	.34**	(.72)				
LMX-7	4.66	.84	.66**	.67**	.64**	.47**	.42**	(.82)			
Job satisfaction	4.46	1.33	.40**	.40**	.30**	.29**	.24**	.39**	(.92)		
Organizational commitment	4.53	1.14	.45**	.48**	.37**	.23**	.20**	.51**	.74**	(.92)	
Intention to quit	3.69	1.59	-.34**	-.29**	-.33**	-.11	-.19*	-.31**	-.63**	-.62**	(.94)

Note: [a]*p* < .05, **p* < .01. [b]Numbers in parentheses are coefficient alphas.

GENERAL DISCUSSION

In the present research, we first identified the domains and contents of LMX in the Chinese context with an inductive research methodology. A total of 77 middle-level managers participated in the Study 1, and a total of 771 useful statements were collected from them. Based on these statements, eleven categories of LMX were identified. Four of these categories, that is, loyalty, trust, liking, and assiduity, are similar to the major LMX dimensions that have been investigated in the Western LMX literature (Graen, 2003). These categories corresponded to loyalty, trust, affect, and professional respect respectively. This suggested LMX was a cross-culture phenomenon. We also found seven emic categories that are specific in the context of China. They are intimacy, job-related support, favoritism, personal friendship, assiduity, performance recognition, obligation, and considering.

Based on these results, we developed an indigenous measure of LMX and test its reliability and validity in the Study 2. We found that there are three etic dimensions that are common to the results in the Western literature, that is, contribution, liking and loyalty. Graen would call these commitment to the relationship, mutual liking, and trust and respect combined (Graen, 2003). Two emic dimensions that are specific to the Chinese organizational context, were closeness and personal interaction. The results of the discriminant validity, content validity, and criteria-related validity test showed that the indigenous measure of LMX has acceptable validity.

Due to the influence of national culture, the Chinese content of LMX has an emphasis on the personal interaction, and not like Western counterpart that has an emphasis on job-related content. The correlation between personal interaction and LMX-7 was .42 and lower than with the other Chinese subscales. For example, closeness is an emic dimension is the new measure. According to Hofstede (1980), China is a country with high power distance. Because of power complex (Hwang, 1997), Chinese subordinates would be more initiative to build a good relationship with their direct supervisor to increase their feeling of security, gain more favorable results in reward allocation, and even their power. Closeness implied the guanxi between a dyad is good, and they interacted frequently not only in the context of organizations, but also in their personal lives. The correlation between closeness and LMX-7 was .67 and higher than with other Chinese subscales.

The other emic dimension is personal interaction. According to Hwang (1987), Greenberg and Cohen (1982), supervisors would interact with their in-group subordinates by a mixed rule of need norm and equity rule (Greenberg & Cohen 1982; Leventhal, 1976), which implied that supervisors would satisfy subordinates need of affection, warmth, safety, and attachment in their interactive process, so it was not surprising to find that supervisors involved into the personal life of subordinates. Tsui and Farh (1997) also found that a different set of exchange principles governed the relationship with individuals having particularistic ties, and the relationship with them had both utilitarian and expressive components.

It is interesting to note that both of the two emic dimensions are not directly related to the work domain between a leader and his/her subordinates. According to the traditional perspective, LMX is strictly adhered to the working relationship between leader and members and the correlations between LMX-7 and contribution (or commitment), closeness (or trust and respect), Liking were .66, .67 and .64 respectively and with loyalty and personal interaction were .47 and .42. We are open to discuss on this issue that if these work unrelated dimensions should be included in the measure of Chinese LMX. We also call for other empirical studies in China to focus and investigate the domain and dimensions of LMX specifically in the Chinese organization context. We started from scratch to develop a Chinese version of the American developed LMX-7. We succeeded with two of our subscales, namely, contribution (or commitment), closeness (or trust and respect). As Graen (2003) pointed out, LMX-7 has not included liking because it was found in numerous studies that LMX-7 without liking added predicted performance and organizational commitment as judged by both hard and soft criteria. Clearly, liking is related to LMX-7, but adding it to LMX-7 only reduces its LMX-7's prediction of performance.

CONCLUSION

In this study, we develop from scratch in China a scale to measure leader-member exchange in the Chinese context. Results show that it has acceptable reliability and validity and could be used as a parallel measure of LMX instrument in the PRC in future relevant studies. One weakness of the study was the relatively small size of the sample, and the lack of cross-validation samples. In the future, we would aim at a refined version of our scale with stronger validity evidence. Now we have three parallel forms of Chinese LMX measures (Wang, Law, Hackett, Wang, &Chen, 2005; Li, Wang & Law, 2005)

REFERENCES

Allen. V. L., & Wilder, D. A. (1975). Categorization, belief similarity, and intergroup discrimination. *Journal of Personality and Social Psychology, 6*, 971-977.

Anderson, J. C., & Gerbing, D. W. (1991). Predicting the performance of measures in a confirmatory factor analysis with a pretest assessment of their substantive validities. *Journal of Applied Psychology*, 76, 732-741.

Bauer, M. W., & Gaskell, G. (1999). Toward a paradigm for research on social representations. *Journal for Theory of Social Behavior*, 29,163-186.

Billig, M., & Tajfel, H. (1973). Social categorization and similarity of inter-group behavior. *European Journal of Social Psychology*, 3, 27-52.

Blau, P. M. (1964). *Exchange and power social life*. New York: Wiley.

Bluedorn, A. (1982). A unified model of turnover from organizations. *Human Relations*, 35, 135-153.

Bond, M. H. (Ed.). (1986). *The psychology of the Chinese people*. Hong Kong, China: Oxford University Press.

Butterfield, F. (1983). *China: Alive in bitter sea*. London: Coronet.

Dienesch, M., & Liden, R. C. (1986). Leader-member exchange model of leadership: A critique and further development. *Academy of Management Review*, 3, 618-634.

Duarte, N. T., Goodson, J. R., & Klich, N. R. (1994). Effects of dyadic quality and duration on performance appraisal. *Academy of Management Journal*, 37, 499-521.

Dunegan, K. J., Duchon, D., & Uhl-Bien, M. (1992). Examining the link between leader-member exchange and subordinate performance: The role of task analyzability and variety as moderators. *Journal of Management*, 1, 59-76.

Engle, E. M., & Lord, R. G. (1997). Implicit theories, self-schemas, and leader-member exchange. *The Academy of Management Journal*, 40, 988-1010.

Farh, J. L., & Cheng, B. S. (2000). A cultural analysis of paternalistic leadership in Chinese organizations. In J. T. Li, A. S. Tsui, & E. Weldon (Eds.), *Management and organizations in the Chinese context* (pp. 84-127). London: Macmillan Press.

Finkelstein, S. (1992). Power in top management teams: Dimensions, measurement, and validation. *Academy of Management Journal*, 35, 505-538.

Gerstner, C. R., & Day, D. V. (1997). Meta-analytic review of leader-member exchange theory: Correlates and construct issues. *Journal of Applied Psychology*, 82, 827-844.

Graen, G. B. (Ed.). (2003). Interpersonal workplace theory at the crossroads. In *LMX leadership: The series: Vol. 1. Dealing with diversity* (pp. 145-182). Greenwich, CT: Information Age.

Graen, G., & Cashman, J. F. (1975). A role-making model in formal organizations: A developmental approach. In J.G. Hunt & L. L. Larson (Eds.), *Leadership frontiers* (pp.143-165). Kent. OH: Kent State Press.

Graen, G. B., Hui, C., & Gu, Q. L. (2004). A new approach to intercultural cooperation. In G. B. Graen (Ed.), *LMX leadership: The series: Vol. 2. New frontiers of leadership* (pp. 225-246). Greenwich, CT: Information Age.

Graen, G. B., Liden, R. C., & Hoel, W. (1982). Role of leadership in the employee withdrawal process. *Journal of Apply Psychology*, 67, 868-872.

Graen, G. B., & Scandura, T. A. (1987). Toward a psychology of dyadic organizing. In L. L. Cummings & B. M. Staw (Eds.), *Research in organizational behavior* (pp. 175-208). Greenwich, CT: JAI Press.

Graen, G. B., & Uhl-Bien, M. (1995). Development of leader-member exchange (LMX) theory of leadership over 25 years: Applying a multi-level multi-domain perspective. *Leadership Quarterly, 6,* 219-247.

Graen, G. B., & Scandura, T. A. (1987). Toward a psychology of dyadic organizing. In L. L. Cummings & B. M. Staw (Eds.), *Research in organizational behavior,* (Vol. 9, pp. 175-208). Greenwich, CT: JAI Press.

Greenberg, J., & Cohen. R. L. (1982). Why justice? Normative and instrumental interpretations. In J. Greenberg & R. L. Cohen (Eds.), *Equity and justice in social behavior* (pp. 437-446). New York: Academic.

Hofstede, G. (1980). *Culture's consequences: International differences in work-related values.* Beverly Hills, CA: Sage.

Hofstede, G. (1991). *Cultures and organizations: Software of the mind.* London: McGraw-Hill.

Holtgraves, T. (1997). Styles of language use: Individual and cultural variability in conversational indirectness. *Journal of Personality and Social Psychology, 73,* 624-637.

Hsu, F. L. K. (1981). *The Americans and the Chinese: Passage to differences* (3rd ed.). Honolulu: University of Hawaii Press.

Hui, C., Eastman, K., & Yee, C. (1995). The relationship between individualism-collectivism and satisfaction at the workplace. *Applied Psychology: An International Review, 44,* 276-282.

Hui, C., & Luk, C. (1997). Industrial/organizational psychology. In J. Berry, M. Segall, & C. Kagitcibasi (Eds.), *Handbook of cross-cultural psychology* (Vol. 3, pp. 371-412). Needham Heights, MA: Allyn & Bacon.

Hwang, K. K. (1987). Face and favor: Chinese power game. *American Journal of Sociology, 92,* 944-974.

Hwang, K.K. (1997). Guanxi and Mientze: Conflict resolution in Chinese society. *Intercultural Communication Studies, 7,* 17-42.

Kerlinger, F. N. (1986). *Foundations of behavioral research.* Fort Worth, TX: Holt, Rinehart and Winston.

Kim, H., & Markus, H. R. (1999). Deviance or uniqueness, harmony or conformity? A cultural analysis, *Journal of Personality and Social Psychology, 77,* 785-800.

Kitayama, S., Markus, H. R., Matsumoto, H., & Norasakkunkit, V. (1997). Individual and collective processes in the construction of the self: Self-enhancement in the United States and self-criticism in Japan. *Journal of Personality and Social Psychology, 72,* 1245-1267.

LaGrace, R. R. (1990). Leader-member exchange: Antecedents and consequences of the cadre and hired hand. *Journal of Personal Selling and Sales Management, 10,* 11-19.

Law, K. S., Lee, C., Farh, L., & Pillutla, M. (2001, July). *Organizational justice perceptions of employees in China: A grounded investigation.* Paper presented at the 2001 International Conference of the Global Business and Technology Association, Istanbul, Turkey.

Leventhal, G. S. (1976). The distribution of reward and resources in groups and organizations. In L. Berkowitz (Ed.), *Advances in experimental social psychology,* (Vol. 9, pp. 91-131). New York: Academic.

Liden, R. C., & Graen, G. (1980). Generalizability of the vertical dyad linkage model of leadership. *Academy of Management Journal, 23*, 451-465.

Liden, R. C., & Maslyn, J. M. (1998. Multidimensionality of leader-member exchange: An empirical assessment through scale development. *Journal of Management, 24*, 43-72.

Liu, X. F., Wang, H., & Law, K. (2005). *Leader-member exchange in the People's Republic of China: Dimensions, development, and validity.* The 6th conference Industrial and Organizational Psychology Society, Brisbane.

Masterson, S. S., Lewis, K., Goldman, B. M., & Taylor, M. S. (2000. Integrating justice and social exchange: The differing effects of fair procedures and treatment on work relationships. *Academy of Management Journal, 4*, 736-748.

Mowday, R. T., Steers, R. M., & Porter, L. W. (1979). The measurement of organizational commitment. *Journal of Vocational Behavior, 14*, 224-247.

Ng, S. H., & Zhu, Y. (2001). Attributing causality and remembering events in individual- and group-acting situations: A Beijing, Hong Kong, and Wellington comparison. *Asian Journal of Social Psychology, 4*, 39-52.

Ohbuchi, K., Fukushima, O., & Tedeschi, J. T. (1999. Cultural values in conflict management: Goal orientation, goal attainment, and tactical decision. *Journal of Cross Culture Psychology, 30*, 51-71.

Parsons, T. (1949). *The structure of social action.* New York: Free Press.

Phillips, A. S., & Bedeian, A. G. (1994). Leader-follower exchange quality: The role of personal and interpersonal attributes. *Academy of Management Journal, 17*, 990-1001.

Rhee, E., Uleman, J., & Lee, H. (1996). Variations in collectivism and individualism by ingroup and culture: Confirmatory factor analysis. *Journal of Personality and Social Psychology, 71*, 1037-1054.

Triandis, H. C. (1995). *Individualism & collectivism.* Boulder, CO: Westview Press.

Triandis H. C. (2001). Individualism-collectivism and personality. *Journal of Personality, 69*, 907-924.

Tsui, A. S., Egan, T. D., & O'Reilly, C. A. (1992). Being different: Relational demography and organizational attachment. *Administrative Science Quarterly, 37*, 549-580.

Tsui, A. S., & Farh, L. J. (1997). Where guanxi matters: Relational demography and guanxi in the Chinese context. *Work and Occupations, 24*, 56-79.

Van de Vijver, F., & Leung, K. (1977). *Methods and data analysis for cross-cultural research.* London: Sage.

Xin, K. R., Tsui, A. S., Wang, H., Zhang, Z., & Chen, W. (2002). Corporate culture in Chinese state-owned enterprises: An inductive analysis of dimensions and influences. In A. S. Tsui & C. M. Lau (Eds.), *The management of enterprises in the People's Republic of China* (pp. 415-444). Boston: Kluwer Academic Press.

Wayne S. J., Shore, L. M., & Liden, R. C. (1997). Perceived organizational support and leader-member exchange: A social exchange perspective. *Academy of Management Journal, 40*, 82-111.

Wagner, W. (1998). Social representations and beyond: Brute facts, symbolic coping and domesticated world. *Culture and Psychology, 4*, 297-329.

Wang, H., Law, K. S., Hackett, R. D., Wang, D., & Chen, Z. X. (2004). Leader-member exchange as a mediator of the relationship between transformational leadership and followers' performance and organizational citizenship behavior. *Academy of Management Journal, 48*(3), 420-432.

Yang, K. S. (1993). Chinese social orientation: An integrative analysis. In L. Y. Cheng, F. M. C. Cheung, & C. N. Chen (Eds.), *Psychotherapy for the Chinese: Selected papers from the first international conference* (pp. 19-56). Hong Kong: The Chinese University of Hong Kong.

Yukl, G. (1981). *Leadership in organizations.* Englewood Cliffs, NJ: Prentice-Hall.

CHAPTER 8

EXAMINING COMPONENT MEASURES OF TEAM LEADER-MEMBER EXCHANGE

Using Item Response Theory

**Charles A. Scherbaum, Loren J. Naidoo,
and Jennifer M. Ferreter**

Leader-member exchange (LMX) has developed into one of the most dominant modern theories of leadership (Graen, 2003; Liden, Sparrowe, & Wayne, 1997). Yet, the research has not taken advantage of more recently developed psychometric techniques such as item response theory (IRT). This chapter offers IRT as a set of tools for enhancing the understanding of LMX measures and provides an introduction to conducting IRT analyses. The newly developed measure of team LMX and MMX were subjected to IRT analyses and the findings indicate that this 6-item measure that includes 4 items from the classic LMX-7 measure supports Graen, Hui, and Taylor's (2004) work on the psychometric quality of team LMX and MMX. Results are compared to a previous IRT analysis of LMX-MDM.

New Multinational Network Sharing
pp. 129–156
Copyright © 2007 by Information Age Publishing
All rights of reproduction in any form reserved.

INTRODUCTION

Leader-member exchange (LMX) theory examines leadership as a dyadic relationship between a leader and his or her followers (Dansereau, Cashman, & Graen, 1973; Graen, Novak, & Sommerkamp, 1982). Since its inception in the early 1970s, LMX theory has inspired considerable theoretical and empirical research (Graen 2003; Graen & Uhl-Bien, 1995; Liden, Sparrowe, & Wayne, 1997). This research has produced a variety of measures for assessing and examining LMX. As part of that development, there has been keen interest in understanding the psychometric properties of these measures (Graen 2003; Graen & Uhl-Bien, 1995; Liden et al., 1997; Schriesheim, Castro, & Cogliser, 1999). Common to all of the research on the psychometric properties of LMX measures is a general reliance on classical measurement theory techniques. Over the last 4 decades, measurement theory has evolved rapidly and several techniques have been developed (e.g., generalizability theory, item response theory) that liberate researchers from the assumptions and limitations of classical measurement theory.

Modern measurement techniques have been used to advance our understanding in a variety of domains of organizational research. However, they are rarely used in leadership research (see Craig & Gustafson, 1998 or Scherbaum, Finlinson, Barden, & Tamanini, 2006 for two exceptions). This situation is regrettable as modern psychometric techniques can provide insights over and above those gained from classical psychometric techniques (Embretson & Reise, 2000; Reise & Henson, 2003). It is particularly the case with areas of research, such as LMX, where the constructs are primarily assessed using self-report or other-report questionnaire measures and the conceptualization of the constructs is becoming more complex (e.g., Marion & Uhl-Bien, 2001; Schriesheim et al., 1999).

In this chapter, we focus on one of the modern developments, item response theory (IRT), and how it can be applied to enhance the understanding of LMX measures. IRT is a family of techniques for understanding the psychometric properties of measures and relationships between properties of the measures and the individuals completing those measures. We argue that using IRT techniques to gain a better understanding of the measures used to support LMX theories and constructs is a prudent course for LMX research to take. Thus, the purpose of this chapter is to introduce IRT to LMX researchers as a set of tools that can be used to gain a further understanding of LMX measures and how they can be used best. In the subsequent sections, we review the basic IRT framework, describe the IRT models and their assumptions, discuss the advantages of IRT, and explicate how IRT can be used to enhance research on the measurement of LMX. We note several of the practical considerations when conducting IRT analyses, as well as provide an example using IRT with data from Graen, Hui, and Taylor's (2004) LMX-SLX measure.

Examining the Psychometric Properties of Leader-Member Exchange Measures

Although substantial research has been devoted to the measurement of LMX, this research has relied on classical measurement techniques to establish the psychometric properties of the scores from LMX measures. Classical measurement theory, also know as the "true score" model, is based on the notion that an observed score on a measure is composed of the true score for that construct that is assessed by the measure and random error. Based on classical measurement theory, a variety of techniques have been developed that allow researchers to assess the reliability and validity of scores and the measurement properties of items. These techniques have been very useful for evaluating the quality of the psychometric properties of scores and have become increasingly sophisticated (e.g., covariance structure modeling techniques). Nevertheless, psychometric techniques based on classical measurement theory have a number of well-known limitations (see the subsequent sections or Hambleton, Swaminathan, & Rogers, 1991 for a review of these limitations). These limitations are not fatal, but they can shape the nature of the conclusions that one may draw from scores on a measure and the questions that one may ask.

Modern measurement theory offers several approaches that overcome many of the limitations of classical measurement theory. These techniques have been used in a variety of areas in the organizational sciences. However, these techniques have been used infrequently in leadership research (Scherbaum et al., 2006). The lack of use is unfortunate because modern psychometric techniques can provide researchers with additional knowledge about the properties and best uses of their measures beyond what classical measurement techniques provide. Although there are several modern psychometric techniques that have been developed (see Shavelson & Webb, 1991 for an introduction to generalizability theory), the most commonly used is IRT. In the subsequent sections, we describe basic concepts in IRT, the mathematical model that underlies one of the most frequently used IRT models, the advantages, the limitations, and the situations in which it is appropriate to use IRT.

Item Response Theory

Item response theory (IRT) is a model-based (i.e., mathematical) approach to understanding the nonlinear relationships between individual characteristics (e.g., LMX), item characteristics (e.g., item discrimination), and individuals' response patterns (Drasgow & Hulin, 1990). Classical psychometric procedures rely on total scores, means, and correlations as a basis for the person and item parameters. IRT, on the other hand, estimates latent parameters for the persons (i.e., the characteristic underlying the total scores) and items using the responses from the sample of data. The relationship between the latent person and item parameters in IRT is probabilistic, such that one can estimate the probability of an individual with a particular level of the latent characteristic selecting a particular option.

These probabilistic relationships can be demonstrated graphically using an item characteristic curve (ICC). ICCs graph the relationship between the latent characteristic (called theta and labeled θ in IRT) underlying the responses to an item and the probability of particular response to an item (labeled $P(\theta)$ in IRT). Many ICCs take an S-shaped curve, such as the logistic or normal ogive (Crocker & Algina, 1986). However, the exact shape of the relationship is determined by the IRT model used and the item parameters included in the model.

Figure 8.1 presents a generic representation of an ICC from an IRT model called the two-parameter logistic model. Although more details are provided in the subsequent sections, this particular IRT model is used with dichotomous data. For example consider an item about the quality of an exchange relationship where the response options are "yes" or "no" (no = 0, yes = 1). In the figure, the latent characteristic, θ, is along the x-axis and the probability of a particular response, $P(\theta)$, is along the y-axis. The values of θ are normally distributed and expressed as z-scores. For example, an individual with $\theta = 1$, has a value of LMX that is one standard deviation above the mean. Using Figure 8.1, we see that as the level of LMX increases (i.e., moves to the right), the probability of selecting the option scored 'yes' increases. For any level of θ, we can determine the $P(\theta)$ by finding the height of the curve at that particular value of θ.

As noted above, IRT is based on mathematical models and there are a variety of different mathematical models that comprise IRT. Before elaborating on the different types of IRT models and the equations underlying them, we describe some of the general advantages for LMX researchers of IRT over classical measurement theory approaches.

General Advantages of Item Response Theory

Both IRT and classical psychometric techniques estimate parameters for the persons and items using the responses from the sample of data. With classical techniques, the interpretation of the item parameters (e.g., item discrimination, item means) depends on the distribution of the char-

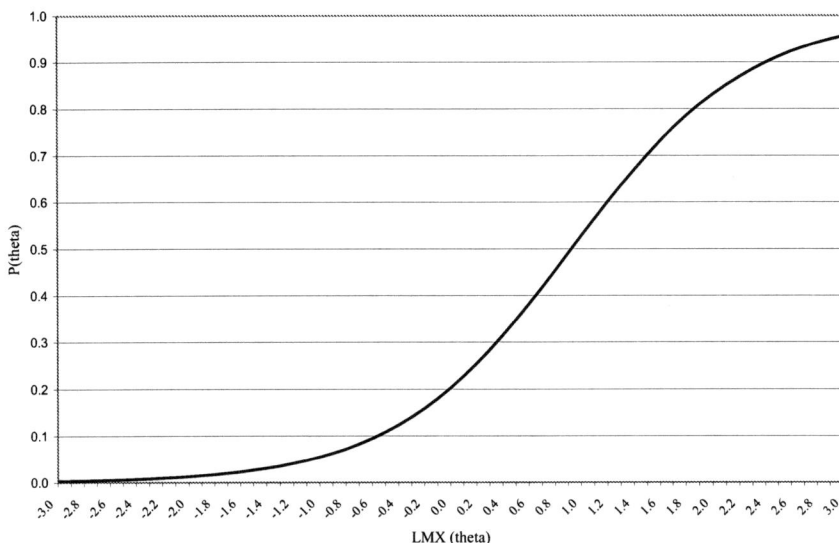

Figure 8.1.   Generic item characteristic curve for a two-parameter logistic model.

acteristic in the sample and the person parameters (e.g., level of LMX) depends on the particular items on a measure. For example, one needs to know the mean for each item to make interpretations about an individual's level of LMX. With IRT, the estimated person and item parameters are invariant. That is, the item parameters do not completely depend on the distribution of the characteristic in the sample and the person parameters do not completely depend on the particular items on a measure (Hambleton et al., 1991). Therefore, the item parameters are not needed to interpret the person parameters and vice versa. Moreover, the IRT item and person parameters are on the same metric (i.e., z-scores). Therefore, the level of a characteristic an individual possesses can be compared to the level of the characteristic required to endorse the item. With classical techniques, individuals can only be compared to other individuals or an external standard (e.g., a cut score).

Due to the invariance property of IRT, unbiased estimates of the item parameters can be estimated from unrepresentative samples (Embretson & Reise, 2000). In many cases, organizational research, including leadership research, is conducted using samples that may not be representative of the populations for which generalizations are desired (Dipboye & Flanagan, 1979; Scandura & Williams, 2000). Because the item parameters are not independent of the person parameters in the classical approach to psychometrics, the parameter estimates may be biased resulting in inconsistent results and possibly inappropriate conclusions based on these biased parameter estimates.

One of the most fundamental concepts in psychometrics is the standard error of measurement (Embretson & Reise, 2000). The standard error of measurement is an indication of how well a characteristic is assessed by a measure. In classical psychometric approaches, the standard error of measurement is constant across all levels of a characteristic. That is, these techniques require the assumption that the characteristic is assessed with equal precision at any level of the characteristic. However, it may very well be the case that different levels of the characteristic are measured with different levels of precision. For example, an LMX measure may be more precise for individuals with average levels of exchange quality than for individuals with high or low levels of exchange quality. IRT allows for the examination of this possibility.

The standard error of measurement is estimated for each level of the latent characteristic. As a result, researchers can have a clear picture of the quality of measurement at any level of the characteristic. This aspect is particularly important for LMX research that uses scores from an LMX measure to form different follower groups (e.g., in-groups and out-groups). If these groupings are used as the basis for theory testing or personnel decisions, then high levels of measurement precision at the ranges of LMX where the groups are separated are critical.

A second major advantage of IRT is that the amount of psychometric information an item provides about the latent characteristic can be determined for any level of the latent characteristic, which is called the item information function (IIF). The IIF indicates how well the item is working for each level of the characteristic that a measure assesses. It may be the case that a measure of LMX contains several items that provide a substantial amount of information about the quality of the exchange between subordinates and supervisors and other items may provide very little information. As an example, the IIF estimated for the item, "How satisfied is your colleague with your work" (see Graen et al., 2004) is presented in Figure 8.2. As can be seen in the figure, this item provides the maximum amount of information at below average levels of exchange quality and it provides information over a considerable range of the latent characteristic (i.e., ± 2 SD from the mean).

In addition, the amount of information provided by the entire measure can also be computed as the test information function. The test information function is the sum of the item information functions. The square root of the test information function for a given level of the latent characteristic demonstrates an inverse relationship with the standard error of measurement for that level of the characteristic. Therefore, different LMX measures can be evaluated in terms of how well they assess LMX at

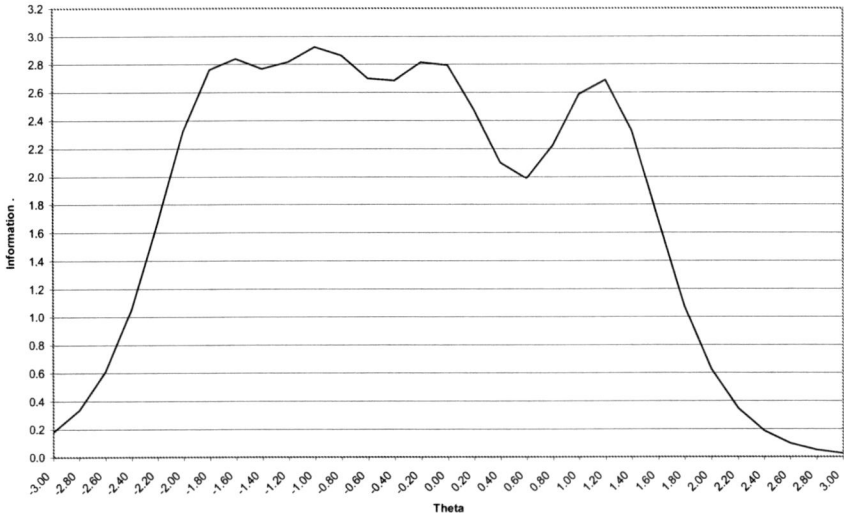

Figure 8.2.   Item information function for item 1 on the LMX-SLX.

different points on the LMX continuum. One could use this information to develop or revise LMX measures such that they provide high amounts of information at particular ranges of LMX. One could also use it to select measures that work best at the particular ranges of LMX that are of substantive interest. Alternatively, one could identify which items on an existing or newly developed LMX measure are unnecessary, and therefore, shorten the measure without sacrificing the usefulness of the entire measure (Stanton, Sinar, Balzer, & Smith, 2002). With classical methods, it is not possible to truly identify the contribution of a single item because the psychometric indices depend on the other items (Lord, 1980). This property of IRT is a major advantage over classical methods and is extremely useful for LMX research as modifications of LMX measures have been common, but the impact of these modifications is not well understood (Keller & Dansereau, 2001). The test and item information functions, as well as the standard error of measurement, provide a set of tools for LMX researchers to empirically examine the impact of modifying existing LMX measures.

One major implication of these first two advantages is that the classical psychometric approach to reliability does not apply to IRT. Classical psychometric techniques examine reliability as a function of an entire measure. In IRT, reliability is examined at the item level and at each level of the latent characteristic. Thus, there is no single reliability estimate. Nevertheless, a composite reliability index can be estimated. The composite reliability index provides an estimate of the average reliability across all of the levels of the latent characteristic and all of the items.

Types of IRT Models

IRT is best classified as a family of different mathematical models. There are different models that are appropriate for a variety of situations. Although not an exhaustive taxonomy, these models can be classified based on the dimensionality of the data, the nature of the underlying psychological response process, the type of data used, and the number of parameters estimated (see van der Linden & Hambleton, 1997 for additional classifications and models). These different categories are by no means mutually exclusive. In fact two overarching distinctions are assumptions about dimensionality of the data and the underlying psychological response process that cut across most of the categories.

IRT models make the assumption that either a unidimensional or multidimensional latent construct underlies the data. The unidimensional models assume that only one latent characteristic underlies the response to the items on a measure. These models are the most commonly used and are explained in more detail below. Multidimensional IRT (MIRT) models examine multiple latent characteristics underlying responses to the items on a measure (see Ackerman, 1994, 1996; Ackerman, Gierl, & Walker, 2003 for a detailed treatment). For example, MIRT could be used with data from measures that require ratings of the contribution of oneself, as well as others in a workgroup. MIRT analyses model both of these latent characteristics, and therefore, provide a value for each latent characteristic for each individual. As many organizational and leadership phenomena are multidimensional, the models have the potential to contribute to organizational research. However, MIRT has received little attention from organizational researchers. It is understandable given the complexity of these models and the evolving state of the literature and software for these models.

Nevertheless, MIRT offers a viable option for using IRT with a variety of organizational and leadership phenomena. For example, there has been some discussion about the dimensionality of the LMX construct (Dienesch & Liden, 1986; Graen & Uhl-Bien, 1995; Liden & Maslyn, 1998; Schriesheim et al., 1999). Some researchers have proposed measures that capture the multidimensional nature of LMX (e.g., LMX-MDM; Liden & Maslyn, 1998), but the evidence supporting the multidimensionality of these measures is inconsistent (e.g., Scherbaum et al., 2006). An approach to examining the inconsistency is to compare the results from a unidimensional to a multidimensional IRT model using the data from a measure such as the LMX-MDM to determine the dimensionality.

IRT models can also be distinguished based on the assumption about the underlying psychological response process. More specifically, models can differ in their assumptions about the relationship between the selection of response options and the level of the latent characteristic. For "cumulative" IRT models, the assumption is that there is an increased probability of selecting the correct or higher-order response options as the level of the latent characteristic increases (Embretson & Reise, 2000). That is, the relationship between the response choice and the level of the latent characteristic is monotonic. Thus, individuals with the highest levels of the latent characteristic will have the highest scores on a given item. The ICC in Figure 8.1 demonstrates a cumulative model. Many of the well-known IRT models (e.g., Samejima's, 1969, graded response model, Master's, 1982, partial credit model) are cumulative models.

Another possible assumption is that the relationship is nonmonotonic. More specifically, there is an ideal point for each individual on the continuum of a latent characteristic and the response option nearest the ideal point will be selected. Consequently, the individuals with a level of the latent characteristic that is closest to the level expressed in the item will have the highest scores on a given item. This notion is based the research of Coombs (1964) and Thurstone (1931) on ideal point response processes. This class of IRT models is referred to as "unfolding" models (Roberts, 1995; Roberts, Donoghue, & Laughlin, 2000).

In this chapter, we focus on unidimensional, cumulative models given their frequency of use and wide applicability to many measurement issues. Moreover, many of the measures used in leadership are likely sufficiently unidimensional to warrant the use of unidimensional IRT (Scherbaum et al., 2006). The unidimensional, cumulative IRT models can be classified based on the type of data that the model requires. Some models require dichotomously scored data. With this type of data, there are two response options to an item (e.g., agree or disagree) or the data are scored to produce two categories (e.g., correct or incorrect). Logistic IRT models can be used with these types of data (see Hambleton et al., 1991 for a detailed treatment of these models). Other types of models require polytomously scored data. With this type of data, there are three or more response options that can be graded (e.g., ranging from strongly disagree to strongly agree) or nominal (e.g., multiple-choice response options). Graded data are ordered such that higher ordered options reflect greater levels of the latent construct (e.g., Likert-type response options). There are several models that are appropriate with graded response data including Samejima's (1969) graded response model, Master's (1982) partial credit model, and Andrich's (1978a, 1978b) rating scale model. We present Samejima's graded response model in much more detail in the subsequent section (see van der Linden & Hambleton, 1997, for a detailed treatment of the other graded response models). Nominal data do not have a natural ordering. There are several models that are appropriate for nominal data including Bock's (1972) nominal model and Thissen and Steinberg's (1984) multiple-choice model (see van der Linden & Hambleton, 1997, for a detailed treatment of these models).

The models for dichotomous and polytomous models also can be categorized based on the number of item parameters that are estimated. In the logistic models for dichotomous data, there are three item parameters that can be estimated. The first parameter is an item location parameter (or item difficulty parameter). It represents the level of the latent characteristic that is needed to endorse the option scored as "1". Logistic models that include only a location parameter are called one-parameter logistic models (1-PL) or Rasch models (see Bond & Fox, 2001, for a detailed treatment of Rasch models). The second parameter is an item discrimination parameter. This parameter represents how well an item discriminates between individuals with different, but similar levels of the latent characteristic. These models are called 2-PL models. The third parameter is a pseudo-guessing parameter. This parameter represents the impact of guessing behavior on the ICC. These models are called 3-PL models. Polytomous models can also differ in the number of parameters estimated. For example, Thissen and Steinberg's (1984) multiple-choice model estimates a parameter related to guessing behavior, where Bock's (1972) nominal model does not. Additionally, Samejima's (1969) model, Master's (1982) model, and Andrich's (1978a, 1978b) model each incorporates a different number of item parameters.

Samejima's (1969) Graded Response Model

In most leadership, attitudinal, and personality research, the measures utilize response options that are ordered (e.g., Likert-type response options) and the data are used to make conclusions concerning the level of the construct that is assessed by the measure. As noted above, graded response models can be used in these situations. In these models, the IRT analysis examines the relationships between item or option parameters, person parameters, and the selection of a particular response option. For cumulative, unidimensional graded response models, it is assumed that the value of the latent characteristic (e.g., the level of LMX) is smaller for individuals who choose the first response option (e.g., strongly disagree) than for individuals who choose the second response option (e.g., disagree) in an ordered response set.

The relationship between the estimate of the latent characteristic, the response option characteristics, and the probability of selecting a particular option is presented graphically with an option characteristic curve (OCC). As an example, the OCC for the item, "My colleague would help me with my job problem" from the LMX-SLX (Graen et al., 2004) is presented in Figure 8.3. This item is rated on a 5-point scale with the anchors of *strongly disagree* and *strongly agree*. In the figure, the estimate of the latent characteristic (i.e., level of LMX) is along the x-axis and the probability of selecting a particular response option at a given level of LMX is along the y-axis. Using the first response option (i.e., strongly disagree) as an example, the probability of selecting this option is greatest for individuals with low levels of exchange quality (< –2.0) and the probability becomes smaller as the exchange quality increases. The fifth response option (i.e., strongly agree), on the other hand, demonstrates the reverse pattern. The probability of selecting the option is small for individuals with low levels of exchange quality and the probability increases as the level of exchange quality increases (> 0.0).

Samejima's (1969) graded response model (GRM) is one unidimensional, cumulative graded model that is often used in organizational research. In Samejima's GRM, two types of parameters associated with the items are estimated. The first is an option location parameter. The location parameter is referred to as the "threshold" parameter. This parameter refers to the probability of an individual with a given level of the latent

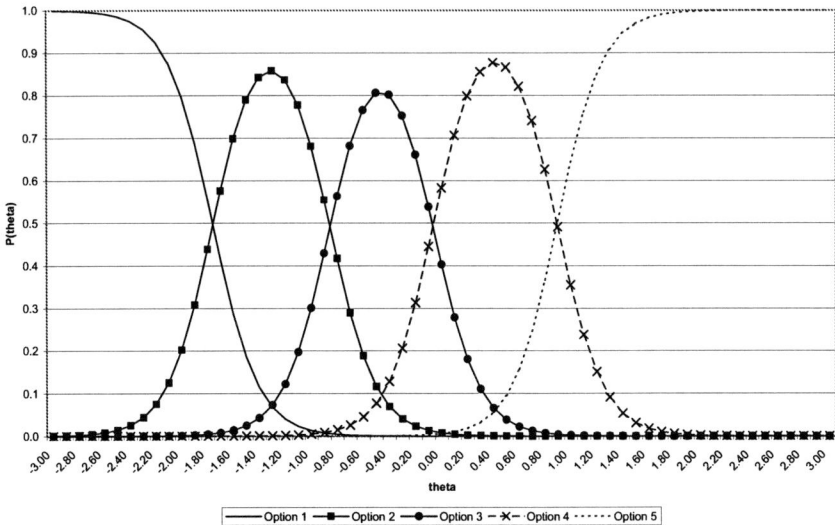

Figure 8.3.   Option characteristic curve for item 2 on the LMX-SLX.

characteristic selecting a given option (e.g., disagree) *or* any of the subsequent higher ordered options (e.g., neutral, agree, and strongly agree). Specifically, this parameter is the point on the theta scale where there is a 50% chance that a given option *or* any of the higher ordered options will be selected (i.e., $P(\theta) = 0.50$). In other words, this parameter represents the thresholds between the response options. The second parameter is the discrimination parameter. This parameter represents how well an option discriminates between individuals at different levels of the latent characteristic. The larger the value, the better the option is at discriminating between individuals at different levels of the latent characteristic.

To estimate the OCCs, one first estimates the boundary response functions. Boundary response functions are the cumulative probability of selecting a response option equal to or greater than the current response option. Option location parameters are estimated for $m_i - 1$ boundary response functions where m_i equals the number of response options. Each boundary response function has a location parameter, but only one discrimination parameter is estimated for each item in Samejima's (1969) GRM. Therefore, on an LMX measure with five response options, four location parameters and only one discrimination parameter are estimated. The boundary response functions are used to estimate the OCC. Mathematically, the boundary response function is expressed as,

$$P^*_{ik}(\theta) = \frac{e^{Da_i(\theta - b_{ik})}}{1 + e^{Da_i(\theta - b_{ik})}} \tag{1}$$

where $P^*_{ik}(\theta)$ is the probability of a respondent at a particular level of the latent characteristic, theta, responding to option k or any of the other higher ordered options on item i, b_{ik} is the option location parameter, a_i is the discrimination parameter, D is a scaling constant equal to 1.702, and e represents an exponential function. Thus, the probability of selecting option k is a function of the level of the latent characteristic, the location of the option, and the level of discrimination. In essence, the boundary response functions are estimated by utilizing a two-parameter logistic IRT model on the response option data.

From the boundary response functions, the probability of selecting a particular option and the OCC are estimated. The probability of selecting a particular option, $P^*_{ik}(\theta)$, is determined by subtracting the boundary response functions for each option. Mathematically, it is represented as,

$$P_{ik}(\theta) = P^*_{i(k-1)}(\theta) - P^*_{ik}(\theta) \tag{2}$$

where the probability of selecting an option is a function of the conditional probability of responding above the threshold parameter (i.e., b_{ik}) for option $k - 1$ minus the conditional probability of responding above the threshold parameter for option k. For example, on a four-option item $P_{ik}(\theta)$ is as follows,

$$P_{i0} = 1 - P_{i1}^{*}(\theta) \qquad \text{for option 1,}$$

$$P_{i1} = P_{i1}^{*}(\theta) - P_{i2}^{*}(\theta) \qquad \text{for option 2,} \qquad (3)$$

$$P_{i2} = P_{i2}^{*}(\theta) - P_{i3}^{*}(\theta) \qquad \text{for option 3,}$$

$$P_{i3} = P_{i3}^{*}(\theta) - 0 \qquad \text{for option 4.}$$

The probabilities are computed for each response option at each level of theta and serve as the basis for the OCC.

Testing the Specific Assumptions of Item Response Theory Models

IRT models can be considered strong models because they require several assumptions that are much more stringent than what is required by classical measurement theory. Each IRT model requires slightly different assumptions. All IRT analyses should include explicit tests of the assumptions required by the model and the fit of the model to the data. The model examined in detail in this chapter requires two assumptions: unidimensionality and local independence.

Samejima's (1969) GRM and many IRT models assume that the construct underlying the responses to the items is unidimensional. There are several different approaches to establishing the veracity of the unidimensionality assumption (see Embretson & Reise, 2000 or Hambleton et al., 1991 for a full review). Typically these approaches consist of exploratory factor analysis with alternative factor retention rules (e.g., parallel analysis, Horn, 1965), confirmatory factor analysis, or variations of factor analysis. For example, with dichotomous data, full information factor analysis (Bock, Gibbons, & Muraki, 1988) is one technique that can be used to assess dimensionality. With polytomous data, modified parallel analysis (MPA; Drasgow & Lissak, 1983) is one technique that can be used. MPA estimates eigenvalues from a randomly generated dataset (i.e., data generated by chance processes) that satisfies the IRT unidimensionality assumption. The random dataset is created using the item parameters from the real data. Thus, it reflects what the data should look like if they are unidimensional. A factor analysis is performed on the random data and the real data. The real eigenvalues extracted from the actual data are compared to the chance eigenvalues. If the second eigenvalue from the real data is greater than the second eigenvalue from the chance data, multidimensionality is said to exist.

Given that there is not agreement about the dimensionality of some LMX measures, there might be multidimensionality in some situations. Several researchers have argued that strict unidimensionality is not necessary to use the unidimensional IRT model (e.g., Drasgow & Parsons, 1983; Reckase, 1979). These authors contend that the unidimensionality assumption is reasonably met if there is a dominant factor in the data. More specifically, some authors have argued that as a rule of thumb the first factor needs to account for at least 20% of the total variance for the item parameters to be stable (Reckase, 1979). However, this rule of thumb should only be used in conjunction with other criteria for identifying the number of factors in the data.

The second IRT assumption is local independence. Local independence requires that the latent characteristic specified in the IRT model accounts for the relationship between the items. That is, responses to the items are uncorrelated after controlling for the latent characteristic. If unidimensionality is met, then the local independence assumption is also usually met (Hambleton et al., 1991). However, local independence can be met even when the unidimensionality assumption is not. There are a number of explicit statistical tests that can be used to examine local independence (see Yen's, 1984, Q3 statistic or Chen & Thissen's, 1997, G^2 statistic for examples). Although not typically reported in IRT research, researchers are well advised to examine local independence as the confidence in the estimated item and person parameters depends on the veracity of the model assumptions.

Although not an explicit assumption, IRT methods also assume that the selected IRT model fits the data. Model fit can be assessed in a variety of ways (Hambleton et al., 1991) and verifying the veracity of the two assumptions listed above is part of the model fit process. In comparison to covariance modeling techniques (e.g., confirmatory factor analysis), there are no well-established methods or rules of thumb for assessing model fit (Hambleton et al., 1991). One of the more widely used tests of fit in organizational research is the chi-square procedure described by Drasgow, Levine, Tsien, Williams, and Mead (1995). This procedure forms indices of the difference between the expected frequency of responses for the options and the observed frequency of responses for the options. Drasgow et al. recommend that χ^2 values less than or equal to 3.0 indicate good fit. This procedure has been operationalized in a very user-friendly program call MODFIT.[1]

When Should LMX Researchers Use IRT Methods?

An important question to ask is, "should I use classical psychometric techniques or IRT techniques?" In some cases, classical techniques will provide all of the information that is needed and IRT techniques are unnecessary (Fan, 1998; Hambleton & Jones, 1993). In other cases, it is quite the opposite. As a general rule, if a simpler analysis will be sufficient, then use it. Although there are many criteria that can be used to choose between IRT and classical techniques (e.g., knowledge, resources), we highlight a few that are related to the advantages of IRT for LMX researchers that were discussed above (see Hambleton & Jones, 1993 or Reise & Henson, 2003 for additional discussion of choosing between IRT and classical methods).

Two important criteria are the purpose of the analysis and the intended use of the results. If the purpose is to generate support for the use of an LMX measure as a basis for high stakes decisions, then a more sophisticated analysis such as IRT might be prudent. If you are performing routine analyses on an existing LMX measure or the use of the measure has little consequence, then classical analyses may be more appropriate. Also, in situations where new LMX measures are being created or existing LMX measures need to be modified, the use of IRT is advisable, especially when the initial focus is on the reliability of scores from the measure.

As previously noted, one can use the item and test information functions from an IRT analysis to understand how the psychometric properties would change if an LMX measure were to be modified. For example, these indices can be used to determine which items on an LMX measure are unnecessary. Items that provide little information only add length to the measure without increasing the psychometric information. Removing these items will shorten the measure without negatively impacting the properties of the scores. Small modifications of established LMX measures have been common (Keller & Dansereau, 2001). However, the impact of these modifications is not typically reported and these modifications complicate comparisons of the results between LMX studies. IRT analyses could provide clarity about the impact of those modifications, as well as provide researchers with some tools to better compare results across studies and measures. These comparisons are important given that the measure was found to be a moderator of the relationships between LMX and organizationally relevant outcome variables (Gerstner & Day,

1997). Additionally, these indices can be used to compare the information provided by two different LMX measures by computing the ratio of the test information functions. This ratio is referred to as the relative efficiency of the measures (Hambleton et al., 1991). The relative efficiency can be computed at each level of the latent characteristic, theta, and then averaged across levels of theta.

The third criterion concerns the constancy of the standard error of measurement (SEM) and reliability across the levels of interest on LMX. In instances where it is known that the SEM is not constant, IRT is a better option as it can account for and model the variability in the SEM. In other words, IRT is a better choice if one has a good reason to believe that reliability varies across different levels of LMX. If one can assume reasonable constancy in the SEM and reliability, the choice of the classical procedures is appropriate and may offer some advantages (e.g., ease of analysis and interpretation).

The fourth criterion concerns the nature of the sample from which the LMX data were collected. If the sample is unrepresentative of the larger population, then IRT analyses are a better choice than classical analyses. As the parameters derived from a classical analysis are sample dependent, unrepresentative samples will lead to biased parameters. IRT analysis can produce unbiased estimates from unrepresentative samples (Embretson & Reise, 2000).

General Issues in Conducting IRT Analyses

Of course, IRT analyses have a number of caveats and potential limitations conceptually and practically. For example, IRT carries several strong assumptions that are not required by classical psychometric techniques. The confidence in the results from an IRT analysis will depend on the degree to which the assumptions are met. Although IRT models are robust to modest violations of these assumptions (Drasgow & Hulin, 1990), explicit tests of these assumptions are required. In some cases, the assumptions may preclude the use of IRT analyses.

A primary consideration, especially for LMX research, is the sample size requirements. IRT requires sample sizes for many of the models that often exceed what is typically used in LMX research. The simplest models (e.g., Rasch model) can require sample sizes in excess of 150 respondents and more complex models can require substantially more respondents when estimating both person and item parameters (Zickar, 2001). There are no firm rules about the required sample sizes. However, Reise and Yu (1990) have reported that the ratio of the total number of parameters that are estimated to the sample size should be greater than 5.0 for the parameters to be stable. This ratio can be computed as follows:

$$5.0 \leq \frac{\text{Sample Size}}{\text{Number of Parameters per Item * Number of Items}} \quad (4)$$

When estimating only one set of parameters, such as estimating person parameters from previously established item parameters, smaller sample sizes are sufficient. Nevertheless, the sample size requirements may limit the use of IRT for some areas of research (e.g., LMX research on CEOs of multinationals).

IRT analyses require item level data. That is, one needs the actual responses to the LMX items to perform the analyses. In some situations, data at this level may not be available or may be of low quality. For example, the data may only be retained at total score level or there may be privacy concerns that prevent the release of this type of data. These two possibilities are concerns for LMX researchers wishing to conduct secondary analyses of existing data. Alternatively, the item level data may contain substantial missing data. Thus, the quality and the form of the data will impact the possibility of conducting IRT analyses.

An additional consideration is the complexity and software required for performing IRT analyses. These analyses require special software and often several different programs are needed to perform the tests of the assumptions and parameter estimation. Subsequent advanced analyses that use the estimated IRT parameters as input require the use of even more programs. As a result, IRT analyses can take a substantial amount of time. Complicating matters is that until recently, the majority of the IRT software was DOS-based and required some understanding of FORTRAN. However, more sources are becoming available to guide researchers with limited experience in utilizing IRT techniques.[2] To illustrate the use of item response theory and the software, we report an IRT analysis that was performed using data from Graen et al.'s (2004) LMX-SLX measure.

EMPIRICAL EXAMPLE

Data

The data used in this example of IRT analyses were drawn from wave 3 of studies 2 and 3 in Graen et al. (2004). The sample consisted of 252 engineering students taking part of a program in which they developed or modified a product for a client organization. The students worked in 84 different teams with three individuals in each team. Each student provided ratings of the other two students on the team. In total, there were

486 usable ratings. To determine the adequacy of this sample size, one can enter 486 for the sample size, 6 items, and 5 parameters per item into Equation 4. The resulting ratio of person to parameters is 16.2, which is greater than the minimum 5.0 ratio advocated by Reise and Yu (1990). An important point to note is that using multiple ratings from the same source does violate the assumption of independent observations. However, previous research has shown that the violation of this assumption does not have an appreciable impact on the estimated IRT parameters (Craig & Kaiser, 2003).

Members of each team completed the LMX-SLX. This measure can be used to assess the exchange quality of relationships with supervisors, subordinates, or coworkers. Only the ratings on the coworkers were used in these analyses. The reader is referred to Graen et al. (2004) for a detailed treatment of the development of this measure. The LMX-SLX consists of six items that are rated on five point scales with anchors ranging from strongly disagree to strong agree. Higher scores represent higher levels of leader-member exchange. The measure contains no reverse scored items. An example item is, "My (colleague, supervisor, or subordinate) has respect for my capabilities?" A complete list of the items is presented in Table 8.1.

Analyses

Classical psychometric analyses. Before the IRT analyses, we conducted a classical item analysis. In this analysis, we estimated the item discrimination and item location. The item discrimination is the corrected item-total correlation and the item location is the item mean.

Parameter estimation, information functions, and standard errors of measurement. We computed the marginal maximum likelihood estimates of the item parameters and the expected a posteriori estimates of the person parameters in Samejima's (1969) graded response model using MULTI-LOG (Thissen, Chen, & Bock, 2003).[3] We used the program defaults in the analyses. MULTILOG computed the IIFs, TIF, and the SEM.

Tests of IRT assumptions and model fit. To examine the fit of Samejima's model to the data, we used the Drasgow et al. (1995) chi-square procedure. We conducted a modified parallel analyses to examine the dimensionality of the data.

Results

Classical psychometric analyses. The internal consistency of the responses on the LMX-SLX was high, $\alpha = 0.95$. Table 8.1 presents the classical mea-

**Table 8.1.   Item Parameters From the
Classical Item Analysis of the LMX-SLX**

Item	CITC	M	SD
*How satisfied is your (colleague, supervisor, or subordinate) with your work?	0.84	3.52	1.12
*My (colleague, supervisor, or subordinate) would help me with my job problem?	0.90	3.61	1.16
*My (colleague, supervisor, or subordinate) has confidence in my ideas?	0.89	3.59	1.09
My (colleague, supervisor, or subordinate) has trust that I would carry my workload?	0.88	3.64	1.12
My (colleague, supervisor, or subordinate) has respect for my capabilities?	0.89	3.65	1.09
*I have an excellent working relationship with my (colleague, supervisor, or subordinate).	0.85	3.59	1.08

Note: CITC = corrected item-total correlation. *Original LMX-7 items.

surement theory indices of item discrimination and location. The indices indicate that the items demonstrate high levels of discrimination and are fairly similar in the level of discrimination. The mean item score is slightly above the midpoint on the scale indicating a slight negative skew in the data. The item scores ranged the entire rating scale. Together both pieces of information suggest that there is quite a bit of variability in exchange quality. This type of variability is beneficial for parameter estimation and generalizability of the subsequent IRT analyses.

Tests of IRT model assumptions and model fit. The results of the MPA indicated that the unidimensionality assumption was met (see Figure 8.4). The second eigenvalue for the real data (0.128) was smaller than the second eigenvalue for the chance dataset (0.821). Moreover, the first eigenvalue accounted for more than 83% of the variance. The test of fit indicated that the fit of the model to the data was less than ideal. The average value for the χ^2 was 4.12 ($SD = .57$). Thus, some caution is warrant when interpreting the results of these analyses. It is likely that the larger than desired value of the chi-square statistic is a result of an unfolding response process on some of the items (Scherbaum et al., 2006).

IRT parameter estimates. The item parameters are presented in Table 8.2. As can be seen in the table, the a parameters indicate that most of the items do quite well at distinguishing between individuals with similar, but differing levels of LMX. The values of the discrimination parameter range from 3.26 to 5.79. More importantly, these results indicate that the items on the measures have an appreciable relationship with LMX as the

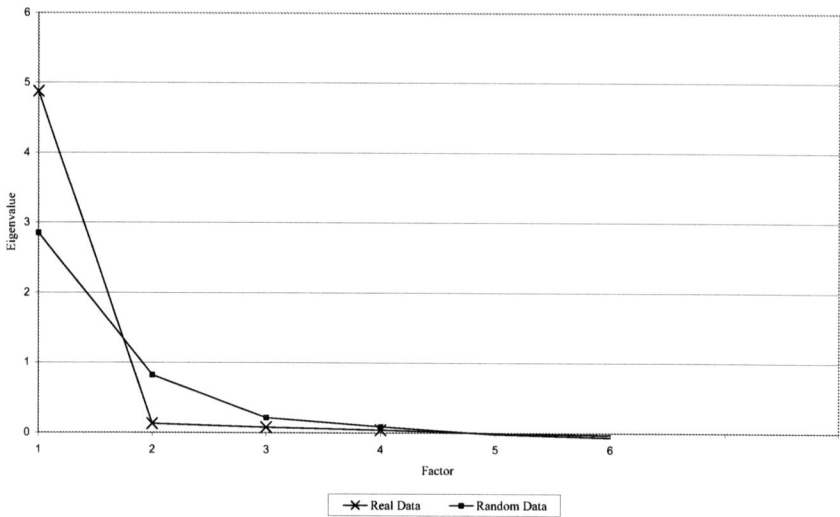

Figure 8.4.   Results of the modified parallel analysis of the LMX-SLX.

a parameter can be thought of in similar terms as a factor loading of an item on the latent construct in a confirmatory factor analysis (Meade & Lautenschlager, 2004). Given these results, the LMX-SLX should be useful in situations when scores on the measure are used to differentiate individuals in terms of their levels of LMX.

The location parameters of the items displayed some desirable properties. Again, the location parameters indicate the level of the latent characteristic required to endorse a given option or any of the higher order options. The parameters were negative for the options indicating lower levels of exchange quality, were close to zero for the parameters representing the thresholds from response option number 2 to 3 and 3 to 4, and were positive for the options indicating the highest levels of exchange quality (see Table 8.2).

Item and test information functions. Table 8.2 contains the maximum value of the item information functions. Overall, the items provide quite a bit of information, but there is also considerable variability in the amount of information provided. The test information function and standard error of measurement are presented in Figure 8.5. As demonstrated in the Figure, the level of measurement precision is greatest between the values of theta of –2.40 and 1.40. Beyond this range, there is more error than information. However, given that the values of theta are standardized scores and the slight negative skew in the data, the measure does a good job of assessing the quality of leader-member exchange for most individu-

Table 8.2.   Item Parameters from Samejima's Graded Response Model

Item	a	b_1	b_2	b_3	b_4	Max IIF
*How satisfied is your (colleague, supervisor, or subordinate) with your work?	3.26	−1.76	−0.94	−0.05	1.17	2.92
*My (colleague, supervisor, or subordinate) would help me with my job problem?	5.68	−1.76	−0.86	−0.06	0.90	8.06
*My (colleague, supervisor, or subordinate) has confidence in my ideas?	5.79	−1.96	−0.90	−0.01	0.96	8.44
My (colleague, supervisor, or subordinate) has trust that I would carry my workload?	4.59	−1.97	−0.95	−0.04	0.88	5.38
My (colleague, supervisor, or subordinate) has respect for my capabilities?	4.59	−1.98	−0.95	−0.17	0.97	5.44
*I have an excellent working relationship with my (colleague, supervisor, or subordinate).	3.69	−2.08	−1.00	0.00	1.01	3.55

Note: a = discrimination parameter; b = location parameter; *Max IIF* = maximum value of the item information function; *Original LMX-7 items.

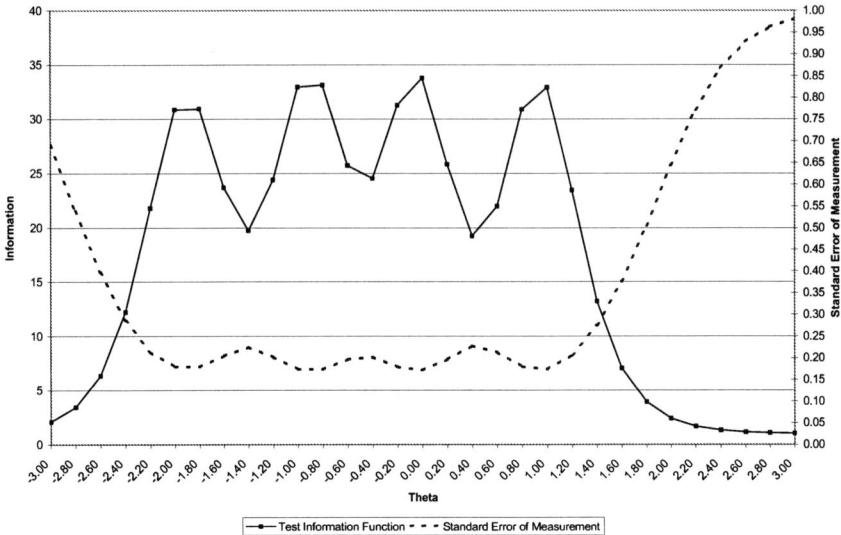

Figure 8.5.   Test information function and the standard error of measurement for LMX-SLX.

als with the exception of those with the most extreme scores (i.e., the maximum score and near the minimum score). Outside the range of –2.40 and 1.40, we have less confidence in the reliability of scores. It would not be advisable to use those scores to differentiate individuals into different groups. However, given the extremity, it is not likely that a researcher would be using those scores for the purposes of differentiation. Scores within the –2.40 and 1.40 are more likely to be used. Thus, this measure provides a considerable about of psychometric information in the ranges that are of interest to researchers. This type of information cannot be estimated in classical measurement analyses and thus demonstrates the utility of IRT with these types of measures.

CONCLUSIONS

Measurement and the psychometric properties of measures have received quite a bit of attention from LMX researchers. The purpose of this chapter was to aid those efforts by introducing a new set of tools that LMX researchers can use to better understand and revise their measures, as well as assist with developing new measures. Specifically, we have attempted to provide an introductory treatment of IRT and demonstrate how it can be used to further the measurement of LMX. Certainly, some aspects of this demonstration are less than ideal (e.g., multiple observations from each respondent, model fit). Nevertheless, we believe our demonstration is a sound example of using IRT to examine the psychometric properties of an LMX measure.

This demonstration also supports Graen et al.'s (2004) previous research on the psychometric quality of the LMX-SLX. We found that this measure is very useful for distinguishing between individuals with similar, but different levels of LMX. It also provides a considerable amount of information for individuals within a range of two standard deviations below the mean and one standard deviation above the mean. Moreover, the results of the IRT analysis on the LMX-SLX are comparable to Scherbaum et al.'s (2006) results from the IRT analysis of Liden and Maslyn's (1998) LMX-MDM. The results from both measures demonstrate that the items are highly discriminating and provide considerable amounts of information for values of latent characteristic that range between one standard deviation above and below the mean. The results also indicate that there is a little more variability in the values of the parameters for the LMX-MDM than the LMX-SLX. The values in the a parameter from the LMX-SLX are more consistent and on average the items on the LMX-SLX provide greater amounts of psychometric information. The LMX-SLX is also slightly more efficient. The ratio of the information functions from the two measures (i.e., the relative efficiency) indicates that the LMX-MDM performs as if it contained 40% more items than the LMX-SLX, but it contains 50% more items. However, it is important to note that these comparisons are qualitative and ad hoc. Also, these comparisons are based only on reliability considerations, not validity. Stronger conclusions could be made from a direct comparison of the measures using data collected from the same sample. In conclusion, we highlight some additional directions for researchers wishing to incorporate IRT into their LMX research.

Additional Uses for Item Response Theory in LMX Research

Beyond estimating the item parameters, person parameters, and information functions, there are a number of advanced uses of IRT. Several of these uses are widespread, but may be difficult to apply to LMX research (e.g., computer adaptive testing). Other uses have considerable potential for LMX research. We focus on two of these uses, differential item functioning and mixed-measurement models.

LMX research has long been focused on examining this construct in different sub-populations (e.g., strong, medium, and weak LMX) and more recently focused on different cultural and national groups (e.g., Graen & Wakabayashi, 1994; Graen, Wakabayashi, Graen, & Graen, 1990). One issue to be concerned with in this type of research is the measurement equivalence of the item parameters in different groups of respondents. Measurement equivalence asks the question of whether the measure functions in a psychometrically comparable manner in different groups. If a measure does not, then it is not meaningful to compare the scores from the two groups. It is like comparing apples to oranges. A lack of equivalence can be a result of respondents differentially using the rating scale or continuum, differences in the construct assessed, or true differences in the level construct (Liu, Borg, & Spector, 2004).

Item response theory provides a set of techniques called differential item functioning (DIF) that can be used to assess measurement equivalence (see Meade & Lautenschlager, 2004, or Raju, Laffitte, & Byrne, 2002, for a comparison of IRT and alternative techniques for assessing measurement equivalence). These analyses examine if different groups of respondents have OCCs that differ beyond what would be expected due to simple variability in the sample parameters. DIF is examined for each item on a measure and the cumulative effect of the differential item functioning on the entire measure can also be examined (i.e., differential test functioning; Raju, van der Linden, & Fleer, 1995).

If a measure or item is equivalent, there should be little difference between the OCCs for different groups. To examine potential differences, these analyses compare the probabilies of selecting particular response options on an item after equating the parameter estimates from the two groups (see Embretson & Reise, 2000 for a detailed description of equating) and matching individuals from different groups on the level of the latent characteristic. If differential item functioning exists, it is an indication that an item does not work in an equivalent manner for different groups. For example, if DIF is occurring, individuals from one group will have a greater probability of selecting an option on an LMX item than individuals from another group despite the fact that they possess the same level of LMX. There are a variety of techniques that can be used to detect differential item and test functioning and the interested reader should consult Millsap and Everson (1993) or Camilli and Shepard (1994) for a review of the various methods.

More recently, a family of IRT models called mixed measurement models (Rost, 1991, 1997) have been developed that approach DIF from a different direction. These models are a combination of latent class analysis and IRT. In DIF analyses, manifest classes in the data are identified a priori and analyses are performed to examine these manifest classes. In mixed measurement models, the analyses attempt to identify the latent classes that might exist in the data (e.g., level of exchange quality). That is, these models identify subgroups within a larger population. For example, these analyses could be used to identify groups of individuals with differential exchange relationships with a manager. In these analyses, one may discover that the latent and manifest classes are not the same.

ACKNOWLEDGMENT

The authors would like to thank Drs. George Graen, Chun Hui and Lisa Taylor for the use of their data.

NOTES

1. The MODFIT program can be freely downloaded at http://io.psych.uiuc.edu/irt/downloads.asp
2. An excellent series of tutorials on conducting IRT analysis can be found on the Web site of the IRT modeling lab at the University of Illinois at Urbana-Champagne: http://work.psych.uiuc.edu/irt/main_tutorial.asp
3. The Multilog program can be purchased from Scientific Software International.

REFERENCES

Ackerman, T. A. (1994). Using multidimensional item response theory to understand what items and tests are measuring. *Applied Measurement in Education, 7*, 255-278.

Ackerman, T. A. (1996). Developments in multidimensional item response theory. *Applied Psychological Measurement, 20*, 309-310.

Ackerman, T. A., Gierl, M. J., & Walker, C. M. (2003). Using multidimensional item response theory to evaluate educational and psychological tests. *Educational Measurement: Issues & Practice, 22*, 37-53.

Andrich, D. (1978a). A rating formulation for ordered response categories. *Psychometrika, 43*, 561-573.

Andrich, D. (1978b). Application of a psychometric rating model to ordered categories which are scored with successive integers. *Applied Psychological Measurement, 2*, 581-594.

Bock, R. D. (1972). Estimating item parameters and latent ability when responses are scored in two or more nominal categories. *Psychometrika, 37*, 29-51.

Bock, R. D., Gibbons, R., & Muraki, E. (1988). Full-information item factor analysis. *Applied Psychological Measurement, 12*, 261-280.

Bond, T. G., & Fox, C. M. (2001). *Applying the Rasch model: Fundamental measurement in the human sciences*. Mahwah, NJ: Erlbaum.

Camilli, G., & Shepard, L. (1994). *Methods for identifying biased test items*. Thousand Oaks, CA: Sage.

Chen, W. H., & Thissen, D. (1997). Local dependence indices for item pairs using item response theory. *Journal of Educational and Behavioral Statistics, 22*, 265-289.

Coombs, C. H. (1964). *A theory of data*. New York: Wiley.

Craig, S. B., & Gustafson, S. B. (1998). Perceived leader integrity scale: An instrument for assessing employee perceptions of leader. *Leadership Quarterly, 9*, 127-145.

Craig, S. B., & Kaiser, R. B. (2003). Applying item response theory to multisource performance ratings: What are the consequences of violating the independent observations assumption? *Organizational Research Methods, 6*, 44-60.

Crocker, L., & Algina, J. (1986). *Introduction to classical and modern test theory*. New York: Holt, Rinehart, and Winston.

Dansereau, F., Cashman, J. F., & Graen, G. B. (1973). Instrumentality theory and equity theory as complementary approaches in predicting the relationship of leadership and turnover among managers. *Organizational Behavior and Human Performance, 10*, 184-220.

Dienesch, R. M., & Liden, R. C. (1986). Leader-member exchange model of leadership: A critique and further development. *Academy of Management Review, 11*, 618-634.

Dipboye, R. L., & Flanagan, M. F. (1979). Research settings in industrial and organizational psychology: Are findings in the field more generalizable than in the laboratory? *American Psychologist, 34*, 141-150.

Drasgow, F., & Hulin, C. L. (1990). Item response theory. In M. D. Dunnette & L. M. Hough (Eds.), *Handbook of industrial and organizational psychology* (2nd ed., Vol. 1, pp. 577-636). Palo Alto, CA: Consulting Psychologists' Press.

Drasgow, F., Levine, M. V., Tsien, S., Williams, B., & Mead, A. (1995). Fitting polytomous item response theory models to multiple-choice tests. *Applied Psychological Measurement, 19*, 143-165.

Drasgow, F., & Lissak, R. (1983). Modified parallel analysis: A procedure for examining the latent dimensionality of dichotomously scored item responses. *Journal of Applied Psychology, 68*, 363-373.

Drasgow, F., & Parsons, C. K. (1983). Application of unidimensional item response theory models to multidimensional data. *Applied Psychological Measurement, 7*, 189-199.

Embretson, S. E., & Reise, S. P. (2000). *Item response theory for psychologists.* Mahwah, NJ: Erlbaum.

Fan, X. (1998). Item response theory and classical test theory: An empirical comparison of their item/person statistics. *Educational and Psychological Measurement, 58*, 357-381.

Gerstner, C. R., & Day, D. V. (1997). Meta-analytic review of leader-member exchange theory: Correlates and construct issues. *Journal of Applied Psychology, 82*, 827-844.

Graen, G. B. (2003). Interpersonal workplace theory at the crossroads: LMX and transformational theory as special cases of role making in work organizations. In G. Graen's (Ed.), *LMX leadership: The series: Vol. 1. Dealing with diversity* (pp. 145-182). Greenwich, CT: Information Age.

Graen, G. B., Hui, C., & Taylor, E. (2004). A new approach to leadership: Upward, downward, and horizontal differentiation. In G. Graen's (Ed.), *LMX leadership: The series: Vol. 2. New frontiers of leadership* (pp. 33-66). Greenwich, CT: Information Age.

Graen, G. B., Novak, M. A., & Sommerkamp, P. (1982). The effects of leader-member exchange and job design on productivity and job satisfaction: Testing a dual attachment model. *Organizational Behavior and Human Performance, 30*, 109-131.

Graen, G. B., & Uhl-Bien, M. (1995). Relationship-based approach to leadership: Development of leader-member exchange (LMX) theory of leadership over 25 years: Applying a multi-level multi-domain perspective. *Leadership Quarterly, 6*, 219-247.

Graen, G. B., & Wakabayashi, M. (1994). Cross-cultural leadership-making: Bridging American & Japanese diversity for team advantage. In H. C. Triandis, M. D. Dunnette & L. M. Hough (Eds.), *Handbook of industrial and organizational psychology* (Vol. 4, pp. 415-446). Palo Alto, CA: Consulting Psychologist Press.

Graen, G. B., Wakabayashi, M., Graen, M. R., & Graen, M. G. (1990). International generalizability of American hypotheses about Japanese management progress: A strong inference investigation. *Leadership Quarterly, 1*, 1-23.

Hambleton, R. K., & Jones, R. W. (1993). Comparison of classical test theory and item response theory and their applications to test development. *Educational Measurement: Issues & Practice, 12*, 38-47.

Hambleton, R. K., Swaminathan, H., & Rogers, H. J. (1991). *Fundamentals of item response theory*. Newbury Park, CA: Sage.

Horn, J. L. (1965). A rationale and test for the number of factors in factor analysis. *Psychometrika, 30,* 179-185.

Keller, T., & Dansereau, F. (2001). The effect of adding items to scales: An illustrative case of LMX. *Organizational Research Methods, 4,* 131-143.

Liden, R. C., & Maslyn, J. M. (1998). Multidimensionality of leader-member exchange: An empirical assessment through scale development. *Journal of Management, 24,* 43-72.

Liden, R. C., Sparrowe, R. T., & Wayne, S. J. (1997). Leader-member exchange theory: The past and potential for the future. In G. R. Ferris (Ed.), *Research in personnel and human resources management* (Vol. 15, pp. 47-119). Stamford, CT: JAI Press.

Liu, C., Borg, I., & Spector, P. E. (2004). Measurement equivalence of the german job satisfaction survey used in a multinational organization: Implications of Schwartz's culture model. *Journal of Applied Psychology, 89,* 1070-1082.

Lord, F. M. (1980). *Application of item response theory to practical testing problems.* Hillsdale, NJ: Erlbaum.

Marion, R., & Uhl-Bien, M. (2001). Leadership in complex organizations. *Leadership Quarterly, 12,* 389-418.

Masters, G. N. (1982). A Rasch model for partial credit scoring. *Psychometrika, 47,* 149-174.

Meade, A. W., & Lautenschlager, G. J. (2004). A comparison of item response theory and confirmatory factor analytic methodologies for establishing measurement equivalence/invariance. *Organizational Research Methods, 7,* 361-388.

Millsap, R. E., & Everson, H. T. (1993). Methodology review: Statistical approaches for assessing measurement bias. *Applied Psychological Measurement, 17,* 297-334.

Raju, N. S., Laffitte, L. J., & Byrne, B. M. (2002). Measurement equivalence: A comparison of methods based on confirmatory factor analysis and item response theory. *Journal of Applied Psychology, 87,* 517-529.

Raju, N. S., van der Linden, W., & Fleer, P. F. (1995). IRT-based internal measures of differential functioning of items and tests. *Applied Psychological Measurement, 19,* 353-368.

Reckase, M. D. (1979). Unifactor latent trait models applied to multifactor tests: Results and implications. *Journal of Educational Statistics, 4,* 207-230.

Reise, S. P., & Henson, J. M. (2003). A discussion of modern versus traditional psychometrics as applied to personality assessment scales. *Journal of Personality Assessment, 81,* 93-103.

Reise, S. P., & Yu, J. (1990). Parameter recovery in the graded response model using MULTILOG. *Journal of Educational Measurement, 27,* 133-144.

Roberts, J. S. (1995). Item response theory approaches to attitude measurement. (Doctoral dissertation, University of South Carolina, Columbia, 1995). *Dissertation Abstracts International, 56,* 7089B.

Roberts, J. S., Donoghue, J. R., & Laughlin, J. E. (2000). A general item response theory model for unfolding unidimensional polytomous responses. *Applied Psychological Measurement, 24,* 3-32.

Rost, J. (1991). A logistic mixture distribution model for polychotomous item responses. *British Journal of Mathematical & Statistical Psychology, 44*, 75-92.

Rost, J. (1997). Logistic mixture models. In W. van der Linden & R. Hambleton (Eds.), *Handbook of modern item response theory* (pp. 449-463). New York: Springer.

Samejima, F. (1969). Estimation of latent ability using a response pattern of graded scores. *Psychometrika, 34*, 1-100.

Scandura, T. A., & Williams, E. A. (2000). Research methodology in management: Current practices, trends, and implications for future research. *Academy of Management Journal 43*, 1248-1264.

Scherbaum, C. A., Finlinson, S., Barden, K., & Tamanini, K. (2006). Applications of item response theory to measurement issues in leadership research. *Leadership Quarterly, 17*, 366-386.

Schriesheim, C. A., Castro, S. L., & Cogliser, C. C. (1999). Leader-member exchange (LMX) research: a comprehensive review of theory, measurement, and data-analytic practices. *Leadership Quarterly, 10*, 63-113.

Shavelson, R. J., & Webb, N.M. (1991). *Generalizability theory: A primer*. Newbury Park, CA: Sage.

Stanton, J. M., Sinar, E. F., Balzer, W. K., & Smith, P. C. (2002). Issues and strategies for reducing the length of self-report scales. *Personnel Psychology 55*, 167-194.

Thissen, D., Chen, W. H., & Bock, R. D. (2003). *MULTILOG users' guide*. Chicago: Scientific Software.

Thissen, D., & Steinberg, L. (1984). A response model for multiple choice items. *Psychometrika, 49*, 501-519.

Thurstone, L. L. (1931). The measurement of social attitudes. *Abnormal and Social Psychology, 26*, 249-269.

van der Linden, W. J., & Hambleton, R. K. (Eds.). (1997). *Handbook of modern item response theory*. New York: Springer.

Yen, W. M. (1984). Effects of local independence on the fit and equating performance of the three-parameter logistic model. *Applied Psychological Measurement, 8*, 125-145.

Zickar, M. J. (2001). Conquering the next frontier: Modeling personality data with item response theory. In B. W. Roberts & R. Hogan (Eds.), *Personality psychology in the workplace* (pp. 141-160). Washington, DC: American Psychological Association.

CHAPTER 9

THE JOB CHARACTERISTICS MODEL AND LMX-MMX LEADERSHIP

Yitzhak Fried, Ariel S. Levi, and Gregory Laurence

The Job Characteristics Model (JCM) focuses on the fit between the job's motivating potential and the jobholder as the basis for explaining the relationship between job enrichment and employee reactions. The theory, however, fails to systematically analyze the process which determines the level of fit between the job and the jobholder. In this paper we systematically analyze how the incorporation of LMX-MMX components into the JCM premises would enhance our knowledge and understanding of the leader's role in influencing and facilitating the fit between job and jobholder. We specifically focus on how LMX-MMX may facilitate the fit between the job and the job incumbent by: (a) helping the individual to better manage the demands of his/her current job; and (b) helping the individual to proactively change (craft) the job characteristics to create a better fit with his or her own needs and abilities. We also discuss how future research can help further integrate the two literatures to enhance our understanding of employees' psychological and behavioral reactions in the area of job design.

New Multinational Network Sharing
pp. 157–196
Copyright © 2007 by Information Age Publishing
All rights of reproduction in any form reserved.

INTRODUCTION

The area of work design has generated much interest and research during the past few decades (e.g., Fried & Ferris, 1987; Grant, 2007; Morgeson & Campion, 2003; Oldham, 1996; Parker & Wall, 1998; Parker, Wall, & Cordery, 2001; Taber & Taylor, 1990). This interest has been prompted by recent and increasingly rapid changes in the work environment (e.g., Fried, Oldham & Cummings, 1998; Fried, Snider, Hadani, & Levi, 2006; Kulik, Oldham, & Hackman, 1987; Parker et al., 2001; Seers, 2004). Such changes include the rapid development of technology and information technology, the growth of both knowledge-based and service industries, greater diversity in the composition of the work force, and the increasing variety of career paths within and between organizations and across national boundaries. In such a dynamic work environment, rigidly defined jobs may serve as barriers to organizational success (Cascio, 2003; Parker et al., 2001; Rousseau & Fried, 2001). Organizations have indeed found that in order to better compete in the emerging economy they need to organize work in a fluid and dynamic fashion capable of responding flexibly to rapid change (Cascio, 2003; Fried, Snider, Hadani, & Levi, 2006; Parker et al., 2001).

Most of the contemporary research on job design has drawn on Hackman and Oldham's Job Characteristics Model (JCM; Fried et al., 1998; Fried et al., in press; Hackman & Oldham, 1980; Humphrey, Nahrgang, & Morgeson, in press; Parker et al., 2001). The JCM is based on a person-environment fit framework (Kulik et al., 1987). It focuses on the fit between the motivating potential of the job (i.e., job characteristics) and the jobholder's needs, abilities, and work-related constraints in predicting individual job- related psychological and behavioral outcomes. The JCM assumes that the better the fit between the individual jobholder and his or her job (i.e., between the individual needs, opportunities, and capabilities and the demands or characteristics of the job), the better the individual's work outcomes in terms of attitudes, motivation, and performance (Hackman & Oldham, 1980; Kulik et al., 1987). However, the theory fails to fully and systematically address the process by which organizations may optimize the fit between the job and the individual (cf. Ilgen & Hollenbeck, 1992). Understanding this process by which fit (i.e., congruence) develops between individuals and their jobs has increased in importance, as uncertainty, fluidity, and change have become increasingly dominant characteristics of the information age (Cascio, 2003; Parker et al., 2001).

In this paper we demonstrate how systematically incorporating the construct of leadership into the JCM can enhance our knowledge and understanding of the role of the leader in influencing and facilitating the process of fit between the job and the jobholder.

Our analysis integrating leadership with the JCM draws on leader-member exchange (LMX) theory, which is unique among leadership theories in its emphasis on the dyadic exchange relationships between supervisors and each of their subordinates (e.g., Graen 2003; Graen & Uhl-Bien, 1995; Janssen & Van Yperen, 2004). In accordance with LMX theory (Graen; Uhl-Bien, Graen & Scandura, 2000), we propose that the leader, through a dynamic relationship with the employee, can play a critical role in facilitating a better fit between the individual jobholder and the job characteristics proposed by the JCM.

We will discuss in turn the two ways in which this process can take place. First, the leader can help the subordinate better manage his or her current job demands. Here we focus on how the leader can contribute to the fit between the job characteristics and the subordinate's personality (growth need orientation), knowledge and skills, and social and physical contexts. Second, the leader can help the individual proactively change (remake) the job characteristics to create a better fit with his or her needs and abilities. "Job crafting" complements theories of job design; instead of the design of the job eliciting attitudes and motivation, which is the focus of the JCM and the job design literature in general, job crafting focuses on the motivation and opportunity to proactively bring about changes in one's current job characteristics (e.g., Wrzesniewski & Dutton, 2001). In addition, we will also analyze the role of member-member exchange (MMX) quality in facilitating the fit between the jobholder and job properties. While the leader has greater formal power than peers to influence the job incumbent's work career and experience, the pattern of the relationships with peers may also play an important supportive role in facilitating employee experiences at work (Humphrey et al., in press; Sherony & Green, 2002). In the following paragraphs we will discuss the major characteristics of the JCM and LMX, and then discuss the role of both LMX and MMX in facilitating the fit between the job and the individual incumbent.

THE JOB CHARACTERISTICS MODEL (JCM)

The JCM posits that five core job characteristics (skill variety, task identity, task significance, autonomy, and job feedback) contribute positively to individual work outcomes (e.g., high work motivation, job satisfaction, performance and reduced absenteeism) via the mediating effect of three psychological states (experienced meaningfulness, experienced responsibility, and knowledge of results).

Skill variety refers to the degree to which a job requires a variety of different activities in carrying out the work, involving the use of a number of different skills and talents of the person. *Task identity* refers to the degree to which a job requires completion of a whole, identifiable piece of work, that is, doing a job from beginning to end with a visible outcome. *Task significance* refers to the degree to which the job has a substantial impact on the lives of other people in the immediate organization or in the world at large. *Autonomy* refers to the degree to which the job provides substantial freedom, independence, and discretion to the individual in scheduling the work and in determining the procedures to be used in carrying it out. *Job feedback* refers to the degree to which carrying out the work activities of the job provides the individual with direct and clear information about the effectiveness of his or her performance (Hackman & Oldham, 1980).

The JCM posits that jobs that are high on these five core job characteristics are enriched and complex, and therefore are experienced by employees as stimulating and challenging. This, in turn, leads to positive psychological states. Specifically, skill variety, task identity, and task significance contribute to experienced meaningfulness of the work; work autonomy contributes to experienced responsibility for outcomes of the work; and job feedback contributes to knowledge of the actual results of the work activities. These positive psychological states contribute to positive work outcomes, including work motivation, overall job satisfaction, growth satisfaction, and work performance and effectiveness (Hackman & Oldham, 1980).

In addition, three variables moderate the relationships among the key variables described above: knowledge and skills needed to accomplish the job successfully, context satisfaction (satisfaction with supervisors, peers, compensation, and job security), and growth need strength (GNS), which refers to individuals' need for personal accomplishment, learning, and development (Hackman & Oldham, 1980). The theory argues that job complexity will have the strongest positive effect on individual attitudes and performance when there is a fit between the complex job characteristics and the three moderators. Specifically, when individuals have high GNS (they strive to be involved in challenging jobs), high knowledge and skills (they have the capabilities needed to accomplish the jobs successfully), and a high level of satisfaction with their supervisor, co-workers, pay, and job security, these enable them to focus on their job without distractions. On the other hand, if GNS and knowledge and skills are low, individuals will lack the motivation and ability to successfully pursue complex jobs. Further, if they are not satisfied with their supervisors, co-workers, pay, and job security, they will be distracted and will find it difficult to focus and concentrate on the job (Hackman & Oldham, 1980).

The JCM does recognize the importance of the leader/supervisor (as part of context satisfaction) in affecting individual reactions to job characteristics (e.g., Hackman & Oldham, 1980). However, the JCM appears to adopt the concept of the average leadership style (ALS) toward employees, and tends to neglect the important role of the dyadic relationship between the leader and his or her subordinates (Graen, 2003). Moreover, the JCM's consideration of the role of the leader is largely limited to the leader's effect on the contribution of the core job characteristics to employee reactions. There is no systematic discussion in the model of the important contribution of the leader in actively enhancing employees' abilities and motivation in coping with demanding job requirements, or in facilitating job crafting, which involves proactively changing the job characteristics to improve their fit with individual motivation and capabilities.

Current Evidence on the JCM

Numerous studies provide general support for the major premises of the model, although only limited or mixed support for some of its components (e.g. Fried, 1991; Fried & Ferris, 1987; Humphrey et al., in press; Parker et al., 2001). More specifically, studies have generally supported the multidimensional assumption of the JCM (Fried & Ferris, 1986). However, not all studies have supported the a priori five dimensions (Parker et al., 2001). While some studies have supported the a priori five core job characteristics proposed by the model (e.g., Katz, 1978a, 1978b; Lee & Klein, 1982), others have suggested a reduced number (e.g., Gaines & Jermier, 1983; Pokorney, Gilmore, & Beehr, 1980). However, a comprehensive study by Fried and Ferris (1986) of 7,000 employees across different jobs and occupations supported the prevalence of the five core job dimensions. The study suggested that, among employees having the capacity to differentiate among work dimensions (e.g., managers, educated, and younger employees), the results of self-report surveys indeed supported the prevalence of five core job characteristics, as proposed by the JCM (see also, Oldham, 1996).

Moreover, results also provided general support for the mediating effects of the proposed psychological states, although questions are raised about the validity of the expected relationship of each job characteristic with its particular psychological state (e.g., Fried & Ferris, 1987; Humphrey et al., in press; Parker et al., 2001). Results suggest that the core job characteristics are related to both their specified and unspecified psychological states (Fried & Ferris, 1987; Johns, Xie, & Fang, 1992). These results may, at least in part, reflect the problem of multicolinearity caused by researchers' tendency to assess all features of the theory using a single self-report tool. Overall, however, research appears to support the role of psychological states as mediators of the job characteristics-employee reactions relationships. In a comprehensive meta-analysis, Fried and Ferris (1987) found support for the mediating role of the psychological states, by indicating that the relationships between these psychological states and psychological outcomes were stronger than the relationships between the core job characteristics and these outcomes. Similarly, Johns, Xie, and Fang (1992) concluded, based on a sophisticated analysis in a study on the validity of the JCM among managers, that "results provide relatively good support for the basic (unmoderated) JCM, and especially for the mediating role of the psychological states" (p. 674). Support for the mediating role of the psychological states is also provided by the literature on psychological empowerment, which closely corresponds to the three psychological states. More specifically, Parker et al. (2001) indicate that key components of empowerment (meaning, impact, and self-determination) are very closely related to the three psychological states of the JCM. Moreover, evidence suggests that psychological empowerment does mediate the relationship between work characteristics and affective outcomes (Liden, Wayne, & Sparrow, 2000; Parker et al., 2001). Finally, in their recent meta-analysis, Humphrey et al. (in press) used a sophisticated multi-step mediation process to examine the mediating effect of the psychological states across a large number of studies. They found that experienced meaningfulness was the primary mediator between job characteristics and outcomes.

From the standpoint of practicality, the most important part of the JCM is the hypothesized relationship between the core job characteristics and attitudinal and behavioral outcomes. Overall, research supports the hypothesized relationship between the core job characteristics and attitudinal (psychological) outcomes (job satisfaction, growth satisfaction and internal motivation) (Fried, 1991; Fried & Ferris, 1987; Johns et al., 1992; Parker et al., 2001). In their meta-analysis, Fried and Ferris (1987) reported moderate relationships between the core job characteristics and the three attitudinal outcomes. The relationship between the core job characteristics and behavioral outcomes (performance and absenteeism) has been shown to be substantially weaker (e.g., Humphrey et al., in press; Fried & Ferris, 1987; Kopelman, 1985; Oldham, 1996; Parker et al., 2001). Moreover, much of the variance of performance remains unexplained (e.g., Fried & Ferris, 1987). We note here that Humphrey et al. (in press), in their recent comprehensive meta-analysis (based on 259 studies and close to 220,000 participants), supported the pattern of results reported by Fried and Ferris (1987). More specifically, Humphrey et al. indicated that their results on the relationship between the core job characteristics and outcomes were generally stronger than the results reported by Fried and Ferris (1987), with the exception of the variable of absenteeism. It should also be noted that Humphrey et al. have distinguished among 14 work characteristics (cf. Morgeson & Humphrey, 2006, on the issue of extended work characteristics).

In addition, the hypothesized effects of the three moderators in the model have received mixed support. In fairness, though, there has not been much systematic research to cover the effect of all moderators proposed in the JCM (e.g., Fried & Ferris, 1987; Oldham, 1996). Studies that have examined this issue have focused primarily on the moderating effect of GNS. The results suggest that GNS does moderate the relationship between job characteristics and job satisfaction and performance (see reviews by Fried & Ferris, 1987; Loher, Noe, Moeller, & Fitzgerald, 1985; Oldham, 1996; Spector, 1985).

Relatively few studies have examined the moderating role of context satisfaction, and there is hardly any evidence on the moderating effect of indicators of knowledge and skills (see e.g., Fried & Ferris, 1987; Johns et al., 1992; Oldham, 1996; Tiegs, Tetrick, & Fried, 1992). Overall, studies have provided little support for the hypothesized moderating effect of context satisfaction. Some studies have provided results in the predicted directions (Oldham, Hackman, & Pearce, 1976; Orpen, 1979), but only a few of the findings were statistically supported (Oldham, 1996). Moreover, other studies reported a moderating effect of context but in a direction opposite of that predicted by the JCM (Bottger & Chew, 1986; Champoux, 1981; Johns et al., 1992). However, it is possible that the failure to find systematic effects for the moderating role of context satisfaction may have been due to a failure to take into account the differential effect of the other variables in the employee work environment, such as leadership. Indeed, Oldham and Cummings (1996) supported the moderating effect of two strong contributors of supervisory satisfaction: supervisory level of non-controlling and supportive behaviors on performance. They reported an interaction between job complexity and supervisory behavioral style on performance, such that employees were most likely to write patent disclosures over a two-year period when job complexity was high and their supervisors exhibited non-controlling and supportive behaviors. This study suggests that incorporating leadership behavior and interaction with employees in research on job design is important for validly assessing the effect of job characteristics on performance. This is especially likely to be relevant in an era in which creativity and innovation are increasingly becoming an integral part of performance (cf. Rousseau & Fried, 2001). The potential importance of context satisfaction (as the above findings demonstrate) suggests that by incorporating the dynamic influence of the leader and peers (through the dyadic relationships with employees) into the context of job design, we will be able to improve our understanding of the contribution of job characteristics to work outcomes.

LEADER-MEMBER EXCHANGE AND MEMBER-MEMBER EXCHANGE THEORY (LMX AND MMX)

The central concept of LMX is "that effective leadership processes occur when leaders and followers are able to develop mature leadership relationships (partnerships) and thus gain access to the many benefits these relationships bring" (Graen & Uhl-Bien, 1995, p. 225). The theory is based on the concepts of social and economic exchange and role making. Concerning the exchange component, the theory distinguishes between high quality exchange relationships, which are based on social exchange, versus low quality exchange relationships, which are based on economic exchange. Low-quality exchange relationships represent formal, preliminary contractual exchanges, which are characterized by hierarchy-based downward influence and distance between the managers and their employees. In contrast, high quality exchange relationships represent mutual trust, respect, and obligation, which produce joint influence between the employees and the supervisor which go above and beyond the formally defined work contracts (e.g., Janssen & Van Yepren, 2004). High quality exchange relationships are also characterized by generalized reciprocity in which the obligations of one party to the other are indefinite in terms of time and quality (Sparrowe & Liden, 1997, 2005).

The concepts of "role taking" and "role making" are directly related to the type of relationships between the parties (Graen & Cashman, 1975; Graen & Scandura, 1987; Graen & Uhl-Bien, 1995). "Role taking" is associated with low quality exchange relationships, in which the employees comply with their job requirements based on the formal employment contract. This is the "stranger" ("not my job") phase. Here the leaders provide their employees only what is needed to accomplish their jobs, and the employees do only what is formally required. In "role making," one can differentiate between the "acquaintance" or testing stage, and the "mature partnership" stage. In the "acquaintance" stage there is a gradual increase in social exchange between the supervisors and employees above the employment contracts, and greater sharing of information and resources. However, initially these exchanges are relatively limited in scope and time. In the "mature partnership" stage both leaders and followers share the highest level of mutual trust, respect, and commitment, which serve as the basis for a long-term reciprocal relationship (generalized reciprocity) in which each side relies on the other to achieve their interests. For example, employees may engage in more responsible and complex tasks than their formal job requires, either because their supervisors asked them to do so or because they persuaded the supervisors to enable them to engage in these tasks. In either case, they know that they can rely on their superiors to help them in training, resources, and whatever other support is necessary to successfully accomplish their jobs. The leaders also know that they can rely on these employees to be committed to pursue these tasks successfully. These leaders also know that when necessary, they can rely on these employees to help them (e.g., staying late at their personal expense to meet deadlines). Thus, both sides are empowered and motivated to expend energy mutually beyond their formal work contract and rules (Graen & Uhl-Bien, 1995). The above three stages may develop sequentially over time, although in some dyads the relationships may not develop much beyond the stranger phase. Thus, role making is do-it-yourself dyadic job enrichment for a true leader and member at the mature partner stage.

In addition to the importance of the quality of the relationship between the leader and members as a determinant of the reactions of the latter, the relations among the members themselves can also play an important role in affecting employee reactions (e.g., Graen, 2003; Keup, Bruning, & Seers, 2004; Seers, Petty, & Cashman, 1995; Sherony & Green, 2002). For example, the quality of MMX may have a direct effect on employees' ability to function, particularly in jobs characterized by high interdependence. Such jobs require a high degree of interaction, exchange of information, and cooperation among the members (Humphrey et al., in press). The quality of the interaction and cooperation among the members is largely influenced by the quality of MMX (cf. Keup et al., 2004; Sherony & Green, 2002). MMX may also contribute to employees' ability to function, by affecting their relationship with the leader. Thus, for example, an individual who develops close relationships with peers who are close to the leader may use these relationships to establish a good relationship with the leader, resulting in high LMX (e.g., Sparrowe & Liden, 1997). Similarly, a bad relationship between an individual and peers who have established a good relationship with the leader, would hinder the relationship between this individual and the leader, resulting in low LMX (e.g., Sparrowe & Liden, 1997).

Current Evidence on the Effect of LMX and MMX

Studies on the effect of LMX have provided support for the positive effect of high-quality LMX on such outcomes as performance, organizational commitment, employee citizenship behavior, job satisfaction, enhanced career development opportunities, and delegation and participation in decision making (i.e., increase in job enrichment) (see, e.g.,

Graen, 2003; Gerstner & Day, 1997; Uhl-Bien et al., 2000). Similar to the findings concerning the effect of job characteristics, research indicates a stronger relationship between LMX and psychological outcomes (e.g., organizational commitment, job satisfaction) than behavioral outcomes (rated performance, turnover) (Gerstner & Day, 1997).

Studies on performance as a criterion have produced some inconsistent results (see, e.g., Dienesch & Liden, 1986; Dunegan, Duchon, & Uhl-Bien, 1992; Miner, 1980; Vecchio & Gobdel, 1984). These results support further examination of contextual variables as moderators affecting the exchange process (cf. Green, Anderson, & Shivers, 1996; Graen & Wakabayashi, 1992). One of these contextual variables is job design. It is possible, for example, that LMX will be more effective in contributing to employee performance if it results in an increased fit between the job's motivating potential and the jobholder, and will be less effective if it fails to address the issue of individual-job fit (cf. Liden, Wayne, & Sparrowe, 2000; Rousseau & Fried, 2001; Parker et al., 2001).

Concerning MMX, the available findings do support its significant contribution to individual experiences and reactions at work (e.g., Graen, Hui, & Taylor, 2006; Keup et al., 2004; Sherony & Green, 2002; Uhl-Bien, Graen, & Uhl-Bien, 1995). We argue that similar to LMX, the contribution of MMX can be better understood if it is discussed in the context of the contingencies of job design.

We will now discuss the role of LMX and MMX in facilitating the fit between the job's motivating potential and the jobholder. We will first analyze how the leader and group members may facilitate the fit between the jobholder and his or her job characteristics by helping to enhance the fit between the individual GNS and the characteristics of the job; by contributing to subordinates' knowledge and skills; by creating positive climate among group members to enhance group interaction and collaboration; and by reducing constraints for pursuing complex jobs associated with the physical work environment, particularly noise and social interference related to workspace characteristics. We will then analyze how the leader and group members may help facilitate job change (crafting) as an active process to enhance the fit between the job characteristics and the jobholder's needs and capabilities.

LMX AND MMX AND FIT BETWEEN THE JOBHOLDER'S AND THE JOB CHARACTERISTICS

JCM argues that the key for a positive effect of job design on employee reactions is the fit between the core job characteristics and GNS, knowledge and skills, and context satisfaction (satisfaction with the supervisor, peers, income, and job security). The leader can adopt a variety of human resource related activities to enhance the fit between the job and the individual (cf. Uhl-Bien et al., 2000). We will discuss these activities in reference to each one of the moderators.

Knowledge and Skills

The growing knowledge-based sector of the economy and the rapid technological changes associated with this growth have contributed to the increased importance of employee knowledge and skills, and consequently opportunities for skill acquisition (Parker et al., 2001). Updating and upgrading employee skills and knowledge is needed not only to meet new demands and challenges at work, but also to maintain high opportunities for mobility in an era in which job change and transfer are becoming more and more prevalent (Lawler & Fingold, 2000).

Leaders may play an important role in providing employees with opportunities for skill and knowledge acquisition by encouraging employees' involvement in training and development programs (Uhl-Bien et al., 2000). Leaders, based on their dyadic interaction with, and knowledge of, different subordinates, may be able to determine the differential needs of these individuals for particular knowledge and skills, and design their training and development programs accordingly (cf. Uhl-Bien et al., 2000). However, without a supportive organizational culture and organization-wide training and development plans, the power of the immediate leader to provide adequate opportunities for acquisition of new knowledge and skills may be limited (Uhl-Bien et al., 2000).

In addition, the leader may play an important role in helping subordinates better manage the increased complexity of their work. To illustrate, the use of modern technology to improve timely feedback may adversely affect employees' ability to process information effectively (e.g., Aiello & Kolb, 1995). For example, the growing use of electronic job feedback (electronic performance monitoring) may create a situation in which there is too much feedback which, rather than improving performance, may contribute to mental overload, experience of stress, and consequently reduced performance (e.g., Aiello & Kolb, 1995; Parker et al., 2001). In this situation, the leader may play an important role in helping the subordinate by, for example, providing access to appropriate training and professional assistance in processing, interpreting, and applying the increased load of information. This assistance by the leader is important to enable the employee to maintain his or her ability to successfully manage complex assignments. However, more research is needed on the contribution of the leader and coworkers to employees' ability to manage challenging tasks, as changes in technology and increased volume of information when jobs are enriched and complex, makes it increasingly difficult for the individual to process and apply this information to work, and consequently to successfully manage his or her job independently (cf. Parker et al., 2001).

Context Satisfaction

According to the JCM, context satisfaction consists of four components: pay, job security, coworkers, and supervisors. The leader can, to one degree or another, potentially affect each of these context variables and by doing so can affect employees' reactions to job enrichment.

LMX and Satisfaction With Supervisor, Pay, and Job Security

Naturally, high quality LMX can be expected to contribute to high *satisfaction with the supervisor. Satisfaction with pay* can be also increased if a pay raise is perceived to be based on valid performance appraisal criteria and procedures. An important part of high quality LMX is the trust that subordinates have that the performance appraisal criteria and processes are being implemented in a valid way by the supervisor, so that subordinates' pay reflects their performance contribution (cf. Uhl-Bien et al., 2000). Thus, the role of the leader is to make sure that the performance evaluation system is transparent, understood, and accepted by the followers as fair (e.g., Graen et al., 2006).

Similarly, supervisors can contribute to higher *satisfaction with job security* by taking the following steps: implementing fair and transparent criteria and processes layoff decisions, when such decisions have to be made; helping followers acquire new skills that will serve them well in searching for new jobs; and establishing a formal system to help employees find alternative jobs. It should be noted, however, that the ability of the supervisor to contribute to subordinates' satisfaction with pay and job security may be limited by the policies put in place, and the resources made available, by the organization's leadership. Thus, for example, the effort of a supervisor to practice valid performance evaluation reviews to determine pay may not be successful if the organization fails to adopt valid procedures and criteria as a basis for evaluation, or if it fails to consistently use the performance appraisal system to make administrative decisions concerning pay raises, promotions, or layoffs (cf. Parker et al., 2001; Uhl-Bien et al., 2000).

LMX Satisfaction With Coworkers and MMX

The leader can also be instrumental in enhancing *satisfaction with co-workers*. Peers' satisfaction with one another has become an important issue in the contemporary organization because of the growing use and importance of collaboration and teamwork (e.g., Hackman, 1990, 2002; Hollenbeck, Ilgen, Sago, Hedlund, Major, & Philips, 1995; Uhl-Bien et al., 2000). The concept of member-member exchange (MMX) quality represents the nature of the relationship between the group members. Similar to LMX quality, high MMX quality is associated with exchange of information resources and support among coworkers above and beyond what is formally required. This relationship is characterized by mutual trust, respect, and obligation. On the other hand, low MMX quality is associated with the minimal required exchange, and is characterized by low levels of trust, respect, and obligation between the focal co-workers (Keup, Bruning, & Seers, 2004; Seers, 1989; Seers, Petty, & Cashman, 1995; Sherony & Green, 2002).

The quality of MMX that is associated with coworker satisfaction (see e.g., Seers, 1989) is often affected by the quality of LMX (Graen et al., 2006; Sherony & Green, 2002; Sparrow & Liden, 1997). For example, in accord, with Heider's (1958) balance theory, high quality relationships between the leader and each member of the group are expected to result in high MMX quality among the peers in the group. If, however, the group is divided between an in-group for which LMX is high, versus an out-group for which LMX is low, the out-group members are likely to develop feelings of resentment (Sherony & Green, 2002). As a result, members will experience relationships that are diverse in quality, resulting in an adverse effect on individual reactions. Indeed, Sherony and Green (2002) reported that greater diversity in employees' MMX relationships was negatively related to their organizational commitment. This supports the recommendation that supervisors should develop an atmosphere conducive to development of high quality MMX, so as to produce high quality collaboration among the group members and an increased ability to manage the challenge of complex jobs (cf. Sherony & Green, 2002; Uhl-Bien et al. 2000). More research is needed to investigate how changes initiated by the leader and the organization on these context variables can affect employees' context satisfaction and their reactions to job characteristics. In addition, research is needed to systematically examine the process by which the quality of LMX and MMX can influence employees' context satisfaction and subsequent reactions to job characteristics.

LMX and Satisfaction From Work-Family Relationship

The JCM does not include the work-family relationship as part of context satisfaction. However, the increased demands and pressures on employees in the competitive work environment, and the increased number of women at work, has increased the potential for work-family conflict (Oldham, 1996; Parker et al. 2001). Work-family conflict may hinder work performance, especially when the work is complex and thus requires consistent levels of focus and concentration. High quality LMX has been shown to reduce role conflict (Uhl-Bien et al., 2000). Thus, when the quality of LMX is high, the leader may be more flexible and generous in accommodating the subordinates' family needs (expecting, in return, that it will improve job performance) than when the quality of LMX is poor. Research is needed to explore what types of adjustments leaders may use to reduce work-family conflict (e.g., working from home, flexible work hours, supporting day care services), and which of these are most effective in enabling the employee to manage complex and challenging jobs.

LMX, Individual Job Enrichment, and MMX

One of the challenges a leader faces is how to maintain a balance between individual job enrichment and high quality MMX, as these two constructs may be in conflict with one another (Drach-Zahavy, 2004). Specifically, job enrichment emphasizes employees' exclusive control over their job. This is associated with high autonomy, high skill level, access to job feedback, and responsibility and accountability with respect to over all aspects of the job. In contrast, a high quality of MMX requires sharing ideas and information, helping one another learn on the job, and providing support in accomplishing challenging assignments. Hence, enriched job design may hinder supportive relationships among group members. Indeed, in a study of 56 health care teams, Drach-Zahavy (2004) found a negative relationship between job enrichment and team support.

The leader could play a major role in minimizing this conflict. For example, the leader may set clear ground rules to encourage high quality MMX relationships among group members, help clarify expectations concerning relationships among group members, and reward high quality MMX relationships through the performance appraisal and reward system (Drach-Zhavy, 2004; Graen & Scandura, 1987; Uhl-Bien et al., 2000). To help facilitate group norms of open interpersonal relationships and support among group members, the leader may also consider implementing experiential sensitivity training programs (Hackman & Oldham, 1980). Anderson and Williams (1996) reported that when the leader helped develop norms of helping behaviors, it led team members to engage in higher levels of seeking and providing support. Moreover, Drach-Zahavy (2004) supported the important role of the leader in balancing between individual job enrichment and group members' support and collaboration. They found that when job enrichment was high, it was accompanied by team support, but only when leader support for such a collaborative relationship was high. Clearly, more research is needed to explore the role of the leader and group members in balancing between individual job enrichment and teamwork and support.

LMX-MMX and Additional Situational Moderators: The Effect of Noise and Workspace Characteristics

In the past decades, it has become evident that characteristics of the physical work environment such as health hazards, temperature, and noise adversely affect employee reactions, such as by contributing higher levels of experienced stress (e.g., Humphrey et al., in press). Moreover, growing evidence indicates that the physical work environment plays an important role in determining the relative effectiveness of demanding (i.e., complex) jobs in both industrial and office settings (e.g., Melamed, Fried, & Froom, 2001; Oldham, Cummings, & Zhou, 1995). This is because these characteristics may either hinder or facilitate employees' ability to focus on their jobs (Melamed et al., 2004). Moreover, the complexity of the configurations of variables that interact with job design is related to additional outcomes that the JCM does not address, such as stress and health-related outcomes (Humphrey et al., in press; Oldham, 1996). This may further increase the challenge leaders face in eliciting and maintaining high performance among employees. In particular, research supports the moderating effect of noise and workspace characteristics (e.g., spatial density, number of enclosures surrounding a work area) on the relation between work demands and level of job complexity and work-related outcomes (e.g., Fried et al., 2002; Melamed et al., 2001; 2004; Oldham et al., 1995). Therefore, we focus on the effect of workspace characteristics and noise, and the potential role of the leader in reducing their adverse effects on employee reactions to job characteristics.

NOISE IN THE INDUSTRIAL WORK SETTING

Evidence indicates that noise is the most prevalent stressor in the physical work environment for the industrial work force in the United States and

Europe (Fried et al., 2002; Kjelberg, 1990; Tempest, 1985). Exposure to even moderate levels of noise has been shown to adversely affect psychological and health-related outcomes (e.g., Kryter, 1994; Sawada, 1993). Given this finding, a relevant question is whether noise moderates the relation between job complexity and employee reactions. Research on a large and representative sample of industrial employees in Israel has indicated that chronic noise, even at a moderate level, tends to adversely affect the contribution of job complexity to attitudinal (job satisfaction; distress), behavioral (absenteeism), and health-related (blood pressure, injuries) outcomes (see, e.g., Fried, Melamed, & Ben-David, 2002; Melamed et al., 2001; 2004).

Interestingly, the results indicate that when noise is high, high job complexity is detrimental to all these outcomes. Consistent with these findings, a series of experiments has shown that adverse physiological indicators such as blood pressure, muscle tension, heart rate, and cortisol are more likely to occur when people are involved in cognitively demanding tasks in a noisy environment (e.g., Hanson, Schellekens, Veldman, & Muller, 1993; Ray, Brady, & Emurian, 1984; Taffala & Evans, 1997). These findings can be explained by the information overload model, under which the combination of noise and cognitively demanding tasks increases the burden on the limited cognitive capacity of the affected employees (see, e.g., Cohen, 1980). Thus, because higher job complexity is associated with greater job challenge and greater use of cognitive capacity, the difficulty of performing well in a noisy environment will be noticeably greater for individuals whose jobs are complex rather than simple (e.g., Cohen, 1980; Fried et al., 2002). This in turn further contributes to stress-related psychological and physiological reactions such as job dissatisfaction, sickness, absence, and higher blood pressure (cf. Cohen, 1980; Fried et al., 2002; Melamed et al., 2001).

It is important to note that these results regarding the effect of noise are consistent with the general premise of the JCM that under some conditions individuals may not react as positively, and may possibly react negatively, to the presence of job complexity (Hackman & Oldham, 1980). However, these findings further indicate that job complexity may have some noticeable adverse effects on employee reactions. Thus, under adverse physical conditions such as high noise, not only does job complexity fail to positively contribute to individual reactions, but it is *detrimental* to these reactions. This result further supports the notion that under certain adverse circumstances, job complexity may become a source of stress to employees (e.g., Parker et al., 2001), and as such may contribute to stress-related outcomes such as sickness or high blood pressure (e.g., Fried et al., 2002; Melamed et al., 2001). Moreover, Fried et al. (2002) also reported that the interactive effect of job complexity and noise had stronger adverse effects on women than on men, as indicated by a higher level of absenteeism among the former than the latter.

On the basis of the above findings, one can conclude that it is important for leaders in industrial settings to consider how to reduce the adverse effect of noise on employees' ability to complete complex and challenging jobs. One mechanism the leader may consider is to select people who have higher ability to function under noise. For example, the leader may select individuals with high "screening ability" who are able to concentrate on their challenging tasks despite the destructive effect of noise (cf. Oldham et al., 1995; Fried, 1990). Moreover, the leader may place higher priority on the design and maintenance of quiet work environments (Fried et al., 2002), given the finding that even a moderate level of noise may, over time, have deleterious effects on employee well-being and job performance. While supervisors typically have a limited influence on the physical characteristics of the workplace, they may be able to help those who are most adversely affected by noise by, for example, relocating them to quieter work settings if feasible. The leader may also consider installing technology to reduce the noise level.

A fruitful direction for future research would be to examine how the quality of LMX and MMX is affected by the increased difficulty in task accomplishment faced by employees in noisy environments. Concerning LMX, it is possible that subordinates who find it difficult to function because noise hinders their ability to accomplish their challenging job (e.g., Cohen, 1980), will come to rely more on the leader, consequently strengthening the intensity and quality of LMX. Concerning MMX, it is possible that the cognitive demands needed for subordinates to accomplish challenging tasks in the presence of noise will deplete their cognitive resources, reducing their ability and desire to interact with others (cf. Cohen, 1980), thus leading to a reduction in MMX quality. However, an alternative possibility is that the destructive effect of noise on subordinates' ability to accomplish complex jobs in a noisy environment will lead them to increase collaboration and mutual support for the benefit of all, leading to an increase in MMX quality.

Workspace Characteristics and Social Interferences

Today, most employees work in an office environment, which makes the study of the effect of the architecture of the office environment highly relevant (e.g., Oldham et al., 1995; Oldham, Kulik, & Stepina, 1991). In office settings, employees may suffer from social interferences caused by workspace characteristics, such as high spatial density (little space available to an individual in a given area), high social density, close interpersonal distance, or few work station physical boundaries such as walls or partitions, which in turn may adversely affect their ability to concentrate and perform on the job (e.g., Oldham et al., 1995). Moreover, these work-space-related interferences are expected to have the strongest detrimental effect on performance when job complexity is high, because of the importance of focus and concentration in such jobs (see review by Oldham et al., 1995). However, while studies appear to support the interactive effect of job characteristics and workspace characteristics on individual reactions, they do not provide a clear picture of the pattern of these interactions (Fried, Slowik, Ben-David, & Tiegs, 2001; Oldham et al., 1995).

One possible explanation for the inconsistent findings is that high social distractions may reduce the capacity to handle complex jobs among some individuals, but not others. For example, in a study of office employees, Fried et al. (2001) found that individuals reacted psychologically most negatively to an environment characterized by high social density (high number of employees within a radius of 15 feet of the target employee) when job complexity and tenure were high simultaneously. Fried et al. (2001) suggested that, given their long work experience and knowledge and skills which were acquired over the years, the completion of a complex task by employees with high tenure may require less cognitive effort and attention, relative to low-tenure employees. This in turn may reduce the experienced stimulation and consequent interest in the job for long tenured people (cf. Katz, 1978a, 1978b), resulting in increased sensitivity to distractions (Fried et al., 2001). Clearly, more research is needed on this issue.

On the basis of the above findings one can conclude that when considering the effect of job complexity on work outcomes, it is important for the organization to take into account the mitigating effects of different characteristics of the physical work environment, as well as the potential differential effects of these characteristics on different demographics. More specifically, when job complexity and social interferences are high, supervisors may focus their efforts on reducing those interferences, for example, by developing and promoting norms of social behavior at work that promote consideration and respect toward others. The leader may focus particularly on protecting employees with low tenure, because of their higher vulnerability to interferences at work. However, the challenge of the leader is to walk a fine line between the desire to reduce social interferences which are detrimental to work performance when the job is complex and demanding, and desire to promote high quality levels of MMX, associated with high levels of social interaction, exchange of ideas, and mutual support at work. High MMX is particularly beneficial when the work environment is complex and challenging. It is conceivable that rules that aim to restrict social interference may also adversely affect the level of interaction among coworkers, if these rules are too strict. Therefore, the leader's challenge is to find appropriate ways to balance the two objectives of reduced social interference, on one hand, and the promotion of helpful social interaction, on the other. We need more research on the role of the leader in balancing between the reduction of social interference and the promotion of social interaction and exchange of ideas to better accomplish complex and challenging assignments at work.

Growth Need Strength (GNS)

As indicated, evidence suggests that GNS does moderate the relationship between job characteristics and work outcomes (satisfaction and performance) (e.g., Fried & Ferris, 1987; Oldham, 1996). If GNS is high and job characteristics are low, employees will feel frustrated, adversely affecting their performance. Leaders may help create a better fit between the characteristics of the job and the individual GNS through the selection process (cf. Uhl-Bien et al., 2000). Moreover, given the increased importance of collaborative relationships between group members at work, it is also important for the leader to select people who have the potential to form relationships and work well with others (Uhl-Bien et al., 2000).

However, it is also possible that individuals can be trained to improve their relational ability (Uhl-Bien et al., 2000). Such training could help enhance the LMX quality of the leader and the MMX quality of the subordinates. Training supervisors to develop better quality relationships with their followers may help the leader use these improved LMX relationships as a mechanism to help improve performance, for those high in GNS. Graen, Novak, and Sommerkamp's field experiment (1982), and Graen, Scandura, and Graen's replication (1986) reported that when managers were trained to improve the LMX relationships and expressed their desire to each of their subordinates to have better quality relationships with them, performance on difficult tasks was improved only for subordinates with high GNS. Although these replicated experimental findings strongly support the JCM, there is a clear need for more studies to explore the interaction between leadership and JCM.

LMX AND MMX AND JOB CRAFTING

The increased level of environmental uncertainty and complexity, and the need to rely on greater product or service customization in order to compete, dictates a reliance on dynamic forms of job redesign (crafting) associated with delegation of important responsibilities to individual employees and teams (Parker et al., 2001; Miner, 1987; Wrzesniewski & Dutton, 2001). We propose that LMX and MMX can play an important role in facilitating job crafting.

The JCM does not address the possibility of informal processes of change in job characteristics based on interaction between job incumbents and their social environment (supervisors and peers). However, a number of theories in the literature strongly suggest that employees are expected to be involved in changing their job characteristics over time, thereby contributing to changes in work outcomes. Dawis and Lofquist (1984), for example, discuss in their theory of work adjustment the role of "activeness" by the job incumbent in the process of changing the environment to achieve better fit. Similarly, in their job-role differentiation theory, Ilgen and Hollenbeck (1992) discuss how incumbents are involved in a negotiated process of "emergent task elements" toward "amendments" of their original job descriptions. Further, the role of leadership in the process of role making may be crucial, as suggested by LMX (e.g., Graen, 2003; Graen & Scandura,1987; Liden, Wayne, & Stillwell, 1993; Uhl-Bien et al., 2000). As indicated above, this theory supports a process of negotiation between job incumbents and their superiors, leading to changes in their job responsibilities. Analyzing the dyadic relationships between leaders and followers in the context of job design can improve our understanding of the dynamic process by which job design is established, along with its subsequent effects on individual psychological and behavioral outcomes.

Consistent with the LMX, the social exchange between the leader and the individual subordinate is an important determinant of the individual level of job enrichment, associated with the core job characteristics (e.g., Bauer & Green, 1996; Lapierre, Hackett, & Taggar, 2006; Liden, Wayne, & Stilwell, 1993). The notion is that the reciprocal relationship between the leader and the follower (subordinate) will affect the opportunities of the follower to be engaged in enriched and empowered jobs (e.g., Bauer & Green, 1996; Keller & Dansereau, 1995; Graen, Liden, & Hoel, 1982). That is, leaders are likely to provide their subordinates with opportunities for enriched work if these subordinates have gained their trust and respect by successfully fulfilling their formal performance expectations (Bauer & Green, 1996). Thus, positive leader expectations of a follower are expected to prompt the leader to delegate to the follower challenging task assignments associated with higher core job characteristics (cf. Bauer & Green, 1996; Keller & Dansereau, 1995; Scandura, Graen, & Novak, 1986; Liden & Graen, 1980). As a result, followers gain the opportunity to engage in more challenging and important responsibilities, resulting in an increased experience of empowerment and intrinsic motivation, and consequently their job performance and contribution to the organization

(Liden et al., 1993; Uhl Bien et al., 2000). In contrast, when followers fail to satisfy the leader's expectations with regard to work performance, the leader is likely to assign the followers to routine, mundane tasks, with little opportunity for growth and development (Leana, 1986; Liden et al., 1993).

This analysis suggests that successful crafting of enriched jobs requires a mature partnership between the leader and followers, associated with generalized reciprocity. Such a partnership entails high trust and respect by the leader in the subordinate's capabilities and commitment (obligation) to pursue his or her complex job successfully. The failure of a subordinate to perform well on the job will reflect badly not only on the subordinate but on the leader as well. From the standpoint of the employees, they need to trust the leader's commitment and respect his or her ability to provide the needed assistance and support for their success. In other words, there is a need for high compatibility between the characteristics of the job, and employees' motivation and abilities to meet their job challenges (cf. Hackman & Oldham, 1980; Parker et al., 2001; Wright & Cordery, 1999).

Summary Research on LMX and Job Crafting

Relatively little research has been conducted on the relationship between LMX and job enrichment (job characteristics) (Cogliser & Schriesheim, 2000; Duchon, Green, & Taber, 1986; Dunegan et al., 1992; Lapierre et al., 2006; Liden et al., 2000; Scandura et al., 1986). Overall, studies have supported the expected relationship between LMX and job enrichment, such that higher LMX was related to higher job characteristics, supporting the notion that LMX may contribute to changes in job characteristics. Most studies, however, have focused on only some of the core characteristics identified by the JCM. Lapierre et al. (2006) is the only study that focused on the focal five core job characteristics, while Liden et al focused on four of the five (excluding autonomy). Only a few of the studies failed to support the expected positive relationship between LMX and job characteristics. Duchon et al. (1986) reported a nonsignificant relationship between LMX and job characteristics. However, as Lapierre et al. (2006) pointed out, this may be due to the study's use of a dichotomous measure of LMX quality and its use of a sample of high school students with limited options for job enrichment. Dunegan et al. (1992) reported a positive but nonsignificant correlation between skill variety and LMX. Lapierre et al. (2006) further indicated that job characteristics mediate the relation between family interference with work (FIW) and LMX, such that FIW adversely affects the involvement in enriched jobs, which, in turn, reduces LMX quality. Overall, these findings provide support for the notion that high quality LMX contributes to an increase in job enrichment (job characteristics). However, the cross sectional nature of the studies does not allow an inference of causality, and evidence from longitudinal studies on the relation between LMX and job design is scarce. However, the findings of these cross-sectional studies received support from the longitudinal study of Bauer and Green (1996) who indicated that leaders tend to use increased levels of delegation of responsibility and latitude as a reward for employees who showed higher levels of performance. Moreover, the increased responsibility and latitude for the employee, granted by the leader, was found to be strongly related to better quality of exchange. Future research should focus more specifically on how changes in responsibility and latitude affect particular job characteristics. For example, it is plausible that increases in responsibility and latitude in decision making will be associated not only with higher autonomy (most obvious) but also with the remaining core characteristics: skill variety, task identity, task significance, and job feedback. Research could shed light on the relative effect of leaders' delegation of authority and responsibility on each of these core job characteristics.

MMX and Job Crafting

Although less obvious theoretically, high quality exchange among group members (MMX or team-member exchange; TMX) may also contribute to higher levels of job characteristics. Liden et al. (2000) reported a positive relationship between TMX and measures of job characteristics (task identity, task significance, skill variety, and feedback). When the quality of the TMX relationship is high, co-workers provide each other with work-related expertise and feedback, which should increase the experience of both job feedback and skill variety. Moreover, the exchange of input, advice, and resources may also contribute to peers' perceptions of competence and control, associated with the experience of autonomy and task identity (cf. Liden et al., 2000). We clearly need more studies, longitudinal in nature, on the effect of both LMX and MMX or TMX on the circumstances under which changes in job characteristics occur, the characteristics of the changes, and the process by which these changes occur.

LMX, Job Design and Work Outcomes

The relationship between LMX and job design in reference to work outcomes such as satisfaction and performance has also been studied. Seers and Graen (1984) reported main effects of both job characteristics and LMX on subordinate performance, but failed to show interactions between the two. They concluded that both job characteristics and LMX contribute independently to job-related outcomes. Similarly, Liden et al (2000) also supported the effects of both LMX and job characteristics. Specifically, the relationship between job characteristics and work satisfaction was mediated by the meaning and competence dimensions of empowerment. The meaning dimension also mediated the relationship between job characteristics and work satisfaction. In contrast, empowerment did not mediate the relation between LMX and the outcome variables. However, LMX was directly related to organizational commitment.

In contrast, Dunegan et al. (1992) found an interaction between LMX and job characteristics on performance. They reported that LMX and performance were positively related when task challenge (based on the measures of skill variety and analyzability) was either very high or very low. However, when task challenge was moderately high, no relationship was found between LMX and performance. The explanation for these findings (see Dunegan et al., 1992) is that when the task is routine, supportive and considerate behavior by the leader, which are important in a high quality dyad, would help employees perform better than would their counterparts with low LMX quality. Moreover, when the job is characterized by high demand and challenge, the solutions are not easily analyzable, and therefore the additional guidance and support provided by high quality dyads would result in higher performance. In contrast, when the task challenge is moderate, employees can focus on the motivational aspects of the job and accomplish it without the help of the leader. This notion of the need for leadership support when job complexity is either high or low, rather then moderate, is also supported by the results reported by Xie and Johns (1995). The authors found that job exhaustion was high in situations of high and low job complexity, and low when job complexity was moderate.

The findings of Dunegan et al. are consistent with permanent leadership theories such as Fiedler's LPC model (1964, 1967), the House path-goal model (1971), Hersey & Blanchard's situational leadership theory (1969, 1988), and Vroom and Yetton's Decision Tree approach (1973), which recognize that to one degree or another, a leader's effect is a function of the subordinate's task characteristics. Therefore, designing and crafting the appropriate level of job characteristics is in the interest of both the leader and the employee, and can further contribute to both high performance and LMX (cf. Bauer & Green, 1996). However, the involvement of leaders and subordinates in job crafting is a complex process, which is influenced (moderated) by individual differences (personality, demographics) concerning the need or desire to engage in challenging tasks, and situational constraints (e.g., task interdependence, structure) that may affect individual ability to successfully pursue challenging tasks. We now discuss both of these issues.

INDIVIDUAL DIFFERENCES, LMX, MMX, AND JOB CRAFTING

The JCM assumes that individuals high on GNS will respond more positively to enriched jobs than will individuals low on GNS. However, GNS can not only affect how people react to a current level of job design, but can also serve as an important determinant in crafting changes in one's job complexity. Specifically, Wrzesniewski and Dutton (2001), argued that individual motivation for job crafting is based on multiple needs: need for control over job and work meaning, need for positive self-image, and need for human connection with others (see also, Fried & Slowik, 2004). Individuals with personalities characterized by GNS, or, more broadly, openness to experience, are likely to be higher in these needs than are others (cf. Fried, Hollenbeck, Slowik, Tiegs, & Ben-David, 1999). Furthermore, the ability of an individual to change his or her job also depends on opportunities to do so (Wrzesniewski & Dutton, 2001).

An important contextual factor that should affect the pursuit of such changes is the relationship of the incumbent with his or her supervisor. High quality LMX and MMX are likely to create openness by the supervisor and peers to support a change in job characteristics by the incumbent. Fried et al. (1999) found in two different samples that individuals were more likely to enhance their job decision latitude if both interpersonal satisfaction with supervisors and peers and GNS (study 1) and openness to experience (study 2) were high simultaneously. Moreover, in high quality LMX relationships, supervisors are more likely to take the initiative to provide the interested incumbents (i.e., those with high GNS) the opportunities for growth. Indeed, Graen, Scandura, and Graen (1986) and Graen, Novak, and Sommerkamp (1992) provided evidence that individuals who are high on GNS respond more favorably than do low GNS individuals (in terms of performance, satisfaction, and motivation) to growth opportunities, represented by vertical collaboration with the leader initiated by the latter. Moreover, growth opportunities provided by the leader can also explain why employees may respond more positively to relatively unstimulating jobs, knowing that these jobs are linked to future career growth (Graen et al., 1982, 1986; Fried & Slowik, 2004).

Therefore, GNS should be studied not only as a moderator of the relation between the current level of job design and individual reactions, but also as an important determinant of LMX quality, which helps produce a higher level of job enrichment for the individuals. That is, high GNS individuals will tend to more successfully meet challenges at work than will low GNS individuals. High GNS individuals are also expected to perform well in nonchallenging tasks if they believe that good performance will help them negotiate increased responsibilities and engagement in challenging jobs in the future. Such high-quality performance, in turn, is likely to enhance the trust and respect of the leader with these individuals, and consequently to either initiate delegation of responsibilities and decision making to the employees or respond positively to these employees' requests to enrich their jobs by taking on increased autonomy, decision latitude, and challenging assignments that require more complex skills. The ability to negotiate with the leader an increase in job enrichment will also raise the level of trust and respect toward the leader by these individuals, resulting in high LMX quality. In a positive feedback cycle, this high quality LMX will further increase the likelihood that employees will be successful in negotiating further enrichment of their jobs (cf. Wrzesniewski & Dutton, 2001). Much remains to be learned about the negotiation process between the leader and the follower in the context of employee job design and career paths. Considering the context of time (career path) as it affects exchange negotiation can enrich our understanding of employee responses to their current job characteristics in light of expectations (or lack of) for future career growth (Fried & Slowik, 2004; Graen et al., 1982, 1986).

Conceptually, high quality LMX may also help in establishing a better match between individuals who are low on GNS and job characteristics. Individuals low on GNS who perceive their jobs to be too demanding at certain points in their career, either because of increased job demands or because of family matters that require time and attention, may use the positive relationship with the leader to negotiate a job with somewhat lower responsibilities and complexity. A leader may be amenable to such changes if he or she concludes that the motivation and performance of these subordinates will deteriorate unless their job characteristics match their growth need level. However, such a decision by the leader is not consistent with organization's goal of enhancing employee involvement and contributions at work. Thus research is needed to explore the conditions under which leaders may agree to reduce employees' responsibilities and the level of their job characteristics, and under what conditions this decision will be permanent or temporary.

Moreover, changes in job characteristics based on negotiations between leaders and followers may also be influenced by demographic differences such as career stage. Katz (1978a, 1978b, 1980), for example, supported the notion that employees' interest in challenging tasks differs according to their career levels. Their interest in complex and challenging jobs tend to be high earlier in their career and lower at later stages of their career. Hambrick and Fukutomi (1991) portrayed a similar pattern among CEOs.

These findings suggest that to keep high quality LMX and high productivity by employees, leaders should offer job enrichment as incentives and rewards only for those who value it and are committed to job success, contingent on personality and demographic differences.

Finally, changes in job characteristics may also be influenced by the level of job characteristics of others in the network (Oldham, 1996). Studies have suggested that individuals often compare their own job characteristics (e.g., skill variety, autonomy) to the job characteristics of their counterparts and respond to their job characteristics according to this comparison (Montagno, 1985; Oldham, Kulik, Ambrose, Stepina, & Brand, 1986; Oldham, Nottenburg, Kassner, Ferris, Fedor, & Masters, 1982). Consistent with equity theory, these studies indicated that employees whose jobs were similar in complexity to the jobs of referent others exhibited higher internal motivation than did employees whose jobs were not similar in complexity to those of referent others.

These results support the notion that leader involvement in changes (crafting) of subordinates' jobs should reflect the subordinates' perception (based on the comparative process described above) of what constitutes an appropriate change in the job. Moreover, the leader should be aware that a change in the job characteristics of one employee may require a change in the job characteristics of others, as the latter are likely to evaluate their job complexity in reference to the ones whose jobs had been changed. In sum, the issue of fairness should be an important guideline for the leader involved in job crafting (cf. Graen et al., 2006). Research is needed on the processes and outcomes that are perceived as fair with respect to job crafting in different organizational settings.

Situational Characteristics, LMX, MMX and Job Crafting

Some situational characteristics such as low task interdependence or high resource and mission uncertainty tend to contribute to opportunities to increase job enrichment (e.g., Miner, 1987; Parker et al., 2001). However, in other situations, such as assembly-line technology (high task interdependence) or structures associated with high formalization, centralization, or organizational hierarchies, jobs are typically characterized by standardized routines and low job characteristics, such as skill variety, task identity, autonomy, and significance (e.g., Gannon & Paine, 1974; Oldham & Hackman, 1981; Pierce & Dunham, 1978). Such technological and structural constraints will make it difficult to craft the job characteristics toward higher job enrichment (cf. Oldham & Hackman, 1981). Interestingly, in this situation, providing the employees with higher control (autonomy) over their work may not be sufficient to compensate for the simplicity of the task assignments and may actually have adverse effects on employee performance. More specifically, the literature suggests that the contribution of autonomy to employees' motivation and performance tends to be contingent on the simplicity of the tasks for which the employee is responsible. Research conducted by Mullarkey, Jackson, Wall, Wilson, and Grey-Taylor (1997), and Wright and Cordery (1999) demonstrated that having a high level of control (corresponding to a high level of autonomy) over work does not necessarily mean employees experience a high level of motivation and satisfaction at work. Instead, high control over the work environment contributes to positive reactions only when these employees are involved in challenging, non-routine operations associated with production uncertainty. On the other hand, a high level of control over one's work tends to lead to low motivation and satisfaction when the work is routine and predictable (e.g., Wright & Cordery, 1999). In such cases, the lack of challenge contributes to frustration and boredom. Thus, high autonomy may contribute to motivation and performance when the tasks are nonroutine. When the tasks are routine, high autonomy may be detrimental to employees' motivation, effort, and performance (cf. Pearce & Ravlin, 1987). Janz, Colquitt, and Noe (1997) reported similar results with regard to team autonomy. They reported that among knowledge workers, the positive effect of team autonomy over planning and work processes on team motivation was reduced when task interdependence increased.

With respect to the constructs of the JCM, skill variety, task identity, and task significance largely correspond to the construct of job simplicity. Jobs that are high on these three job dimensions are typically more complex and non-routine, and contribute to experienced meaningfulness and empowerment. The reverse is also true: simple and routine jobs are associated with low levels on these dimensions. The JCM, however, does not recognize the potential effect of job simplicity on the contribution of autonomy to employee reactions. In fact, the theory posits that employees who are working in relatively simple jobs characterized by lower levels of skill variety, task identity, and significance can still feel motivated if autonomy and job feedback are high (Hackman & Oldham, 1980). The evidence discussed above, however, indicates that if job simplicity is high, high control over work accomplishments (high autonomy) may actually contribute to increased negative reactions among employees because of the increased frustration of having high control over a simple, non-challenging job. We clearly need more studies to explore the pattern of interactions among the core job characteristics in explaining employee reactions. However, the current evidence suggests that the contribution of autonomy on employee reactions is contingent on the level of other job characteristics in the model. This further suggests that in the process of facilitating job design or job crafting, the leader should be aware of the importance of the fit between job complexity/simplicity and autonomy. Addressing job design from the standpoint of only one or a few job characteristics, rather than all five characteristics, may not produce the expected results, and in some cases may result in adverse outcomes.

Changing the Relational Characteristics of the Job

When leaders find it difficult to facilitate changes in job characteristics that would satisfy employees' desire for growth (because of the reasons described above), they may focus instead on changing the relational architecture of the jobs to shape employee motivation (e.g., Grant, 2007). More specifically, the literature supports the notion that people care about positively affecting other people's lives, and that a major purpose of employees at work is to make a positive difference in others' lives (Colby, Sippola, & Phelps, 2001; Ruiz-Quintanilla & England, 1996). The JCM has recognized this important need by including task significance as one of the five core job characteristics (Hackman & Oldham, 1980). However, the theory focuses on how the structure of task significance (and the structure of all other task characteristics) affects employees' experience of meaningfulness and motivation at work, and neglects to recognize the importance of the relational part of task significance on meaningfulness and work motivation (Grant, 2007). That is, employees may be engaged in jobs with high task significance (impact on others), but the degree to which they experience the meaningfulness and motivation associated with task significance may vary, contingent on the degree to which they are aware and therefore also psychologically attached to the beneficiaries (Grant, 2007; Stone & Gueutal, 1985). One can expect that the higher the interaction with beneficiaries, the higher is the experience of task significance, and therefore the higher is the experience of psychological meaningfulness and motivation at work. To test this proposition, Grant, Campbell, Chen, Cottone, Lapedis, and Lee (2007) conducted a longitudinal field experiment with fundraising callers soliciting alumni donations to a university. They tested whether introducing callers to one beneficiary of their work—a student who received a scholarship funded by the donations that they raised—would increase their motivation. They measured motivation in terms of two behavioral indicators: persistence, the amount of time that callers spent on the phone, and performance, the amount of money that callers raised. Relative to their baseline levels and to callers in two control groups, callers who met the beneficiary increased significantly in both persistence and performance. Subsequent experiments suggested that the interaction with beneficiaries enabled callers to experience their jobs as higher in task significance, thereby increasing their motivation.

Moreover, direct relationships with beneficiaries may also affect other job characteristics (Kulik et al., 1987). For example, increased interaction with beneficiaries can increase opportunities for direct feedback from people who are recipients of work outputs. In addition, skill variety may increase because of the need to exercise interpersonal skills in facilitating the interaction with the beneficiaries, as well as the use of additional skills in completing the tasks in response to the beneficiaries' feedback. Finally, the experience of autonomy may also increase because individuals need to decide how to most effectively manage the relationships with the beneficiaries (Kulik et al., 1987).

Therefore, managers can intensify employees' positive psychological experiences associated with core job characteristics by increasing the opportunities for contact with the intended beneficiaries. The opportunities for managers to enhance contact with beneficiaries has been on the rise, because of the significant growth of the service sector, in which work is defined in terms of relationships (e.g., Parker et al., 2001). For example, a textbook editor who is introduced to students who benefit from the editing is likely to experience higher task significance than is his or her counterpart who is working in isolation from the customers, because of increased awareness of the impact of the job (Grant, 2007). Similarly, production teams that interact with their customers are likely to develop higher awareness and experience of task significance than do production teams that are isolated from their customers (Grant, 2007; Hackman, 1990). One example from the business world is Microsoft, which established a program in which developers were able to observe users testing new programs (Cusumano & Selby, 1995; Grant, 2007). Future research would benefit from further exploring the relative effect of leaders focusing on changes in job characteristics versus changes in relational characteristics, and the degree to which these two types of changes affect employee reactions.

CONCLUSION

In the current paper we have analyzed how the premises of the two theories—the JCM and LMX leadership theory—can be integrated to enhance our understanding of the dynamics of leadership and changes in job design. More studies are needed to clarify the conceptual and empirical links between these two theories. Our aim is that the discussion and suggestions presented in the paper will serve as a basis for future research concerning the integration between the two theories. However, available findings and their implications suggest that linking the two theories will help provide a more precise understanding of individual reactions at work. We will illustrate this point with a few examples.

A central debate in the LMX literature is whether leaders can successfully manage and maintain large numbers of high quality relations with subordinates (Uhl-Bien et al., 2000). Sparrowe and Liden (1997) represent the approach that argues that " if a leader attempts to develop generalized reciprocity (high quality relationships) with each member, his or her own performance may suffer from an overinvestment in redundant contacts" (p. 545). Uhl-Bien et al., on the other hand, argue for quality relationships between the leader and all subordinates. They argue that

> to the extent that managers and subordinates are not maximizing their ability to work together by having poor working relationships, organizational effectiveness necessarily suffers....Organizations that can generate more of these relationships would clearly have a competitive advantage over organizations that are willing to accept fewer. (p. 177)

One way to balance these two approaches is to incorporate job enrichment as a substitute for leadership on the basis of Kerr and Jermier"s (1978) "substitutes for leadership" model, which argues that leadership effectiveness can be improved by identifying the situational variables that can substitute for the effects of the behavior of a leader. The idea here is that people who are engaged in jobs with high complexity may be sufficiently motivated and skilled to manage their jobs without the help of the leader (cf. Kerr & Jermier, 1978; Morgeson, Johnson, Campion, Medsker, & Mumford, 2006). This, in turn, will provide the leader with the time and resources to promote high quality relationships with other employees who need his or her help to accomplish their jobs successfully. So far, studies that have examined job characteristics as a substitute for leadership have produced inconsistent results (see, e.g., Dunegan, Uhl-Bien, & Duchon, 2002; Morgeson et al., 2006; Podsakoff, MacKenzie, & Bommer, 1996; Whittington, Goodwin, & Murray, 2004).

However, it is possible that this research has not taken into account the complexity of variables' effects in exploring this issue. For example, scholars have generally assumed that leadership substitution will occur when job complexity is high. However, Dunegan et al. (1992) reported that when the task challenge is moderate (rather than high or low), employees seem most able to effectively focus on the motivational aspects of the job and accomplish it without the help of the leader. This suggests that research should examine more carefully the nonlinear relation between LMX and job complexity. Moreover, research should also explore how individual differences in such variables as need for autonomy or self-esteem will affect individual performance in a situation of high job complexity and low leader involvement (cf. Uhl-Bien et al., 2000). It is conceivable, for example, that individuals with high need for autonomy and self-esteem will function better in a "leaderless" situation, in which they need to overcome challenging assignments with no or minimal help from the leader, than will their counterparts with low need for autonomy and low self-esteem. In sum, there is a need to develop and examine more complex models to improve our understanding of the conditions under which job enrichment may serve as a successful substitute for leadership.

Moreover, research has supported the notion that high LMX quality will be associated with increases in job complexity. However, the associations reported in the literature are moderate in size, thus supporting the need to study these relationships in context (e.g., Rousseau & Fried, 2001). For example, enriching employees' jobs and delegating authority and decision making latitude is often associated with the supervisor becoming a facilitator and mentor (Parker et al., 2001). Supervisors may be reluctant to relinquish their traditional authority and power or share them with employees if they are personally insecure or have high need for power, or if the organization fails to adopt a system in which the new roles of the supervisor are recognized, embraced, and rewarded. Thus research in LMX should explore the relationship between the quality of LMX and changes in job enrichment by incorporating the context of the leader's personality and the organizational support for the change in supervisory role.

From the standpoint of the JCM, the inconsistent results of context satisfaction as a moderator (in which some studies supported the expected moderating effect of context satisfaction, while other studies reported the highest relationship between job characteristics and satisfaction when dissatisfaction from context was high, rather than low), may further support the complex effect of job complexity, as discussed above. It may be that under some conditions, low context satisfaction (e.g., low satisfaction with LMX) causes people to be distracted from work and thus respond less positively to job complexity, while in other cases, such low satisfaction with LMX causes people to insulate themselves from the unpleasant situation by focusing on the job (Oldham, 1996). This may also be the case when people are unhappy with the quality of MMX. Sherony and Green (2002) reported that coworkers remained satisfied with their jobs despite relatively high diversity in MMX relationships that caused a negative relationship with organizational commitment. As Sherony & Green have suggested, it may be that high variation in the quality of MMX may not affect the pleasure associated with enriched tasks. The question future research should address is under what conditions low quality LMX and MMX will affect the positive influence of job characteristics on employee reactions, and what are the underlying reasons for the change in relationships.

Finally, in our analysis we have assumed that high quality LMX plays an important role in the successful pursuit of job crafting. This, however, may not always be true. It may be that job crafting is a self-initiated process by subordinates, in response to poor leadership and poor LMX (cf. Sparrowe & Liden, 1987, 2005). Subordinates may be involved individually or collectively in job crafting to enhance their job stimulation if they feel neglected and conclude that their leaders are incompetent or indifferent and are unable to help them reach their career goals. In such a situation, it is conceivable that employees will attempt to take their fate into their own hands, by, for example, finding another job, of, if they are unsuccessful, engaging in job crafting to increase their job challenge. It is also conceivable that in changing their jobs these individuals will need the support and collaboration of their peers, which will contribute to high MMX. In other words, low LMX quality between the leader and subordinates may contribute to high MMX quality, which will help the subordinates achieve their goal of job enrichment (cf. Kulik et al., 1987; Sparrowe & Liden, 1997). Given this possibility, research should explore the role of MMX in job crafting when LMX quality is low. Research should also investigate whether job crafting that was facilitated or assisted by the supervisor has similar effects on the employee, compared to job crafting that was initiated and carried out by the individual without the help of the supervisor (cf. Kulik et al., 1987).

In this paper we have attempted to analyze how LMX-MMX can improve our knowledge and understanding of the JCM in the current complex and changing global economy. Only limited research has attempted to incorporate the two theories. We hope that this analysis will serve as the basis for future research directions, as well as for organizational leaders to better apply the principles of JCM at work.

ACKNOWLEDGMENT

We are indebted to Adam Grant and George Graen for their helpful comments and suggestions on an earlier version of this article

REFERENCES

Aiello, J. R., & Kolb, K. J. (1995). Electronic performance monitoring and social context: Impact on productivity and stress. *Journal of Applied Psychology, 80*(3), 339-364.

Bauer, T. N., & Green, S. G. (1996). Development of leader-member exchange: A longitudinal test. *Academy of Management Journal, 39*(6), 1538-1568.

Bottger, P. C., & Chew, I. K. H. (1986). The job characteristics model and growth satisfaction: Main effects of assimilation of work experience and context satisfaction. *Human Relations, 39*(6), 575-594.

Cascio, W. F. (2003). Changes in workers, work, and organizations. In W. Borman, R. Klimoski, & D. Ilgen (Eds.), *Handbook of psychology, volume twelve: Industrial and organizational psychology* (pp. 401-422). New York: Wiley.

Champoux, J. E. (1981). The moderating effect of work context satisfactions on the curvilinear relationship between job scope and affective response. *Human Relations, 34*(6), 503-515.

Cogliser, C. C., & Schriesheim, C. A. (2000). Exploring work unit context and leader-member exchange: A multi-level perspective. *Journal of Organizational Behavior, 21*(5), 487-511.

Cohen, S. (1980). Aftereffects of stress on human performance and social behavior: A review of research and theory. *Psychological Bulletin, 88*, 82-108.

Colby, A., Sippola, L., & Phelps, E. (2001). Social responsibility and paid work in contemporary American life. In A. Rossi (Ed.), *Caring and doing for others: social responsibility in the domain of family, work, and community* (pp. 349-399). Chicago: University of Chicago Press.

Cusumano, M., & Selby, R. W. (1996). How Microsoft competes. *Research Technology Management, 39*(1), 26-31.

Dawis, R. V., & Lofquist, L. H. (1984). *A psychological theory of work adjustment.* Minneapolis: University of Minnesota Press.

Dienesch, R. M., & Liden, R. C. (1986). Leader-member exchange model of leadership: A critique and further development. *The Academy of Management Review, 11*(3), 618-634.

Drach-Zahavy, A. (2004). The proficiency trap: How to balance enriched job designs and the team's need for support. *Journal of Organizational Behavior 25*(8), 979-996.

Duchon, D., Green, S. G., & Taber, T. G. (1986). Vertical dyad linkage: A longitudinal assessment of antecedents, measures, and consequences. *Journal of Applied Psychology, 71*(1), 56-61.

Dunegan, K. J., Duchon, D., & Uhl-Bien, M. (1992). Examining the link between leader-member exchange and subordinate performance: The role of task analyzability and variety as moderators. *Journal of Management, 18*(1), 59-76.

Dunegan, K. J., Uhl-Bien, M., & Duchon, D. (2002). LMX and subordinate performance: The moderating effects of task characteristics. *Journal of Business and Psychology, 17*(2), 275-285.

Fiedler, F. E. (1964). A contingency model of leadership effectiveness. In L. Berkowitz (Ed.), *Advances in experimental social psychology, 70*, 149-190. New York: Academic Press.

Fiedler, F. E. (1967). *A theory of leadership effectiveness.* New York: McGraw-Hill.

Fried, Y. (1990). Workspace characteristics, behavioral interferences, and screening ability as joint predictors of employee reactions: An examination of the intensification approach. *Journal of Organizational Behavior, 11*, 267-280.

Fried, Y. (1991). Meta-analytic comparison of the job diagnostic survey and job characteristics inventory as correlates of work satisfaction and performance. *Journal of Applied Psychology, 76,* 690-697.

Fried, Y., & Ferris, G. R. (1986). The dimensionality of job characteristics: Some neglected issues. *Journal of Applied Psychology, 71*(3), 419-426.

Fried, Y., & Ferris, G. R. (1987). The validity of the job characteristics model: Areview and meta-analysis. *Personnel Psychology, 40*(2), 287-322.

Fried, Y., Hollenbeck J. R., Slowik, L. H., Tiegs, R. B., & Ben-David, H. A. (1999). Changes in job decision latitude: The influence of personality and interpersonal satisfaction. *Journal of Vocational Behavior, 54,* 233-243.

Fried, Y., Melamed, S., & Ben-David, H. A. (2002). The joint effects of noise, job complexity, and gender on employee sickness absence: An exploratory study across 21 organizations—The CORDIS study. *Journal of Occupational and Organizational Psychology, 75,* 131-144.

Fried, Y., Oldham, G. R., & Cummings, L. A. (1998). Job design. In M. People & M. Warener (Eds.), *International encyclopedia of business and management* (pp. 523-543). London: International Thompson.

Fried, Y., & Slowik, L. H. (2004). Enriching goal-setting theory with time: An integrated approach. *Academy of Management Review, 29*(3), 404-422.

Fried, Y., Slowik, L., Ben-David, H. A., & Tiegs, R. B. (2001). Exploring the relationship between workspace density and employee attitudinal reactions: An integrative model. *Journal of Occupational and Organizational Psychology, 74,* 359-372.

Fried, Y., Snidrr, C., Hadani, M., & Levi, A. S. (2006). Job design. In S. G. Rogelberg (Ed.), *The encyclopedia of industrial and organizational psychology* (Vol. 1, pp. 392-396). Thousand Oaks, CA: Sage.

Gaines, J., & Jermier, J. M. (1983). Emotional exhaustion in a high stress organization. *Academy of Management Journal, 26*(4), 567-586.

Gannon, M. J., & Paine, F. T. (1974). Unity of command and job attitudes of managers in a bureaucratic organization. *Journal of Applied Psychology, 59*(3), 392-394.

Gerstner, C. R. & Day, D. V. (1997). Meta-analytic review of leader-member exchange theory: Correlates and construct issues. *Journal of Applied Psychology 82*(6), 827-844.

Graen, G. B. (Ed.). (2003). Interpersonal workplace theory at the crossroads. In *LMX leadership: The series: Vol. 1. Dealing with diversity* (pp. 145-182), Greenwich, CT: Information Age.

Graen, G. B., & Cashman, J. (1975). A role making model of leadership in formal organizations: A developmental approach. In J. G. Hunt & L. L. Larson (Eds.), *Leadership frontiers* (pp. 143-166). Kent, OH: Kent State University Press.

Graen, G. B., Hui, C., & Taylor, E. T. (2006). Experience-based learning about LMX leadership and fairness in project teams: A dyadic directional approach. *Academy of Management Learning and Education, 5*(4), 448-460.

Graen, G. B., Liden, R. C., & Hoel, W. (1982). Role of leadership in the employee withdrawal process. *Journal of Applied Psychology, 67*(6), 868-872.

Graen, G. B., Novak, M. A., & Sommerkamp, P. (1982). The effects of leader-member exchange and job design on productivity and satisfaction: Testing a dual attachment model. *Organizational Behavior and Human Performance, 30*, 109-131.

Graen, G. B., & Scandura T. A. (1987). Toward a psychology of dyadic organizing. *Research in Organizational Behavior, 9*, 175-208.

Graen, G. B., Scandura, T. A., & Graen, M. (1986). A field experimental test of the moderating effects of growth need strength on productivity. *Journal of Applied Psychology, 71*(3), 484-491.

Graen, G. B., & Uhl-Bien, M. (1995). Relationship-based approach to leadership: Development of leader-member exchange (LMX) theory of leadership over 25 years: Applying a multi-level multi-domain perspective. *The Leadership Quarterly, 6*(2), 219-247.

Graen, G. B., & Wakabayashi, M. (1992). Cross-cultural leadership making: Bridging American and Japanese diversity for team advantage. In H. C. Triandis, M. D. Dunette, & L. M. Hough (Eds.), *Handbook of industrial and organizational psychology, 4*, 415-446. Palo Alto, CA: Consulting Psychologists Press.

Grant, A. M. (2007). Relational job design and the motivation to make a prosocial difference. *Academy of Management Review, 32*(2), 393-417.

Grant, A. M., Campbell, E. M., Chen, G., Cottone, K., Lapedis, D., & Lee, K. (2007). Impact and the art of motivation maintenance: The effects of contact with beneficiaries on persistence behavior. *Organizational Behavior and Human Decision Processes, 103*(1), 53-67.

Green, S. G., Anderson, S. E., & Shivers, S. L. (1996). Demographic and organizational influences on leader-member exchange and related work attitudes. *Organizational Behavior and Human Decision Processes, 66*(2), 203-224.

Hackman, J. R. (1990). *Groups that work (and those that don't)*. San Francisco: Josey-Bass.

Hackman, J. R. (2002). *Leading teams: Setting the stage for great performances*. Boston: Harvard Business School Press.

Hackman, J. R., & Oldham, G. R. (1980). *Work redesign*. Reading, MA: Addison-Wesley, Reading.

Hambrick, D. C., & Fukutomi, G. D. S. (1991). The seasons of a CEO's tenure. *Academy of Management Review, 16*(4), 719-743.

Hanson, E. K. S., Schellekens, J. M. H., Veldman, J. B. P., & Mulder, L. J. M. (1993). Psychomotor and cardiovascular consequences of mental effort and noise. *Human Movement Science, 12*, 607-626.

Heider, F. (1958). *The psychology of interpersonal relations*. New York: Wiley.

Hersey, P., & Blanchard, K. H. (1969). Life cycle theory of leadership. *Training and Development Journal, 23*(2), 26-34.

Hersey, P., & Blanchard, K. H. (1988). *Management of organizational behavior: Utilizing human resources* (5th ed.). Englewood Cliffs, NJ: Prentice-Hall.

Hollenbeck, J. R., Ilgen, D. R., Sego, D. R., & Hedlund, J., Major, & Phillips. (1995). Multilevel theory of team decision making: Decision performance in teams incorporating distributed expertise. *Journal of Applied Psychology, 80*(2), 292-317.

House, R. J. (1971). A path-goal theory of leader effectiveness. *Administrative Science Quarterly, 16,* 556-571.

Humphrey, S. E., Nahrgang, J. D., & Morgeson, F. P. (in press). Integrating motivational, social, and contextual work design futures: A meta-analytic summary and theoretical extension of the work design literature. *Journal of Applied Psychology.*

Ilgen, D. R., & Hollenbeck, J. R. (1992). The structure of work: Job design and roles. In M. D. Dunnette & L. M. Hough (Eds.), *Handbook of industrial and organizational psychology* (Vol. 2, pp. 165-208). Palo Alto, CA: Consulting Psychologists Press.

Janssen, O., & Van Yperen, N. W. (2004). Employees' goal orientations, The quality of leader-member exchange, and the outcomes of job performance and job satisfaction. *Academy of Management Journal, 47*(3), 369-384.

Janz, B. D., Colquitt, J. A., & Noe, R. A. (1997). Knowledge worker team effectiveness: The role of autonomy, interdependence, team development, and contextual support variables. *Personnel Psychology, 50*(4), 877-905.

Johns, G., Xie, J. L., & Fang, Y. (1992). Mediating and moderating effects in job design. *Journal of Management, 18*(4), 657-676.

Katz, R. (1978a). The influence of job longevity on employee reactions to task characteristics. *Human Relations, 31*(8), 703-725.

Katz, R. (1978b). Job longevity as a situational factor in job satisfaction. *Administrative Science Quarterly, 23*(2), 204-233.

Katz, R. (1980). Time and work: toward an integrative perspective. *Research in Organizational Behavior, 2,* 81-127.

Keller, T., & Dansereau, F. (1995). Leadership and empowerment: A social exchange perspective. *Human Relations, 48*(2), 127-147.

Kerr, S. & Jermier, J. M. (1978). Substitutes for leadership: their meaning and measurement. *Organizational Behavior and Human Performance, 22*(3), 375.

Keup, L., Bruning, N. S., & Seers, A. (2004). Members, leaders and the team: Extending LMX to co-worker relationships. *The Canadian Journal of Administrative Sciences,* 1-14.

Kjelberg, A. (1990). Subjective, behavioral and psychophysiological effects of noise. *Scandinavian Journal of Work, Environment and Health, 16,* 29-38.

Kopelman, R. (1985). Job redesign and productivity: A review of the evidence. *National Productivity Review, 4,* 237-255.

Kryter, K. D. (1994). *The handbook of hearing and the effects of noise: Physiology, psychology, and public health.* New York: Academic Press.

Kulik, C. T., Oldham, G. R., & Hackman, J. R. (1987). Work design as an approach to person-environment fit. *Journal of Vocational Behavior, 31,* 278-296.

Lapierre, L. M., Hackett, R. D., & Taggar, S. (2006). A test of the links between family, interference with work, job enrichment and leader-member exchange. *Applied Psychology, 55*(4), 489-511.

Lawler, E. E., III, & Finegold, D. (2000). Individualizing the organization: Past, present, and future. *Organizational Dynamics, 29*(1), 1-15.

Leana, C. R. (1986). Predictors and consequences of delegation. *Academy of Management Journal, 29*(4), 754-775.

Lee, R. & Klein, A. R. (1982). Structure of the job diagnostic survey for public sector occupations. *Journal of Applied Psychology, 67*(4), 515-519.

Liden, R. C., & Graen, G. B. (1980). Generalizability of the vertical dyad linkage model of leadership. *Academy of Management Journal, 23*(3), 451-465.

Liden, R. C., Wayne, S. J., & Stillwell, D. (1993). A longitudinal study on the early development of leader-member exchanges. *Journal of Applied Psychology, 78*(4), 662-674.

Liden, R. C., Wayne, S. J., & Sparrowe, R. A. (2000). An examination of the mediating role of psychological empowerment on the relations between the job, interpersonal relationships, and work outcomes. *Journal of Applied Psychology 85*(3), 407-416.

Loher, B. T., Noe, R. A., Moeller, N. L, & Fitzgerald, M. P. (1985). A meta-analysis of the relation of job characteristics to job satisfaction. *Journal of Applied Psychology, 70*(2), 280-289.

Melamed, S., Fried, Y., Froom, P. (2001). The interaction effect of chronic exposure to noise and job complexity on changes in blood pressure and job satisfaction: A longitudinal study of industrial employees. *Journal of Occupational Health Psychology, 6*, 182-195.

Melamed, S., Fried, Y., & Froom, P. (2004). The joint effect of noise exposure and job complexity on distress and injury risk among men and women: the cardiovascular occupational risk factors determination in Israel study. *Journal of Occupational and Environmental Medicine, 46*(10), 1023-1032.

Miner, A. S. (1987). Idiosyncratic jobs in formalized organizations. *Administrative Science Quarterly, 32*(3), 327-351.

Miner, J. B. (1980). The role of managerial and professional motivation in the career success of management professors. *Academy of Management Journal, 23*(3), 487-508.

Montagno, R. V. (1985). The effects of comparison others and prior experience on responses to task design. *Academy of Management Journal, 28*(2), 491-499.

Morgeson, F. P., & Campion, M. A. (2003). Work design. In W. C. Borman, D. R. Ilgen, & R. J. Klimoski (Eds.), *Handbook of psychology: Industrial and organizational psychology* (Vol. 12, pp. 423-452). Hoboken, NJ: Wiley.

Morgeson, F. P., & Humphrey, S. E. (2006). The work design questionnaire (WDQ): Developing and validating a comprehensive measure for assessing design and the nature of work. *Journal of Applied Psychology, 91*, 1321-1339.

Morgeson, F. P., Johnson, M. D., Campion, M. A., Medsker, G. J., & Mumford, T. V. (2006). Understanding reactions to job redesign: A quasi-experimental investigation of the moderating effects of organizational context on perceptions of performance behavior. *Personnel Psychology, 59*, 333-363.

Mullarkey, S., Jackson, P. R., Wall, T. D., Wilson, J. R., & Grey-Taylor, S. M. (1997). The impact of technology characteristics and job control on worker mental health. *Journal of Organizational Behavior, 18*(5), 471-490.

Oldham, G. R. (1996). Job design. In C. L. Cooper & I. T. Robertson (Eds.), *International review of industrial and organizational psychology* (pp. 33-60). Chichester, United Kingdom: Wiley.

Oldham, G. R., & Cummings, A. (1996). Employee creativity: Personal and contextual factors at work. *Academy of Management Journal, 39*(3), 607-634.

Oldham, G. R., Cummings, A., & Zhou, J. (1995). The spatial configuration of organizations: A review of the literature and some new research directions. In G. Ferris (Ed.), *Research in personnel and human resources management* (Vol. 13, pp. 1-37). Greenwich, CT: JAI Press.

Oldham, G. R., & Hackman, J. R. (1981). Relationships between organizational structure and employee reactions: Comparing alternative frameworks. *Administrative Science Quarterly, 26*(1), 66-84.

Oldham, G. R., Hackman, J. R., & Pearce, J. L. (1976). Conditions under which employees respond positively to enriched work. *Journal of Applied Psychology, 61*(4), 395-403.

Oldham, G. R., Kulik, C. T., Ambrose, M. L., Stepina, L. P., & Brand, J. F. (1986). Relations between job facet comparisons and employee reactions. *Organizational Behavior and Human Decision Processes, 38*(1), 28-48.

Oldham, G. R., Kulik, C. T., & Stepina, L. P. (1991). Physical environments and employee reactions: Effects of stimulus-screening skills and job complexity. *Academy of Management Journal, 34,* 929-938.

Oldham, G. R., Nottenburg, G., Kassner, M. W., Ferris, G., Fedor, D., & Masters, M. (1982). The selection and consequences of job comparisons. *Organizational Behavior and Human Performance, 29*(1), 84-111.

Orpen, C. (1979). The effects of job enrichment on employee satisfaction, motivation, involvement, and performance: A field experiment. *Human Relations 32*(3), 189-217.

Parker, S. K., & Wall, T. D. (1998). *Job and work design: Organizing work to promote well-being and effectiveness.* Thousand Oaks, CA: Sage.

Parker, S. K., Wall, T. D., & Cordery J. L. (2001). Future work design research and practice: Towards an elaborated model of work design. *Journal of Occupational and Organizational Psychology,* 74: 413-440.

Pearce, J. A., II, & Ravlin, E. C. (1987). The design and activation of self-regulating work groups. *Human Relations, 40*(11), 751-783.

Pierce, J. L., & Dunham, R. B. (1978). The measurement of perceived job characteristics: The job diagnostic survey versus the job characteristics inventory. *Academy of Management Journal, 21*(1), 123-129.

Podsakoff, P. M., MacKenzie, S. B., & Bommer, W. H. (1996). Transformational leader behaviors and substitutes for leadership as determinants of employee satisfaction, commitment, trust, and organizational citizenship behaviors. *Journal of Management, 22*(2), 259-237.

Pokorney, J. J., Gilmore, D. C., & Beehr, T. A. (1980). Job diagnostic survey dimensions: Moderating effect of growth needs and correspondence with dimensions of job rating form. *Organizational Behavior and Human Performance, 26*(2), 222.

Ray, R., Brady, J. V., & Emurian, H. H. (1984). Cardiovascular effects of noise during complex task performance. *International Journal of Psychophysiology, 1,* 335-340.

Rousseau, D. M., & Fried, Y. (2001). Location, location, location: Contextualizing organizational research. *Journal of Organizational Behavior, 22*(1), 1-13.

Ruiz-Quintanilla, S. A., & England, G. W. (1996). How working is defined: Structure and stability. *Journal of Organizational Behavior, 17,* 515-541.

Sawada, Y. (1993). Reprodycibal increases in blood pressure during intermittent noise exposure: Underlying haemodynamic mechanisms specific to passive coping. *European Journal of Applied Physiology, 67,* 367-374.

Scandura, T. A., Graen, G. B., & Novak, M. A. (1986). When managers decide not to decide autocratically: An investigation of leader-member exchange and decision influence. *Journal of Applied Psychology, 71*(4), 579-584.

Seers, A. (2004). Interpersonal workplace theory at a crossroads. In G. B. Graen (Ed.), *LMX leadership: The series: Vol. 2. New frontiers of leadership* (pp. 1-31). Greenwich, CT: Information Age.

Seers, A., & Graen, G. B. (1984). The dual attachment concept: A longitudinal investigation of the combination of task characteristics and leader-member exchange. *Organizational Behavior and Human Performance, 33*(3), 283-306.

Seers, A., Petty, M., & Cashman, J. F. (1995). Team-member exchange under team and traditional management. *Group & Organization Management, 20*(1), 18-39.

Sherony, K. M., & Green, S. G. (2002). Coworker exchange: Relationships between coworkers, leader-member exchange, and work attitudes. *Journal of Applied Psychology, 87*(3), 542-548.

Sparrowe, R. D., & Liden, R. C. (1997). Process and structure in leader-member exchange. *The Academy of Management Review, 22*(2), 522-552.

Sparrowe, R. D., & Liden, R. C. (2005). Two routes to influence: Integrating leader-member exchange and social network perspectives. *Administrative Science Quarterly, 50*(4), 505-535.

Spector, P. E. (1985). Higher-order need strength as a moderator of the job scope-employee outcome relationship: A meta-analysis. *Journal of Occupational Psychology, 58*(2), 119-127.

Stone, E. F., & Gueutal, H. G. (1985). An empirical derivation of the dimensions along which characteristics of jobs are perceived. *Academy of Management Journal, 28*(2), 376-397.

Taber, T. D., & Taylor, E. (1990). A review and evaluation of the psychometric properties of the job diagnostic survey. *Personnel Psychology, 43,* 467-500.

Tafalla, R .J., & Evans, G. W. (1997). Noise, physiology, and human performance: The potential role of effort. *Journal of Occupational Health Psychology, 2,* 148-155.

Tempest, W. (Ed.). (1985). Noise in industry. In *The noise handbook* (pp. 179-194). , London: Academic Press.

Tiegs, R. B., Tetrick, L. E., & Fried, Y. (1992). Growth need strength and context satisfactions as moderators of the relations of the job characteristics model. *Journal of Management, 18*(3), 575-593.

Uhl-Bien, M., Graen, G. B., & Scandura, T. A. (2000). Implications of leader-member exchange (LMX) for strategic human resource management systems: Relationships as social capital for competitive advantage. *Research in Personnel and Human Resource Management, 18,* 137-185.

Vecchio, R. P., & Gobdel, B. C. (1984). The vertical dyad linkage model of leadership: Problems and prospects. *Organizational Behavior and Human Performance, 34*(1), 5-20.

Vroom, V. H., & Yetton, P. (1973). *Leadership and decision making.* Pittsburgh, PA: University of Pittsburgh Press.

Whittington, J. L., Goodwin, V. L., & Murray, B. (2004). Transformational leadership, goal difficulty, and job design: Independent and interactive effects on employee outcomes. *Leadership Quarterly, 15*(5), 593-606.

Wright, B. M., & Cordery, J. L. (1999). Production uncertainty as a contextual moderator of employee reactions to job design. *Journal of Applied Psychology 84*(3), 456-462.

Wrzesniewski, A., & Dutton, J. E. (2001). Crafting a job: Revisioning employees as active crafters of their work. *Academy of Management Review, 26*(2), 179-202.

Xie, I. L., & Johns, G. (1995). Job scope and stress: Can job scope be too high? *Academy of Management Journal, 38,* 1288-1309.

CHAPTER 10

INTEGRATING GRAEN'S LMX LEADERSHIP THEORY AND HACKMAN'S JOB CHARACTERISTICS MODEL

GEORGE B. GRAEN

Two independent but well researched models of behavior in organizations are placed together following the results of strong inference research. In addition, fundamental questions are exchanged between Hackman and Graen within the University of Illinois functional approach.

INTRODUCTION

After reading Fried, Levi and Laurence's (this volume) very thorough and excellent review of the research literature on Hackman's job characteristic model of job enrichment and their various attempts to integrate it with the LMX leadership theory literature (Graen & Graen, this volume) I was challenged to try my hand at such an integration. Following is a description of my thinking.

New Multinational Network Sharing
pp. 197–209
Copyright © 2007 by Information Age Publishing
All rights of reproduction in any form reserved.

CONTINGENCY EFFECT OF NEEDS

Perhaps, the most convincing set of field experiments testing the moderating effect of growth need strength GNS, Hackman and Oldham (1976), was reported by Graen and his colleagues (Graen, Novak, & Sommerkamp, 1982; Graen, Scandura, & Graen, 1986). In these studies, they found that training managers in the theory and methods of LMX and then having the managers make LMX improvement offers to each of their subordinates produced hard performance improvements over time by their subordinates that were moderated dramatically as predicted by growth need strength (Hackman's measure). These improvements were found for the LMX trained manager's people, but not for those whose manager was trained in leadership "management by objectives" (MBO).

These findings were replicated in a follow-on field experiment that trained the former control group of managers in LMX theory and methods (new experimental group). This experiment showed that subsequent performance improvements by technicians reporting to the new LMX trained managers were again moderated by GNS, but not for the new control group technicians. In both field experiments, the top one-third of the LMX trained manager's technicians improve their average performance over 6 months by 50% compared to the lower two-thirds on GNS.

As shown in Figure 10.1, Graen and his doctoral students' field experiments at the IRS are diagrammed in terms of the experimental (LMX

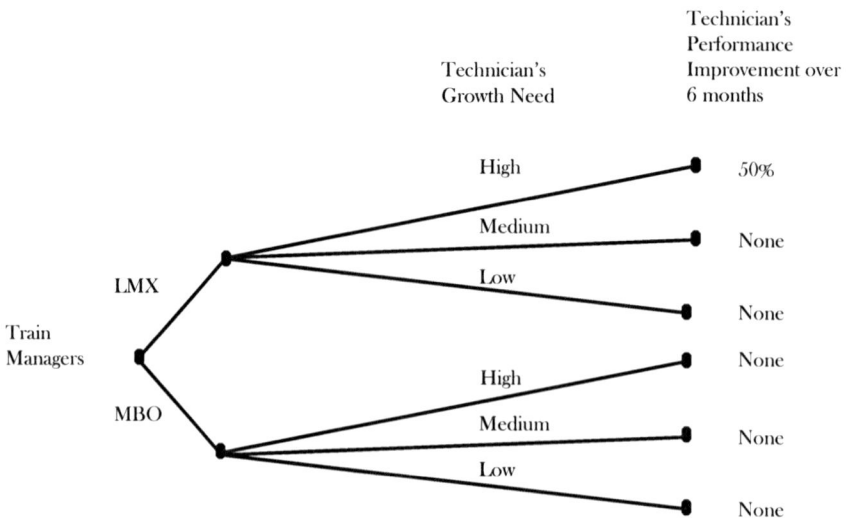

Figure 10.1.   Graen's replicated experimental findings.

training) and control (MOB training) of managers, GNS of subordinates, (top, middle, bottom third) and subsequent performance gain from before to after the interview. Hackman stated that this was the best demonstration of his fundamental model of new job enrichment opportunities moderated by GNS producing gains in job performance (Hackman & Oldham, 1976) and others agree with Hackman's assessment (Gerstner & Day, 1997).

As can be seen in Figure 10.1, beginning at the left, managers were randomly assigned to the experimental group or the control group. Those in the experimental group were given 6 days of LMX leadership training over 6 weeks (1 day a week) and those in the control group were given 6 days of MBO leadership training over 6 weeks. After the training the managers met with each of their subordinates for at least 30 minutes to offer them new LMX opportunities or not. The results in terms of computer generated productivity gains showed that the highest third on GNS in the experimental condition improved their performance significantly more than all of the other five groups. The results were precisely as Hackman's Job Characteristics Model (JCM) predicted. Only those extremely high on growth needs accepted the offer of their LMX leadership trained manager and were motivated enough to improve their performance. These results also were compatible with Graen's leader-member exchange (LMX) model (Graen, 2003). Clearly, when an LMX leadership trained manager makes an offer to improve their working relationship, those with strong growth needs, good relational skills, relevant knowledge and skill, and not satisfied with the content of the job would be expected to accept the offer. This experiment only considered GNS, but the accepters of the challenge were probably favorable also on one or more of the other three proposed antecedents.

The finding that only the top third was receptive to the offer was confirmed in a replication experiment a year later in the same computer processing organization that again studied the same departments of computer technicians. This cutoff score of the top one third on GNS would likely vary by occupation with the more highly educated ones producing larger percentages of LMX offer accepters. In young management samples 50% and over are expected to accept. It seems unreasonable that employees would not accept LMX leadership offers, but they don't. In the above studies two thirds rejected the offer based on their performance improvement. All employees received the offer using a trained script, but many "prefer to only do my job." This is self-selection by the employees and their legal right. Of course in the ongoing organizations, managers also may select who is given the LMX leadership offer. Although we know that 100% acceptance is the optimal, we seldom find it (Graen, Hui, & Taylor, 2006).

Although we feel quite confident in the GNS moderating effect on LMX leadership development, we need to test the other theoretical moderators. Clearly, accepting the LMX offer requires that the follower be in a position to survive the developmental process and become mature partners. Other moderators of getting and accepting the LMX offer found in research are expected mutual respect, trust and commitment with the leader (Graen, 2006). This discussion emphasizes the preconditions for subordinate accepting the LMX offer that normally are estimated by the leader before making the offer (Graen, 2006). Sometimes, the subordinate can successfully influence an offer from a reluctant manager and make the process work. This case will be discussed later.

ROLE ENHANCEMENT UNDER STRESS

Another series of three field simulations addressed the question of role making in response to fear of team failure and was reported by Graen and his colleagues (Graen, Hui & Taylor, 2004, 2006). These studies are described in Figure 10.2. As shown, team leaders under fear of team failure either challenged their team to do the new role making needed for their team to succeed or did not. Those team members who accepted their leader's challenge improve their roles and their teams' overall performance. In these studies LMX leadership behavior was moderated by team LMX on team performance and team processing effectiveness.

In the above studies, teams of three engineers with a designated project leader were organized into project teams and given design projects to be completed in six months. The deadline was not flexible. Measurements were taken three times during the six month period. About 40 teams were involved in each of the three studies (120 teams total). Results of all three studies showed the same findings. For those teams whose leader challenged them at the choice point to reorganize, the stronger the LMX and MMX, the more successful the teams were in terms of both team outcome and final process. For these teams, outcomes were predicted equally well by all three team LMX (looking up and looking down) and MMX (peer). In all cases, the stronger the LMX or MMX the better the team outcomes. It should be noted that the original study of these project teams was thus formally replicated twice in subsequent years.

These findings support the integrated LMX-JCM model in that role making is an informal job enrichment process through using leadership sharing and support. For teams the more acting leaders the better, In project teams, the teammates typically take too much time planning and leave too little time for executing the plan. With a fixed deadline, they know that they will not meet the deadline with a good product. Thus, they

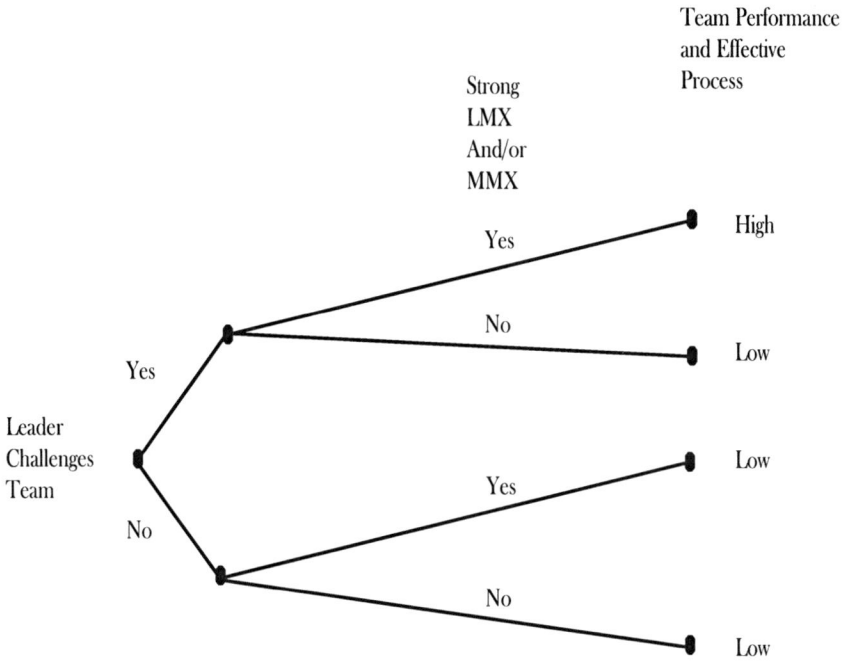

Figure 10.2.   Graen, Hui, and Taylor (2006) replicated findings.

expect team failure, unless their roles are changed. If the leader challenges teammates (an act of leadership) and they accept (result of leadership) the role making, they are likely to succeed as a team.

Informal roles can be changed as carefully planned team building through gradual LMX leadership development or as a team scrambling through emotional challenges to overcome unforeseen threats. Moreover, informal roles can be changed by initial efforts of nonleaders on the team in both of the above manners.

Finally, for those members who persist in their LMX process create more valuable human assets for the team and improved team performance, process, and reactions on the job. LMX leaders or MMX members do not treat these antecedents as mutually exclusive and choose based on some combination of desirable attributes. The first two are usually sought, but others may be included as well. All should be given some consideration. Overall, this should be a model of do-it-yourself (DIY) total network enhancement containing enriched job components, networks and leadership sharing by LMX leaders, improved self-efficacy due to learning, and rewards to the more intrinsic (content) seeker.

Antecedents ⟶	Process ⟶	Outcomes*
What LMX	**LMX &/or**	
Leader	**MMX**	**For LMX**
Looks For	**Seeks**	
		Leadership
GNS ...	**Highest**	**Growth**	**Sharing**
Relational			**Network**
Skills ...	**High**	**Negotiate**	**Development**
Knowledge &			**Enhancement**
Skills ...	**High**	**Learning**	**K & S**
Content			**Improved**
Satisfaction ...	**Low**	**Enrichment**	**Content**

Note: *Organizational outcomes are improved performance, process, and reations.

Figure 10.3.   Integrated model of LMX and MMX and JCM.

R.I.P. JOB ENRICHMENT

My personal theory about the cooling of interest in the job enrichment movement is that it did not take into account the existing LMX structures in theory and simply ignored them in practice. Without building a new LMX structure, enrichments in employee's formal jobs, as defined by Hackman's JCM, cannot survive over time due to supervisory resistance. Also, many job enrichment attempts were based on unrealistic cost cutting assumptions by management, such that, increased responsibilities in the name of job enrichment did not need to be fairly compensated at any time by the organization. Clearly, a formal program of job enrichment in terms of increased responsibilities make the implicit promise of forthcoming fair compensation. The trade-off of intrinsic satisfaction on the job for pay is a cruel myth and grossly unfair. Those fooled by this assumption of forthcoming reward felt cheated by their organization (Graen, 1966a, 1966b, 1968, 1969, 1970).

Post mortems of failed job enrichment attempts revealed that it was like dropping an 800 pound gorilla into a pool of water, you witness a huge splash and turbulent water, but after the gorilla leaves the pool nothing has been changed, because water seeks its own level. Job enrichment programs were based on several faculty assumptions: (1) Every employee wants a more enriched job; (2) More interesting and challenging work itself can be traded off for fair pay; (3) Present LMX and MMX structures and functions will support the job enrichment program whole heartedly, even when the new responsibilities and authority impoverish the supervisors; (4) The job enrichment program will lower labor costs by increasing productivity and reducing total pay. Unfortunately, none of these assumptions were ever tested and only questioned during post mortems. Let us not repeat our historic mistakes.

LMX leadership makes it transparent that those members who take on greater responsibility will receive greater compensation in the form of bonuses, stock options, faster promotions, sabbaticals and the like. Only a foolish leader would attempt to cheat their critical followers. LMX leadership must be built on a firm foundation of mutual trust, respect and commitment to the relationship. Incidentally, it's okay for LMX leaders to remind even their mature partners that in the final analysis they are most formally accountable to the team upstairs. But for a leader to become an autocratic commander is poison to strong LMX and MMX relationships.

SUGGESTED INTEGRATIVE MODEL

My integrated model is shown in Figure 10.3. As can be seen, antecedents lead to process that subsequently lead to outcomes for both followers and leaders. Three of my antecedents are from Hackman's JCM model (Hackman & Oldham, 1976, 1980) and one (Relational Skills) is from the LMX leadership model (Graen, 2003). As shown, LMX leaders look for these individual differences in their subordinates and seek those with the target values. For GNS, they seek the highest, for relation skills, and knowledge and skill, they seek high values, but for content satisfaction they seek low values. Once invited by the LMX leader or MMX colleague to begin the process, those with enough confidence are likely to accept. The content enriched differs depending on the attribute. Those with highest growth need strength, experience a professional growth process with their leader. Those with high relational skills undertake a negotiating practicum with their leader and those with job knowledge and skills take on advanced courses of study sponsored by their leader. Finally, the low content (Hackman used context) satisfaction followers undergo an enrichment of their job content.

Expanded Integration

Going beyond the integrated model, I suggest a few additional moderators. In general, any variable that can reasonable be advanced as one that would convince a potential follower to accept an LMX or MMX offer could be a moderator between accepting the performance augmenting offer or not. Variables suggested for this would include clear as opposed to ambiguous self-concept (Shamir, House, & Arthur, 1993), optimism (Graen, 1989) of both leader and follower, and risk taker, romantic and type A personality, (Graen, 2003). Those who refuse such an LMX offer take themselves out of the possibility of a faster track career with the present train engineer. The main difference between accepting an LMX offer and reacting favorably to an imposed job enrichment are that (1) Your supervisor must support his/her LMX offer but may not impact an outside supplier of job enrichment, and (2) The job incumbent has a choice with the LMX offer, but not with the enriched job.

Prerequisites for Role Making

According to this integration of JCM and LMX leadership theory, each team member can have different needs, skills and job attitudes. These member characteristics must be understood by the team leader so as not to reward with "A" while member needs to be rewarded by "B". This is the first rule of LMX leadership, *Understand the individual differences of team members and give them the opportunity to fulfill their dreams by putting the team first and their needs second and fulfilling both the first and the second* (Graen, 1989). If one of your followers needs professional growth above all, provide ways to grow. If another of your followers needs to exercise his/her relational skills, give him/her opportunities to negotiate for the team with the networks. For those who desire advanced technical expertise above all else, provide the training opportunities. Finally, for those who seek content satisfaction, meaningful job enrichment would be appropriate. However, there is no free lunch.

The second rule of LMX leadership is, *Establish contingencies for need fulfillment carefully and make them flexible but predictable* (Graen, 1968). When contingencies are changed frequently, they become random and meaningless as motivational incentives. The third rule of LMX leadership is, *Allow team members to engage in authentic role making as long as they are trusted and making progress toward paying their way on the team* (Graen, in press). The team members as well as their leader are involved in role making at the same time. If a member has cheated the team by playing games for personal advantage, the team members as well as the team leader have been cheated. However, if a member just cannot complete the climb to mature partner, they are not punished but respected for attempting to climb to the top of the mountain. As long as the member who failed had a responsible chance to succeed and failed through no lack of effort, the member is valued and the team eats the costs.

The fourth rule of LMX leadership is, *Ensure that those on the team who climb to the top of the mountain and share leadership with the formal leader be properly acknowledged formally by promotion, visibility upstairs, and overall upward mobility*. This point was discussed above in terms of fairness.

The fifth rule of LMX leadership is, *Make certain that the shared leadership to the top of the mountain are themselves valued instruments of career progress*. This means leadership sharing for the future leaders, network development and maintenance for the future executive coordinators, relevant high tech training for the future gurus, and improved content for the future technology managers.

The sixth rule of LMX leadership is, *Role making is a reciprocal process that can be initiated by any team member and offered to the team leader*. A parallel process such as the one presented in Figure 10.3, applies to the member. Prospective team members should consider their own needs, knowledge and skills, and job attitudes and assess their chances that the team leader will deliver. If the offer is accepted the process can unfold much like the one that the leader initiated, but more of the burden of keeping the process going until completion rests with the member.

The seventh rule of LMX leadership is, *Make every feasible effort to develop mature partners of all team members and encourage MMX leaderships within the team's networks*. Research suggests that the more strong LMXs and MMXs in a team the better for the team (Graen et al., 2006). Team leaders must make some early investments in developing team human assets but the payoffs can be most gratifying for the team when the storm hits.

Next, we turn to an exchange about fundamental questions concerning the construct of organizational leadership. Hackman and Wageman (2007) revisit the leadership issues that have not been answered by the "flash in the pan" that was called the job enrichment movement. They understand that established LMX leadership structures and processes do not take kindly to outside interference by job enrichment gurus who arbitrarily destroy the established reward structure of the team. In contrast, it looks favorably on team initiated improvements.

ASKING THE RIGHT QUESTIONS

Hackman and Wageman (2007) presented some new and insightful directions for leadership research. These new directions were stated by rejecting questions that have not been answered and probably cannot be and accepting new questions that should be addressed through research. This was accomplished economically by stating and discussing only five questions. We welcome Hackman and Wageman's (2007) new directions for leadership research as a sign that leadership can be understood by researching when, where, and how it is activated and makes a difference in team performance and process effectiveness (Graen, Hui, Taylor, 2006). However, we think that Hackman and Wageman (2007) understate the changes of direction needed to extract useful leadership models from the huge and tangled morass of pedestrian thinking in which it's covered.

Hackman and Wageman organize their article around their five reject-accept questions suggesting new directions. We shall discuss how each of the questions appears far too timid for real progress in sorting out the chaff from the grain. In fairness, we point out that the critiqued article was a critique of five companion articles in the issue and made a substantial contribution to the literature.

Question 1: "Not do leaders make a difference, but under what conditions does leadership matter?" We would state this as a larger new direction question: In what contexts (C) do actors (team leader's, team member's and relevant network member's characteristics (A), and behaviors (B) matter? The difference between these two questions, we think, is that the former underspecified the inclusiveness of the emergent leadership processes. Our new model of *Sharing Network Leadership* (Graen & Graen, 2006) and *New Multinational Network Sharing* (Graen & Graen, this volume) avoid the "leader attribution error" by focusing on all relevant actors, behaviors, and contexts in predicting and understanding team and network performance and process effectiveness.

Question 2: "Not what are the traits of leaders, but how do leader's personal attributes interact with situational properties to shape outcomes?" We would restate this question as: How do the actors' characteristics and behavior interact over time with context variables? Again the focus should be expanded to include the relevant set of actor, behaviors, contexts, and not focused on one actor's attributes. Clearly, leaders must be defined by their convincing others to follow them until some goal is reached or mission concluded, but not by the attainment of a particular position in an organization.

Question 3: "Not do there exist common dimensions on which all leaders can be arrayed, but are good and poor leaders qualitatively different phenomena?" We would restate this as: What set of actors, behavior and contexts lead to the most effective team and network outcomes? We feel that there are too many arrangements of A, B, Cs for failure in complex and dynamic leadership relevant problem scenarios to learn very much from failures compared to what we can learn from successive partial successes (small wins).

Question #4: "Not how leaders and followers differ, but how can leadership models be reframed so they treat all systems members as both leaders and followers?" We would prefer this question be: How can leadership models be framed to include all system members as leaders and followers who share network leadership within the proper contexts and involve the appropriate behavior to achieve team and network performance and process effectiveness. Our two volumes on this question present both the genotypical and phenotypical versions (Graen & Graen, 2006, and this volume). Clearly, all system members act, react, and double interact, and the dynamics of this process are well understood but tragically avoided for deepseated psychological reasons by many Western and Eastern managers.

Question 5: "Not what should be taught in leadership courses, but how can leaders be helped to learn?" We would prefer that the question read: How can all system members be helped to learn when, where and how leadership intervention may be useful and at what cost? The functional approach to team and network performance and process effectiveness goes far beyond the romance of the great personality and its simplistic "holy grail" of leader as superman or superwoman. Clearly, leader "wannabes" can't learn their craft alone in front of a mirror, but they must learn to live authentically in the world of systems with actors, behaviors, and contexts. Only over time, in both crisis and calm can one learn the ABCs of that emergent phenomena we label "leadership" when a more descriptive but less sexy construct is informal team or network cooperation. An example of this training is described by Graen, Hui, and Taylor (2006) and suggested by Hackman and O'Connor (2004).

CONCLUSIONS

In the last 5 years, LMX leadership has been integrated with a large number of different areas of research that were once seen as independent via *LMX Leadership: The Series*. We continue this tradition by attempting to integrate LMX with JCM. We acknowledge the masterful work of the JCM experts and put forth our suggested model which has some strong research support. Also, we suggested some new research questions about the construct of leadership based on the University of Illinois "functional" approach.

REFERENCES

Gerstner, C. R., & Day, D. V. (1997). A meta-analytic review of the leader-member exchange literature: Correlates and construct issues. *Journal of Applied Psychology, 82,* 827-844.

Graen, G. B. (1966a). Motivator and hygiene dimensions for research and development engineers. *Journal of Applied Psychology, 50*, 563-566.

Graen, G. B. (1966b). Addendum to "An empirical test of the Herzberg two-factor theory." *Journal of Applied Psychology, 50*, 551-555.

Graen, G. B. (1968). *Approach for testing multiple hypotheses concerning the motivational effects of work role treatments on managerial behaviors.* James McKeen Cattell Award Winner, American Psychological Association, Division of Industrial and Organizational Psychology.

Graen, G. B. (1969). Instrumentality theory of work motivation: Some experimental results and suggested modifications [Whole issue]. *Journal of Applied Psychology Monograph, 53* (2, Part 2).

Graen, G. B. (1970). Review of Robert N. Ford, *Motivation through the work itself. Contemporary Psychology, 15*, 291-294.

Graen, G. B. (1989). *Unwritten rules for your career: 15 secrets for fast-track success.* New York: Wiley.

Graen, G. B. (Ed.). (2003). Interpersonal workplace theory at the crossroads: LMX and Transformational theory as special cases of role making in work organizations. In *LMX leadership: The series: Vol. 1. Dealing with diversity* (pp. 145-182). Greenwich, CT: Information Age.

Graen, G. B. (Ed.). (2006). To share or not to share leadership: New LMX-MMX network leadership or charismatic leadership on creative projects. In *LMX leadership: The series: Vol. 4. Sharing network leadership* (pp. 25-36). Greenwich, CT: Information Age.

Graen, G. B. (in press). Letter to the editor. *Academy of Management Perspectives.*

Graen, G. B., & Graen, J. A. (Eds.). (2006). *LMX leadership: The series: Vol. 4. Sharing network leadership.* Greenwich, CT: Information Age.

Graen, G. B., Hui, C., & Taylor, E. A. (2004). A new approach to team leadership: Upward, downward, and horizontal differentiation. In G. B. Graen (Ed.), *LMX leadership: The series: Vol. 2. New frontiers of leadership* (pp. 33-66). Greenwich, CT: Information Age.

Graen, G. B., Hui, C., & Taylor, E. A. (2006). Experience-based learning about LMX leadership and fairness in project teams: A dyadic directional approach. *Academy of Management Learning and Education, 5*(4), 448-460.

Graen, G. B., Novak, M., & Sommerkamp, P. (1982). The effects of leader-member exchange and job design on productivity and satisfaction: Testing a dual attachment model. *Organizational Behavior and Human Performance, 30*, 109-131.

Graen, G. B., Scandura, T., & Graen, M. R. (1986). A field experimental test of the moderating effects of growth need strength on productivity. *Journal of Applied Psychology, 71*, 484-491.

Hackman, J. R., & O'Connor, M. (2004). *What makes a great analytic team?* Washington, DC: CIA.

Hackman, J. R., & Oldham, G. R. (1976). Motivation through the design of work: Test of a theory. *Organizational Behavior and Human Performance, 16*, 250-279.

Hackman, J. R., & Oldham, G. R. (1980). *Work redesign.* Reading, MA: Addison-Wesley.

Hackman, J. R., & Wageman, R. (2007). Asking the right questions about leadership. *American Psychologist, 62*, 1, 43-47.

Shamir, B., House, R. J., & Arthur, M. B. (1993). The motivational effects of charismatic leadership: A self-concept based theory. *Organization Science, 4*, 577-594.

CHAPTER 11

EMERGING INTEGRATION OF ORGANIZATIONAL LEADERSHIP

Summary and Conclusions

George B. Graen

The mission of this book is to suggest ways that leadership researchers may understand the conditions that lead to changes in functions, such as, cycles of tactical failures creating operational problems contributing to strategy changes with testing at all three parts from microleadership to mesoleadership to macroleadership (induction) or the reverse (deduction). These cycles travel through particular overlapping networks of communications and leadership and are beginning to be investigated in both the People's Republic of China and the United States. Such new research is refreshing in our information age. The many contributions of the various chapters are outlined in terms of the various levels of an overall approach to efficiently identifying and understanding these network cycles. Finally, suggestions are made for future research using our new multinational leadership sharing (Marion & Uhl-Bien, 2001).

New Multinational Network Sharing
pp. 211–229
Copyright © 2007 by Information Age Publishing
All rights of reproduction in any form reserved.

INTRODUCTION

Gelfand, Erez, and Aycan (2007), suggest five new directions for research on cross-national issues: (1) Studies similar to our investigation of Chinese managers reporting to Western bosses in Shanghai; (2) Studies of historical theories of leadership such as those by Chen and Lee's (2007) on Chinese leadership theories from Confucius to Farh; (3) Studies of cross-cultural conflict resolution such as the studies of Cheng, Tjosvold, and Peng (this volume); (4) Studies using hierarchical methods such as Graen and Lau's (2005); and (5) Studies seeking cultural similarities and differences using cooperative methods such as Tjosvold and Van Kippenberg's (2007). These five new directions should serve to expand our often one-note approach to our world song. Clearly, our focus on the individualism—collectivism dimension(s) of cultures hides a multitude of different deep-level variables such as past history and current circumstance. Acceptance of such surface-level concepts leads to national stereotypes and caricatures that insult one's cross-cultural intelligence (Graen, 2006a). These five suggestions for research have already begun to be implemented by innovating organizations and researchers. Now, we should set our sights much higher. The field is ready for a great leap forward to integrating the two disciplines of management research. To this higher purpose we dedicate this book.

My goal for this volume of *LMX Leadership: The Series* is to enhance the acceleration of the field of management of organizations toward more useful emergent integration of the three functional approaches: top-down (macro approach), bottom-up (micro approach) and connecting top-down to bottom-up (meso approach). My objective is to help understand how the three approaches are connected via overlapping informal communications networks. What are needed are functional investigations of the connections between networks to permit the process of integration to advance.

A POSSIBLE INTEGRATION OF TWO DISCIPLINES

Organizational theory and organizational behavior are at a crossroads. Each must choose between (a) remaining in its parallel universe within business schools and (b) seeking an integration of the complementary strengths of each for the benefit of greater understanding of the human side of organizations.

Clearly during my two-score and 7 years of studying organizations and the individuals and groups within them (Graen, 2002), I have been repeatedly frustrated by the allegiance of researchers and scholars to their "schools" and their majors as doctoral students. The parallel worlds of organizational theory (macro) and organizational behavior (micro) have become dysfunctional in our attempts to unify our understanding and predict what goes on in organizations. We need to put away the toys of our youth and develop the new tools of our adulthood in terms of integrating our roots in sociology and psychology.

I may have a bias for this because my doctoral program at the University of Minnesota was split between organizational psychology and industrial sociology and at the University of Illinois, I worked with industrial/organizational psychologists, industrial sociologists, economists, and experts in communications and cultural studies. I also had the fortunate opportunity to be an exchange professor at Keio University in Tokyo for a year, a Fulbright professor at Nagoya University, Nagoya, Japan, and at the University of Science and Technology in Hong Kong and a Fulbright researcher at Chinese University of Hong Kong, Donghau University, Shanghai and Hangzhou, University, Hangzhou, China. My research partners in Japan first and then China gave me a deep appreciation for the larger multinational picture in organizational studies. Finally, my editing of *LMX Leadership: The Series* brought me into contact with some of the brightest minds in the larger field of management studies.

Over the past 50 years management research has morphed from describing surface-level formal organization and mechanistic organizational forms to analyzing deep-level processes such as role-making, sense-making and strategy-making. Clearly, architecture of the formal organization and its systems account for most organizational behavior under conditions of environmental calm, clarity, and certainty, but fails significantly when faced with turbulence, ambiguity, and uncertainty. What is emerging from this research is movement that suggests leadership should be trichotomized into macrostrategic leadership, mesostrategic leadership, and microstrategic leadership (Boal & Hooijberg, 2000).

When I was a university student in the 1950s, the leading business journals had long outgrown autobiographic stories of U.S. business heroes, had finished a brief infatuation with decision sciences, and were beginning a full-fledged affair with behavioral sciences. However, the behavioral sciences were forced by the retired business people into the so-called "functional areas of business" (FAB) such as, finance, strategy, supervision and management, human resources, marketing, production, engineering, and the like. Accordingly, the Academy of Management also was divided into FAB. What FAB did was to partition organizational problems and solutions into separate departments of schools and colleges of business. This partitioning allowed specialization but made little sense to Simon, March and later Weick (Graen, 2006b) who conceived of organizations as decision systems designed and implemented by humans with little regard for FAB. Today, their continued efforts have begun to yield converts to their more research-based approach to the field of organizations. As I read Simon, March, and Weick, even the organizational behavior of strategizing was part of a flow of behavior by human decision makers to detect, make sense out of and cope with events over time and space. They saw the same humans operating at many separate parts of many networks to energize the microsystems that were transformed into mesosystems that were converted into macrosystems or some other pattern. Humans employing technology, but following the general laws of the basic behavioral sciences, enact these emergent human networks to make sense of and adapt to environmental changes. We call these pragmatic action patterns "informal" because they fill in the gaps in the "formal" (written procedure).

Role-Making Processes

LMX Leadership: The Series (Graen, 2003, 2004, 2005; Graen & Graen, 2006, this volume) is focused on forwarding this view integrated with that of the formal legal view which assumes that organizations are legal entities that can contract for and command compliance to specific orderly human behavior. These entities are human inventions that must justify their existence by producing a product or service and can hire and compensate humans for outlined formal roles that encourage legal compliance with all written rules and procedures. Although lawyers love its perfectly defensible logic, it does not always predict human behavior when under stress. Because many formal plans are incomplete and inflexible, they become obsolete, even as general guides, and require unwritten human organizing to allow sense making, role making, and strategy making to survive.

Role-Making is Informal

According to this view (Graen, 1976, 1989), humans react in two very different ways to formal roles in organizations. Most people submit to "role-taking" (Katz & Kahn, 1978) in which humans accept all the formal rules and procedures for their jobs religiously. Other people enact Graen's "role-making" (1976) in which humans negotiate new and more open-ended rules and procedures for their jobs with significant others in their networks. Because the formal organization is a legal fiction designed to minimize exposure to any challenges or lawsuits first and foremost and organizational efficiency and effectiveness secondly, the threat of legal punishment for role-making is ever-present. However, market demands require that informal systems be developed and used to make organizations adapt to their environments. Thus, to make sense out of human systems, informal systems need to be understood along with the formal system demands factored into the equations. We need to focus on how the informal networks change the rules of the game for organizational members and change strategy, operations, and tactics.

Clearly, formal organization plans are incomplete as illustrated by the British labor unions tactic of "work to rule," by which union members only follow the written (formal) rules and take no informal action. Without needed informal actions, their organizations slowly grind to a halt. Human's have limited rationality and cannot anticipate every contingency of an organization's future situation, thus their best formal plans for organizations need to be open to human sense making over time. We have too long been in denial about the necessity to understand organized and complex informal human network behavior.

When the norms of rationality hold, the bureaucracy model is reasonably descriptive, but when the conditions become highly ambiguous, the model must be enlarged to include network organizations such as Hewlett-Packard (Ouchi, 1978, 1980, 1981; Ouchi & Wilkins, 1978; Wilkins & Ouchi, 1983). Networks are organizational forms that emerge to penetrated dysfunctional organizational boundaries. Through networks the evolution of organizational forms seems to move from simple to more and more complex: macrostrategic leadership, mesostrategic leadership, and microstrategic leadership (Allison, 1969, 1971; Allison & Zelikow, 1999).

A Fruitful Beginning

Leader-member exchange theory (LMX) was recommended to guide research on the new overlapping networks model of leadership (Orton & Dhillon, 2006, p, 141).

> Fortunately, LMX theory is grounded in theories of enactment, in which leaders/managers and members jointly construct the environment to which they must then respond (Weick, 1979)—a process referred to by Graen and his colleagues as "role-making" (Uhl-Bien, Graen, & Scandura, 2000). Because LMX is grounded in enactment theories, it is better able than most theories of leadership to explain how leadership influences strategy, and how strategy influences leadership. Enactment theories explain how microstrategic actions shape the creation of portfolios of mesostrategic options, and how portfolios of mesostrategic options shape the creation of macrostrategic organizational directions (Mintzberg & McHugh, 1985). Enactment

theories also explain how integrated macrostrategic cultures can influence differentiated mesostrategic subcultures, and how differentiated mesostrategic subcultures can explain fragmented microstrategic individual networks (Martin, 1992; Meyerson, 2001; Meyerson & Martin, 1987). Recent developments in LMX theory show that "scalability," or the ability to explain leadership phenomena at multiple levels of analysis, and the additional ability to explain interactions between those levels of analysis, are continuing advantages of LMX theory (Graen, 2004).

Orton and Weick (1990) make the distinction between "strong" leadership (Ouchi, 1980; Perrow, 1967; Peters & Waterman, 1982) and "subtle" leadership.

What is less well-developed is Orton and Weick's notion of "subtle" leadership. Although it is tempting to sort "strong leadership" into Graen's category of leadership and sort "subtle leadership" into Graen's category of "managership," a more accurate way to describe subtle leadership would be to connect it to the processes of role-making in which the manager builds social capital into the network one relationship at a time (Uhl-Bien, Graen, & Scandura, 2000). Orton and Weick described subtle leadership as the awareness of system fragmentation and a willingness to engage that fragmented system.

Other researchers have suggested that loose coupling calls for subtle leadership. For example, Boynton and Zmud (1987) counseled information systems professionals who, because of the dispersal of computer technology, will find themselves in more loosely coupled systems, to try "to simultaneously provide centralized direction and coordination while recognizing the value of increased discretion" (p. 62). Similarly, Weick (1982) counseled educational administrators to be more attentive to the "glue" that holds loosely coupled systems together: "Since channels are unpredictable, administrators must get out of the office and spend lots of time one-on-one—both to remind people of central visions and to assist them in applying these visions to their own activities" (p. 676). Therefore, this one-on-one or subtle leadership implies sensitivity to diverse system components (Kaplan, 1982) and the ability to control systems through conversation (Gronn, 1983). (Orton & Dhillon, 2006, p. 146)

MACROSTRATEGIC LEADERSHIP, MICROSTRATEGIC LEADERSHIP, AND MESOSTRATEGIC LEADERSHIP

The Honda case study described over a 20-year period how Honda motorcycle company launched a U.S. subsidiary that dominated the U.S. market and drove out the European competitors. Only Harley-Davidson who found a nostalgia niché for its old technology machines survived and prospered among U.S. manufacturers.

Honda D

The Boston Consulting Group (BGC, 1975) analysis of this success concluded that the Japanese manufacturers lead by Honda Motors had a three-legged strategy: (1) build market share, (2) maximize production, and (3) benefit from economies of both scale and scope (BCG, 1975). This was Honda A. In contrast, Honda B, emphasized microstrategic leadership of successive approximation to cope with a series of found choices (Pascale, 1984). Later came Honda C by Rumelt (1996) that emphasized a mesostrategic leadership explanation. Graen prefers an integration of all three types of leadership for Honda D. In his studies of the Toyota system in Japan, Australia, China, and North American, Graen and Wakabayashi find that the system is pragmatic and seeks solutions to problems through continuous and discrete improvements at all levels and all functions (Graen & Wakabayashi, 1994; Graen, Dharwadkar, Grewal, & Wakabayashi, 2006).

According to Graen's Honda D, executives at Honda decided to enter the U.S. market with their motorcycles that were dominant in Japan and Asia. They carefully launched a small exploratory presence in the United States and proceeded by trial and error and sense making to discover how to enter the U.S. market. Following their microstrategic leadership orientation to be pragmatic and take what is given, they were more welcome in Los Angles, had fewer problems with their smaller bikes, and found a ready demand for their high technology small bikes. U.S. consumers for motorcycles wanted toys that could go off-road and handle well and perform reliably in races on both tracks and highways. The Hell's Angels or Harley images did not accept "rice burners." In North America, real men wanted the "wild one" Brando and Fonda image, but in the United States Honda found the younger generation of racers who preferred the newer, faster, and more maneuverable, forgiving, and reliable Japanese bikes. Honda proceeded from microstrategic leadership to mesostrategic leadership, and finally, to macrostrategic leadership. The BCG's reconstruction of Honda's outstanding success in the United States was overdetermined by its focus on formal organization and MBA-type analysis. The mesostrategic leadership view of putting what worked into operations was overlooked as was the microstrategic leadership perspective of problem finding, alternative generation, and solution making (Graen, 1989).

The Toyota systems as understood by the Japanese executives are based on all three levels of strategic leadership. After a system is created and functioning properly, the Toyota way prescribes an over arching search for continuous and discrete improvement of all systems to create the better way. This typically starts with microstrategic leadership finding a problem with the current system. This leads to microlevel problem-solving attempts. When a successful modification cannot be found the mesostrategic leadership steps in to problem solve and challenge operations to changes in the design. When changes lead to macrostrategic problems, this level must take action (induction). The changed macrostrategy also will lead to mesostrategic changes and these to microstrategic changes (deductive).

In sum, the conception of formal organizations designed by genius engineers to be operated by average people doesn't describe competitive organizations. Organizations that must adapt to survive and prosper must be superior to their competition. As I jokingly tell my scuba students on shark dives, you do not need to swim faster than the great white, you only need to swim faster than your buddy.

Clearly, we need to use this integration of macro-, meso-, and microstrategic leadership to force a shot-gun marriage of organizational theory and organizational behavior. As we see it, they have been living in sin for some time now and we would like to perform the ceremony with the children called role-making and role-taking, bounded rationality, sense-making, continuous improvement, and the unnamed others present.

Our studies in mainland China support the trichotomized overlapping network model of strategic leadership in terms of the Sino-foreign ventures and the new private China ventures (Graen, Hui, & Gu, 2005). Shanghai is the growing tip of postmodern China and our studies of the new organizational forms show the emergence of the trichotomized model in new private companies. China has become the manufacturing capital of the world and it likely will be so for decades, if not centuries. She has more than her share of huge problems, such as over a hundred unique cultures demanding to be heard and about 1.3 billion people to support, a government that ignores the fact that all capitalistic activity is against the obsolete communist law, festering inequalities of opportunity and wealth, and a provincial versus central government struggling for political power to name a few. China also will be the research bed for the new theory of trichotomized strategic leadership. It is becoming the new test-bed of organizational studies (Tjosvold & Leung, 2004).

A NEW APPROACH

Orton and Dhillon (2006, p. 160) state the case for integration clearly:

> In conclusion, we think that LMX theory, because of its roots in enactment research and "role-making," is well-positioned to attack the following three projects that we believe are necessary for the useful and emerging field of

strategic leadership (Boal & Hooijberg, 2000): (1) help transform the leadership research from its outdated roots in command-and-control bureaucracies from before World-War-II to a post-Simon-March-Weick environment of loosely coupled networks and schizoid incoherence; (2) get more involved in the project of mapping a shared repertoire of meso-strategic options that are generated and maintained by organizations, consulting firms, and academia; and (3) start asking questions about the interaction of generic macro-strategies, meso-strategic options, and micro-strategic actions over time. We hope that our notes here are a small win that can help LMX research and strategic leadership research move in a sensible direction (Weick, 1982).

We are flattered by such an assignment, but we are ready and willing to answer the plea of Orton and Dhillon. We implore with our colleagues to leave the safe ports of organizational theory and organizational behavior and join with other members of the Society of Organizing Brothers and Sisters (SOB) and cooperate to attach the emerging field of strategic leadership from micro to meso to macro functions and processes.

A key process in the creation and operation of the overlapping networks sharing model of organization is relational leadership that is defined as an emergent social influence process that can be instrumental in fostering emergent coordination and emergent change. It is not an entity, but temporal evaluations of it (LMX & MMX) can be treated as relative states of the process as can shared network leadership. In this definition, **LMX or MMX specifies the magnitude of readiness for sharing network leadership**. The magnitude of shared network leadership (SNL) is a measure of relational leadership potential for coordination and change. These dyadic measures can be summed to meaningful collectivity levels and used to understand and predict collectivity outcomes (see Graen, Hui, & Taylor, 2006). SNL at any level of collectivity only can be a contributing condition to coordination and change outcomes and it can be used for good or ill from various perspectives. For example, it can grow some parts of an organization and sell other parts as in Kodak today. Shared informal communications networks function similarly as shared friendship networks, shared ethnic networks, and nationality networks.

CONTRIBUTIONS

Informal communications networks in new organizations usually are formed based on need-to-know considerations and gradually opened through validated working relations with individuals from different reference groups. Once opened for information, influence follows and may create new subnetworks that cut across friendship, ethnic, and national differences. Information is the key and trust, respect and commitment are necessary conditions for SNL.

Research suggests that our genotypic model of these processes works similarly in the vastly different national cultures of China, America, and Japan, although the phenotypic models many be quite different (Graen, 2006a). In this book, we describe both the genotype model (chapter 1) and the phenotypic model (chapter 2). Next, in chapter three, we discussed the need for and successful application of cooperative conflict methods to find a better "third way" to "True Cultural Bonding" TCB between Easterners and Westerners. The extensive and intensive research of Tjosvold and his associates provide massive evidence that two very different national cultures do not prevent the finding of a better third way and True Cultural Bonding.

The important intervention clearly is the training to employ the "cooperative frame" approach (CFA) to identifying and reducing or resolving conflict and to stay away from the "competitive frame" or the "denial/avoidance frame." In chapter 2, we present a set of conflicts between Western managers and their Chinese managers who reported directly to them. Although the Chinese MBA students were reluctant to complain about their Western bosses, they relented under the patient encouragement of their major professor. Once they trusted the American researcher, they described the many organizational practices and bosses behaviors that made them feel like audience and not players. They said that they feared being labeled as "job hoppers," but as audience members they would not grow professionally and not be promoted to more responsible positions. They prayed for the use of the cooperative frame between them and their Western bosses. Failing this they were forced to change companies and accept the pain of moving. Also in chapter 2, we describe briefly some of the major Chinese leadership theories and schools. Do to the tremendous demand in China for young Chinese managers and technicians, the cooperative frame approach (CFA) should be used routinely in multinational ventures in China. Those employing the CFA should be trained to understand that its use is only an intervention in an ongoing process of organizing networks and producing new true cultural bonding opportunities. After the new, more multinational friendly processes have been put into operation, employees must test them to determine to what extent they allow multinational network leadership sharing.

Our experience in China suggests that these cooperative frame programs should be instituted from the top down and backed by top down oversight. It is too easy for Western managers to avoid the work of authentic cooperative framework programs with their Chinese subordinates. Unfortunately, many follow the path of least resistance and increase the costs of turnover.

Wing Lam's piece on understanding how you are coming across to your boss alerts the reader to an important contributor to the emergent process of sharing network leadership. If you go to your boss for information and advice to improve your performance, you must be careful that your motives are in line and honest. Otherwise, you may be damaging your objective every time you ask your boss. When the boss attributes your apparent improvement seeking as driven by a motive of presentation, it insults the boss' intelligence that he/she was naive enough to be fooled. Clearly, the search for performance and self-improvement using your boss requires the attribution of compatible motives by the boss. This model also applies to team leaders who ask their members for augmented commitment to their team's mission. If members attribute these requests as driven by the leader's self-servicing motives, poorer relations will result between leader and members. Members also do not like to be played for fools by their team leaders. The genotype of this works similarly in both China and America.

Along these lines of the moderating effect of LMX, a recent study by Sparrow, Soetjipto, and Kraimer (2006) found that a leader's influence strategies with followers helping the team depended on their LMX relationship: (1) Frequency of inspirational lectures had a negative relationship with helping their coworkers (extra role behavior) for weak LMX and none for strong LMX, (2) Frequency of consultative sessions had a positive relationship with helping behavior for weak LMX and none for strong LMX, and (3) Frequencies of promised contingent rewards had a positive relationship for strong LMX and a negative relationship for weak LMX. Moreover, without the influence of LMX as a moderator, none of these three influence strategies worked. Without a strong LMX relationship, a supervisor's influence attempts to get a subordinate to help peers were either ignored or produced the opposite result. This study and the one by Wang and his associates (Wang, Law, Hackett, Wang, & Chen (2004) support again the primacy of LMX before leader behavior to influence followers has any positive contribution. A two-filter process model incorporating the above findings is presented in Figure 11.1.

Returning to a focus on China, Chen and Lam in chapter four review the research on LMX leadership theory done in China with domestic employees. They find that the LMX theory works for the Chinese at least at the genotypic level. The particular behaviors involved for both leader and member have yet to be specified, but we know that the Chinese LMX (CLMX) measure predicts performance and citizenship behavior (Hackett, Farh, Song, & Lapierre, 2003). The extent that leader and member

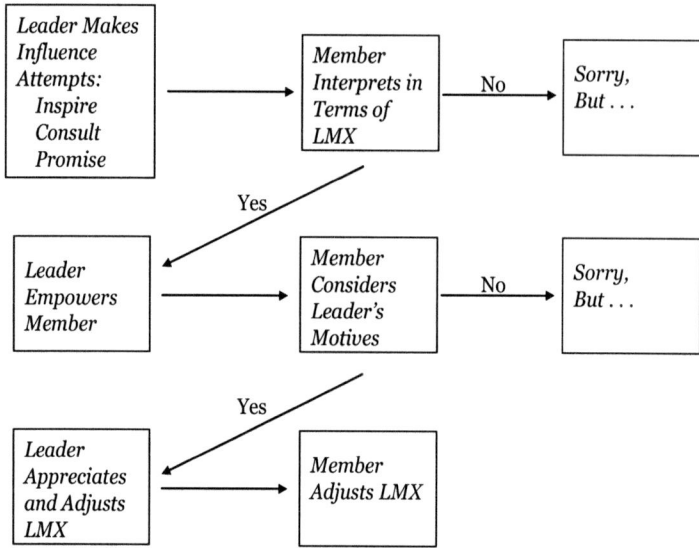

Figure 11.1.   Two-filter model of member compliance to extrarole requests.

engage in leadership sharing or network sharing needs to be researched in China.

Chen and Lam also share something about what it feels like to be raised in mainland China during the last 30 years or so after the death of Chairman Mao. They represent the generation of Chinese yuppies (young, urban professionals) from coastal China. Clearly, these yuppies will become quite rich and form the new middle class.

In their chapter, Wang, Liu and Law develop a new measure of Chinese LMX (CLMX) based on Chinese employee's experiences in modern Chinese companies. Although they explored some characteristically Chinese content dimensions along with some bicultural content dimensions, those uniquely Chinese turn out not to be validly related to performance outcomes. But, the Sino-American dimensions were valid correlates. This supports the content similarity of the LMX content for the American-developed LMX-7 and Wang and associates' (2004) CLMX.

Also along this same theme, Scherbaum, Naidoo, and Ferreter apply the latest psychometric analysis techniques to a new measure of team LMX called LMX-SLX (sharing leadership exchange). They conclude that the items of LMX-SLX are properly sensitive and differentiating as were those of a parallel measure called LMX-MDM. These authors are continuing they psychometrix analysis of LMX-SLX relating to predictive validity of the items using item response theory (IRT) that will be reported in volume 6 of this series.

A successful way to innovate business relations augmented by new technology was described in detail by Michael Graen's Creation of Wal-Mart team of Procter & Gamble. By employing the latest information technology, a cooperative framework on both sides, and support from the top-down, P&G and Wal-Mart developed new long-term relations that are the envy of manufacturers and retailers worldwide. Although the process of creating a new set of relations between giant corporations takes time and active cooperation, the transformed interface is seen as well worth the costs. Moreover, once this new cooperative network emerged, many innovations implementing new technology was feasible as described by a key team member. This chapter should be studied closely by those who seek to make a difference in their organization.

Finally, Fried, Levi and Laurence review the evidence of the job characteristic model (JCM) and develop an integration of it with the LMX leadership theory. The review is very comprehensive and exhaustive. They find support for the JCM. In addition, to this review they stimulated some previous thinking by Graen about the clear connection between JCM and the preconditions for LMX role making.

SHARING NETWORK LEADERSHIP MODEL

Based solidly on relational leadership research cited in our *LMX Leadership: The Series*, the new sharing network leadership (SNL) team plan is presented in outline form in seven steps as follows.

1. Team leader outlines the plan and asks for suggestions regarding all team missions and all members' contributions.
2. Team leader and members cooperatively develop contingency plans A, B, and C for team and network structure and processing.
3. Team leader and members carefully commit to sharing network leadership within and between other teams in networks.
4. Team leader and members share important networks.
5. Team leader and members negotiate cooperative role making adjustment to the plan as needed for sustainable excellence.
6. Team leader and members negotiate joint missions with other teams' members.
7. Overlapping networks move process from micro (immediate concern for people conflicts) to meso (design concern for operations

conflicts) to macro (planning concern with environmental compatibility of organization in the future).

As shown, the model begins at the micro level with actors in three different structural positions: team leader, team member, and relevant network member outside of the team. The first three steps involve only the team leader and the team members developing their plans for internal and external structure and functioning. At step four, the third set of actors are involved in developing and sharing networks. Based on the progress of step four, the team negotiates changes in missions and contributions needed to attain sustainable excellence. In steps five and six the teams negotiates compatible changes in within and between networks.

Finally, in step seven, the flows within the larger organization are from micro (people) to meso (operations) to macro (organization and environment). This plan promotes small and large changes to sustainable excellence and is incompatible with modern bureaucratic organizations. This model may also develop hardening of its arteries, but only after bureaucratic organizations are long extinct.

This SNL model of informal, continuously adaptable overlapping team organization is an emergent process model. It allows the formally structured organization to retain its illusion of stability and at the same time permits the informal organization to be adaptable to environmental changes. In this organization, lawyers can defend the fiction and employees can sail their ship through the stormy sea. This model of emergent organization requires top-down support to implement successfully. Necessary ingredients for a successful new multinational network sharing (NMNS) project are shown in Table 11.1.

Next we turn to an early business case of cooperation from the top-down of an American multinational young Chinese college graduates dur-

Table 11.1.   New Multinational Network Sharing Intervention

- Top-down support and participation.
- Incentives to encourage full cooperation.
- Procedure for correcting resistance to cooperation.
- Regular progress reports to top.
- Appointed project teams of most transcultural from all sides and relevant demographics.
- Local coaches for project teams.
- Appropriate budget and authority.
- Appeal process.
- Active support from all sides.
- Commitment of top management to long-term integration of venture into local culture.
- Sharing network leadership between cultures.
- Growing commitment to "The Third Way" for the entire venture to make all systems whether formal or informal work equally well for all sides.

**Table 11.2.   Criteria for Promotion of
Chinese Managers Judged Ability to do Success Action in the Future**

Success Actions
• Build the Business: Breakthrough results
• Leadership: Envision and energize change
• Risk Taking: Bias toward action
• Innovation: Leverage technology
• Problem Solving: Exploit opportunities
• Collaboration: Understand, discuss, and resolve impediments
• Mastery: Learn and share

ing the Deng era. Unfortunately this early success was not followed very well by later Sino-Western ventures in China resulting in many undocumented losses.

A Pioneer Venture

One of the first Western corporations recruiting Chinese college graduates after Deng opened the door was Procter & Gamble. P&G recruited from those judged to be the top 10 schools in China and trained their selected recruits using weekend seminars by professors from Chinese University in Hong Kong. These new hires were promised a new apartment if they stayed with P&G for 10 years. These Chinese managers were very successful in their new ventures and are the stuff of business legends.

The criteria used for promotion of these Chinese managers was genotypically similar to that used for all managers in the corporation as shown in Table 11.2, however, phenotypically the means were quite different. Moreover, the development of these valuable managers was based on understanding the Chinese way of doing business, cooperatively seeking accommodations between the U.S. way and the Chinese way, and giving the Chinese managers as much opportunity as they could handle.

These criteria for promotion were translated into Chinese business terms cooperatively and creatively. For example, when the trucking companies refused to deliver P&G products to the customer stores in China, the young Chinese managers recruited three-wheeled bicycle delivery people to deliver their products until the truckers accepted a settlement of their issues. These actions scored points on all of the Chinese criteria for promotion, because it helped build the business, showed leadership, took risks, was innovative and collaborative, and showed unique mastery of an opportunity unknown to non-Chinese employees. These Chinese mangers were allowed to use their unique knowledge of the Chinese way and connections to make the P&G business in China a most successful venture. I was told that the venture did not lose a single Chinese manager that they wanted to keep. This is a sharp contrast to some ventures in our studies. Curiously, it took P&G in Japan much longer to accept and learn the Japanese way of doing business. As in China, those ventures that made major investments in recruiting the best managers and allowing them to teach the Western managers how to do business successfully in Japan did better than those who do not.

CONCLUSION

In conclusion, the new frontiers of leadership are keys to understanding the impact of informal organizational networks on the resultant behavior of organizations as microactions moves to meso-options and to macrostrategizing. The door to putting human and organizational structures clearly together is open and we hope that we have lit a few candles at the door. Do not fear organizational dynamics because they are the next leap forward.

We have presented the latest thinking and research in applying the *Sharing Network Leadership* (SNL) model to the multinational organization focusing on Sino-Western and Sino-Nippon ventures. Based on the contributions of both scholars and practioners, we developed a new process for resolving cross-cultural conflicts using cooperative frameworks to identify and resolve them over time. Fundamental to this cooperative top-down approach to building a mutually endorsed "third culture" for ventures is the strong assumption that surface-level information about similarities and differences between national cultures can generate only oversimplified and misleading cultural stereotypes and caricatures that only contribute negatively to our cooperative approach. Only deep-level understanding of two cultures can aid our process of resolving deep-level, cultural conflicts. China and India with over a billion people each are the future areas of rapid development. Both recently emerged from the dark ages of feudalism and embraced their age of the scientific and industrial revolution. We have focused on China, because more of our research attention has been focused on the new emerging middle kingdom. The world's systems will be changed by the new realities. Whether the future is dominated by cooperation or domination will be determined by future events. At the present time, either model can become accepted. We pray for cooperation and we work against domination where it can be destructive. We seek the cross-national leadership that can help us enact the correct path.

REFERENCES

Allison, G. T. (1969). Conceptual models and the Cuban missile crisis. *The American Political Science Review, 63*, 689-718.

Allison, G. T. (1971). *Essence of decision: Explaining the Cuban Missile Crisis.* Boston: Little, Brown.

Allison, G. T., & Zelikow, P. (1999). *Essence of decision: Explaining the Cuban Missile Crisis* (2nd ed.). New York: Addison Wesley Longman.

Boston Consulting Group. (1975). *Strategy alternatives for the British motorcycle industry.* Boston: Author.

Boal, K. B., & Hooijberg, R. (2000). Strategic leadership research: Moving on. *Leadership Quarterly, 11*, 515-549.

Boynton, A. C., & Zmud, R. W. (1987). Information technology planning in the 1990's: Directions for practice and research. *MIS Quarterly, 11*, 59-71.

Chen, C. C., & Lee, Y. -T. (2007). *Business leadership in China: Philosophies, theories & practices.* London: Cambridge University Press.

Gelfand, M. J., Erez, M., & Aycan, Z. (2007). Cross-cultural organizational behavior. *Annual Review of* Psychology, *58*, 479-514.

Graen, G. (1976). Role making processes within complex organizations. In M.D. Dunnette (Ed.), *Handbook of industrial and organizational psychology* (pp. 1201-1245). Chicago: Rand McNally.

Graen, G. B. (1989). *Unwritten rules for your career: 15 secrets for fast-track success.* New York: Wiley.

Graen, G. B. (2002). It's about LMXs stupid: Collect high quality data, follow it, trust LMXs and seek serendipity always. In A. Bedeian (Ed.), *Management laureates: A collection of autobiographical essays* (6th ed., pp. 52-81). Greenwich, CT: JAI Press.

Graen, G. B. (Ed.). (2003). *LMX leadership: The series: Vol. 1. Dealing with diversity.* Greenwich, CT: Information Age.

Graen, G. B. (Ed.). (2004). *LMX leadership: The series: Vol. 2. New frontiers of leadership.* Greenwich, CT: Information Age.

Graen, G. B. (Ed.). (2005). *LMX leadership: The serie:s Vol. 3. Global organizing designs.* Greenwich, CT: Information Age.

Graen, G. B. (2006a). In the eye of the beholder: Cross-cultural lesson in leadership from project GLOBE. *Academy of Management Perspectives, 20*, 95-101.

Graen, G. B. (2006b). Post Simon, March, Weick, and Graen. In G. B. Graen & J. A. Graen (Eds.), *LMX leadership: The series Vol 4. Sharing network leadership* (pp. 269-278). Greenwich, CT: Information Age.

Graen, G. B., Dharwadkar, R. Grewal, R., & Wakabayashi, M. (2006). Japanese career progress over the long haul: An empirical examination. *Journal of International Business Studies, 37*, 148-161.

Graen, G. B., & Graen, J. A. (Ed.). (2006). *LMX leadership: The series: Vol. 4. Sharing network leadership.* Greenwich, CT: Information Age.

Graen, G. B., Hui, C., & Gu, Q. L. (2005). A new approach to intercultural cooperation, In G B. Graen (Ed.). *LMX leadership: The series: Vol. 2. New frontiers of leadership* (pp. 225-246). Greenwich, CT: Information Age.

Graen, G. B., Hui, C., & Taylor, E. A. (2006).Experience-based learning about LMX leadership and fairness in project teams: A dyadic directional approach. *Academy of Management Learning and Education*, *5*, 448-460.

Graen, G. B., & Lau, D. (2005). Proper levels of analysis, hierarchical linear models, and leadership theories. In G. B. Graen (Ed.), *LMX leadership: The series: Vol. 3. Global organizing designs* (pp. 237-271). Greenwich, CT: Information Age.

Graen, G. B., & Wakabayashi, M. (1994). Cross-cultural leadership-making: Bridging American and Japanese diversity for team advantage. In H. C. Triandis, M. D. Dunnette, & L. M. Hough (Eds.), *Handbook of industrial and organizational psychology* (Vol. 4, pp. 415-446). New York: Consulting Psychologist Press.

Gronn, P. C. (1983). Talk as work: The accomplishment of school administration. *Administrative Science Quarterly*, *28*, 1-21.

Hackett, R. D., Farh, J. L., Song, L. J., & Lapierre, L. M. (2003). LMX and organizational citizenship behavior: Examining the links within and across Western and Chinese samples. In G. Graen (Ed.), *LMX leadership: The series: Vol. 1. Dealing with diversity* (pp. 219-263). Greenwich, CT: Information Age.

Kaplan, R. E. (1982). Intervention in a loosely organized system: An encounter with non-being. *The Journal of Applied Behavioral Science*, *18*(4), 415-432.

Katz, D., & Kahn, R. (1978). *The social psychology of organizations* (2nd ed.). New York: Wiley.

Marion, R., & Uhl-Bien, M. (2001). Leadership in complex organization. *Leadership Quarterly*, *12*, 389-418.

Martin, J. (1992). *Cultures in organizations: Three perspectives*. New York: Oxford University Press.

Meyerson, D. (2001). *Tempered radicals: How people use difference to inspire change at work*. Boston: Harvard Business School Press.

Meyerson, D., & Martin, J. (1987). Cultural change: An integration of three different views. *Journal of Management Studies*, *24*, 623-647.

Mintzberg, H., & McHugh, A. (1985). Strategy formation in an adhocracy. *Administrative Science Quarterly*, *30*, 160-197.

Orton, J. D., & Dhillon, G. (2006). Macrostrategic, meso-strategic, and microstrategic leadership processes in loosely coupled networks. In G. B. Graen (Ed.), *LMX leadership: The series: Vol. 4. Sharing network leadership* (pp. 137-167). Greenwich, CT: Information Age.

Orton, J. D., & Weick, K. E. (1990). Loosely coupled systems: A reconceptualization. *Academy of Management Review*, *15*, 203-223.

Ouchi, W. G. (1978). Coupled versus uncoupled control in organizational hierarchies. In M. W. Meyer et al. (Eds.), *Environments and organizations* (pp. 264-289). San Francisco: Jossey-Bass.

Ouchi, W. G. (1980). Markets, bureaucracies, and clans. *Administrative Science Quarterly*, *25*, 129-141.

Ouchi, W. G. (1981). *Theory Z: How American business can beat the Japanese challenge*. Reading, MA: Addison-Wesley.

Ouchi, W. G., & Wilkins, A. L. (1978). Organizational entitativity: The problem of boundaries, units, and loose couplings. In D. V. Gibson (Ed.), *Seminars on organizations at Stanford, academic year, 1977-1978* (Vol. 4, pp. 17-21). Palo Alto, CA: Stanford University Press.

Pascale, R. T. (1984). Perspectives on strategy: The real story behind Honda's success. *California Management Review, 26*(3), 47-72.

Perrow, C. (1967). A framework for the comparative analysis of organizations. *American Sociological Review, 32*(3), 194-208.

Peters, T. J., & Waterman, R. H. (1982). *In search of excellence: Lessons from America's best-run companies*. New York: Harper & Row.

Rumelt, R. (1996). The many faces of Honda. *California Management Review, 38*(4), 103-111.

Sparrowe, R. T., Soetjipto, B. W., & Kraimer, M. (2006). Do leaders' influence tactics relate to members' helping behavior? It depends on the quality of the LMX relationship. *Academy of Management Journal, 49*(6), 1194-1208.

Tjosvold, D., & Leung, K. (2004). *Leading in high growth Asia: Managing relationship for teamwork and change*. London: World Scientific.

Tjosvold, D., & Van Kippenberg, B. (2007). *Power and interdependence in organizations*. Cambridge, United Kingdom: Cambridge University Press.

Uhl-Bien, M., Graen, G. B., & Scandura, T. A. (2000). Implications of leader-member exchange (LMX) for strategic human resource management systems: Relationships as social capital for competitive advantage. In G. Ferris (Ed.), *Research in personnel and human resources management* (Vol. 18, pp. 137-185). Stamford, CT: JAI Press.

Wang, H., Law, K. S., Hackett, R. D., Wang, D., & Chen, Z. X. (2004). Leader-member exchange as a mediator of the relationship between transformational leadership and followers' performance and organizational citizenship behavior. *Academy of Management Journal, 48*(3), 420-432.

Weick, K. E. (1979). *The social psychology of organizing* (2nd ed.). Reading, MA: Addison-Wesley.

Weick, K. E. (1982). Administering education in loosely coupled schools. *Phi Delta Kappan*, 673-676.

Wilkins, A. L., & Ouchi, W. G. (1983). Efficient cultures: Exploring the relationship between culture and organizational performance. *Administrative Science Quarterly, 28*, 468-481.

ABOUT THE AUTHORS

Yi Feng Chen is an assistant professor in the Management Department, Lingnan University in Hong Kong. Her research interests are cross-cultural management, cooperative and competitive relationships in China, conflict management, leadership and teamwork, the role of Chinese values and thoughts. She received Outstanding Doctoral Research Award by Emerald Group Publishing and the EFMD, 2006; The Finalist of the Best Doctoral Student Paper Award at the 4th Asia Academy of Management Conference, 2004; and Outstanding Paper Award at the 16th Annual IACM Conference, 2003.

Ziguang Chen is an associate professor of organizational behavior and human resource management at the Department of Management, City University of Hong Kong, Hong Kong SAR. He received his PhD in international management and development from Nagoya University, Japan. His research focuses on human resource issues in China, including managerial skill practices, cross-cultural human resource development, and leader-member exchange in Chinese firms. His publications appear in *Journal of Applied Psychology, Journal of Organizational Behavior, Management and Organization Review*, and *International Journal of Human Resource Management*.

Jennifer M. Ferreter is a doctoral student in industrial and organizational psychology at Baruch College, City University of New York. Her current research areas incorporate personnel selection, international human resource management, applied psychometrics, and employee engagement and satisfaction. She is currently a research fellow for the City University of New York's Office of Academic Affairs.

Yitzhak Fried is a professor of organizational behavior and human resources, in the Management Department, Whitman School of Management, Syracuse University. He received his PhD from the University of Illinois at Urbana-Champaign. His research focus is on the contribution of context in the areas of job and office design, work stress, motivation, performance appraisal, and diversity. His work has appeared in leading journals in the field, including the *Academy of Management Review, Journal of Applied Psychology, Personnel Psychology, Journal of Organizational Behavior, Journal of Occupational and Organizational Psychology, Journal of Occupational Health Psychology, Journal of Vocational Behavior,* and *Human Relations.* Between 1998 and 2001 he served as the associate-editor-in-chief of the *International Journal of Organizational Behavior.*

George B. Graen, emeritus professor of international organizational psychology, University of Illinois, Champaign-Urbana is a founding and board member of the Society of Organizational Behavior (SOB), a Paul Harris Fellow and volunteer to Thailand for International Rotary, and a member of Artists of Northwest Arkansas. He is a grandad of four, dad of two sons and 48-year husband of Joni. He is the internationally known father of one of the most dominant theory and methods for developing successful LMX and MMX leaders and followers and building effective teams and networks in organizations both domestic and multinational. He grew up in North Minneapolis, married his high school sweetheart and served his country before going on to the University of Minnesota majoring in psychology with Marv Dunnette and staying for all three degrees. He taught at University of Illinois for 10 years, at the University of Cincinnati for 20 years, at the University of Louisiana (Cajun U) for 4 years and 1 year at Keio University in Tokyo and Nagoya University, the University of Science and Technology in Hong Kong, and Dong Hua University in Shanghai, China. He continues to edit *LMX Leadership: The Series* and creating new insights through new LMX theory and research, consulting globally and enjoying life on Beaver Lake in Northwest Arkansas.

Michael R. Graen has been employed by Procter & Gamble since September 1982. He joined P&G after receiving a BA in information systems and an MBA in management from the University of Cincinnati. Mike has held numerous roles with Procter & Gamble including foodservice and lodging products systems, corporate data center manager, and the systems manager for the Cape Girardeau Paper plant. Since 1989, Mike has been associated with the Wal-Mart Global Customer Team. His role has been to lead the information technology organization to align P&G and Wal-Mart systems on a Worldwide basis. This has resulted in the global implementation of EDI systems, Linking P&G and Wal-Mart systems to exchange data, and to promote the use of Data Sharing to drive up sales and reduce costs. Mike has been actively working with industry groups and third party service providers to create an environment of sharing data to understand consumers.

Wing LAM is an assistant professor in the Department of Management and Marketing at the Hong Kong Polytechnic University. She received her PhD from the same university. Her research interests include human resource management in China, feedback-seeking behavior in organizations, leadership, emotional labor, and emotional intelligence. She has publications in *Academy of Management Journal* and *Journal of Applied Psychology*.

Gregory Laurence is a PhD student in organizational behavior at the Whitman School of Management, Syracuse University. He holds an MBA from the Whitman School as well as an MA in international relations from the Maxwell School of Citizenship and Public Affairs, also at Syracuse University. His interests lie in the areas of national and organizational culture, intercultural relations, and conflict.

Kenneth Law is an active researcher in the Chinese University of Hong Kong. His area of expertise is human resource management and management in Chinese context. He has published more than two dozen articles in leading research journals. His major research areas are personnel selection, human resource research methods, organizational citizenship behaviors, compensation management, and HRM and OB issues of Chinese management. Professor Law is currently serving as an associate editor of the *Academy of Management Journal*. He has served in the editorial board of the *Academy of Management Journal* (AMJ) for three consecutive terms. He is also the consulting editor of the *Journal of Occupational and Organizational Psychology*, and responsible for providing additional methodological comments to the editor if needed.

Ariel Levi, PhD, Yale University, is senior lecturer in the Department of Business at Wayne State University. He teaches courses in organizational behavior, human resource management, and organizational development and change. Dr. Levi's research focuses on judgment and decision making at the group and individual level, and on individual reactions to affirmative action and diversity programs. He has published in academic journals in the areas of judgment, decision making, performance appraisal, and diversity management. He is a member of the Decision Sciences Institute, the Academy of Management, and the Society for Industrial and Organizational Psychology.

Xuefeng Liu is an assistant professor in the Department of Human Resources Management, School of International Business Administration, Shanghai University of Finance & Economics and received a PhD from Peking University, Beijing, China. Research interests include leadership, conflict management, communications and negotiation.

Loren J. Naidoo is an assistant professor of industrial and organizational psychology at Baruch College, the City University of New York. He received his PhD in industrial and organizational psychology from the University of Akron. Dr. Naidoo's research interests include leadership, motivation, emotions, organizational justice, performance appraisal, attitude measurement and behavior regulation. His research has appeared in a variety of outlets including *Leadership Quarterly* and *Personality and Social Psychology Bulletin*. He has also served as a consultant for organizations in the United States and Canada.

Chunyan Peng is a student and research assistant in the Management Department, Lingnan University, Hong Kong. She earned her bachelors degree in psychology from Beijing Normal University, China, in 2004. Her research interests include cooperation and competition and conflict management. She has conducted studies on managerial decision making, government-business cooperation, and working with competitors. She has given a paper at an academic conference and published in the *Asia Pacific Journal of Management*. Her thesis is on conflict avoidance between local employees and foreign managers.

Charles A. Scherbaum is an assistant professor of psychology at Baruch College in the City University of New York. He received his PhD and M.S. in industrial and organizational psychology from Ohio University. His research focuses on personnel selection, work motivation, quantitative methods, and applied psychometrics. Dr. Scherbaum's research has been published in a variety of outlets including *Personnel Psychology*, *Leadership Quarterly*, *Organizational Research Methods*, and *Journal of Applied Social Psychology*.

Dean Tjosvold is the Henry Y. W. Fong Chair Professor of Management, Lingnan University, Hong Kong, and the director of the Hong Kong Cooperative Learning Center. After graduating from Princeton University, he earned his masters degree in history and his PhD in the social psychology of organizations at the University of Minnesota, both in 1972. He has taught at Pennsylvania State University, Simon Fraser University, and was visiting professor at National University of Singapore, the State University of Groningen in The Netherlands, Hong Kong University of Science and Technology, and City University of Hong Kong. He is past president of the International Association of Conflict Management. In 1992, Simon Fraser University awarded him a university professorship for his research contributions. He received the American Education Research Association's Outstanding Contribution to Cooperative Learning Award in 1998. His review of cooperative and competitive conflict was recognized as the best article in *Applied Psychology: An International Review* for 1998. He was elected to the Academy of Management Board of Governors in 2004. He has also received outstanding paper awards from the International Association of Conflict Management. He has published over 200 articles, 20 books, 30 book chapters, and 100 conference papers on managing conflict, cooperation and competition, decision-making, power, and other management issues. He is now Asian editor, the *Journal of World Business*, and has served on several editorial boards, including the *Academy of Management Review*, *Journal of Organizational Behavior*, *Journal of Occupational and Organizational Psychology* and *Journal of Management*. His books have been selected by Fortune, Business Week, Newbridge, and Executive Book Clubs and translated into Chinese and Spanish. With colleagues, he has written books on teamwork, leadership, and conflict management in China published in Chinese. He is a partner in his family's health care business that has 900 employees and is based in Minnesota.

Hui Wang is an associate professor of organizational management at the Guanghua School of Management, Peking University. He received his PhD in management of organizations from Hong Kong University of Science and Technology. His research interests include leadership behavior, organizational culture, and firm performance, especially in the context of Chinese organizations.

Printed in the United States
88320LV00003B/205-210/A